HOUSES, VILLAS, AND PALACES
IN THE ROMAN WORLD

HOUSES, VILLAS, AND PALACES IN THE ROMAN WORLD

Alexander G. McKay

THE JOHNS HOPKINS UNIVERSITY PRESS

BALTIMORE AND LONDON

For
Jean,
Julie, and Danae

Published by arrangement with Thames and Hudson, London
© 1975 Thames and Hudson
All rights reserved
Hardcover edition originally published in the United States by
Cornell University Press, 1975
Printed in the United States of America on acid-free paper

Johns Hopkins Paperbacks edition, 1998
9 8 7 6 5 4 3 2 1

The Johns Hopkins University Press
2715 North Charles Street
Baltimore, Maryland 21218-4363
The Johns Hopkins Press Ltd., London

Library of Congress Cataloging-in-Publication Data

McKay, Alexander Gordon, 1924–
    Houses, villas, and palaces in the Roman world / Alexander G. McKay. —
Johns Hopkins paperbacks ed.
        p.   cm.
    Originally published: Ithaca, N.Y. : Cornell University Press, 1975, in series :
Aspects of Greek and Roman life.
    Includes bibliographical references and index.
    ISBN 0-8018-5904-2 (pbk. : alk. paper)
    1. Architecture, Domestic—Rome.   I. Title.
NA324.M32   1998
728´.09376—dc21   97-51608
                                                                             CIP

A catalog record for this book is available from the British Library.

CONTENTS

FOREWORD 6

I THE ETRUSCAN BACKGROUND 11

II ITALIAN TOWN HOUSES: POMPEII,

HERCULANEUM AND COSA 30

III ROME AND OSTIA: DOMUS AND PALATIUM 64

IV ITALIAN MULTIPLE DWELLINGS 80

V ITALIAN VILLAS: RURAL, SUBURBAN AND MARITIME 100

VI ROMAN INTERIOR FURNISHING AND DECORATION 136

VII EUROPEAN PROVINCES AND BRITAIN 156

VIII EASTERN PROVINCES AND NORTH AFRICA 210

NOTES 238

BIBLIOGRAPHY 259

ARCHITECTURAL GLOSSARY 269

LIST OF ILLUSTRATIONS 272

SOURCES OF ILLUSTRATIONS 279

INDEX 280

FOREWORD

MODERN ARCHAEOLOGY has made impressive advances in the recovery and study of the private buildings of Greeks and Romans of practically every time and a large variety of places. The Greek house, since Bertha Carr Rider's history was first published,[1] has come much more sharply into focus and has yielded structures which, however perishable, reflect a sense of dignity, a sensitivity to family needs, and an aesthetic sense quite compatible with the other achievements of the Greek spirit. The sweeping generalization, still repeated in some popular histories, that the Greeks sought the communal civic centre or *palaestra* or temple compound because their homes were so nondescript and unpleasant has been totally dispelled by the marvellous finds at Olynthus and Delos, and more recently in Attica and Athens itself.[2] The humble fifth-century shop-dwelling of Simon the Shoemaker, Socrates' pupil, and the *atelier* home of Mikion the Athenian sculptor, evidence an unexpected degree of utility and comfort.[3] The tradition of ancient Greek house design persists, in evolution, into the present day, often with a startling similarity of attitude to domestic life.[4] There is also a constant sense of living persons in the recovered homes of the ancient Greeks and Romans, an intimacy which transcends time and recreates a family's private travails and prosperity with uncanny detail. The reconstructed *cubiculum* of the Boscoreale Villa in the Metropolitan Museum of New York, and the splendidly reconstructed Roman house at Augst (Switzerland) are only a sample of what may be done under skilled direction and with adequate funds.[5]

60, 61

The venturesome engineering genius of Hippodamus, the Milesian town-planner, and others of the same profession who remain anonymous, revolutionized Greek city plans in fifth-century Hellas and Magna Graecia and undoubtedly sparked off new patterns of house design as a complement to his chess-board communities.[6] But the patterns of living from time immemorial were hard to break in any age. Nero endeavoured to intervene paternalistically after the Great Fire of AD 64, to rectify the problems of urban confusion in Rome; but even his panache and engineering insight could not instil new patterns of living. The mass of the Roman citizenry remained cloistered in their *botteghe oscure*, dreaming regretfully of pastoral landscapes or distant shores, but enthralled by the bustle and gaiety and diversity of the metropolis. Juvenal's Umbricius preferred Cumae, a Campanian ghost-town, to the ruthless, impersonal capital; but his was a rare instance of total withdrawal from the urban excitement and the rewards of 'bread and circuses' which emperors provided for their restless subjects.

The country towns of Italy give evidence of inviting dwellings more systematically and spaciously planned than their metropolitan counterparts – the very image of W.H. Auden's satiric lines on the follies of pre-Munich England: *Those who fancy themselves as foxes | Or desire a special setting for spooning | Erect their villas at the right places, | Airtight, lighted, elaborately warmed.* There was the additional premium of maintaining a garden and of dazzling one's guests with a mural reproduction of a famous master or with an impressive mosaic floor. Town houses tended to cling to the traditional atrium plan but with innovative developments involving peristyles, porticoes and vistas in ways which excite admiration even today.

We have much to learn from the interior decoration of Olynthian, Delian, Campanian and provincial dwellings from the standpoint of furnishing and decoration. There are some astonishing anticipations of Renaissance and Baroque interiors, and of surrealistic, abstract murals of unusual distinction and modernity. The removal of wall-paintings from their original settings has fortunately ceased and the enlightened excavators of Stabiae and Pompeii and elsewhere have taken appropriate measures to safeguard their survival *in situ* for the delight and instruction of visitors.

Ancient writers, both Greek and Roman, often interlace their works with references to house forms, interiors, furnishings, and the like. Homer, the Greek tragedians, the orators, philosophers and biographers offer accounts and verdicts as graphic and as valuable as any epigraphical or archaeological material. Vergil, whose palaces are reflections of Hellenistic mansions,[7] Horace, Pliny the Elder and his nephew Pliny the Younger, and the native satirists, abound in allusions to domestic forms. Their references are as impartial and as liberal as my own. The palaces of emperors, imperial legates and client kings, the luxury villas of wealthy aristocrats and pretentious freedmen in the Neapolitan environs, and the stately homes of provincial *domini* and commercial magnates, compete for attention with the houses of the common folk where simplicity, economy, charm and utility were often powerful factors in the design.

The daughter towns of Rome overseas cause one to respect the magnitude of the imperial mission – *parcere subiectis et debellare superbos* – 'to show mercy to the conquered and to war down the arrogant'.[8] Rome brought and maintained a rule which must have seemed oppressive and demanding to some, but to the majority Imperium Romanum guaranteed peace for a longer term than had been known before or would be experienced later. The *colonus*, whether soldier or landed proprietor, in cantonal capital or on isolated ranches, remained loyal to Rome through thick and thin. There was a monotony in the Roman foundations, as steadfast and constricted as Baltimore and Philadelphia in colonial America, evident particularly in the civic housing. Timgad, Volubilis, Silchester and Verulamium, Italica and Ephesus bring the visitor into touch with an environment of shocking modernity. High-rise apartments, compact and appealing civic squares, grandiose public buildings and temples, shopping centres and commercial piles, along with the congestion, the confusion and the ugliness of over-populated cities, are a shared experience. Rome is a veritable mirror of our own civilization but it offers no easy answers to the enigmatic problems of our own city life. Britain, for all its remoteness, provides us with a better rounded picture of life in the Imperial provinces than any other province. Londinium, Silchester, Verulamium, and Lincoln could hardly aspire to the eminence of Alexandria, Antioch, Pergamum or Trier; they enable us nevertheless, by dint of painstaking archaeological recovery and research, to understand aspects of Roman life more completely and more rewardingly than almost any other places, even in Italy itself.

The enterprise and the innovating energies of architects and builders throughout the Empire are endlessly fascinating. Obviously the repertoire which can be outlined in this volume includes only a small proportion of those known and excavated; the bibliography relating to each chapter must be explored for additional examples and more extensive review. Testimony to the enterprise and genius of provincial architects and builders throughout the Roman world is immense. A separate volume, the size of the present study, would hardly encompass the innumerable provincial adaptations and innovations in house design.

My purpose has been to provide a readable, informative, and up-to-date survey of the subject, to offer a representative selection of figures and photographs which may illuminate the printed word and inform the imagination. The choice of examples has been arbitrary but deliberate. Student and amateur should find the compilation useful if only because no other single study provides comparable coverage.

Carl Blegen, Alan Wace, Homer Thompson, Walter Graham and many others have by their work as excavators and by their lucid reports greatly expanded the repertoire and the understanding of Hellenic housing. Italy's offering, undeniably more diversified than that of peninsular Greece and the Islands, is indebted on many accounts to Amedeo Maiuri, whose persistence and good fortune are legendary; and to Alfonso de Franciscis, present Superintendent of Antiquities for Campania, Frank E. Brown, Lawrence J. Richardson Jr, John B. Ward-Perkins and the members of the British School in Rome, Erik Sjøqvist, Richard Stillwell, Axel Boëthius and very many others. For recent finds and scholarly reports in Roman provincial areas I am repeatedly aware of the important contributions made by Franz Miltner and Hermann Vetters, Raymond Thouvenot, John B. Ward-Perkins and Richard Goodchild, A. Grenier and K. M. Swoboda, M. I. Rostovtzeff, Sir Ian Richmond, Sheppard Frere, Barry Cunliffe, A. L. F. Rivet, and a host of others.

I owe a debt of gratitude to more scholars than I may politely name for their counsel and assistance during fifteen years of lectures, the late Commendatore Amedeo Maiuri, Professor Libero d'Orsi, the indefatigable excavator of Stabiae, John B.Ward-Perkins, Dr Edward Togo Salmon, Dr Claudio Pellegrino Sestieri, Dr Robert F.Paget and, particularly, to Dr Axel Boëthius. The late Dr Ernest Nash, of the Fototeca Unione in Rome, was always helpful with advice and with photographs from his thesaurus of material. J.Appleton Thayer, Honorary President of the Vergilian Society of America, has provided constant encouragement and has endorsed my repeated appointments as Director of the Vergilian Society's Overseas Programme at Cumae, the very heart of Campanian archaeology. The kind invitation of Professor H.H.Scullard to provide a volume for his enterprising series and the patient assistance of the editors of Thames and Hudson, must not go unmentioned. My indebtedness to Paul MacKendrick's compendia of archaeological history and finds and to Edith Wightman's recent study of Roman Trier is repeatedly evident; to Joan Liversidge and Sheppard Frere I am beholden for detailed aspects of daily life and interior furnishings in their magisterial reports and writings. Finally, infinite thanks are owing to my wife Jean and to Mrs Veronica Morrison for their constant energy and care in typing the manuscript.

A.G.M.

Hamilton, Canada

CHAPTER I

THE ETRUSCAN
BACKGROUND

*The territory occupied by the Tyrrhenians
produces every crop and because of
their intensive cultivation of the land
they enjoy an abundance of produce,
not only adequate for their own sustenance,
but contributing also to abundant enjoyment and luxury. For example, twice
daily they spread costly tables and set
on them everything appropriate to
excessive luxury, providing brightly
coloured couches and having available a
multitude of silver goblets of every
description and servants in no small
number; some of the attendants are
exceedingly handsome and some wear
clothing more costly than befits the status
of a slave. Their dwellings are of every
description and idiosyncrasy, not only
those of the majority of their free citizenry
but those of the slaves as well.*
Diodorus Siculus V, 40

THE ENIGMA OF ETRUSCAN ORIGINS remains unsolved.[9] Even the
ancients could find no easy or generally acceptable solution to the
problem of the original home of the Etruscans. The limited
number of surviving inscriptions has not provided a sufficient
sample to enable scholars fully to decipher the language of the
Etruscans in Italy. However, judging by the words which can be
interpreted with some certitude, the language is neither Indo-
European nor Semitic. The ancients were as uncertain as modern
scholars regarding the homeland of the Etruscans: Herodotus of
Halicarnassus regarded the Etruscans as Lydians, *émigrés* from
Asia Minor to Italy during a time of famine and general travail;[10]
Dionysius, a native of the same Asiatic Greek city who flourished

in the time of Augustus, regarded them as local and indigenous, a non-invading people, associated with Italy from earliest times.[11] The thesis, which argues for an original habitat across the Alps, now lacks supporters.

One opinion today favours a succession of 'invasions'.[12] The first wave and settlement, during the Iron Age, brought settlers to the territory of Tuscany and Latium, a cremating people with some affinities with northern Europe. These seaborne invaders from the eastern Mediterranean, arriving between 1000 and 900 BC, quickly overwhelmed the resident Bronze Age people, a peaceful agrarian folk, and ushered in a new era of piratical and military ventures. At the outset of the Orientalizing period, another migratory band of easterners, self-styled Rasenna, reached the shores of Tuscany and inaugurated a new phase of culture among the earlier 'Villanovans'. Called Tyrsenoi (evidently a non-Greek word) by Herodotus and Thucydides, Tyrrhenoi and Tyrsenoi, Tusci and Etrusci by Greeks and Italians, these latter-day immigrants from a highly sophisticated environment soon acquired an alphabetic script, borrowed probably from the Greeks at Cumae (post-750 BC), to record the Etruscan language. This last stage in the invasion process marked the beginnings of the rise of Etruria to a position of dominance in central and northern Italy.

There is no certainty regarding the Villanovan contribution to the evolution of the later Italic or Etruscan house types. But domestic forms tend to be influenced by locale and climatic conditions far more than temples and tombs, and the Villanovans of the Early Iron Age must have evolved forms which were suitable to the climate of Tuscany before the arrival of the Tyrsenoi.

Villanovan housing consisted basically of the humble pastoral dwelling, which finds its counterpart in the *capanne* of modern Italy; there are also traces of the rectangular *megaron* form peculiar to the Geometric period in Greece.

The shepherd's hut, judging by the forms of ash urn found in Villanovan cemeteries in central Italy and Latium in particular, was a basic building constructed of wattle and daub, with a steep thatched roof of two slopes and overhanging eaves. Sometimes the roof provided a triangular air-space to permit the escape of smoke

I, 2

and to admit light. The ridge-pole was often decorated with ornamental horns, birds and the like, startlingly similar to the later Etruscan penchant for locating terracotta statues on the roof-tree of Etruscan temples during the late archaic and early classical periods. Such huts provided the most common form of habitation for the Palatine village which antedated Rome, and the same forms must have served the Villanovans elsewhere. Judging by the tombs and by house remains, there was a predilection among the Etruscans for rectangular buildings with a gable roof.

Tomb and temple remains, as well as Vitruvius' comments, shed some light on the design and construction of the earliest fully-fledged Etruscan houses of the archaic period. Etruscan temple architecture, certainly by the end of the sixth century BC, seems to have adhered with characteristic conservatism to certain canonical forms. The temple usually consisted of a building on a high podium with frontal emphasis and single approach. It was provided with a deep porch in front and with either a single room in the rear, or a large room divided into three separate *cellae*. Vitruvius states that the *tuscanicae dispositiones*, as outlined, were consistent. Orientation and axiality are basic to the conception of the temple.[13] The pitch roof was designed to project for a considerable distance over the side walls, presumably to protect the vulnerable painted surfaces of the terracotta revetments and the stuccoed surfaces of the side walls of the building.

3; 1

Fig. 1 Cosa. Capitolium, plan.
Boëthius & Ward-Perkins, fig. 64

The massive side and rear walls were of brick and frame construction, supported on stone or tufa foundations. The deep shadowy porch exhibited wooden columns and, unlike the Greek temple, there was no surrounding colonnade. The porch columns, rarely numbering more than six, with four front columns and two *in antis* (i.e. between the projecting wings of the side walls), reflected the interior division of the *cella*. Basically non-Greek and, in the view of the ancients, heavy-headed, sprawling, and ungainly, this architectural scheme, excluding the high podium and processional steps, is reflected many times in the early rock-cut chamber tombs of Caere and Tarquinii.

Etruscan masons, working in the tufaceous hills of the Etruscan setting, took great pains to reproduce the design of contemporary buildings, religious and secular, in fashioning the tombs of wealthy Etruscans.[14] Less perishable than the materials which inspired their design, the ceilings of the outer porches frequently reflected the elaborate wooden beams of the model above ground. Tombs at Caere tend to reproduce all the details of the characteristically heavy woodwork, ridge-beam, rafters, laths, and sometimes even coffering, with the greatest detail. Although Holloway and others have properly identified many of the tomb paintings as reflections of outdoor pavilions, with land-and seascape elements appropriately introduced into the banquet-performance sequence, many of these dank, desperately deteriorating interiors also give evidence of the marvellous carpentry, elegant roofing, door posts and lintels which must have characterized the homes of the *lucumones* and wealthy bourgeoisie. Strabo, Vitruvius and Dionysius of Halicarnassus praise in unison the abundant resources of fine timber for constructional purposes in the forests of central Italy, and these tomb interiors and the abundance of terracotta protective revetments are a vindication of their remarks for the classical era.[15] On occasion, as for example in the Tomb of the Capitals at Caere, the porch or atrium court contains columns cut from the same tufa rock, providing a kind of monumental approach or propylaea to the inner chambers. The walls of the interior are often pierced with windows and always with doors, further reflections of the house type above ground. Often the large vestibule was provided with benches

and chairs, 'petrified' versions of furniture used in the city of the   5
living, where client waited patiently on *patronus*. The porch usually
opened into a central chamber with two side apartments (*alae*) to complete the triadic design, again reminiscent of temple architecture.

There can be little doubt that early Etruscan towns and housing
owed much to the Near East. Their sanctuaries, central to the
strongly religious regimen of the state and of political life, probably reflect Oriental origins, but we should not discard the possi-
bility of imported forms being superimposed or grafted on to
indigenous elements. By 550 BC urban planning was a reality in
the Etruscan cities, once again, no doubt, the product of Near
Eastern experimentation – Hippodamus of Miletus was certainly
not the first to pioneer in rational town-planning – and new
domestic forms responded to the new regularity of plan in
Etruria. The Regolini-Galassi tomb at Caere with its fabulous
treasures, the beehive tombs at Vetulonia and important finds
at Casal Marittimo, Populonia, Volterra and Sesto Fiorentino all
bespeak Oriental luxury and lead one to imagine early influences
from the East. Certainly Boëthius and Gjerstad have accepted
that the pattern of the earliest atrium houses and the associated
tombs derive from a traditional Etruscan design which is related
to the Oriental one-storey 'liwan' style of architecture still
evident in Syria and throughout the Near East.[16]

Actual house foundations from the archaic period at Veii
indicate that the rectangular houses may have adopted the Greek
megaron plan, with a shallow antechamber and a deep back room
where the hearth was installed.[17] At Rome the Regia, traditionally
ascribed to Numa Pompilius, second of Rome's kings, followed
the same conservative pattern, but was supplemented by an open
courtyard containing a well. This ancient building design, though
frequently reconstructed, followed the same conservative pattern   2
throughout its history as the abode of the Pontifex Maximus.[18]
Perhaps the most interesting feature of the Orvieto tombs
is their alignment along a single street, suggesting that even as
early as the sixth century the Etruscans organized their towns
on a chess-board or grid plan of streets intersecting at right angles.

Tomb types and excavation finds indicate that the Etruscans
during the archaic period did not restrict their house designs to

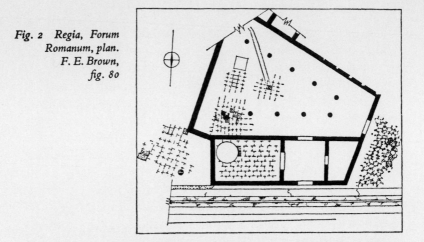

Fig. 2 Regia, Forum Romanum, plan. F. E. Brown, fig. 80

any single plan. The chamber-tombs at Caere provide testimony, also, for the diversity of door designs in the domestic scene. Many of the door-frames are elegantly designed and decorated, suggesting that the originals were wooden and heavy, handsomely decorated with bronze studs, as suggested by the false doorway represented on the rear wall of the Tomb of the Augurs at Tarquinii (c. 540–530 BC).[19] The door jambs customarily slope slightly inwards and are occasionally provided with a raised border curved in a hawk's beak at the corners of the T-frame.

6

The literary testimony on the 'Tuscan' house has been a matter of contention for many years. A contemporary of Cicero, M. Terentius Varro, polymath and grammarian, suggested that the Romans derived the atrium, the word and the convention, from the Etruscan town of Atria (Adria).[20] He also defined and explained the expression *cavum aedium*, the hollow of the house, as 'the roofed-over area inside the house walls which is left open for the use of everyone', implying that the atrium was a waiting room designed to receive and accommodate clients and visitors.

Vitruvius supplies us with more valuable testimony on the atrium house.[21] The Augustan military engineer and architect does not state that the atrium was an Etruscan legacy from the city at the mouth of the Po, but he does use the adjective Tuscan in his account of the various sorts of atrium.

Using the word atrium as a synonym for Varro's *cavum aedium*, he enlarges on the Tuscan atrium as comprising a roof supported on two heavy beams running the entire length of the room and framing the long sides of the *compluvium*, the light, air and rain aperture familiar to us from Campanian houses in Pompeii and Herculaneum. The short sides were marked by beams hung between the main beams. From this resulting rectangle the roof sloped upward and outward in four directions. A moderately elaborate wooden ceiling is thoroughly characteristic of the Etruscans, and is reflected in the tomb ceilings carved in tufa. Vitruvius indicates too that there were no columns at the corners of the *impluvium* (the catch-basin laid into the floor) to support the frame of the *compluvium* (skylight). The impluviate atrium, in Vitruvius' description, was probably a common phenomenon in the Hellenistic cities of Campania by the mid-third century BC.

The less elaborate form, with hip or gable roof and no skylight, would logically be the earlier. This completely roofed form, called testudinate from its likeness to a tortoise shell, with pitch roof and a roof-tree running the entire length of the house, follows the Varronian description. Presumably, before the *compluvium* punctured the roof, the major light to penetrate the 'dark' room came from the opened front door, from the window in the rear wall of the *tablinum* (the master's *salon* facing the door and opening on to the atrium) and from the *alae* or side apartments which were also provided with windows.

The impluviate house is almost certainly a product of the Hellenistic period. The origins of the basic plan, called Tuscan by Varro and Vitruvius long after the event, are problematical. Until very recently, only the intrepid were prepared to argue in favour of an Etruscan origin for the characteristic Roman house type, Vitruvius and Varro notwithstanding.

Patroni, however, did make some challenging suggestions regarding the basic house type.[22] He postulated the existence of an archetypal Italian farmhouse with a single main room, and with smaller rooms (*alae*) facing south on to an open courtyard. In his hypothetical dwelling, additional rooms or sheds might line the sides of the yard, leaving space between them and the rooms on the northern side for easy circulation.

3, 4

If one were to accept this somewhat formalized plan as essential to the later atrium house, several important phases in its evolution

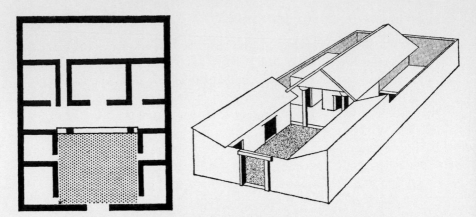

Fig. 3 (left)   *Domus Italica, prototype plan (Patroni). J. W. Graham, fig. 22*
Fig. 4 (right)   *Domus Italica, prototype reconstruction (Patroni). J. W. Graham, fig. 25*

to the refined form of testudinate or impluviate atrium have to be assumed. The transfer of this basic ranch, or farmhouse, to an urban or town environment would necessitate several changes: most important, the extensions of the courtyard alongside the central main room would become *alae* in the urban dwelling, designed to accommodate the owner's family, or the portrait busts of the ancestors; and the courtyard, with its original well or cistern, would also undergo restrictions in area and function. Walter Graham has argued that the 'deep overhanging eaves, familiar from the architecture of the early Etruscan temples, would tend to project well over the court; their eventual further extension would result in the court becoming, in effect, a high *room* – the atrium – with a rectangular opening of considerable size in its roof.'[23] One may agree that this evolution might be the direct ancestor to the compluviate atrium house, but the change did not happen overnight, and the testudinate form would appear to be an essential stage in the evolution.

Until recently, Patroni's 'farmhouse' was discarded in discussions of the Roman house type. Tombs and ash urns seemed to have little bearing on this primal dwelling. Recently, however, archaeologists have shown a keener interest in the recovery of Etruscan cities, in the study of the city planning, and in domestic architecture and furnishings. Though less dazzling than the necropolis finds and certainly more costly and laborious, the recent finds at Marzabotto have virtually revolutionized our notions of Etruscan house architecture.

Founded *c.* 520 BC as an Etruscan outpost in the Apennines, fifteen miles south of Felsina (modern Bologna) on the Reno River, colonial Marzabotto (the ancient name remains uncertain) occupies a glorious site perched high above the river, and embraced by the steep slopes of mountains. The ruins uncovered by the Italian excavators Brizio and, more recently, Mansuelli have provided marvellously convincing support for Patroni's

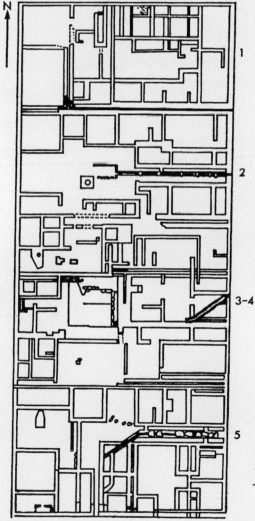

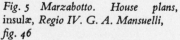

Fig. 5 Marzabotto. House plans, insulæ, Regio IV. G. A. Mansuelli, fig. 46

5 theory.[24] Contemporary with the supposed domestic tomb architecture at Caere and Tarquinii, Marzabotto's master-plan antedates 'Hippodamian' gridiron planning elsewhere in Magna Graecia and Sicily. Designed like Olynthus, Piraeus, Naples, Capua, Selinus and Paestum (Poseidonia), Marzabotto offered its progressive inhabitants a rationally planned city. The broad streets, running east–west, were crossed by a single wide street and a number of other narrow streets, running north–south. The wide avenues, equivalent to the later *decumanus* arteries, measured fifteen yards across. Five yards were reserved on both sides of raised pavements, the central five being for wheeled traffic. All the streets were paved with river pebbles; major arteries had common sewers on either side while narrow streets, five yards across, had a single drain running down one side. Regularity in Etruscan town-planning seems to be reflected in the Caeretan cemeteries but even more remarkably in the Crocefisso necropolis of Orvieto. The corbelled chamber-tombs, surmounted with the familiar earthen tumulus and stelae, appear in rectangular blocks of widths varying from four to ten yards, all accessible by means of a network of straight streets, evidently initiated *c*. 550 BC, only slightly prior to the comparable arrangements of the town site at Marzabotto.

House remains at Marzabotto are limited to the stone founda-
7 tions below floor level. The superstructure, which was almost certainly of timber or timber-framed, has vanished completely. Even in the discernible plans recovered by archaeology we cannot in every instance distinguish the original features from alterations and additions inevitably made during the century or more that the city was inhabited.[25] The houses varied considerably in size, but normally included a paved central courtyard around which the living-quarters were somewhat haphazardly arranged. The courtyard usually contained a well or cistern and there was frequently provision for drainage into the main drain in the adjoining street. The city drainage system was very carefully planned and executed, with a uniform flow from north to south and from east to west. The residential remains at Marzabotto are of interest and importance primarily because they were designed as city homes attached to one another by party walls, following

the established pattern in Greek cities. Small rectangular rooms opening on to the street probably served as dwellings, shops and workshops for the proletariat, prototypes of the *tabernae* found at Pompeii, Herculaneum and Ostia. None of the city residences contained a garden, although the cobbled or pebbled courtyards may have made provision for plants and shrubs (both figure prominently in Etruscan wall-paintings), as well as providing open-air accommodation for household services such as laundry and cooking.[26]

Brizio's earlier excavations at the site produced a building which he identified as a partial prototype of the atrium house. Supplied with the customary entrance passage (*fauces*), adjacent shops, rear shops, and rooms, it also contained a large courtyard, which he proclaimed to be an unroofed predecessor of the atrium, even before Patroni's theory became common knowledge. When restored symmetrically, following the guide-lines suggested by Brizio, the resultant house plan has strong ties with the developed atrium house. Indeed, Brizio's house was a mansion, a *casa signorile*, property of some wealthy 'merchant prince' in this progressive outpost of Etruscan civilization in the mountains.

Guido Mansuelli's more recent diggings have exposed two additional recognizable prototypes for the atrium house, complete with *alae*, *tablinum* and axial *fauces*. One example (Ins. IV i, 2) measures 59 feet in front and extends the entire width of the block, 37 yards. The house is oriented to the west. The inner courtyard, paved with pebbles and equipped with a well, measures 28 ft 3 in. by 38 ft 9 in. Another comparable house (Ins. IV i, 6) measures 75 ft 6 in. across the façade. It is equipped with *fauces*, roughly trapezoidal, measuring 8 ft 2 in. at the point of entry and 6 ft 7 in. at the point of access into the court, and 59 ft in length. The central area or courtyard measures 32 ft 9 in. by 39 ft 4 in. and has a central well. Both houses have the same triple arrangement of rooms at the rear of the court, the central *tablinum*, and two *alae*.

It now appears from these fifth-century examples at Marzabotto, the Etruscan Pompeii, that the atrium house was probably an Etruscan innovation. The central hall and axial plan, suggested in the rock-cut tomb interiors, now emerges above ground, and well before the Hellenistic period when most authorities assume that the house type came into existence. Patroni's hypothetical farmhouse now appears in a more sophisticated and regularized form within an urban environment. The courtyard wells, exemplified at Marzabotto, would ultimately yield to the *compluvium-impluvium* arrangement. As cities became more populous and the pressure on building space intensified, the courtyard wells yielded to the *compluvium* and cistern arrangement familiar in Pompeii, Herculaneum and Ostia at a later date. To ensure that the householder would have a constant supply of clean water readily accessible for the multiple uses of the family, the slope of the courtyard roof, as Graham has suggested, was reversed, thereby providing another ample room spacious enough for the family or clients' entertainment and used, with a vaulted cistern beneath the *compluvium*, to serve the family's needs.

6, 7

The older practices, inherited from the farmhouse and from earlier, less crowded towns, of locating tanks and cisterns outside the house walls to collect rainwater from the testudinate or other roofs yielded to a more private and more dependable system of storage within the house confines.

Two early atrium-style houses have been detected in the Etruscan territory. The Atrium House at Cosa (ancient Ansedonia), north of Rome, is equipped with a Tuscan atrium in the

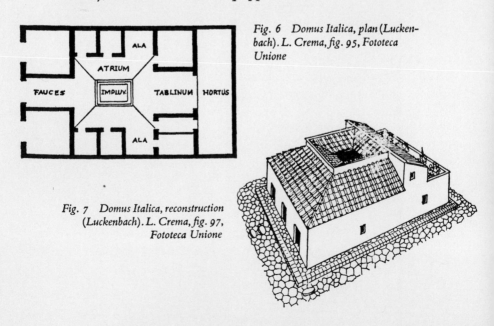

Fig. 6   Domus Italica, plan (Luckenbach). L. Crema, fig. 95, Fototeca Unione

Fig. 7   Domus Italica, reconstruction (Luckenbach). L. Crema, fig. 97, Fototeca Unione

Vitruvian definition, replete with rectangular *compluvium* and vaulted cistern.[27] This was not a private domicile, but rather an *atrium publicum*, a public building containing offices which opened on to the forum. Another Tuscan atrium house, of modest scale and dating from the late Republican era, has been found at Vetulonia.

The magnificent Hellenistic chamber-tomb of the Volumnii (*c.* 150–100 BC) near Perugia in the Umbrian hills reproduces the plan of an Etruscan palace in the yellowish sandstone of the region.[28] The tomb interior is entered through a small vestibule   8 and comprises a long rectangular atrium, with a high pitched and gabled roof and an alcove, or *tablinum*, at the far side of the atrium. Side rooms (*alae*) are located to the right and left of the *tablinum*, and from each wing another room opens up in line with the *tablinum*. Two small bedchambers (*cubicula*) interrupt the side walls of the atrium between the *alae* and the front wall. The steeply pitched roof of the atrium suggests a testudinate roof of the Vitruvian order; the elegant coffering and ceiling decoration attest the celebrated woodworking craft of the Etruscans.

The palatial residences of the *lucomones* and the wealthier burghers ennobled the Etruscan cities but were hardly characteristic.[29] Marzabotto's workshops, as separate entities or tenant quarters incorporated in house façades, must have spilt their wares on to the pavements and afforded simple, sometimes mean, garret or back-room quarters for their proprietors. San Giovenale,   9 a typical hill-town, has also yielded crowded lower-class housing of small, rectangular design on one slope, along with some fine mid-sixth-century terrace houses perched on substructures of ashlar work in tufa and enjoying a marvellous prospect. Houses on the north slope, no doubt a preferred sector, had entrances on the long sides by way of alleys.

Hellenistic Etruscan house architecture finds parallels in the fourth- and third-century BC houses at Pompeii, the House of the Surgeon and the House of Sallust, and at Herculaneum, in the   19; *11,* Samnite House.   *12*

Most impressive testimony to the elaborate nature of the later mansions appears in the rock-cut ornate tomb façades peculiar to the interior of Etruria, at Bieda (ancient Blera), Castel d'Asso,

Norchia, San Giovenale and San Giuliano. All are on the Marta River and its tributaries[30] and offer a fantastic array of house and temple façades, a kind of Etruscan Petra carved into the soft rock of the cliffsides, sometimes in the shape of gabled buildings with a single central doorway, and occasionally two-storeyed, with a colonnaded loggia over the entry, like terrace housing on the south slopes of Pompeii. Perched like eagles' eyries on the cliffside, these late tomb superstructures provide additional insight into the varied situation and elaboration of Etruscan mansions. Houses with porticoes of two, four and even six Doric or Corinthian columns, occasionally of two storeys with the upper storey recessed, are a splendid forecast of Renaissance palaces in Tuscany and Umbria and must have crowned and garlanded many of the lovely hills of Etruria.

A cinerary urn of the second century B C sheds additional light on the architectural details and general magnificence of later Etruscan mansions. The rectangular building, outlined in relief, appears like some fossilized version of the long one-room house with a projecting pitch roof and an arched entrance on the short side. The lower part of the house is of rusticated masonry construction, the upper part wooden. It is possible that here, as in the tomb façades of the Etruscan interior, the upper part represents a second-floor gallery with pilasters. The incised pattern on the long side of the urn probably represents a window providing light for the great hall on the ground floor. The end columns with volute capitals probably allude to a surrounding portico. It is remarkable how closely this Etruscan palace resembles the Florentine palaces of the early Renaissance. Another ash urn from Clusium (Chiusi), now in Berlin's Altes Museum, takes the shape of a fourth-century displuviate manor house on a high podium with wide eaves and a *compluvium* on a low pyramidal roof. A third urn features a projecting roof and an open gallery with small columns, following the pattern of known examples at Herculaneum and Pompeii.

Two other sites have yet to yield up further secrets about Etruscan housing and residential arrangement: Spina and Rusellae. Air photographs of Spina, near one of the seven mouths of the Po, the ancient Penaro, revealed an inhabited area of almost 750

3 Veii. Temple of Minerva, model

4 Caere (Cerveteri). Tomb of the Capitals, interior

1 Hut of Villanovan
period, reconstruction

2 Villanovan hut urn

5 Caere (Cerveteri). Tomb of the Shields and Chairs

6　Tarquinii. Tomb of the Augurs, interior rear wall

7　Marzabotto. Etruscan house foundations

8 Perugia. Tomb of the Volumnii, inner chamber with sepulchral monuments

9　San Giovenale. Etruscan terrace houses

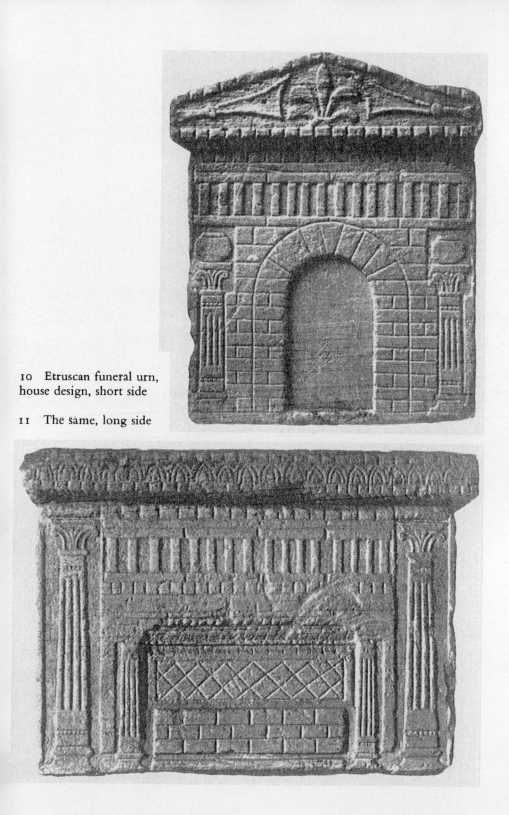

10 Etruscan funeral urn, house design, short side

11 The same, long side

12　Caere (Cerveteri).
Tomb of the Painted
Stuccoes, relief pillars
and walls

13　Chiusi. Etruscan
ash urn, house design

acres, enough to hold a population of 500,000 persons.[31] At this site the *decumanus* (one hundred feet wide) was a canal and the entire city, although organized like Marzabotto along modern city-planning lines, was a sort of Etruscan Venice or Roman Ravenna flourishing during the fifth and fourth centuries BC. Spina's residents, half Greek and half Etruscan, lived like the later Venetians in houses built on piles.

Rusellae (modern Roselle), which has already yielded some splendid sixth-century city walls, fell to the Romans in 302 BC.[32] The walls are the earliest known stone fortifications in Etruria, with a circuit of almost two miles entered by five gates. Traces of an even earlier wall, of the seventh century, have also appeared. Laviosa's excavations are expected to yield additional data on the Etruscan house type.

Tomb interiors supply invaluable information about the interior decoration and furnishing of Etruscan homes through the centuries. It has been argued that the tombs were often tufa versions of the 'baronial' halls and quarters of the Etruscan *lucomones* and tycoons. One may fairly assume also that the furnishings were peculiar not only to the Etruscan warlords and merchants, but equally to the Roman patricians of the archaic and transitional periods before and after the expulsion of the Tarquins (509 BC) and up to the time of the Gallic sack of Rome (*c.* 390 BC).

The documentation is rich and extensive. The tomb was evidently designed to be a dwelling place where the deceased would continue to use and enjoy his life's treasures and conveniences. The wall-paintings offer a brilliant reflection of the Etruscan taste for luxury and refined comfort.

The forms of furnishing were largely Greek-inspired, with some clearly derivative forms from the Assyrian and Egyptian cultures.[33] The throne with solid sides, an Etruscan 'original', had a barrel-shaped, or sometimes rectangular, seat with a rounded back and is the counterpart of our modern armchairs. A fine stone version of the throne with a footstool stands immovable in the Tomb of the Shields and Chairs at Caere. Other versions in bronze and marble feature designs and figure-scenes in relief. The bronze Barberini Chair in Rome's Villa Giulia

5

Museum and the marble Corsini Chair in the Palazzo Corsini in Rome are two splendid examples of the furniture style.[34] Other thrones with carved and rectangular legs have appeared, along with folding stools (ancestor of the Roman curule chair in ivory), benches and couches. The couches are richly illustrated in the tomb-paintings dating from the mid-sixth century to the final years of the Etruscan society.

Most justifiably famous and admired are the full-size terra-cottas of a man and a woman reclining together on a single banqueting couch, both from Caere, which are now in the Louvre and the Villa Giulia collections. The couples are almost certainly man and wife. They date from the last decades of the sixth century BC, and their style and fastidious details are closely paralleled by contemporary Ionian art. The husband and wife motif, oft repeated during the sixth century in the tomb-paintings (see, for instance, the Tomb of Hunting and Fishing, the Tomb of the Old Man and the Tomb of the Painted Vases, all at Tarquinii), is equally common during the fifth century and even where more than a single couch is depicted one may assume, in contrast to Greek practice, that the women sharing the elaborate couches were respectable family members or guests and not courtesans. This assumption is supported by the fact that the context is almost always the 'wake' or funeral banquet and the ceremonial observances offered to the deceased.[35]

Tables, three- and four-legged, followed Greek models closely. The banqueting tables, so often part of the tomb-paintings, were set alongside the couches for convenience's sake. Round, three-legged occasional tables appear in later Etruscan contexts. Chests, household boxes and *cistae*, the characteristic toilet boxes, are normal tomb and grave furnishings. Bronze *cistae*, often superbly decorated with incised scenes and usually round, were designed to hold perfume flasks, mirrors, strigils and other cosmetic aids, even jewellery on occasion. A special product of Praeneste (modern Palestrina) after the fourth century BC, these toilet chests were often mounted on bronze animal paws, sometimes with a domed lid surmounted by handles in the shape of cast groups of satyr and nymph, warriors carrying a dead comrade, etc. These toilet boxes were an original Italic contribution, good-looking and practical – an elegant adornment for the boudoir.

The Tomb of the Augurs (c. 520 BC) introduces a fully developed architectural scheme of wall-painting which remained standard practice for a very long period. The walls are divided into four clearly demarcated zones: dado or floorboard, wall-frieze of subject-matter painting, an entablature of striped bands, and pediments. One may reasonably suppose that the interiors of Etruscan houses were comparably decorated with *genre* or landscape scenes, mythological panels, or family portraits as the time and vogue dictated. Bronze candelabra, a popular export item, provided illumination for the interiors and often assumed grandiosely baroque proportions. Some were extremely elongated in shape, and they were frequently surmounted by a bronze statuette, or supplied with spikes, in the shape of bird beaks, to hold candles and torches. The candelabra supported often equally elaborate oil lamps. Bronze tripods, incense-burners and braziers mounted on wheels, played a useful role in the furnishing of the home, particularly during the winter.

The Tomb of the Painted Stuccoes at Caere is a marvellous revelation of the diversity and richness of interior furnishing. This third-century tomb comprises a single room whose walls provide niches where the dead were placed. As in some mortuary chapels, the more illustrious were placed in thirteen of these wall alcoves, while the less notable remainder (about thirty) of the dear departed were accommodated on morgue-like shelves above the floor level.

The tomb was the property of the Matuna (Mat[h]onius) family, and the name of Ramta Matunai Canatei is carved in the central alcove of the rear wall, the place of honour. The bed or couch, carved in the tufa rock, is supported by lathe-turned feet. Beneath the bed, creatures of the underworld are represented in relief: a serpent-tailed Charon and a triple-headed Cerberus with serpent tail. Two pillows, one piled on top of the other, and a low footstool with a pair of thong sandals on top complete the composition. To the left, a chest, decorated with raised studs or bosses and equipped with a lock, bears a pile of carefully folded linen.

The pillars which frame this central alcove feature a walking-stick, a feather fan, necklaces and garlands, and vases worked in relief. On each pilaster framing the funerary couch there were originally likenesses of the deceased, now mutilated; on the left the male, and on the right the female, both evidently turned towards the bed.

Above the niche and continuing like a frieze around the walls of the tomb there is a fine array of weapons, embodiments of the vocation peculiar to the family. Helmets and shin guards, circular shields, sheathed swords, *phalerae* for the horses' necks, piles of round missiles and war trumpets hang suspended in relief from the upper walls as in some ancient armoury or sanctuary where victorious arms were exhibited. The helmets, some with visors, others with cheek-pieces, are pictured alongside the felt or leather caps which were worn under the metallic helmets to prevent chafing. *Bucrania* (ox skulls), a curved war trumpet and *paterae* (sacrificial bowls) crown the entrance.

12   The pillars in the centre of the chamber are even more revealing of Etruscan daily life. The exhibition space is reserved, economically, for the sides visible from the entrance. The four rectangular panels, about 2 yards high and 2 ft 4 in. across, are decked with household ware of an astonishing variety. Objects which may be identified without question include: a bronze wine jug (*oenochoe*), a terracotta bowl with handles, decorated with a laurel-leaf pattern, ladles and spoons, a basin with tripod, a pestle, a knife-rack holding two wooden-handled knives with iron blades, spits for roasting meat, a pickaxe and machete, a large coil of rope, tongs and pincers – all suspended on nails driven into the supposedly wooden or adobe ceiling supports. A wooden (or bronze) tray with complementary leather pouch has given rise to considerable speculation. Most recently, discarding the suggestion that the table was designed as a board for kneading fettucine or tagliatelle and that the pouch held the flour, Heurgon has argued that the tray is in fact a *tabula lusoria* with folding handles, a gaming table with twelve compartments designed for the counters and dice held in the pouch. Dice, backgammon and tric-trac were popular in the ancient world, and this Etruscan version, perhaps referred to by Varro as the *latrunculi* (little thieves), is another clue to the gamesome nature of the Etruscans, who much earlier, in the Herodotean story, had

invented dice, knuckle-bones and handball to take their minds off the rigours of famine.

Elsewhere, a trolley table, covered with red cloth or leather, may have served as a 'tea-wagon' in the *triclinium* arrangements of the Etruscan *domus*. Slings, an augur's curved staff, a knapsack with attached *patera* and canteen, and a yellowish and sizeable disc of cheese to titillate the appetite and ennoble the pasta make their appearance.

Domestic animals are not forgotten in this transfer to the underworld: a tame marten on a leash plays with a black mouse (or mole?), a goose pecks at the ground, and a sleeping duck and a cat with a lizard in its claws round out the menagerie and complete the catalogue of painted reliefs.

The Tomb of the Volumnii near Perugia, the François Tomb in Vulci, and the celebrated Tomb of the Painted Stuccoes at Caere are mute but illuminating testimony to the sophistication and high style of the Hellenistic period of the Etruscan towns. Maligned and caricatured by their Roman competitors, despised and yet secretly admired and imitated, the Etruscan culture shone brightly until political disorders and the uneasy balance of power between the Etruscan centres made them a prey to the Romans. The death throes came during the civil wars of the period of Marius and Sulla.

What remained was at the heart of Roman practice, in government, religion, art and architecture. The high spirit of their fore-fathers buried in the antique tumuli and the quality of their lives and accomplishments survived in memory and in art, both periodically revived by poets and scholars like Persius and the Emperor Claudius. Horace undoubtedly sought to pay his patron the highest compliment when he recalled that Maecenas was *atavis edite regibus* – 'descended from ancient rulers' – of Etruscan Arretium.

CHAPTER II

ITALIAN TOWN HOUSES: POMPEII, HERCULANEUM AND COSA

14 POMPEII AND HERCULANEUM PROVIDE the best and most complete information available on Italic and Hellenistic–Roman housing from the fourth century BC to the time of the eruption of Vesuvius in AD 79. Both cities had suffered fairly heavy damage from the earthquake of AD 62 (or 63), and many of the houses had undergone considerable renovation and enlargement before the final disaster.[36] The eruption seems to have taken the inhabitants of both cities by surprise. Pompeii was buried in pumice stones (*lapilli*) and light ash (*scoriae*), a destructive but at the same time protective covering which reached a depth of 19–23 feet over the entire site. The nature of the fall-out, light and gradual, seems to have deluded some of the Pompeians into believing that they could survive if they took refuge in their homes, the public baths, *cryptoportici*, etc. All of these individuals perished by asphyxiation, perhaps some two thousand in all, and approximately ten per cent of the total population. Others, after the initial panic, returned to their homes and shops to try to salvage valuables; some returned to loot deserted homes and buildings, and many perished in the attempt. Pliny the Younger's superb eyewitness narrative of the eruption and its effects at Misenum, the Roman naval base where his uncle served as admiral of the fleet, makes us aware of what transpired there on the fateful day:

A cloud was rising, from what mountain observers could not tell, but it was later learned to have been Vesuvius; its likeness and shape are best compared to a [umbrella] pine tree, for it rose on a very long trunk, and then spread out in branches. . . .

It was white at one moment, at others dark and spotted, according to whether it had picked up earth or ashes. . . . Soon afterwards the cloud which I have described began to descend upon the earth and cover the sea; it had already encircled Capri and hidden it from view, and had blotted out the promontory of Misenum. . . . Now ashes, thin as yet, began to fall on us. . . . The fire stopped some distance away from us; darkness came on again, and again the ashes, thick and heavy. We got up repeatedly to shake these off, otherwise we would have been buried and crushed by their weight. . . . At last the fog dissipated into smoke or mist, and then vanished; soon there was real daylight; the sun even shone, though wanly, as where there is an eclipse. Our eyes, still haunted with fear, found everything changed, buried in deep ashes, as if in snow. We returned to Misenum and attended to our physical needs as best we could; then we spent an anxious night between hope and fear.[37]

Pliny's record of the eruption is worthy of the historian Tacitus, to whom Pliny apologetically directed it, and sheds some light on the circumstances and the conduct of the Pompeians during the same disaster, although the burial there was more complete, as also at Stabiae. The fate of Herculaneum was somewhat different. Located only 4½ miles from the volcano, the town was engulfed with a muddy, ashen flow which solidified into a lava blanket. Houses and their contents were hermetically sealed from the corrosive acids which tend to destroy or disfigure art works, and some of the finds at Herculaneum are as well preserved as if they had been buried in the sands of Egypt or Tripolitania. The death toll also seems to have been light, suggesting that the volcanic flow moved slowly enough to permit the evacuation of most of the residents. Although smaller in area (twenty-six acres) and population (four thousand) than Pompeii, Herculaneum has yielded finds of great importance and beauty. The condition of the bronzes recovered from the Villa of the Papyri, the abundance of carbonized wooden remains (tables, bed-frames, door-frames, inner stairs, folding partition doors, storage cabinets, clothes presses, amphora racks, sandals, etc.)

and the valuable papyrus library unearthed in the Suburban Villa are practically without parallel.

Before examining specific examples of non-metropolitan town housing, it is pertinent to keep in mind Vitruvius' comments on the contemporary form (*c.* 25 BC) known to him in Rome and in the provincial towns of Italy. To be sure, the houses of Pompeii and Herculaneum cannot provide us with a complete conspectus of the town houses of Rome, but we can gain from them at least some insight into the life of the capital, where rooms and façades were undoubtedly more grandiose and of costlier fabric and decoration than elsewhere but where the basic design of living was closely similar to life in the provincial towns of Italy.

In his discussion of correct proportions for the main rooms in the town house, Vitruvius emphasizes certain major areas in the architectural design: atrium, *alae, tablinum,* peristyles, dining-rooms, *exedrae* and *oeci,* picture galleries, etc.[38]

The basic floor plan, embodied in Vitruvius' architectural commentary and the excavator's finds, favours axiality and symmetry throughout, at least in the more conservatively designed houses. Between the front door and the street, houses often provided a *vestibulum* where one could step aside from the confusion of the street to find refuge or cover, and equally, to await the summons to the morning *salutatio,* a ritual required of clients daily, in order to present their requests or congratulations to their patrons. The passage inside the front entrance, the *fauces* or 'throat' of the house, led into the atrium or main reception hall. Doors, often of extreme height, were fitted with pivots (*cardines*) which were inserted and rotated in floor and lintel sockets. House doors could be fastened with iron locks or bolts which were located at strategic points to guarantee security against the disturbances and dangers of the streets at night. The atrium court might be entirely roofed over, or, more commonly, equipped with a skylight and elaborate terracotta gutters or drain-pipes which poured the rainwater from the sloping roof into a catch-basin (*impluvium*) below. The earliest *compluvium–impluvium* complexes probably date from the third century, since before that time the most venerable houses in Pompeii lacked the shallow pool in the atrium. Certainly Pliny's allusion to antique atria

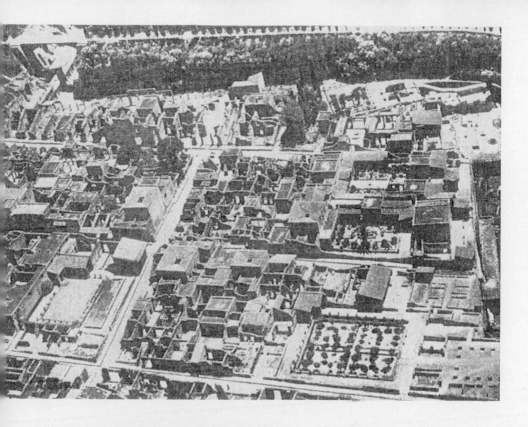

14 Herculaneum. Air
view of the excavations;
House of the Mosaic
Atrium and garden
(right centre)

15 Pompeii. House of
the Silver Wedding,
tetrastyle *oecus*

16 Pompeii. House of
the Dioscuri, atrium and
peristyle

17 Herculaneum. House
of the Wooden partition,
atrium, *impluvium*,
tablinum and garden

18 Pompeii. Villa of
Julia Felix, garden

19 Herculaneum.
Samnite house, atrium
and balcony

20 Pompeii. House of Menander, atrium, *tablinum* and peristyle garden

21 Herculaneum. House of the Neptune and Amphitrite mosaic, atrium, *impluvium*, *tablinum* and mosaic

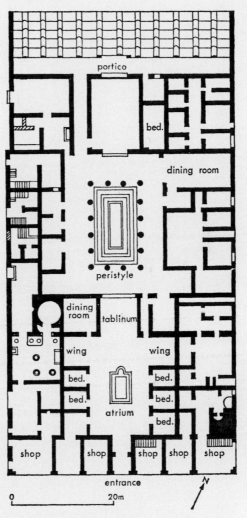

with wax busts (*imagines*, 'impressions') of the ancestors allo-
cated to special cupboards makes no reference to *impluvia*, which
would seem to conflict with the strait-laced character of the
canonical room.

The *tablinum*, which was usually located on the main axis
controlled by the front door and *fauces*, was a large room at the
rear of the atrium, often opening into it along its whole width.
Architecturally the *tablinum* was the most impressive room in the
atrium complex. Originally the master bedroom of the mansion,
later the record room (tablet depository) for family history and

personal documents, the *tablinum* kept its central importance throughout the life-span of the atrium-peristyle house. Wooden screens, folding doors and hangings (*portières*) ensured privacy when required by the *patronus* and guarded against curious passers-by.[39] This was unquestionably where the *patronus* was saluted by his clients, parasites and aides, and acknowledged as an influential support to their designs or professions. Patroni's argument, steadfastly supported by Pierre Grimal, that the real nucleus of the Italic house lay not in the atrium but in the *tablinum* or master's *salon*, has great merit and is probably correct.[40] Two deep recesses on either side of the *tablinum* formed the *alae*. They probably served a dual function at the outset, to provide light for the atrium during an era when the roof did not admit light, and waiting rooms for clients before they were summoned to the reception area. On to the atrium there opened a number of *cubicula*, and usually one or two rooms designed as dining-rooms (*triclinia*). The corridor to the right or left of the *tablinum* connecting the atrium with the garden (*hortus*) was called the *andron*.

This basic floor plan could, of course, undergo numerous variations by the addition of further courtyards, *oeci* and peristyle gardens; but, almost without exception, the basic and characteristic alignment of the atrium house was retained. The Italic architect, like the Etruscan before him, had a fondness for vistas, a concern with the relationship of spaces within the four walls of the town and the country house. The Hellenistic house tended to have rooms grouped around a colonnaded court without any manifest sense of direction, with a completely introspective design. But the Roman and Italic house found meaning, comfort and charm in its axiality, and in the long interior view from the entrance to the *tablinum* and the peristyle garden beyond.

Architectural historians have generally viewed the Campanian town house as an easy marriage of two elements, the Italic atrium dwelling and the Hellenistic peristyle, honourably and lastingly bound together for better or for worse. But there are insuperable archaeological objections to this merger. The peristyle in the Hellenistic houses of Olynthus, Delos and Priene

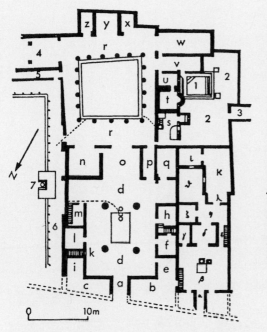

*Fig. 9 Pompeii. House of the Silver Wedding, atrium house, floor plan.
Mau-Kelsey, fig. 141, showing:*
a fauces; d *tetrastyle atrium;*
n *dining-room;* c tablinum; p andron;
r *peristyle;* s *kitchen;* t–v *bath*
(t caldarium; u tepidarium;
v apodyterium); w *summer dining-
room;* x, z *sleeping rooms;* y exedra. 1
*open-air swimming tank, in a small
garden* (2); 3 *corridor leading to another
house and to a side street;* 4 oecus; 5
corridor; 6 *garden, partially excavated;*
7 open-air triclinium: a–i fauces,
*atrium, and other rooms of separate
dwelling connected with the larger house*

was not a garden, but a court, often paved with mosaics, and
generally central to the house design; the Pompeian or Campanian peristyle, on the contrary, was never a court, but a porticoed green space for rest and recreation and for the exhibition
of art works. The Hellenistic peristyle did invade the Italic house
plan but it did so first of all in the atrium, producing the tetrastyle and Corinthian patterns which further enhanced the stature
and focal importance of the atrium in the total fabric. At some
later date, the more elaborate peristyle, modelled after the
palaestra and porticoed civic squares, became an impressive frame
and feature of the formal garden.

The Italic house, in the hill towns of Hirpinum and Samnium,
has not survived in any significant fashion. Judging by the side
comments, often disparaging, made by Livy in his account of
the troubles with Rome, the Samnite dwellings were probably
of a temporary nature, adapted to the needs of the semi-nomadic
herdsmen who moved their dwellings with their flocks. Certainly
the grave furnishings at Aufidena suggest that the Sabine home
life was austere, using simple, unpretentious pottery and basic
eating utensils. The masses must have lived in simple, crude,
presumably one-roomed dwellings, for which the Latin words

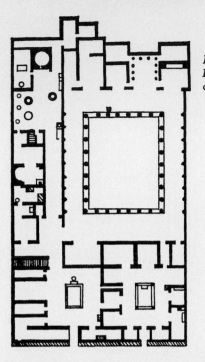

Fig. 10 Pompeii. House of the
Labyrinth, atrium house, Corinthian
oecus, plan

mapalia or tuguria would probably be appropriate, in rustic huts or
rectangular dwellings on the pattern of the Villanovan hut urns
and the 'Hut of Romulus'.[41]

1, 2

Furnishing was almost certainly of the simplest nature. The
Sabellian paintings are of no assistance in the matter of interior
furnishings since the details are invariably Greek, but Cicero's
pronouncement on the Samnites is enlightening in this regard:
'nothing was splendid, nothing elaborate, save their own
persons'.[42]

The House of the Surgeon at Pompeii (VI, i, 10),[43] so called
from the collection of surgical instruments found in it, was built
originally in the fourth or third century BC. Its rectangular
plan, and the absence of Hellenistic additions (peristyle garden,
etc.) mark it as the earliest Italic house so far recovered in
Campania. The massive, severe façade, fashioned from sandstone
blocks quarried from the Sarnus River deposits, and the simple
square atrium with central catch-basin and compluvium probably
reflect something of the sobriety and simplicity of contemporary
well-to-do Samnite houses at Malventum (Beneventum) or
Bovianum.[44] The house walls are laid in successive courses of

11

sandstone with mud bonding. The slits let into the walls like loop-holes to admit light recall the design of the city walls. The *cubicula* are arranged around the atrium, two beside the entrance hall, two on either side of the atrium, followed by two open rooms (*alae*). At the far end, two larger rooms appear on either side of the main *salon* (*tablinum*). Between the *tablinum* and *impluvium* in the atrium court, the architect located the traditional dining table (*cartibulum*), which a more prosperous age transformed into an elegant marble table with elegantly carved legs. Behind the *tablinum* was the walled garden and, in a corner, the shrine of the Lares (*lararium*), the household's protective gods.

Pompeii's House of the Surgeon, in its present state, offers a fine illustration of Vitruvius' *cavaedium tuscanicum*.[45] Although the original building was not provided with skylight and catch-basin, the tufa *impluvium* was added to the original house during the second century B C, adapting an original *cavaedium displuviatum* or *cavaedium testudinatum* to the present design. Vitruvius supplies detailed information on both suggested forms of roofing: 'In the displuviate, there are beams which slope outwards, supporting the roof, and throwing the rainwater off; . . . the testudinate is employed where the span is not great, and where large rooms are provided in upper storeys', the latter implying that the entire

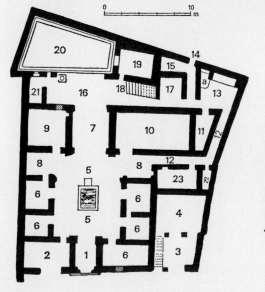

Fig. 11 *Pompeii. House of the Surgeon, plan. Mau-Kelsey, fig. 127, showing:* 1 fauces; 5 atrium; 7 tablinum; 8 alae; 9, 10 dining-rooms; 13 kitchen, with hearth (a); 14 postern; 16 colonnade; 18 stairway to rooms over the rear of the house; 19 room with window opening on the garden; 20 garden

roof was tiled or coffered in the 'tortoise-shell' pattern or cara-pace. Vitruvius also indicates why the displuviate roof form was often superseded by another pattern: 'it is, however, very troublesome to keep in repair, because the pipes, which are intended to hold the water that comes dripping down the walls all round, cannot take it quickly enough as it runs down from the channels, but get too full and run over, thus spoiling the woodwork and the walls of houses of this style [i.e., displuviate].'

The house interior, brightened somewhat during the second phase of construction, was basically cavernous and dark, almost sacrosanct, and awesome in its 'patriarchal' austerity. The only natural light to penetrate the dark interior came from the front door and green area behind, and subsequently through the oak-or beech-beamed skylight which admitted light and air into the residence.

Remodellings, comparable to that detailed in the House of the Surgeon, must have occurred repeatedly in the market town, as the citizens aspired to more conspicuous, more attractive housing and reception areas. Vitruvius comments on the propriety of housing for the different classes:

> the common rooms are those which any of the people have a perfect right to enter, even without an invitation: that is, entrance courts, *cavaedia*, peristyles, and all intended for the like purpose. Hence, men of everyday fortune do not need entrance courts, *tablina*, or an atrium built in the grand style, because such men are more apt to discharge their social obliga-tions by going round to others than to have others come to them.[46]

The rambling one-storey House of Sallust (VI, ii, 4) is another fine example of a pre-Roman house of the Samnite period of Pompeii's history.[47] Contemporary with the House of the Surgeon, it too was constructed entirely of limestone during the late fourth or early third century BC. It follows the pattern of the House of the Surgeon but has four shops along the front, opening on either side of the entrance. The interior rooms were grouped around the central atrium which was probably testudinate. Water was drawn from a well in the first room to the right of the

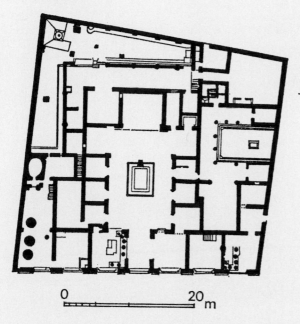

Fig. 12 Pompeii. House of Sallust, plan. Mau–Kelsey, fig. 129

0   20 m

atrium. A portico in the rear served as a prospect for the *tablinum* and the two lateral *oeci*. Considerable remodelling ensued during the second century BC. A new tufa façade was supplied and a tufa *impluvium*, heretofore absent, was set into the atrium with the cistern located in the back garden. The *viridarium* may have been added at the same period. During the early first century AD one of the shops on the left of the *fauces* was redesigned as a hot-food stand (*thermopolium*), seemingly as part of the reconditioning of the house as an inn. The building was subsequently adapted to commercial use with a private apartment incorporated into the design, and after the earthquake of AD 63 a bakery (*pistrinum*) seems to have taken over the antique establishment.

Many of the atrium houses located on the south-west slopes of the town site underwent modification and enlargement as Pompeian affluence and expertise in domestic architecture expanded. Their original plan followed the Italic prototype, sometimes eliminating the *tablinum* in an effort to enlarge the atrium court. During the second century the houses were modified so as to become handsome terrace homes with a supporting portico on the lower levels. The best remains of this compensating and venturesome architectural form appear on the rocky outcropping between the Triangular Forum and the Basilica.[48] Such an innovation, responding probably to the pressure of population and to the scarcity of building lots, was part and parcel of the modifications in Pompeian housing during the second and first centuries BC.

The most extensive innovations followed the Hellenistic trend which swept over Roman (and Etruscan) architecture after the mid-second century BC. Spurred by examples of housing seen in the Hellenistic East (at Rhodes, Miletus, Mitylene, Delos, Priene and Athens), second-century architects, probably Greek, wrought significant changes and remodellings in the fabric of the older houses of the Campanian and Latin towns and cities. In general, the effect was to enlarge the plan of the Pompeian house and render it more spacious and airy, while at the same time suiting the new refinement and pretensions of the wealthy commercial class. The marriage of the Italic and Hellenistic forms produced a novelty in domestic architecture which made itself felt all over the Roman empire for years to come. Building materials were involved in the change of plan and scale, and were, at the same time, partly responsible for the innovations. Cato mentions concrete with an aggregate of chunky stone or brick as the normal building material for *villae rusticae* in his work *De Agricultura*, composed during the first half of the second century BC.[49] The widespread use of *opus caementicium* came with the discovery during the first half of the second century BC of the amazing qualities of *pozzolana* (Puteolan) sand, a common ingredient in the volcanic subsoil of central Italy, including Latium and Campania. Giuseppe Lugli ascribes the first discovery of this 'natural cement' to the period 300–250 BC, and argues that the new find in Campania spread rapidly to Rome and Latium where it was used extensively in the late third and early second centuries.[50] Its use for purposes other than substructures appears in *opus incertum*, a building technique highly favoured by Vitruvius: 'in the *opus incertum*, the rubble, lying in courses and imbricated, makes a wall which, though not beautiful, is stronger than *reticulatum* [the network brick pattern laid into concrete].'[51]

After the third century, the Pompeian architects turned from the local limestone, rough-hewn and square, to volcanic tufa blocks, quarried at nearby Nocera (Nuceria). Tufa, though easy to quarry and susceptible to working, carving and modelling, hardens upon exposure to the atmosphere into a very durable material. Plaster and painted stucco attach easily and permanently to the porous surface of this stone.[52]

Building materials were not the only major revolution in second-century architecture. The standardized pattern of housing underwent significant changes as well. The atrium, once the heart of the house, no longer seemed adequate to the changing times. The architects turned instead, as in the House of Sallust, to the sunny, green spaces and colonnaded settings of peristyle gardens. In house after house, particularly in the newer residential areas, a porticoed court was appended to the atrium complex, replete with sculptures in bronze and marble, fountains and catch-basins, and rooms for rest and recreation with trellised vines and wall-paintings.

The House of the Silver Wedding (V, 2), so named to commemorate the visit of the King and Queen of Italy to Pompeii in 1893, is a superb example of the 'new-style' house. Samnite in its original phase, the modification and enlargement of the second-century house came partly under Augustus and finally under Nero and the Flavian emperors. The atrium is an imposing barrel-vaulted room with four columns (tetrastyle) set at the corners of the *impluvium* basin and a peristyle garden behind.[53] The side adjoining the *tablinum* is elevated following the 'Rhodian' pattern. In his description of the alleged 'Greek' house, Vitruvius comments on the 'Rhodian' peristyle:

> Such apartments have fine entrance courts with imposing front doors of their own; the colonnades of the peristyles are decorated with polished stucco in relief and plain, and with coffered ceilings of woodwork; off the colonnades that face the north they have Cyzicene dining-rooms and picture galleries; to the east, libraries; *exedrae* to the west; and to the south large square rooms of such generous dimensions that four sets of dining couches can easily be arranged in them, with plenty of room for serving and for amusements.[54]

The House of the Silver Wedding subscribes remarkably closely to the Vitruvian example. The peristyle columns were stuccoed with upper revetment and smooth surface below, following the Hellenistic practice of economy and protection against damage. A spacious garden and outdoor dining area were reached from the east side of the peristyle. The south side had the best rooms of all: a large *oecus* with vaulted roof supported by four stucco-faced brick columns imitating porphyry marble; a passageway (*ambulacrum*) opened into *cubicula* with painted decoration, and an *exedra;* another *oecus* opened at the south-west corner and a private bath (comprising *calidarium, tepidarium* and *frigidarium* complex) was located outside in the small garden.

15; 9

The House of Pansa (VI, 1) provided the most elaborate and handsome example of the merging of Hellenistic and Italic domestic forms. Like the House of the Faun this mansion occupied an entire block (*insula*). A Samnite house at its inception, it became in its developed form a sizeable mansion. The original

13

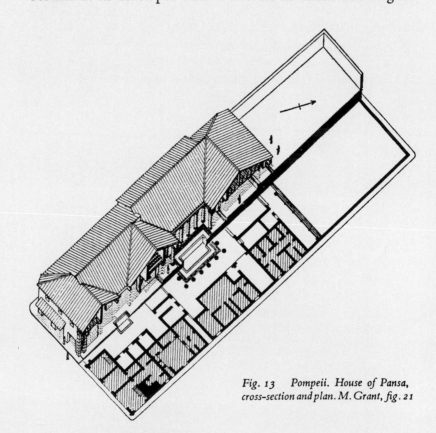

Fig. 13   Pompeii. House of Pansa, cross-section and plan. M. Grant, fig. 21

nucleus is still visible: Tuscan atrium with the usual beamed support, *cubicula*, *alae* and *tablinum*, arranged axially and symmetrically in the front part of the house; the peristyle behind contains a great pool (*piscina*) rather than the usual garden. Behind the peristyle a large hall appears and on the left a kitchen (*culina*), a stable equipped with a latrine, and a garage for carts and wagons.

The extensive garden attached to the rear of the House of   *8, 13*
Pansa – which covered an area of 87 by 160 feet – continues to be cultivated. The French scholar Mazois sketched a plan of the garden at the time of excavation and observed that it was laid out systematically in rectangular plots separated by paths which also served as irrigation ditches. Though flowers may have been included, the garden was obviously a produce garden designed to supply the Pompeian and local markets. The present-day plant-nursery appears to adhere to the ancient plan most assiduously, even to the laying out of identical eight-foot-wide plots.[55]

The House of the Faun (XII, 2–5), named after the bronze figure of the Dancing Faun found in the *impluvium* of the main atrium, is the most spendid house in Pompeii, and probably the best known.[56] Like the earlier houses already described, the House of the Faun was another product of the Samnite period ·during the second century BC, when the Hellenistic influence was invading city planning and architecture. The *fauces*, equipped   *14*
with a massive double door, have the Oscan welcome, HAVE, rendered in the floor mosaic. Two *lararia* appear high up on the vestibule walls, worked in stucco and elaborately decorated. The

Fig. 14   Pompeii. House of the Faun, plan. Mau-Kelsey, fig. 132

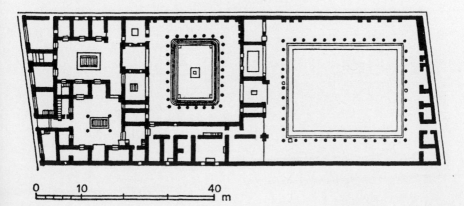

0   10   40
|_____| m

front portion of the house is organized around two atria courts: the first, a Tuscan-type atrium, follows the traditional pattern; the second, tetrastyle, follows the Hellenistic model. The influence of Hellenistic gymnasia and palaestrae is obvious in the two peristyles where the adjoining rooms (*exedrae*) favour the breadth of their gymnasia counterparts. Beside the *tablinum*, facing south on to the Tuscan atrium, two dining-rooms (*triclinia*) appear. Judging by the floor mosaic motifs and the exposure, one was designed for autumn and the other for winter dining. Behind the atria, the architect located the first peristyle with a portico of twenty-eight Ionic columns and a fountain basin in the centre. The walls were covered with decorative stucco. The *exedra* in the centre of the rear wall of the peristyle was emphasized by an entrance with projecting wings (*antae*) and two Corinthian columns stuccoed to resemble porphyry. The floor was covered with the famous Alexander Mosaic and with a Nilotic scene on the mosaic threshold. Two dining-rooms for summer use flank the *exedra*, facing north. On the east side of the house a narrow corridor isolated the kitchen, bath and stable from the rest of the residence. A short service corridor leads from the peristyle garden to another garden with a Doric portico where a postern gate or door (*posticum*) ensured the privacy of the family quarters and recreation and entertainment areas, now far removed from the formal elegance of the atria.

Unquestionably the most spectacular and spacious of the Pompeian gardens was that attached to the House of Marcus 15 Loreius Tiburtinus.[57] The garden was architecturally bound up with the living-quarters and with a terrace equipped with a canal or irrigation channel. Like some prototype of the Villa d'Este fountains, a cascade set into the middle of the open-air terrace, accessible from the atrium, poured water into a fountain house (*nymphaeum*) below, thence into a long channel (*euripus*) which runs the entire length of the garden, framed by trees and flowering shrubs. A marble fountain and pergola marked the midpoint of the canal. At the far end, another shrine housed a statue of a hermaphrodite. The casts of the roots of large plants indicate that the garden was originally shaded by fruit trees planted in serried ranks. Statuettes and herms lined the canal

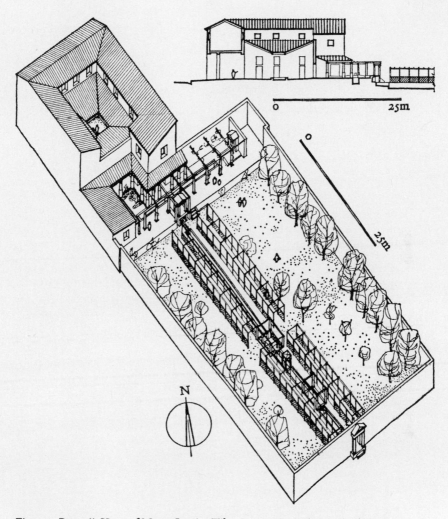

*Fig. 15 Pompeii. House of Marcus Loreius Tiburtinus, section and view. Boëthius &
Ward-Perkins, fig. 121*

banks, while others stood in the intercolumniations of the portico.
At the north end of the garden and at the east end of a terrace,
the architect designed a summer open-air dining-room, fitted
with two dining couches and decorated with wall-paintings, one
of Narcissus and one of Pyramus and Thisbe, both signed by the
Roman painter Lucius.

The absorption of the peristyle into Italic architecture has
occasioned much critical study and debate, particularly in relation

to the development of the atrium. The peristyle, a large open-air garden with a surrounding colonnade (*peristylum*) and informally arranged rooms along the sides and rear wall, was certainly no substitute for the atrium.[58] The ancestral entrance hall managed to retain its original identity throughout the evolution of the house form, but was considerably indebted to the peristyle form in its columnar arrangement. For the atrium, once roofed over, then compluviate, moved towards a columnar aspect in later times. The columns, introduced first at the four corners of the catch-basin, later multiplied into an almost peristyle form. Initially very tall, they shrank ultimately to the height of the peristyle columns in the private sections of the house. The *impluvium*, once a necessary furnishing for the home, became obsolescent with the improved sanitation and drainage systems of late Republican communities, and the catch-basin and cistern beneath were reduced to an ornamental pool connected by lead pipes or terracotta tubes to the city drains on the street façade. Fountains, shrubbery and plants gradually absorbed the space reserved for the *impluvium*, and the tendency to bring the outdoors indoors, exemplified in the wall-paintings, became a charming feature of the Pompeian and Campanian interiors.

The colonnaded gardens may quite conceivably and plausibly derive not from Hellenistic house forms and conventions, but from a merging, in the technical sense a *contaminatio*, of the peristyles employed in gymnasia and palaestrae, and the splendid public and private gardens (*paradeisoi*) of the Near and Middle East. On the other hand, the attached gardens are not always *8, 13* elaborately colonnaded. The House of Pansa, contemporary with the others described, has a walled garden (*hortus conclusus*) with plain walls.

Gardening in Rome, and presumably in the Italian towns like Pompeii and Herculaneum, was an imported art. The earliest known pleasure gardens in Rome were those of the philhellenes P. Cornelius Scipio Aemilianus Africanus Minor and Decimus Junius Brutus Augur in the late second century BC. Lucullus and Pompey the Great, both of whom engaged with the same Asiatic enemy, Mithridates VI Eupator, in Pontus and Cappadocia, were the main instigators of horticulture and impressive gardens in an urban context. Both laid out for themselves great parks which were modelled on Eastern *paradeisoi* and on Hellenistic public gardens. The professional landscape gardeners were almost certainly Greek from the outset. Cicero is the first to use words of Greek derivation, *topiarius* and *ars topiaria*, for 'gardener' and 'gardening'.[59] The Hellenistic Greek gardeners, 'technicians' as is implied by the use of *ars*, ministered, in the first instance, to the urban need for outdoor living space, for areas which would provide fresh air, shade and quiet in the context of an enormous, overcrowded city, largely one of apartment-dwellers. More than this, perhaps, the public gardens in particular served the innate naturalistic urge of the Italians (and their polyglot neighbours), a preoccupation with gardens and landscape which is found in Etruscan paintings of earlier centuries.

Cicero's reference to the landscape gardener, mentioned earlier, also introduces discussion of what was the main objective of landscape gardeners in domestic or larger settings, i.e., to create a tableau. Literature and art repeatedly testify to Roman alertness to the intrinsic beauty of plants and flowers even though their decorative value may have registered most when the landscape artist was commissioned.

Located in a quarter of fashionable residences, the House of the Dioscuri presented its handsome façade to the Via di Mercurio where the pavement is wide and the kerb high.[60] The house was finished *c.* 100 BC and adopted the already classical type of atrium-*tablinum* peristyle. However, the earlier peristyle seems to have been deficient in grandeur and modern luxury. This seems to be the best explanation for the annexation of the neighbouring House of Caetronius (VI, ix, 7), *c.* 30 BC. The two houses were not the work of the same architect. During the last period of the city's life both houses were given a uniform façade of stucco. The Via di Mercurio was evidently not a main traffic artery, nor was it subjected to much wheeled traffic; the ruts which usually scar the streets of Pompeii are almost totally lacking, and the only signs of heavy wear occur at street crossings. The house was admirably situated for access to the forum and the forum baths, and the main arteries of traffic were close by. This advantageous situation may explain why this house, and its neighbours, the

House of the Gilded Amorini (VI, xvi, 7) and the House of the Silver Wedding (V, 2), were built on such grandiose lines.

Richardson has identified the last residents of the house with the Nigidius family, rich business people, merchants involved with import and export and affluent enough, apparently, to live in a double house and to furnish it with decorations of the finest quality. So superior are the wall-paintings that Richardson is able to state that 'the seven painters of the Casa dei Dioscuri cannot be regarded as a fair cross-section of the Fourth Style [50–79 AD] painters of Pompeii, for the house was so splendid that only superior artists were chosen to decorate it'. Instead of assuming, with Richardson, that the annexation of the next-door house was designed to accommodate two families, one might equally argue that the original house, with the superior wall-paintings and all, was diverted to commercial uses, and that the owner chose to quarter himself in a smaller, perhaps quieter, residence.

The short narrow *fauces* which lead into the Corinthian atrium slope slightly, following the normal pattern in Pompeii. The Pompeian architect, as so often in other dwellings, arranged the principal axis from the front door in such a way as to create a vista which would dominate the entire mansion. The small room south of the *fauces* and opening on to them was the doorkeeper's or porter's lodge (*ostiarius*). A wooden stair led to an upper room (*cenaculum*) and bathroom next to where the porter, and possibly other servants, slept. A large window on the upper storey made it possible for late visitors or callers at siesta time to rouse the porter. In the east wall of the porter's bedroom there was evidently a speaking tube connecting the upper room with the atrium.[61]

16   The spacious Corinthian atrium is the most beautiful in Pompeii. The square *impluvium* is ringed by twelve columns, four to each side. The principal axis extends from the street door (west) through the *impluvium* to the *tablinum* (east). There is a fountain on the east rim of the *impluvium*, once supporting a sculpture which was salvaged shortly after the eruption. Another fountain, in the shape of a white marble flower or cluster of leaves covered with tiny frogs and lizards in carved relief, stood originally in the centre of the catch-basin. The bronze key which controlled the jet of water has disappeared, along with the sculptures.[62]

22 Pompeii. House of
the Vettii, garden

23 Cosa. SUNY House,
view from the northeast

24 Ostia. House of Cupid and Psyche, view to *nymphaeum*

25 Rome, Palatine Hill. House of Livia, reticulate brickwork,
wall-paintings and lead pipes

26 Rome, Palatine Hill. Domus Flavia (or Augustana), model of
Domitian's palace, with Circus Maximus in the foreground

In a spacious mansion of Flavian date, it is surprising that the original function of the *impluvium* was not eliminated. Fresh water was certainly abundantly supplied by the water mains of Pompeii, but the architect, and presumably the owners as well, favoured the by then antiquated practice of husbanding rainwater in a cistern beneath the *impluvium*. It has been suggested that rainwater was probably preferred to aqueduct water for laundering or wherever soft water was preferable to hard. And, of course, the cistern water helped to supplement the aqueduct water, which was under heavy strain in the dry months of May through September.

The twelve columns were built around a concrete and brick core. The lower stucco facing was painted red, the upper zone white. The pavement of the atrium and *fauces* followed the usual practice in bourgeois homes of the time and earlier, and was composed of cement and terracotta with added chips and pebbles of brighter colours. Richardson has suggested that the single *ala* which opens on to the atrium at the eastern end of the north wall was originally lined with cabinets and served as the business office or filing room for the owner's business records. Strong boxes (*arcae*) stood on either side of the entry (*cf.* the House of the Vettii, VI, xv, 1).

The modernized *tablinum*, dating from the Flavian period of redecoration, is open to the atrium along its entire front and constitutes the ultimate perspective from the street door through the colonnaded atrium. Richly decorated with wall-paintings, it seems to have served as the main reception room. Householders must normally have devised privacy for the *tablinum* by the use of curtains or draperies or by means of folding doors or shutters after the pattern of the carbonized wooden screen found in the House of the Wooden Partition (Herculaneum iii, 11-12).

17

The kitchen of the House of the Dioscuri resembles its counterpart in the Pompeian House of the Vettii (VI, xv, 1). Spacious, windowless and roofless, basically an open courtyard reminiscent of the Etruscan cortiles at Marzabotto, the room is cheerless and unadorned. The pounded earth floor and coarse plaster walls are practical, but unattractive. The hearth, supplied by fuel bins adjacent to the stove, followed the usual pattern with a covering of broken tile laid in mortar with protective kerbs along the edge. A removable roofing above the hearth protected the fire from rainfall. Work tables and storage shelves for dishes, pans and cutlery would complete the arrangements. A latrine opens off the east end of the kitchen (*culina*). The walls were covered with a fine plaster with a high red dado and white ground panels above, with red and yellow stripes and ornamentation. Slit windows and a rectangular window opened above the sewer at the east end of the sizeable room (7 ft 3 in. by 13 ft 4 in.). The flushing arrangements are unknown, though certainly some provision was made, perhaps channelling rainwater from the roof into the system and thence into the town sewers.

The peristyle is large and impressive, measuring 41 ft 4 in. by 70 ft 6 in. altogether, with a garden area included, measuring 23 ft 10 in. by 47 ft 7 in. Entry into the garden was from the south side of the atrium. A unique instance of the Cyzicene *oecus* opens off the peristyle, according with the Vitruvian description almost precisely: 'these are built with a northern exposure [here, northern and western] and generally command a view of the gardens and have folding doors in the middle. They are also so long and so wide that two sets of dining couches, facing each other with room to pass around them, can be placed therein. On the right and left they have windows which open like folding doors, so that views of the garden may be had from the dining couches through the opened windows.'[63] Richardson suggests, quite plausibly, that musicians and actors might have performed in the east portico of the peristyle and entertained the diners with their songs and antics. The suggestion carries even greater conviction by reason of the subject-matter of the paintings on the peristyle walls directly opposite the *oecus*: Perseus and Andromeda, and Medea contemplating the murder of Jason's sons.

A stable or garage for the family carriage and horses was located at the east end of the north portico of the *viridarium*, at the north end of the east wall. It measures 22 ft wide and 24 ft 11 in. deep.

In spite of many alterations and additions, including the annexing of the neighbouring house, the House of the Dioscuri is one of the most intelligible, rewarding houses for the visitor to Pompeii, for into its fabric are wrought some fine examples of the basic modules and appointments of a rich man's home.

The House of Epidius Rufus (IX, i, 22) is a late Republican house containing the largest polystyle Corinthian atrium at Pompeii, a splendid hall with sixteen Corinthian columns more reminiscent of a public building than a residential factor.[64] A platform also runs along the façade of the house with a short flight of steps at the side and is curiously comparable to the platform in the central building of the official complex at the south end of the Pompeian forum. Surrounding the peristyle atrium, for the house lacks the peristyle garden and has a walled garden (hortus) instead, there are rooms of varying dimensions. Two exedrae, set into the middle of the two longer sides, are provided with two columns in the open wall and have the appearance of small auditoria.

The Samnite House at Herculaneum (V, 1–2) has fauces 19 decorated in Pompeian Style I, which open into an atrium with an upstairs gallery of diminutive Ionic columns connected by a perforated parapet (pluteus) faced with stucco.[65] Although the intercolumnar spaces were originally open, the changed conditions of the house required that all be closed, save on the east side. Before the upstairs rooms were leased out, following the earth- 16 quake of AD 63, there would have been fenestration along the west and north sides of the loggia. The upper storey was extended during the remodelling to project over the street in the form of a gallery running along the entire façade. These rooms, accessible by a private staircase from the adjoining entrance, provided a small apartment to let.

The House of the Mosaic Atrium at Herculaneum (IV, 1–2) takes its name from the black and white chess-board pattern at the point of entry.[66] Fauces, atrium and winter dining-room, 17 rather than the normal tablinum, adhere to the east–west axis of the property. The dining-room, replacing the time-honoured tablinum, follows the oecus Aegyptius design or Egyptian banquet- ing hall detailed by Vitruvius (6, 3, 9). Unusual in its basilican 18 design, with side aisles and a central nave, it offered some distinct and novel advantages by the provision of light through

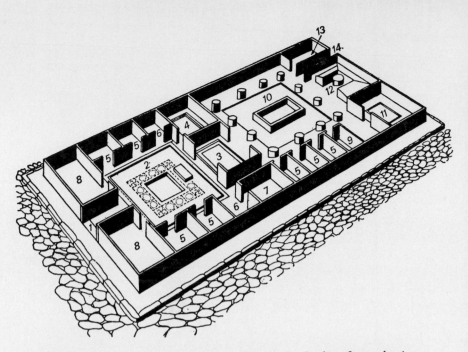

Fig. 16 Herculaneum. Samnite House, schematic plan. V. Catalano, fig. 14, showing: 1 entrance; 2 atrium; 3 tablinum; 4 triclinium; 5 cubicula; 6 alae; 7 storage room; 8 work rooms; 9 kitchen; 10 peristyle, garden and pool; 11 exedra; 12 summer triclinium (oecus); 13 bedroom or stable; 14 service entrance

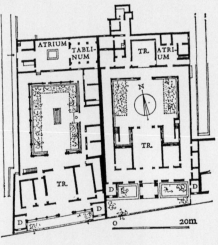

Fig. 17 Herculaneum. House of the Mosaic Atrium (left), and House of the the Stags, right, plans. Boëthius & Ward-Perkins, fig. 110

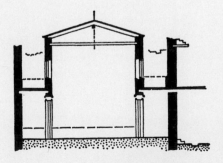

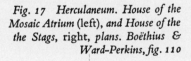

Fig. 18 Herculaneum. House of the Mosaic Atrium, oecus Aegyptius, cross-section

windows in the upper walls of the nave, and a promenading area atop the single-storey side aisles. The peristyle garden is entered by a stair descending at right angles from the atrium. The inter-columniations are walled in and provided with windows and two entrances into the garden. The narrow corridor along the east side of the garden was protected by glass windows. Four *cubicula* with red walls face on to the garden on either side of an *exedra* on a slight elevation. The summer *triclinium* and reception area lie roughly on the north–south axis, facing the garden with its fountain and *impluvium* on one side and the Bay on the other. On either side of the *triclinium* are two additional rooms (*diaetae*) which provided the house owner and his guests with an admirable panoramic view of the Bay. Both have been identified with day bedrooms (*cubicula diurna*) commonly found in patrician houses and villas.

The so-called Vespasianic 'villa' (*praedium*) of Julia Felix (II, iv, 3) at the end of the Street of Abundance (Via dell'Abbondanza) in Pompeii occupies about one-third of a city block, with a large market or commercial flower garden occupying the remainder.[67] The residence of the proprietress, Julia Felix, may also contain another example of the Cyzicene *oecus* described by Vitruvius as uncommon in Italy. The garden of the Villa of Julia Felix was handsomely designed and furnished, with a central fish pond (*euripus*) crossed by marble bridges and with numerous niches to provide shade for the fish. The *porticus* has marble pillars along its western side (comparable to those found recently at Stabiae) and small stuccoed pillars painted green along the southern and eastern sides where a series of rectangular and apsidal niches decorated the garden wall. A rectangular *exedra* opened on the centre of the western side of the *hortus*, behind the portico, with marble couches and a small cascade at the end which provided water for the central spout immediately below and central to the room.

The House of Menander (I, x, 4), marked at the point of entry by Corinthian capitals worked in tufa, is clearly a distinguished home.[68] The atrium, decorated with hunting and landscape scenes (Pompeian Style II), is also provided with a *lararium* and an *exedra* decorated with scenes from the Trojan War. The large

Fig. 19 Herculaneum. *House of the Mosaic Atrium, garden and* cubicula, *reconstruction. V. Catalano, fig. 18*

Fig. 20 Herculaneum. *House of the Mosaic Atrium and House of the Stags, south façade, over city wall, reconstruction. Boëthius & Ward-Perkins, fig. 120*

peristyle, with the intercolumnar spaces once again closed by a low wall, is faced with painted representations of plants and white herons feeding. The two *oeci* on the north side are superbly decorated with paintings and a mosaic floor with a Nilotic scene. The *triclinium*, together with other smaller rooms, opens off the eastern *ambulacrum*. The servant quarters lie in the rear of the house. The rear wall of the portico has a series of rectangular and apsidal alcoves following a pattern which became common during the reign of Nero. The recesses are splendidly painted. One of the wall-paintings offers a portrait of the Hellenistic playwright, Menander, whose name appears on the roll which he is holding and on the hem of his robe. Traces of shelves have been detected in one of the alcoves, suggesting that it was, perhaps, used as a library. A private bath system was located at the end of the west *ambulacrum*. A corridor led to the kitchen and underground store-rooms, in one of which was found a splendid collection of silver, numbering 115 pieces, along with money and jewellery. The dinner service is now exhibited in the National Museum in Naples and is one of the three great silver services to survive from the ancient world.

The House of the Neptune and Amphitrite Mosaic in Herculaneum (V, 6–7) compensated for the lack of space for a peristyle by combining the dining-room and *nymphaeum* (fountain structure) together with the atrium and *tablinum*, to best possible advantage.[69] The atrium, *tablinum* and side rooms on either side of the *tablinum* follow the regular pattern of the Italic and Roman town house. The walls of the *triclinium*, which bordered   21 on the *tablinum*, were decorated with colourful mosaics and paintings of trees and flowers to create the illusion of a peristyle garden. The typical town house, incorporating atrium and peristyle, was gradually reduced with the increase in urban population, and in Herculaneum the colonnaded courtyard behind atrium and *tablinum* is rarely found.

The House of the Tragic Poet (VI, viii, 3–5), opposite the Forum Baths of Pompeii, commands attention and interest from visitors because it is often the first house to be encountered in the tour of the excavations.[70] Celebrated as the residence of Glaucus in Bulwer Lytton's *Last Days of Pompeii*, it owes its name to the discovery of a fine floor mosaic in the *tablinum* depicting a tragic playwright, perhaps Aeschylus, training a satyr chorus for a performance. The householders, judging by the art works found in the house, seem to have been persons of refinement and wealth. The tufa kerbs and fine *opus signinum* pavement in front of the house testify to the careful upkeep of the property required of Pompeian house-owners, and to a concern for an attractive dwelling in an area of comparatively heavy wheel and foot traffic. The House of Pansa lies across the street to the west. At the point of entry, within the vestibule, a black and white mosaic floor-mat confronted the caller with a stern reminder of the owner's desire for privacy. A ferocious hound, chained and girt with a red leather collar, strains threateningly towards the door with an almost unnecessary admonition to Beware of the Dog (*Cave Canem*). The atrium, 28 feet long and 20 feet wide, was paved with black and white marble tesserae, with an interlaced pattern in black bordering the marble *impluvium*. The decoration of the atrium provides one of the richest repertoires of mythological wall-painting in Pompeii and was certainly the most richly decorated room in the entire house – a splendid example of the post-earthquake renovations in the city. The pseudo-peristyle contained five free-standing Doric columns and two engaged columns. A wooden (or iron) parapet connected the columns, which were of stuccoed brick, and the podium and lower part were painted red, the remainder white. The rain spouts attached to the portico roof were fashioned in the shape of terracotta frogs. The *lararium* was located in the north-west corner of the peristyle, against the north wall. A postern gate (*posticum*) enabled the members of the family to come and go by a private door. A large dining-room opens off the peristyle, also richly decorated. Two large shops (*tabernae*) frame the entrance to the house. Usually managed by freedmen or slaves on behalf of the house-owner, these shops may even have served as porters' lodges for the main establishment; both had direct access to the *fauces*.

The House of the Vettii (VI, xv, 1) was a luxurious bourgeois mansion belonging to the Vettii brothers (Aulus Vettius Restitutus and Aulus Vettius Conviva).[71] It is loosely organized around the main axis and canonical constituents of *fauces*, atrium and peristyle.

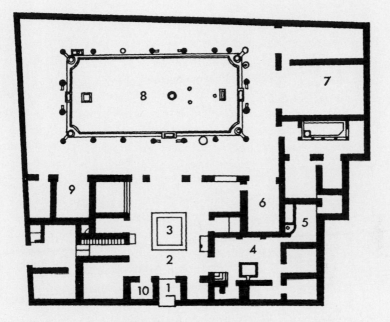

Fig. 21 *Pompeii. House of the Vettii, plan. Nash, Roman Towns, fig. 43a*
1 fauces; 2 atrium; 3 impluvium; 4 atriolum; 5 culina; 6 *red room: Daedalus,*
Ixion, Dionysus and Ariadne; 7 triclinium; 8 peristyle; 9 *yellow room with paintings*
of the Theban legend; 10 *Janitor's room*

Fig. 22 *Pompeii. House of the Vettii, reconstruction. Nash, Roman Towns, fig. 43b*

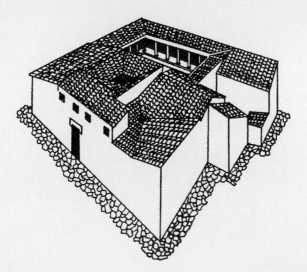

21, 22   There, however, the dictates of the past ended. The entrance, on the east side, opened into the atrium which lacked the usual *tablinum*, although two *alae* opened to the right and left of the peristyle entry. Two storage chests (*arcae*) still stand on either side of the *impluvium*. A small side atrium (*atriolum*) opens on the right of the main *atrium* and is attached to the kitchen and slave quarters. A splendid *lararium*, probably the best known in Pompeii, decorates the *atriolum* wall. A stair led to the upper storey which extended over the south-eastern sector of the mansion. The roof of the peristyle, supported by white-stuccoed columns with ornate stuccoed capitals, is largely restored. The garden has been reconstituted. Holes in the hardened soil and the scientific analysis of carbonized roots of plants and trees assisted the accurate replanting. Between the columns of the peristyle, marble and bronze cupids and satyrs serving as fountain figures occupy their original stations, reflected in the marble catch-basins below. The lead water-pipes have been found and put into use again. The marble garden furniture, tables, Janus-headed busts (Bacchus and Ariadne, Bacchus and a Maenad) remain *in situ*. Three large
22   rooms face on to the peristyle garden: two bedrooms, one with a
62, 63   red, the other with a yellow background and splendid wall-paintings, and a large *oecus* decorated with Cupids and Psyches. The somewhat secluded dining-room opens off a small peristyle on the north side of the house and is the most elegant room in the entire mansion, distinguished for its frieze of Amorini or Cupids engaged in several trades (perhaps those of the freedmen brothers) and amusements, representative of those practised in Pompeii.

The House of the Gilded Amorini (VI, xvi, 7) opposite the Pompeian House of the Vettii is most distinguished for its splendid peristyle.[72] The far end of the garden enclosure is approached by a short flight of steps, like a stage. The back room, with portico and gable (*fastigium*) was probably an elevated dining-room, but related to premises like those adjoining public porticoes. A number of these high, splendid rooms facing on to gardens through a portico have been found in the Campanian excavations, usually equipped with a broad doorway and pediment above. The design finds its best analogy in the *curia* (technically a *conclave*) which stood on a podium halfway along the short side of the porticoed garden or park attached to Pompey's theatre in Rome, an accursed room, technically a *locus sceleratus*, after the assassination of Julius Caesar there in 44 BC.

Besides the House of the Mosaic Atrium, two other aristocratic homes at the southern edge of Herculaneum were designed to take full advantage of the seascape. Their gardens were extended into terraces overlooking the Bay of Naples. It must be remembered, however, that because of the lava flow of past eruptions, in particular that of AD 79, the shore-line has changed markedly and the houses under review are now many hundreds of yards from the shore.

The House of the Telephus Relief (I, 2-3) is one of the most remarkable houses in the city, both for the ingenuity used in its planning in order to provide a sea vista and for its elegant rooms and decoration.[73] The door opens directly into the atrium which is colonnaded on both sides, recalling the *oecus Corinthius* plan. The Tuscan-style roofing was level with the upper storey. Between the red stuccoed columns the owner suspended *oscilla*-marble discs with complementary subject-matter worked in relief on both sides. The *stabula*, accessible from the north side of the atrium, also had an independent entrance from the street, a ramp appropriate to the carts and mules (or donkeys) used by the owner. The peristyle and terraces were located at a lower level, reached by means of a steeply descending ramp from the atrium. The brick columns of the peristyle, with a low *pluteus* (balustrade), frame a rectangular *piscina* (basin) decorated partly with blue plaster. Three rooms open up on the south side of the peristyle garden and behind them, at the end of the corridor which is an extension of the peristyle walk, an open terrace with several rooms appears. The room at the southern limit of the house (30 ft 2 in. by 21 ft 8 in.) has a polychrome marble floor and a spectacular dado composed of panels of cipollino, pavonazzetto and africano marble, framed by bands and punctuated by half-columns with spiral-form flutings and Corinthian capitals. A small room adjacent to the *oecus* contained a neo-Attic relief depicting Achilles in the presence of his mother, Thetis, and treating the wound of the Mysian king, Telephus. Additional rooms on the terrace level beneath the elegant *oecus* have yet to be excavated.

The House of the Stags at Herculaneum (IV, 21) is the most impressive of the seaside residences.[74] Forty-seven yards long,
it covers a major portion of the *insula* which it occupies. Again, to accommodate to the sea view, the architect designed the house in two main sections: the entrance quarter which includes the small testudinate atrium, functioning as a lobby and corridor, the *triclinium* which faces the garden, and the *quadriporticus* with windows, and the service quarter with upstairs accommodation for the servants; the more exclusive garden and terrace quarter overlooks the sea. The enclosed garden area is decorated with marble tables, sculptures and vases. The entrance portal to the inner *triclinium* is adorned with a pediment decorated with a mosaic featuring the head of Oceanus and Cupids riding seahorses. At the sea end of the garden there is a pergola or arbour with four pilasters and two summer rest rooms (*diaetae*) opening on to the unroofed terrace (*solarium*) and the panoramic view. The atrium in this ingeniously planned house (as innovatory as its neighbour, the House of the Mosaic Atrium), serves more as vestibule than as antechamber or reception hall. The servants' stair and upstairs wooden gallery are a clue to the reduced status of the antique hall. The *triclinium*, however, is constructed along grandiose lines, decorated with slender architectural motifs on a luxurious black ground interrupted by red bands and with a floor of marble intarsia. The open wall of the portico enabled the diners to look out over the landscaped garden to the sea beyond. The two marble stags, under attack from hunting dogs, probably stood in the garden originally. The kitchen storage room (*apotheca*) and latrine lay behind the dining area together with an elegant *cubiculum* with marble flooring. The *oecus*, next to the *triclinium*, has a red ground wall and polychrome marble pavement. The outer *triclinium*, with picture windows overlooking the sea, was a summer amenity.

Before examining the SUNY House at Cosa, one must emphasize and reiterate several striking developments and trends in Campanian domestic architecture particularly during the second half of the first century AD, roughly from the time of Claudius to

17, 20

the eruption of Vesuvius during the reign of Titus. The waning
of traditional *mores*, the new-found wealth and the impact of
Hellenistic modes of living all contributed to the atrium's yielding
pride of place and service to the peristyle even during the late
Republic. The wealthy house-owner either expanded his property
to include a peristyle garden or alternatively adapted his atrium
to a peristyle design. The peristyle certainly became the deter-
mining element in house plans of the Imperial age.[75] The widespread use of glass in window panes to brighten an interior *oecus*
or to enable daylight to penetrate rooms opening off peristyle
corridors (e.g., the House of the Mosaic Atrium, Herculaneum)   *19*
facilitated decisive breaks with long-established patterns and plans
of living.[76] The atrium, both in its decoration and general
function, survived in a diminished form often as a mere forecourt
to the peristyle house. The completion of the Augustan aqueduct,
the Aqua Serino, brought plenteous water into Pompeii and
enabled householders with means to install private fountains. The
atrium's *impluvium* was no longer required to collect rainwater
for storage in the cistern below and the high sides of the reflecting
pool or fountain basin were adorned with potted plants which
helped to transform the atrium into a secondary garden. The
peristyle garden, successor to the one-time market garden or
sharply restricted 'back yard' (*hortus* or *heredia*), enabled prosperous house-owners to indulge their fondness for axiality and
vistas to an unprecedented degree. The 'paradise garden' concept
with its bucolic and Dionysiac associations merged with a
traditional love of Nature. The garden became the focus for art
galleries (*pinacothecae*), libraries (*bibliothecae*), lecture halls, meeting rooms, basilicas, and *conclavia* (dining-rooms, bedrooms). All
were equipped with doors or awnings which could be closed in
the forenoon and reopened later to take full advantage of the cool
air and the garden's amenities. Diodorus once referred to peristyles (or *peristoa*) as 'a useful device for avoiding confusion when
crowds are present'.[77] Certainly their original role, as appendages
to atria, whether an Etruscan innovation or a legacy from the
Hellenistic East, gave small forecast of the ultimate elegance and
spectacular loveliness of their successors in Imperial times.

House remains at Cosa, eighty-five miles north-west of Rome

on the Via Aurelia and a day's voyage from the mouth of the
Tiber in ancient times, are distinctive and unsettling. They remind
us that Campanian house patterns were by no means universal in
Italy, that local architects were free to abide by older plans into
later days, and that the perennial axiality and symmetry in
Etruscan house plans and in the derivative Campanian forms were
not essential to the pleasure or the proper function of domiciles.
Cosa's foundation as a Roman maritime colony, combining the
roles of coast-guard station and commercial haven, dates from the
Roman victory over Etruscan Vulci in 273 BC. The excavations
of the American Academy in Rome at Cosa since 1948 have
yielded the earliest extant versions of the *comitium*, *curia*, triumphal arch, basilica, and *atrium publicum*. More recently the State
University of New York at Binghamton undertook to recover
remains of a block of houses between the modern museum and
the ancient forum. One large house has emerged, the so-called
SUNY House, which registers marked contrasts with Campanian
23   plans in domestic architecture.[78] Although the plan incorporates
the features of houses familiar elsewhere in Italy, there is no
23   discernible axis to the arrangement of rooms. The *fauces* do not

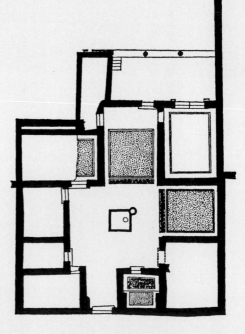

*Fig. 23 Cosa, SUNY
House. V. Bruno,*
Archaeology, *XXIII
(1970), p. 234*

open into the centre of the atrium; the *impluvium* is not central to the atrium area, nor does it align with the *tablinum* behind. The picture window, normally inserted in the *tablinum* wall, is replaced by an entry into the loggia behind. Vincent Bruno, the excavator, has postulated that this 'quality of the unexpected may perhaps be regarded as a symptom of the period in which Roman builders were still experimenting with structural ideas later employed in more rigidly symmetrical compositions'. The *salon* (Room 11), with access to the loggia behind, is decorated in Pompeian Style I, but with a stylistic departure in the socle which shows alternating panels of red and purple. Delian parallels to this unusual scheme have also been adduced for the motif of a string course which bears a pattern of winged *erotes*, in white monochrome, pirouetting through a colourful garland. The paving of Room 11 breaks with the cocciapesto elsewhere in favour of black mortar with white limestone inserts and with a mosaic external frame comparable to a style of flooring in the Pompeian Villa of the Mysteries (Room 47). The bathroom, kitchens and storage space have been cut into the bedrock to the left of the entry; a small *cubiculum*, with First Style decoration, appears to the right of the entry, either a guest room or porter's lodge. The catch-basin fed rainwater into a cistern beneath, and the draw-shaft for raising it appears alongside. Throughout this comfortable middle-class town house there is manifest a desire to guarantee privacy, perhaps asylum, from the manifold activities of the forum nearby. The SUNY House at Cosa, built *c.* 75 BC, is a startling reminder of the important material remains still awaiting the excavator, not least in the area of domestic architecture.

CHAPTER III

ROME AND OSTIA: DOMUS AND PALATIUM

AENEAS' WALK THROUGH ANCIENT PALLANTEUM with Arcadian Evander as guide forecasts much of Augustan Rome.[79] The ancient survivals and the emphasis on humble and contrite hearts fit comfortably with Vergil's sense of the passage and continuity of time and of the essential Roman virtues. Vergil contrasts the Capitolium in Evander's time with his own, 'golden now, once bristling with woods and thickets', and idealizes the pastoral simplicity of Evander's regimen where 'the kindly dawn and birds of morning, singing beneath his thatch roof, roused Evander from his humble abode'.[80] So also, on Aeneas' shield, Vulcan fashioned 'Manlius, warden of the Tarpeian citadel, at his post before the temple, defending the towering Capitol; and below, newly thatched with stiff straw, stood the cottage of Romulus.'[81]

Remains of just such shepherds' huts, similar to modern *capanne*, were found on the Palatine Hill near the Scalae Caci. Their outline and construction were revealed by the remains of postholes on the site and by comparison with cinerary urns in the shape of miniature oval huts found at Alba Longa in the Alban Hills (near modern Castel Gandolfo), as well as in the primitive forum cemetery alongside the Temple of Antoninus and Faustina.[82]

1, 2 The post-holes enabled the archaeologists to reconstruct the general design of the huts as rectangular, but with curved corners, and with a moderately wide entrance on one short side. Sometimes the façade was provided with flanking pillars to carry a porch roof. Roof and walls, of wattle and daub construction, antecedent to *opus craticium*, were supported by timber uprights; outlets for smoke and for illumination were inserted above the entrance, rather like a fanlight, sometimes at both gables. The Palatine huts date between the eighth and seventh centuries BC, i.e., approximating to the canonical date of Rome's foundation (753). Vergil's retrospective view of Rome matched the Augustan design, to provide a future for the past. Both on the Palatine and on the Capitoline Rome nurtured her ancestral huts with their thatched roofs as memorials to her beginnings. As Vergil implies, they were frequently rebuilt and rethatched in the ancient manner.[83]

Huts such as these were the prevailing house type of Iron Age, pre-Etruscan Rome, both on Rome's hills and in the valleys. By the mid-seventh century the first crude brick buildings with stone foundations invaded the rustic environment. By c. 500 BC the Regia, later headquarters of the Pontifex Maximus, had assumed its historical design of a tripartite structure with an open courtyard and dependencies on the north.[84]

The impetus to sturdier, more comfortable, more pretentious architecture undoubtedly came from the Etruscans who, during their hegemony of two centuries or more, organized the forum area and made it practicable by drainage (the Cloaca Maxima), and built, not least, the Temple of the Capitoline Triad. According to tradition, the Regia was the one-time residence of Numa Pompilius, Rome's second king (716–672). Certainly the tripartite building discovered by Frank Brown cannot have been the product of a Sabine architect; its triadic arrangement clearly suggests that the architectural design of the Regia was Etruscan.

Boëthius has argued that after 600 BC the Palatine community, then thoroughly under Etruscan dominion, began to assume the appearance of an Etruscan town.[85] Early Rome's domestic architecture was almost inevitably a direct reflection of Etruscan residences elsewhere, and the mansions of the sixth-century Etruscans and wealthier Roman burghers must have subscribed closely to the atrium-style residences of neighbouring Veii and Caere. There is a curious, probably apocryphal, story relating to Publius Valerius Poplicola's mansion erected after the expulsion of the Tarquins.[86] That patriotic consul (509, 508, 507, 504) was granted a building lot by a grateful Senate on the Velia, but his newly constructed mansion, overlooking the forum, caused so much controversy that he finally razed it himself and resorted to a modest establishment at the foot of the Velia. A second notice relating to Poplicola after his victory over the Sabines (505) is indicative of imported architectural forms. To complement his triumph, Marcus Valerius was honoured with a house built on the Palatine at public expense; and whereas the doors of other houses opened inwards, the Romans constructed his doors to open outwards into the street and thus intimate their perpetual public recognition of his merit by forcing them continually to make way for him.[87] Plutarch appends the comment that the house style was Greek, judging by the comedies where those who are leaving a house make a noise at the door so as to prevent abrupt arrivals or collisions. Plutarch's notice, for what it is worth, seems to reflect the amalgamation of Hellenic architectural forms with what was probably an Etruscan-style *domus*.

The Gallic invasion and destruction of Rome (390 BC) obliterated the significant mansions and public buildings of the day. The Etruscan preference for adobe and wooden construction, judging by the forms reflected in the tombs and at the excavation sites, meant that the cremation would be complete. The post-occupation houses must have remained indebted to the long-established Etruscan forms and responded also to the Hellenistic patterns which became increasingly familiar in the cities of Magna Graecia. The materials of construction and the building techniques, at least until the second century BC, remained the same as before. The old, largely unsafe town was certainly a mud–brick settlement, with *opus craticium* and tufa blocks as more durable components.

The atrium-style of architecture must have persisted in Rome's townscape. Although largely populated by tradesmen, artisans, and plebeian labourers, grander homes stood alongside the *pauperum tabernae*. Livy sheds light on the atrium-house of the Scipio family which stood behind the Tabernae Veteres on the south side of the forum beneath the Palatine with butchers' shops and stalls adjacent.[88] The *patronus-cliens* relationship found the atrium-style house best adapted to the formal procedures and demands of the custom. The Etruscan, perhaps even Italic, preference for axiality and symmetry in house design catered to the formality of the social practice. The bulk of the plebeian citizenry must have lived in the shop-rows of mud–brick, wattle and daub, or occasionally even tufa block construction, sometimes several rickety storeys high.

A revolution in building practices began *c.* 200 B C when Roman construction engineers, who had studied the buildings on Campanian shores, introduced *pozzolana*, a fast-drying volcanic sand, into their old-fashioned mortar of mud or clay.[89] An addiction to 'high-rise' building, already evident before then and no doubt forced on the Romans by the restrictions of the Servian Wall and by their desire to accommodate commercial and industrial establishments on the ground level, had induced them to build to crazy heights with highly inflammable materials. The advent of *opus caementicium* enabled them to build with greater security against collapse and with some insurance against fire.

The Severan *Forma Urbis Romae* (*c.* AD 200) offers dramatic evidence that Rome was then largely an apartment-dwellers' city, with a generous sprinkling of shops, taverns, restaurants, workshops, etc. The evidence for the earlier period is not plentiful but there are sufficient literary allusions to enable us to piece out the imperfections of the archaeological evidence with detailed reports on specific dwellings.

The hills of Rome, particularly the Palatine, Esquiline and Caelian, were favoured zones for high-style mansions. The roster of home-owners in the Germalus zone of the Palatine reads like a 'Who's Who' of late Republican history: Q. Lutatius Catulus, Marius' colleague in arms against the Teutonic hordes in 101; Q. Hortensius Hortalus, eminent lawyer and one-time adversary of Cicero; M. Tullius Cicero (after 63 BC); Seius, and the consular Q. Caecilius Metellus Celer, husband of Catullus' Clodia-Lesbia; the Claudii, in particular Publius Clodius, Cicero's arch-enemy; Lucius Licinius Crassus, the orator, consul in 95 BC, nicknamed 'Palatine Venus' for his luxurious furnishings; Marcus Aemilius Scaurus, who embellished his mansion with fantastic decorations; Publius Cornelius Sulla, the dictator's nephew, and T. Annius Milo, instigator of Clodius' murder at Bovillae in 52.[90]

Clodius' mansion seems to have been converted into a high-class *pensione* by the time it accommodated Cicero's brash *protégé*,

M. Caelius Rufus. The outward and interior show of these
Palatine mansions is often graphically reported, notably by Pliny
the Elder who had an eye for luxury. The millionaire aedile of
58 BC, M. Aemilius Scaurus, furnished his atrium with theatre
columns, some thirty-eight feet high, of black Lucullan (Melian)
marble, far outdoing L. Licinius Crassus who had experimented
earlier with columns of Hymettan marble, six in number, and no
more than twelve feet high.[91] The influx of different types of
marble after the expansion into the Hellenistic Greek East was
steady and dramatic. Marcus Aemilius Lepidus, consul with
Q. Lutatius Catulus (the younger) in 78, first used Numidian
marble for his door-frames and incurred considerable criticism.
The infamous Mamurra, the Formian *eques* who served Caesar as
engineer in Gaul, was first to cover his house-walls with marble
revetments and throughout his mansion used only marble columns
from Carystus and Carrara.[92]

Pliny's reflections on the conspicuous consumption and ostentation of the Lucullan properties in Naples and elsewhere leads
him to comment on the fantastic fluctuations of style which made
the mansion of M. Aemilius Lepidus (consul of 78) a degraded
anachronism by the time of Caesar's assassination.[93] But the
scale of living among wealthy Romans was not always of Scauran
or Lucullan proportions. Cornelius Nepos' Epicurean millionaire
friend, Titus Pomponius Atticus, who was also Cicero's beloved
and faithful correspondent, adopted a different style:

> He had an abundance of money but no one was less inclined to
> excess in buying or in building. And yet he had a dwelling as
> fine as anyone, and enjoyed the best of everything. He had his
> home on the Quirinal in a villa designed by Tamphilus which
> was left to him in his uncle's will. Its charm consisted less in
> its construction than in its park, for the building itself was
> erected in earlier times and was a monument to good taste
> rather than extravagance. He made no changes in it except such
> as lapse of time compelled. The furnishings were modest, not
> abundant, so that it attracted attention in neither direction.[94]

For actual remains of late Republic dwellings, one must probe
beneath the *lararium* of the Domus Flavia on the Palatine to study

the remains of the Casa dei Grifi (House of the Griffins).⁹⁵
Built *c.* 100 BC, its design and interior decoration provide
insight into the elegance of aristocratic late Republican homes.
Closely analogous to the housing on the slope of south-
western Pompeii,⁹⁶ the mansion located its atrium on the Palatine height, with stairs descending to the barrel-vaulted rooms set
into the hillside. All were decorated with floor mosaics, stuccoes,
and paintings best associated with Pompeian Style II. Hanfmann
comments that 'its decoration proves that the capital set fashions
which were closely and faithfully followed in the seaside resorts of
Herculanum [*sic*], Stabiae, and Pompeii'.⁹⁷

The cement-reticulate House of Livia was cleared in 1869 in
the area north of the Apollo Temple on the south side of the
Palatine Hill.⁹⁸ Octavian acquired the property and the house after
its owner, Q. Hortensius Hortalus, son of the celebrated orator
who rivalled Cicero, died at Philippi fighting for Brutus and
Cassius. The house echoes the design of the almost contemporary
Casa dei Grifi. Once again, in an atrium-style house of several
storeys, the architect provided vaulted chambers beneath the
ground floor rooms to furnish a cool retreat during the summer
months. Three of these rooms have survived and their proportions
correspond very closely to Vitruvius' requirements for dining-
rooms;⁹⁹ their length equals their breadth, and all are decorated
with restrained murals of Pompeian Style II. The western room,
which recalls the painted false columns of the Casa dei Grifi,
exhibits garlands of fruit and flowers between columns, similar
to the later Ara Pacis garlands (13–9 BC) and the festal decoration
of a Greek *andron*. The central room features mythological
paintings in the centre of each wall and raised panels with figure   25

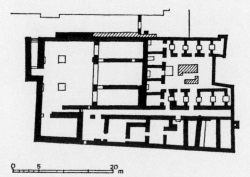

Fig. 24   *Rome, Palatine
Hill. House of Livia, plan.
Nash,* Pictorial Dictionary

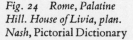

motifs; the ensemble suggests a picture-gallery (pinacotheca). The best preserved mural is a romantic love theme (as appropriate for Scribonia as for Livia) on the south-west wall, depicting Io under the watchful eyes of Argus below a statuette of Juno, with Mercury flying to the rescue. The third room contains more Pompeian Style II decorations with mock columns and ornamental figures.

The official residence of the Princeps has long been identified with the Hortensian town-house on the Palatine but recent excavations around the Apollo temple have produced a secular complex which may be confidently assigned to the head of state. Octavian's pretensions evidently could not be contained within the Hortensian mansion for ever. He therefore undertook to acquire property in its vicinity to enable him to enlarge his domicile. But during the razing and building operations of 36, the zone was struck by lightning and the College of Augurs proclaimed the ground sacrosanct. Undaunted, Octavian

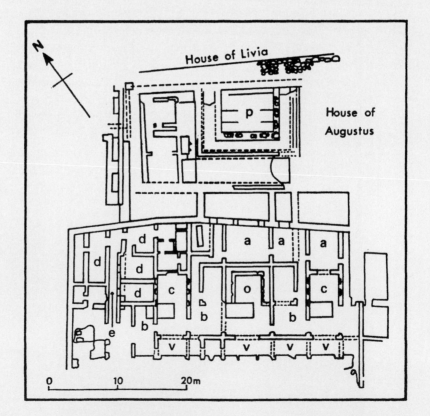

declared his intention to build a Temple of Apollo on the site where
he had originally planned to erect his new residence. The Senate
complied and compensated Octavian for the inconvenience by
building him a residence nearby between 36 and 29. Gianfilippo
Carettoni's excavations since 1956 have revealed the general
design of the Augustan mansion; its top storey lies across a   *25a, 25b*
narrow street from the House of Livia (no doubt the ultimate
residence of the Dowager Empress under Tiberius); the lower
storey is arranged alongside the monumental staircase leading to
the Temple of Apollo Palatinus, guardian and supporter of the
new regime, abiding prophet and guarantor of Rome's destiny.
The main living quarters (d), deliberately designed as a private
sector of the larger mansion, are reached via a narrow hall (e);
the rooms are small, with low undecorated ceilings and simple
geometric mosaics. The upper floor provided additional rooms,
not yet identified, and a portico (p). To the south and east of the
private wing are more elaborate rooms with inlaid marble floors,

*Fig. 25a left   Rome, Palatine Hill. House of Augustus. Carettoni, ILN 6799
(Sept. 20, 1969)*

Fig. 25b below   The same, general plan

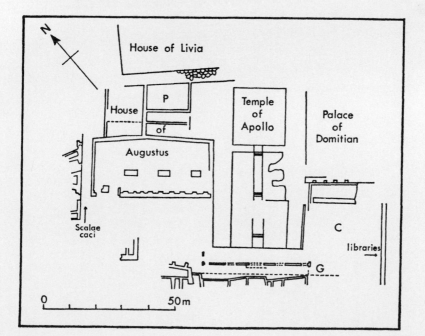

elegant murals and stucco decoration. Windows (v) opened towards the Circus Maximus from the façade of the lower terrace. The central *oecus* (o) has a ledge around the walls with supporting columns and pilasters; two libraries, with wall niches for the volumes, frame the reception area and entertainment salons (b). Rear rooms (a) which lack decoration and paving probably served as storerooms, possibly offices.

Suetonius provides an eyewitness description of the House of Augustus in Hadrianic times merging the later Senatorial gift with the Hortensian *domus* in his account: 'Augustus lived at first near the Forum Romanum above the Ringmaker's Stairs in a house that had belonged to Calvus the orator. Afterwards he lived on the Palatine in the house of Hortensius, which was no less modest, being conspicuous neither for its size nor its decoration, since the porticoes in it were short and had columns of (stuccoed) Alban stone (*peperino*) while the rooms lacked marble decoration or any kind of handsome pavement. Furthermore, for forty years he kept the same bedroom, both in winter and in summer, and although he found by experience that the city in wintertime was rather bad for his health, he nevertheless spent the winter in town. If ever he proposed to do something in secret or without interruption, there was a solitary place at the top of the house which he called his "Syracuse" and "Little Laboratory" (technyphion); his "retreat" was either here or at a freedman's suburban home. However, when he was ill, he used to go to the house of Maecenas (on the Esquiline).'[100] The house doors are described as double, with a straight lintel, with an oak wreath above and a laurel tree on either side.[101]

The House of Augustus was evidently maintained as a museum piece, a relic of less pretentious days, into more spectacular imperial reigns. It certainly was far removed from the prescription of Vitruvius for men of distinction, advocates, orators and their audiences:

For capitalists and farmers of the revenue, somewhat comfortable and showy apartments must be constructed, secure against robbery; for advocates and public speakers, handsome and more roomy, to accommodate meetings; for men of rank who,

from holding offices and magistracies, have social obligations
to their fellow-citizens, lofty entrance courts in regal style, and
most spacious atriums and peristyles, with plantations and
walks of some extent in them, appropriate to their dignity.
They need also libraries, picture galleries and basilicas, finished
in a style similar to that of great public buildings, since public
councils as well as private lawsuits and hearings before arbitra-
tors are very often held in the houses of such men.[102]

Certainly many of Augustus' contemporaries, men like
Maecenas, Messalla and the ubiquitous freedmen engaged in the
service of the state, must have adopted the Vitruvian formula.
The *patronus-cliens* relationship was still persistent, although a
new note of servility was already evident. Augustus' successors,
Tiberius, Caligula, Claudius and Nero, each sought, in his own
fashion, to house himself appropriately and on a grand scale.
The palace of Tiberius, the so-called Domus Tiberiana on the
Palatine, rose impressively on a massive platform (197 yards by
131) on the north-west corner of the hill.[103] The remains today
rest beneath the Renaissance gardens of Cardinal Alessandro
Farnese. The Villa Jovis on Capri and the imperial villa at Albano   *48*
offer insights into characteristic designs favoured by the emperor
but there can be no certainty as to their use in Rome.

Distinguished for the bravura and panache of his life-style and
gifted with an artist's temperament, Nero brought himself and
his architects, Severus and Celer, into the limelight by prodigious
experiments and novel devices in the design of his residences.[104]
Heir to his father's property by the Via Sacra, and to the imperial
palace on the Palatine along with the gardens of the Esquiline,
Nero sought to unite them all by building across the area where
the Arch of Titus and the Church of S. Maria Nova now stand.
Of the immense palace that emerged, the Domus Transitoria,
only meagre sections survived the fire of AD 64 and subsequent
depredations.[105] Hadrian's Temple of Venus and Roma contains
one portion of indeterminate nature; additional elements, the
junction of two corridors and a sunken garden with a *biclinium*
open to the sky, lie beneath Domitian's Domus Flavia. The
grandeur and the extent of the successor mansion, the Domus

Aurea, was Nero's response to the damage occasioned by the holocaust and was, in fact, a monumental example of a country estate lodged in the heart of the city. It is best considered under villa architecture.

Certainly the most impressive palace remains of Imperial Rome are those of the Domus Flavia or Augustana, Domitian's marvellous accommodation on the Palatine.[106] Designed by his architect Rabirius with baroque elegance and impressive symmetry, it functioned as a deliberate, calculated design to enhance the imperial station and presence. Although the Domus Tiberiana seems to have survived the Great Fire of 64, Vespasian showed a marked aversion for the Palatine and its imperial associations.[107]

26; 26

Fig. 26   Rome, Palatine Hill. Domus Flavia (or Augustana), Domitian's Palace. Boëthius & Ward-Perkins, fig. 95. Solid colour indicates buildings at the upper level now in whole or in part upstanding

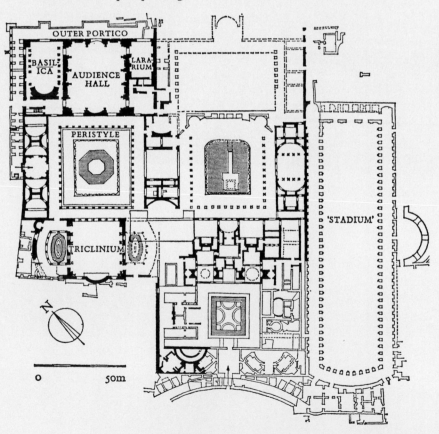

Fire almost certainly sealed the fate of the Palace of Tiberius in 80, and with the gradual destruction and displacement of the Domus Aurea by Vespasian and his son Domitian felt free and entitled to build afresh on the Palatine.

The components of the palace, inaugurated in 92, were grandiose, colourful, and designedly impressive. The platform, which necessitated considerable clearing and the levelling of earlier structures, measured 170 yards wide by 215 yards deep. The west wing, the reception quarter, was accessible from the Clivus Palatinus ascending from the Arch of Titus which served, in its way, as a lower portal for the palace. Access to the official wing was through a courtyard and *porticus* into the state rooms. A basilica, an audience hall (*aula regia*) and a *lararium* constituted the northern sector of the official wing of the palace. The outer portico engulfed the Casa dei Grifi, Caligula's Hall of Isis, and the *nymphaeum* of Nero's Domus Transitoria. The basilica, a rectangular, apsidal hall, used two ranges of Numidian columns to support, ostensibly, the coffered vault; the reception room, a vast chamber measuring 36 yards by 27, was probably designed as a vaulted structure but eventually adopted a panelled ceiling instead. It presented an impressive series of alternating rectangular and curved niches framed by columns of Phrygian marble; the throne, as in the *aula regia* of the Villa Jovis on Capri, stood on a dais in a *48* shallow apse at the south end; imported polychrome marbles covered the entire floor and walls of the room. There was double access from the audience hall to both the basilica and the smaller barrel-vaulted *lararium*, the imperial chapel.

A great peristyle, with *porticus*, opened up behind the audience hall and dominated the central area of the official wing of the palace. It was equipped with a central fountain and a lovely formal garden for the delectation of official visitors and the imperial *entourage*. The columns, of Porta Santa marble with white marble capitals and bases, were surmounted by a rich entablature. The walls, which aroused comment in antiquity and perhaps reflected Domitian's concern for his imperial person, were partly lined with phengites, a Cappadocian gypsum which turned the *porticus* into a hall of mirrors.[108] Small apsidal reception rooms were available on the west side. The *triclinium* or state banqueting hall almost matched the throne room in size and apsidal arrangement. It was in all likelihood assigned a gilded timber roof. The couches of the emperor and his imperial party shared the same dais at the south end and enjoyed the same vista through six immense columns of Egyptian granite into the peristyle garden. Additional granite columns decorated the walls of the banqueting room as well, framing doors and three large windows on either side of the dais that opened on to a pair of elaborate oval *nymphaea*. The imperial platform was paved with porphyry, serpentine, giallo antico and pavonazzeto marble set in a large geometric pattern. The room was illuminated by light coming from the open-air *nymphaea* and from the central peristyle. Rabirius had coped admirably with his commission. 'The old, punctilious rituals of formal greeting, visiting, and dining had been solemnified about that being, the Emperor, who stood above all others. They were now courtly rituals of salutation, audience, and epiphany; the state apartments of the palace were made to contain them.'[109]

The middle zone of the Domus Augustana contained the private residential quarters of the emperor and the monumental entrance portal which was aligned with the Temple of Castor in the forum. Here was the imperial façade, a rectangular composition spreading over the level areas and slopes of the Palatine towards the forum and the Circus Maximus. The main entry was at the lower level of the south façade, some thirty-five feet below. It led into a lower peristyle with an upper storey resting on piers with arches after the fashion of the Ostian cortile apartments. Central to the court was an *impluvium* with an intricate fountain liberally bedecked with sculptures. Stairs on both the east and west sides of the peristyle led to the upper floor. Three domed octagonal halls were set into the hillside on the north side to provide novel, cool *salons*. Another peristyle garden with basin, bridge, and possibly a *cubiculum* on an island, paralleled the western garden.

The east wing of the palace was given over to a vast sunken garden, the so-called Stadium or Hippodrome, 175 yards long and 55 yards wide. Five vaulted chambers recalled the normal starting-gates (*carceres*) at the north end where the Orchestra of Santa Cecilia once provided summer concerts; the turning posts (*metae*) of the garden appeared as fountains near the extremities of the garden which curved in the fashion of a stadium at the south end. A two-storey *porticus*, with a brick pier arcade below and a colonnade above, enclosed the garden on three sides. The longer eastern wall included a large semicircular vaulted *exedra*, probably for exhibitions; the south end accommodated the structure of the imperial box (*pulvinar*) which overlooked the Circus Maximus immediately below.

Alterations and additions by Hadrian and Septimius Severus hardly affected the grand design of Rabirius, and the Domus Augustana remained the official residence of the emperors for centuries to come. Rulers might choose to establish their palaces elsewhere, at Baiae, Tibur (Tivoli), Ravenna, Trier, Constantinople, Casale or Split, but the fantastic fabric of Domitian's palace endured and was available for anyone, upstart or legitimate heir, who claimed the throne.

The Marble Plan of Severan Rome indicates that besides the omnipresent *tabernae*, single- or double-storey, multiple dwellings in the shape of tenements or *pensioni* were the normal accommodation in the capital. The catalogues of the fourteen regions of Rome, the so-called *Curiosum Urbis Romae Regionum XIV* and *Notitia*, reveal that there were 46,602 *insulae* compared with 1,797 private *domus* by the mid-fourth century. They also provide rather surprising figures for *insulae* in Region X (Palatine) – 2,742 and 2,648 respectively. One must suppose that *insula* accommodation in this aristocratic quarter of Rome, the Mons Palatinus and its slopes, must have been largely in private atrium or atrium-peristyle residences which had become boarding-houses. Here, as elsewhere in late Imperial Rome, subdivided town houses probably outnumbered the 'Ostia-type' *insulae*, thereby inducing most Romans to live lives of quiet desperation in declining *pensioni* or poorly constructed *tabernae*.

Ostia's private houses of the Imperial age, of which only twenty have been surely identified by the excavators, must be typical of the forms that survived into Imperial Rome. Atrium-style houses with single-family occupancy, often juxtaposed to a colonnaded or arcaded courtyard, were perennials in the cityscape of most large towns and cities of Italy. The Ostian and Roman population probably preferred tenement living; but independent homes were still built and, of course, the coast-line remained the locale for a host of villas, notably Pliny's Laurentine country place, only five miles distant.

One superb second-century peristyle house survives in Ostia, the House of the Fortuna Annonaria (*c.* AD 150).[110] Its garden court is framed on three sides by travertine columns which were once faced with stucco and probably fluted; a continuous wall runs the entire length of the building on the remaining side, and rooms open off three sides of the courtyard. The entry was from the street on the north side and the *triclinium* is located at the west end. The central room at the eastern end of the garden was heated, the first known instance in Ostia, and probably served as the *cubiculum*. The House of the Round Temple, although combined with an *insula*, offers an equally attractive habitat with an open peristyle-plan court.[111] The street façade incorporates two large shops, each with an inner stair to the *cenaculum* above; two stairs also lead from the street to the upper floors of a three-storey *insula*. A vestibule between the shops leads to the *domus* behind; on the north side, the court opens into the main living-room of the house; three of the four rooms on the west side were heated and another four rooms opened on the east. The house in its extant form of late third-century design, had a wide portico with brick piers and walls of marble veneer. It was conveniently situated for access to the Capitolium and civic square.

27

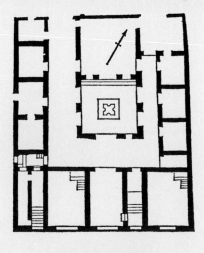

Fig. 27   Ostia. House of the Round Temple. Meiggs, fig. 17

During the third and fourth centuries AD Ostia entered upon a serious economic decline and a steady population decrease. Services were interrupted, security was lacking, and by the end of the fourth or beginning of the fifth century Ostia was virtually derelict, a ghost town with its splendid *insulae* gradually deteriorating and as unsound as Juvenal's disaster areas of an earlier time.[112] But the retreat from the port town was never complete and in some quarters, particularly on the periphery of the city where re-usable materials were more abundant, there was even a partial revival of fortunes. Most of the buildings were one-storey *domus* but with comforts that the *insulae* had never known, such as under-floor heating in certain rooms. The remodelled House of the Fortuna Annonaria was a splendid mansion of fourth-century date. Another, undoubtedly the finest example of the later residences, is the House of Cupid and Psyche (I, xiv, 5) which is unusually elegant and progressive in several respects.[113] 24 The architect adapted the extant half-ruined remains of an earlier cortile-style tenement, replete with shops and a manufacturing establishment, and of course an unspecified number of apartments. The new structure provided a wide central corridor which divided the house into two distinct sectors; on the east, through a Corinthian arcade, one entered a small garden and *nymphaeum* composed of five alternately round and rectangular niches fronted by brick arches springing from diminutive Corinthian columns; on the west side were four small rooms with an inner staircase at the far end giving access to the floor above the west wing, and a lavatory. At the end, the corridor opened into a large room with a niche in one wall. The provision for water display, the elaborate floor mosaics and *opus sectile* marble veneer on the walls, along with the sculptural group which gave its name to the house, befit the wealth and good taste of the owner. Sir Mortimer Wheeler has commented aptly on the total effect as 'one of graciousness, charm and comfort with a hint of the almost eighteenth-century elegance that sometimes marked the later days of the Empire'.[114]

CHAPTER IV

ITALIAN
MULTIPLE DWELLINGS

*A day in the Trastevere for instance, or on
the Campus Martius, is still the best
help in understanding imperial Ostia –
i.e. Rome.*

Axel Boëthius

AFTER THE GALLIC INVASION, Republican Rome retained the
Etruscan atrium-style *domus* as its patriarchal, aristocratic form,
but within a community of workshops, stores, shanties and workmen's housing. Shops (*tabernae*) must have provided living space
for most of the population then as later, either in the rear of the
shop, or in an upper room (*cenaculum*) accessible by stair or ladder
from the shop's interior. The earliest evidence we have of second-
century BC Rome indicates that *domus* and *tabernae* were inter-
mingled, that trade and production shared the same roof with the
resident in a way quite foreign to the practices followed in the
older sectors of provincial towns like Pompeii, where shops and
workshops tended to cluster around the forum and along the
main arteries quite separate from the residential sectors of the
town.[115] Southern Italy, judging by Campanian and Sicilian
remains, followed Greek and Oriental modes at the outset,
although by the first century AD metropolitan building forms had
started to affect the provincial norms.

Boëthius has detected as early as 100 BC in towns like Pompeii
and Praeneste, utility-style housing entirely divorced from the
atrium plan, with rows of independent shops connected by outside stairs to upper storeys (*cenacula*).[116] Study of the detailed
plans of the excavations of Pompeii and, to a lesser degree, of
Herculaneum reveals that, in a diversified repertoire of buildings,
irregular houses, shop-houses, factories, processing and retailing
buildings are omnipresent. The forum baths at Pompeii offer

insight into late Republican tenements; every shop had access to independent apartments above by way of a single stair and corridor on the north façade, of the concrete building.[117] Its design and date (c. 80 BC) suggest two incentives for the building: the pressure of an expanding commercial population, free from the menace of civil war, and the influx of Roman veterans to Sulla's Colonia Cornelia Veneria Pompeiana, ready to reproduce the new architectural modes of the capital. One may assume, judging by the shop-apartment complexes in Pompeii and in the Insula Orientalis of Herculaneum, that both provincial towns were moving towards a reconstruction along Roman lines, no doubt recapitulating the process which sponsored the earlier development of the grandiose *insulae* in Rome.

Frequently, in the Italian towns of Pompeii and Herculaneum, and unquestionably elsewhere in Campania, in Naples, Puteoli, Capua, etc., the needs of an expanding population were met by altering the large older homes. The long established atrium-peristyle house remained the rich man's dwelling, although by late Samnite times the façades might contain *tabernae*. Increasingly, however, during and after the late Republic, older mansions were converted to multiple occupancy. The celebrated Samnite House at Herculaneum (V, 1–2) was altered *16; 19* to incorporate an upstairs apartment reached by a stairway opening off the street; the elegant gallery with its Ionic balustrade overlooking the atrium was blocked in and the lessee was provided with two rooms divided by a wooden plastered partition; the walls were repainted in Pompeian Fourth Style.[118] The House of the Bicentenary, where the alleged imprint of a crucifix was found, was also redesigned as a *pensione* with two upstairs apartments for the shop proprietors.[119] One apartment, at the north-east corner of the house, consisted of two rooms joined by an entrance in a partition wall; another, its neighbour, was linked with the two ground-level shops and enjoyed a private vestibule at street level. The L-shaped suite comprised two bedrooms separated by a living-room with *lararium*, with a hallway to two back bedrooms and a large *triclinium* at the north-west corner. The entire upper storey looked out on the main avenue near the forum and a balcony projected over the pavement below.

8, 13   The one-time grandeur of the House of Pansa did not prevent one owner from advertising his property in a graffito now lost:

> The Insula Arriana Polliana, property of Gnaeus Alleius Nigidius Maius. To rent from the first day of next July: shops with attached upper rooms, gentlemen's quarters upstairs, and the main house. Prospective tenants should apply to Primus, slave of Gnaeus Alleius Nigidius Maius.

A comparable arrangement was offered in connection with the property of Julia Felix:

> On the property of Julia Felix, daughter of Spurius, to rent: the Venus bath for the *élite*, shops, with upper rooms, and second-storey apartments, from the thirteenth day of next August to the thirteenth day of the sixth August thereafter.

Rental units of this nature undoubtedly represent the majority of '*insula*' tenants in the Italian towns, and, no doubt, in the capital also.

28, 29   The Casa a Graticcio in Herculaneum (III, 13–15) is a transitional tenement organized around an inner court.[120] According to Vitruvius, *opus craticium*, which supplies the house's name, implies the use of plastered, timber-framed, wattlework partitions consisting of panels which were filled, luted, and plastered.[121] The bare bones of the structure are exposed today and reveal rather untidy cement work braced by widely spaced brick piers between which was set the framework of wooden beams. The entrance corridor led into an inner court which provided a cell for the janitor and a single *cubiculum*. A shop opened directly on to the street; behind it, absorbing most of the downstairs area, were the work-rooms and storage area of the proprietor. Two additional courts served the rear of the house; one was a survivor from the Samnite house which preceded the *insula* on the lot; the second, in the rear, contained three basins to serve the needs of the ground-floor tenants. The first court contains a large cistern and stairs for use by the tenant of the first floor. The three-room apartment consisted of a bedroom, a dining area and an unspecified room. Carbonized remains of the wooden furniture were found. The dining-room and a corridor leading to a latrine in the rear opened on to the first court and so availed themselves of light and air in a somewhat dingy context. The upper floor also contained another apartment reached by a private stairway from the street. The suite comprised a dining-room and bed-rooms all opening off a central hall and a small covered balcony over the pavement resting on brick columns. The apartment-dweller's food was cooked on a small hearth, with the benefit of a chimney, in the central hall. There are two latrines, one on the ground floor, another on the first floor.

The origins of the Roman *insula* have been hotly debated for many years. The problem remains contentious; the definition of the term may be less elusive. The catalogues of the fourteen regions of Rome, the so-called *Curiosum Urbis Romae Regionum XIV* and *Notitia*, both dating from the mid-fourth century AD, indicate that the Forum Romanum had 3,480 *insulae*, and that the entire city contained 46,602 *insulae* and only 1,797 private houses (*domus*). Meiggs' definition of the *insula* as 'the large, normally high block divided into separate apartments which can be separately let'[122] is convincing for Ostia but not for Rome. The adaptation of the mansion to multiple family occupancy in Pompeii and Herculaneum cannot have been peculiar to the peninsula. Rome's response to the population explosion must have followed comparable lines and the term *insula*, no doubt originally applied to a plot of land bounded by streets, was gradually extended to multiple dwellings which included older homes which had been subdivided into rooming-houses or pensioni and the larger, more commodious multi-storeyed apartment buildings.[123] The Forum and Palatine sectors of Rome abounded in buildings, new and old, wherein units of various sizes were leased to those who sought to live near the city centre for a variety of reasons.

Scholars have, until recently, been inclined to argue that the apartment block, often three or four storeys high, was indigenous to Rome because there were no convincing antecedents in the Near East where shops, fundamental to Roman *insulae*, were either located in the civic centre or clustered along main streets.

Although Strabo indicated that the contemporary Babylonians sought to solve their problem of over-population by means of high-rise housing and that comparable attempts were made in Aradus and Tyre,[124] few archaeologists were prepared to suggest anything more than an analogous experience; direct influence on the sophisticated *insulae* of cosmopolitan Rome seemed unlikely. Testimony elsewhere, at Sicilian Motya, where excavations revealed that Phoenician-Carthaginian skyscrapers had wooden superstructures founded on stone basements, seemed inapplicable to the Roman experiment;[125] Syria, Carthage, and Alexandria, where remains of multi-storeyed buildings have been found, seemed dubious sources of inspiration for the architects of Rome and Ostia.[126] But recent finds at Ephesus provide entirely pertinent analogues, no doubt exemplary patterns, for the Roman *insulae* (*infra*, pp. 213ff). New evidence notwithstanding, Boethius' argument remains plausible, that the tenement house of the Romans evolved naturally from shop-rows with lofts or garrets above, for these were certainly the most common housing of the urban proletariat. Linked by common walls, the *tabernae* were susceptible to enlargement and able to support additional storeys. As the levels increased above the shops and *cenacula* of the street level, sometimes responding to hillsides, there came into being the characteristic and standard form of the ancient megalopolis of Asia Minor or Italy.[127]

One factor was absolutely decisive in the development of high-rise apartments, an element which was peculiar to Italy and so determined the unique character of the Roman *insula*, namely concrete (*opus caementicum*). Developed and used initially in Campania, it was quickly perfected and was in general use in Rome by the second century BC. The discovery not only provided cheap building material but also enabled Rome to cope with its rapidly rising population figures in a entirely new fashion, perhaps as early as the third century.[128]

The rapid growth in population and the turbulence of the last centuries of the Republic engendered serious problems of building and security. While building on a luxurious scale certainly accelerated, one also recalls that the House of Lepidus in Rome, an 'award-winning' mansion in 78 BC, had slipped to one-hundredth place by 43 BC.[129] Alongside the city mansions, Hellenistic-inspired, expensively furnished and acquisitive of green space and gardens, were ranged the new tenements and clumsily adapted *domus* of varying durability and security. The allusions to collapsing apartments, fires, internal problems, jerry-built skyscrapers, cracking walls and weak foundations, recur with awful persistency in the writers of the late Republic and early Empire:[130]

> The building of houses goes on unceasingly in consequence of the collapses and fires and repeated sales (these last, too, go on endlessly); in fact the sales are intentional collapses, so to speak, since the buyers keep razing the houses and building new ones, one after another, to suit their desires.[131]

Or again:

> Here we inhabit a city supported for the most part by slender props: for that is how the bailiff patches up the cracks in the old wall, telling the inmates to sleep at ease under a roof ready to tumble about their ears. No, no, I must live where there are no fires, no nightly alarms. Ucalegon below is already shouting for water and shifting his chattels; smoke is pouring out of your third-floor attic above, but you know nothing of it; for if the alarm begins on the ground floor, the last man to burn will be he who has nothing to shelter him from the rain but the tiles, where the gentle doves lay their eggs.[132]

These are no imaginary terrors, judging by the repeated instances available to us, and the picture is unusually vivid. The crushing anonymity, the loneliness and ugliness of the high-rise apartments or the run-down boarding-houses are repeatedly evidenced. Impoverished writers, Romans in depressed circumstances and immigrants were regularly sentenced to what have been called disposable cubicles for dispensable people. The absence of transportation, horse or carriage, meant that the lower-class citizen had to live near the centre and his trade, and the population density put terrific strain on residential resources. The narrow, winding streets of pre-Neronian Rome, with row-shops, workshops, middle-class housing and mansions set in uneasy contiguity, offered little security and the meanest of amenities to the majority of the urban dwellers. Builders had responded to the need, as early as the third century, by providing multi-level accommodation. Livy records an entertaining and illuminating account of an ox which escaped from the Forum Boarium beside the Tiber and charged into a neighbourhood house to escape its pursuers only to plummet into the street from the third storey![133] The devastation occasioned by the collapse of these multi-storeyed buildings induced Augustus to legislate that the greatest permissible height for houses should be sixty feet, i.e., a maximum of five storeys. To protect his Forum Augusti complex from the danger of fires in the adjacent tenement quarter of the Subura he built a great fire-wall 115 feet high and so screened the *insulae* on the Quirinal from the offensive sight and aroma of that unhappy quarter of the city.[134]

Fires were not the result of delinquency or acts of God. The absence of cooking facilities in the *insulae* prompted Romans to do much of their eating and drinking in restaurants and public houses in the neighbourhood, sometimes located conveniently on the ground floor of the *insula* where they lived. But if the householder chose to cook at home, and hot water was integral to the Italian diet of soup and pasta, there was the constant menace of fire which, once started, spread rapidly. The modern concrete and brick constructions were much more fireproof than the *opus craticium*, 'casa popolare'-style apartments which soared some five or six storeys high so as to accommodate the maximum number of tenants. Vitruvius comments critically on the disadvantages of this kind of construction, shedding light on Juvenal's complaint: 'the main disadvantages are that the movement of the horizontal and vertical beams [through settling] produces cracks in the plaster. When the wall is whitewashed, the wood swells up from the damp, and when it dries, it shrinks and cracks the plaster.'[135] Seneca's tirades and complaints about the perils of tenement living no doubt influenced Nero in his urban renewal projects after the fire of AD 64, when the age of utilitarian architecture of more durable fabric and better disposition dawned.[136] The disaster of 64 urged the provision of an adequate water-supply in every sector of the city thereafter. Regular streets, broad avenues and open spaces were also to supersede the narrow winding streets of antiquity. *Insulae* were not to surpass seventy feet in height; there was to be a ten-foot space between buildings and a flat-roofed *porticus* across the façade of a number of separate buildings from which firemen could manœuvre if necessary. The house occupants were to have their own fire-fighting apparatus. Nero's most perceptive measure, the reduction of timber construction in favour of fire-proof Gabine stone and *peperino*, was largely thwarted. Rubbish and debris from the fire of 64 were partly disposed of in the marshes near Ostia, partly used as strengthening elements in the new concrete construction.[137]

Atrium and peristyle houses, converted tenements and dilapidated *insulae* were to be replaced by brick and concrete structures, with windows on the street, balconies, porticoes and arcades, concrete and stone staircases, and sturdy barrel-vaults. But the scale and the success of the renewal project, Nero's *Urbs Nova*, remains a matter of doubt. Earlier handicaps, though ameliorated, were by no means eradicated.

Vitruvius is generally distrustful of the durability and strength of concrete, which he regarded as reliable only after an interval of eighty years. Nevertheless he passed enthusiastic approval on the specially designed and engineered brick and concrete *insulae* of his day (*c*. 25 BC). No doubt, with Augustus, he welcomed the relief, perhaps only a reprieve, from the nondescript designs, the mud–brick walls and wooden floors, stairs and ceilings that contributed to the back-street holocausts with such appalling frequency, enabling profiteers like Crassus to purchase the buildings and lots for ridiculously low prices for future development.[138]

> Brick walls, unless they attain a thickness of two or three bricks, simply cannot support more than a single storey; certainly not if they are only a foot and a half thick. In view of the present-day status of the city and the unlimited number of its citizens, it is necessary to provide dwellings without number. Therefore, since the ground floors will not allow such a vast population to live in the city, the emergency has made it necessary to elevate our buildings. In these towering structures, comprising stone piers, crowning courses of [baked] brick, and concrete walls to provide floor after floor, the upper

storeys can be partitioned off into rooms to the utmost advantage. The accommodations within the city walls have thus been multiplied as a result of the many storeys rising into the air, and the Roman people now have highly convenient apartments with views.[139]

Roman poets and prose-writers imply a less acceptable situation. They castigate the dishonest contractors who failed to put enough lime into the concrete construction, and Vitruvius' 'superior views' were not every man's lot. Certainly, whenever the chance offered, there was a marked desire to remove to better quarters, to escape the darkness, noise, squalor and lack of privacy of the city tenements. Tacitus records that buildings as high as the Capitoline Hill were often neighbours.[140] Augustus, whose building piety is attested by the restoration of eighty-two temples in the city, showed comparable concern about domestic architecture by trying to safeguard the citizenry against fire and collapsing buildings through stringent building regulations. He even subjected the senators to a reading of Rutilius' *De Modo Aedificiorum* to underscore the seriousness of his intentions to improve urban safety and building standards.[141] For the first time in Rome's history, the security and the quality of Roman life became governmental concerns.

The extant remains of Rome's multiple dwellings are disappointingly few. The apartment house on the slopes of the Capitoline Hill, near the steps to the Church of S. Maria in Aracoeli, has several interesting features: the lower floor was assigned to shops whose proprietors lived above; however, quite distinct from the Ostian pattern, the garret enjoyed 'picture' windows looking into the building's court; the three floors above the *cenacula*, judging by today's impressions, were dark and damp; the façade originally supported a narrow balcony carried on a series of travertine brackets, altered subsequently to provide a two-storey arcade. Besides the evidence of the *Forma Urbis* (c. AD 200), there are other remains in the Aurelian Wall, near the Porta S. Lorenzo, parts of two multiple dwellings in the Church of SS. John and Paul, another beneath the present Galleria 27 Colonna, others on the Via Biberatica in Trajan's Market, on the

27 Rome. Market of Trajan, Via Biberatica, shops and upper rooms

30 Ostia. Air view of the excavations looking northwest, forum
(centre), granaries, theatre and *decumanus maximus* (right)

< 28 Herculaneum. Casa a Graticcio, streetside façade and balcony on
Cardo V

< 29 Herculaneum. Casa a Graticcio, ground floor and second storey,
axonometric plan

31   Ostia. Casa dei Dipinti, garden court, reconstruction drawing
by I. Gismondi

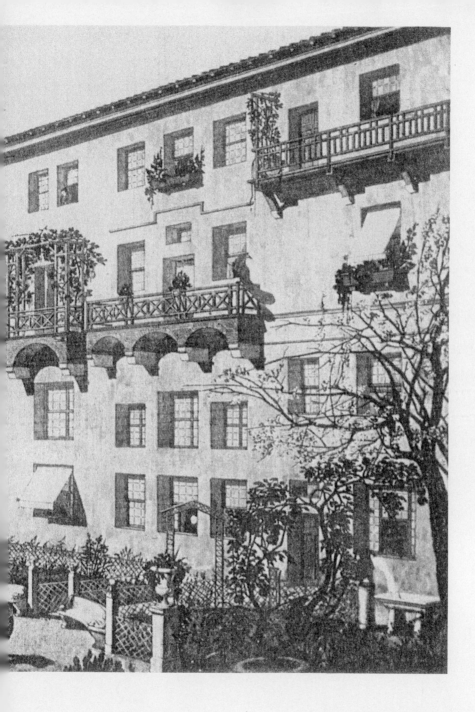

32   Ostia. Caseggiato di Diana, courtyard

33   Ostia. Caseggiato di Diana, south façade along Via di Diana >

34   Ostia. Caseggiato di Diana, axonometric plan >

35 Ostia. Casa delle Volte Dipinte, reconstruction

36 Ostia. *Insulae*, reconstruction model

Via Nova, etc.[142] The common practice was to have a shop or industry on the ground level; sometimes the courts contained gardens or open spaces, and public porticoes abounded. The paucity of remains stems from the continued use of wooden construction, which means that the combustible nature of the tenements continued into later times. Aulus Gellius observed the burning of a whole block from a vantage point on the Esquiline and commented on the high risk attaching to real estate investment;[143] Herodian speaks of fires as a regular occurrence, suggesting that wooden construction was still common in the Urbs.[144]

The final impression of Rome, in both Republican and Imperial times, is largely one of a heterogeneous conglomeration of buildings, residual domus-style mansions, and occasional 'Victorian' revivals, jumbled together with declining mansions which had become rooming houses, patched and precarious tenements, and the new-style brick and concrete skyscrapers with inviting porticoes and shops at the ground level. The pressure of population, the impossible traffic conditions, the menace of collapsing buildings and countless fires tended to worsen the miserable conditions of apartment living. The picture offered by Martial and Juvenal, however affected by poetic licence and exaggeration, suggests a rather cheerless existence for the majority who lived in the tabernae and pergulae of the lower storeys, enclosed behind porticoes, with no direct sunlight and a minimal cubic space of air to breathe. The piazzas may have offered outlets and space for gregarious activity; but the confinement by night must have been nightmarish for the majority of the citizenry.

The port town of Ostia, with its regular town plan and modern services, offers the best testimony from the ancient world for the multiple dwelling. During the period from Trajan to Commodus (AD 98–192), the town affords rich glimpses of the history and the diversity of this building form. Structurally, in Trajan's time, the outer face was composed of opus reticulatum and opus latericium, wherein the recticulate or network tufa pattern of the surface was interlaced horizontally with narrow bands of brickwork at regular intervals. Hadrian's reign (117–138) saw increased use of the brick portion until it finally dominated the facing. *Opus vittatum*, implying alternating courses of brick and tufa, was common between AD 150 and 450.[145]

Most of the Ostian apartments incorporated shops, sometimes behind a protective portico. The shops were closed nightly by means of vertical wooden shutters that fitted into the travertine threshold and lintel blocks, although at night and perhaps during siesta time entry might be made through a small portal set into the larger door. Other doorways, for example the main entry into the apartment house, normally took the form of two wooden leaves which rotated in pivots set into the threshold and lintel blocks, and opened inwards. The one-time introspective aspect of the *domus* was dissipated by the arrival of regular ranks of windows, at first above the mezzanine, then extending into the upper floors. Selunite, mica and glass enabled the householder to bring the outdoors indoors; less affluent flats accommodated double wooden shutters of a pattern still common in Italy. The arcade was an attractive feature of the high-priced apartment

Fig. 28   Ostia. Insula *façade, ground floor* thermopolium, *reconstruction, Boëthius & Ward-Perkins, fig. 111*

houses and public buildings, and could trace lineal descent from the earlier colonnades which appear in Herculaneum and Pompeii. The concrete construction and vaulting of the arcade which supported the skyscraper above often rose to a height of two storeys and offered fireproof protection for residents on the ground and mezzanine levels.

Balconies were another attractive feature of apartment living at Ostia, as well as in the Aracoeli house, in the Porta Tiburtina *insula*, and in the remains on the Via Biberatica in Rome. The balconies were clearly not intended for regular family use and were sometimes completely impracticable; their narrow limits, comparable to contemporary 'survivals' above shop fronts on the Via del Tribunale in Naples, suggest that they were purely ornamental. They may have served as protective traps for objects falling from the roof or windows above. Some were wooden, some rested on barrel-vaulting, others were supported on groin vaults, usually at third-floor level.[146]

Boëthius has discovered four categories of *insulae* at Ostia: (I) a basic structure of ground-level row *tabernae* with living-quarters above; (II) a combination of two-row shops, with apartments, back to back (*cf.* Venice's Mercato Nuovo); (III) a combination of both basic designs around a court; and (IV) Calza's *palazzi di tutti*, an elaboration of the cortile-style *insula* 'combining the usual façade with *tabernae* towards the streets, and inner courts with peristyles, in two or three storeys'.[147]

29–31

This repertoire of standardized patterns is susceptible to variation, but it does recur with almost monotonous consistency. Certainly *insulae* dominated the Ostian city plan. To date, some 78 city blocks have been recovered by the excavators including 364 structures; of these, 205 are obviously apartment houses.

The *tabernae* were among the smallest rental units available and were almost certainly the property of the owner of the apartment block, leased by him or his manager at a figure appropriate to their location. Occasionally the *insula* forfeited the income from shops and workshops by locating luxury suites on the ground floor.

With their appendices, the ground-level shops probably accommodated four persons on the average; the top floors of

Fig. 29 Ostia. Casette tipo, *plan, c. AD 117–38. Meiggs, fig. 12*

Fig. 30 Ostia. Garden house, c. AD 117–38, plan. Meiggs, fig. 11

Fig. 31 Ostia. Insulae, *cross-section and reconstruction. F. E. Brown, fig. 80*

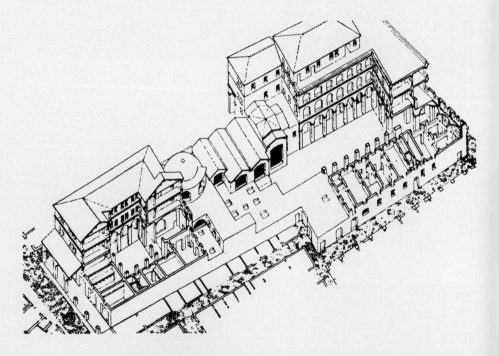

the *insulae*, which rarely exceeded four storeys, probably offered two-room apartments. The largest *insulae* in Ostia certainly accommodated more than one hundred tenants; two exceptionally large complexes, Blocks iii and iv (Regio II), must have housed between 250 and 300 persons apiece.

Who built the apartment houses? Probably private *entrepreneurs* who had sufficient capital to purchase building supplies from the brick factories of the second century AD and to hire the numerous skilled carpenters, artisans and concrete engineers required for the project. The new population density, a consequence of Trajan's harbour installations (AD 100–106), called for additional larger structures. The apartment house had certainly already proved to be a more economical construction than private houses and, with land values soaring and in the face of rising standards of living, builders sought to accommodate ever larger numbers of rent-paying tenants, including the prosperous middle class, in a comparatively small space. The city fathers evidently favoured the new-style high-rise buildings; their compact nature and their fireproof qualities were distinctly attractive when set amidst the grain warehouses of Rome's primary port. The restricted traffic within the city also argued in favour of tenement housing near the city centre and the main avenues of business.

At no stage was Ostia a suburban town, or the dormitory, of Rome as it has been developing in recent times. On the contrary, the absence of private mansions after the first century AD would suggest that the wealthy traders and mercantile magnates preferred to reside in Rome or in coastal villas along Latium's littoral, and to leave the management of their business to trusted freedmen. Even in the high-class apartments, decorations and facilities were modest. Shopkeepers, artisans, service personnel, dockworkers and the like were the labouring citizenry of Ostia. Many of them were immigrants from North Africa and the Greek East and most were, if not slaves, servile by extraction.

Apartment amenities and services were few and far between. Most of the population, one must assume, lived in two rooms without benefit of formal kitchens or latrines. Drain-pipes from the top storeys certainly served to reduce the danger of leakage on the roofs, and occasionally they carried sewage from upstairs apartments. Cooking, as in Rome, was never convenient or capable of providing much variety. Tenants must have prepared their daily meals on portable stoves and braziers, which also provided rudimentary heating in winter. Kleberg's study of hotels, restaurants and cabarets in the Roman period yielded some enlightening statistics on the number of facilities available for the house- and apartment-dweller – particularly in Pompeii, where he detected 20 hotels (*hospitia*, *stabula*) and 118 restaurant-bars clustered, as might be expected, near the city gates or adjacent to public buildings such as baths, gladiatorial barracks, theatres and the like.[148] Ostia's polyglot working-class environment, strangely enough, seems even after extensive rebuilding in the second century AD to have supported only two hotels and fourteen taverns in the areas so far excavated. The paucity is surprising in a seaport with a population somewhere in excess of twenty thousand persons. Several explanations have been advanced for this puzzlingly small number. Taverns were, in Imperial times, certainly in Rome itself, viewed with suspicion by the government; they were regarded as breeding grounds for disaffection, political unrest, and the resort of illegal societies. This factor, combined with imperial edicts against the sale of cooked food and hot water, suggests that taverns were the object of social as well as political reform in Imperial times. Judging by Petronius' account of Marcus Mannicius' inn, and from lively, sometimes scatalogical graffiti on the walls of *tabernae* in Pompeii and elsewhere, many could best be described as whorehouses (*lupanaria*) masquerading behind a restaurant sign.[149] But one must also reckon with the precautionary building regulations of Imperial times which enabled *insulae*-dwellers to maintain private kitchen facilities even when they were dependent on the dole of foodstuffs from the imperial or private largesse. Besides, Ostia's guild houses, the Caseggiato dei Triclini (I, 12, 1), resort of the *fabri tignuarii* (carpenters' union) who numbered 350 in AD 198, the Tempio dei Fabri navales (III, 2, 2), the Tempio and Aula dei Mensores (I, 19, 2–3), and the awesome and elegant Schola di Traiano (IV, 5, 15), all provided the counterpart of modern club life, banquets, burial wakes, and 'locals' which could supplement, for men only, the household regimen of meals and entertainment. And one must also remember that the excavators may yet discover Ostian variations or alternatives in tavern and restaurant design.

Private baths were rare in Ostia in the context of house and apartment block, except for the Domus dei Dioscuri (III, ix, 1), primarily because water could not be raised to floors above the first. But the townsman and his family had no dearth of public baths; hardly anyone was more than five minutes' away from one. Three were impressive structures, benefactions of the Roman government – the Terme di Nettuno, Terme del Foro, and Terme di Porta Marina. Of the fourteen baths so far discovered, these were certainly the most grand; the others, so-called *balnearia*, were often incorporated with palaestrae.[150]

The interior decoration of the *insulae* was normally quite modest. Most of the apartment-house mosaics and paintings seem to have been products of journeyman artists or amateurs, working for small commissions. Mosaics, marble veneer, fine wall-paintings and the like are not usually found in the tenements, though they occasionally appear in the handsome commercial establishments. Lower hallways and entrances were sometimes treated to mosaic floors, while the upper corridors were paved with small bricks laid in concrete in a herring-bone pattern (*opus spicatum*), or with brick tiles (*bipedales*). The walls usually suited the simplicity of the floors and general décor with a mere facing of white plaster. We can tell little about the appearance or the condition of the topmost flats since none has survived, but we may fairly assume that normally the higher one went, the less appealing living conditions became. Certainly none of the Ostian apartments, not even the most luxurious, had arrangements for heating. The salient and redeeming characteristics of Ostian apartment houses are the brick-faced façade, generally unstuccoed, vaulted façade and interior structures, porticoes and balconies, abundant windows, and, very frequently, inner courts for light and air.

Several examples will serve to characterize the range of tenement styles in Imperial Ostia. Many of the second-century AD apartment houses favoured the cortile plan of a central court designed to admit light and ventilation into the inner rooms of

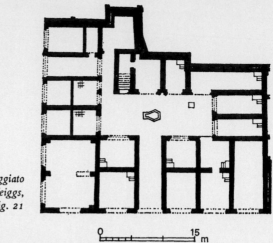

Fig. 32 Ostia. Caseggiato
del Larario, plan. Meiggs,
fig. 21

0 ⊢———————⊣ 15 m

32   the apartment house. The Caseggiato del Larario (I, ix, 3) is a
fairly typical example of the design, although here the court is
surrounded, contrary to normal practice, by a double row of
shops. This apartment house, on a lot measuring 33 yards by 26,
had two entrances, one from the north-east corner of the *decumanus* and one from the Via della Casa del Larario. Both led into
the open court (50 ft 10 in. by 19 ft) with a central fountain and
the array of shops. A staircase led from the cortile to the upper
storeys, of which there were perhaps four. Windows above the
shop entries provided light for the mezzanine apartments, and
their ceilings were, according to size and shape, either barrel-
or cross-vaulted. The upper rooms were accessible from the shops
by inner stairs. Clay pipes built into the walls indicate that the
roof was flat and probably served as a terrace for the residents.
Interior balconies, overlooking the court, may have served to
provide access to the upper storeys but if so, they were wooden,
and appeared on only two sides of the cortile.[151]

The Caseggiato di Diana (Regio I, iii, 3) resembles *insulae* on
the Severan *Forma Urbis*.[152] The ground floor, liberally decorated
with paintings and mosaics, provided multiple shops which were
33, 34   subsequently adapted to incorporate a Mithraeum and a stall. The
second floor, the traditional *piano nobile*, was provided with a
superb balcony and wall-paintings of high quality (Pompeian
Style III); only two apartments were contained on this floor,
one accessible from the street, the other by a wooden staircase

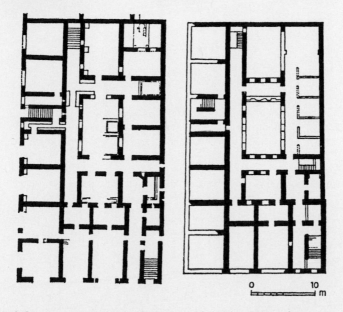

0   10
⊢⊢⊢⊢⊢⊢⊢⊣ m

Fig. 33 left   *Ostia. Caseggiato di Diana, ground floor, plan. Meiggs, fig. 9*
Fig. 34 right   *The same, piano nobile*

from the interior. Judging by the massiveness of the ground-floor walls, three additional storeys completed the fabric. The fountain in the central courtyard was fed by the public aqueduct and was available for common use, including laundry needs and cooking.

The Casa dei Dipinti (I, iv, 4), across the street from the Caseggiato di Diana, is one of the most celebrated apartments in the city.[153] Once again built in the garden-court style, it rose above a lovely garden replete with trees and shrubs, marble basins, benches, and statuary, as elegant as anything in Pompeii or Herculaneum. This luxury apartment house contains three apartments of twelve rooms each, with seven rooms on the ground floor, and five on the second in every instance. The living-room and dining-room were double the normal height (so approximately twenty feet high), the bedrooms had ceilings about ten feet high. In many ways it corresponds closely to the luxury apartments of Rome's contemporary and ultra-fashionable Parioli sector.

32–35
31

The Casa delle Volte Dipinte (III, v, 1) is dated *c.* AD 120.[154] The ground floor, once a single rich man's apartment, exhibits fine wall-paintings and mosaics, and also houses a kitchen and

35

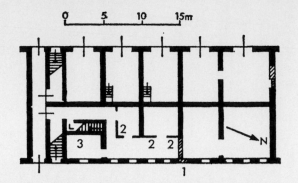

Fig. 35 Ostia. Casa delle Volte Dipinte, plan. Meiggs, fig. 13, showing : 1 original entrance from street, closed when the apartment was reduced; 2 light walls, no longer surviving; 3 paintings

35 latrine. Following the pattern of the *insulae* of Pompeii and Herculaneum, though on a much grander scale, this *insula* undoubtedly began its career as a private mansion and was gradually subdivided for a wealthy clientele. The first storey, accessible from the street by a stairway, seems to have shared the fate of the ground-floor mansion; a second storey probably completed the design.

Ostia, unlike Rome, Pompeii or Herculaneum, was a model town. Its plan sought to end city congestion and the menace of appalling fires and collapsing buildings. Its inhabitants were privileged to enjoy the best fruits of the Imperial genius for engineering and constructional design. Rome undoubtedly remained a slum city in large areas of its sprawling mass, a prey to congestion and claustrophobia, surrounded by noisy cluttered streets, invaded on every side by the clatter of trades and with a host of *botteghe oscure* in almost every quarter. And yet the Roman, for all his addiction to high-density housing, had his share of green space in the many parks and gardens, and the formal, well-sculptured context of the squares which still characterize the Eternal City. Nero, and Augustus before him, first demonstrated that government has a responsibility for the quality of the environment; both employed the skills of planners and the talents of designers with singular, if limited, success.

Ostia was probably never larger than 20,000 souls, in contrast to Rome whose population hovered around 700,000 at its greatest size, and it adopted a residential pattern which, judging by the

Forma Urbis Romae was never really characteristic of Rome.[155] Ostia was almost completely a commercial city, with limited pretensions to culture and art. The massive confusion, the ugliness and the grime of Imperial Rome were absent but instead there was a conventionality, a cityscape which sacrificed diversity to compromises and statistical norms, to externals which were neither too conservative nor too advanced, and so it forfeited the glamour (and the culture) of Rome and the Italian towns. A great flood-tide of races had poured into Rome – Juvenal remarked acerbically that 'the Orontes had flowed into the Tiber', but the amalgam was hearty and basically sensitive and productive.[156] The modern rational design and engineering in Ostia reflect the imperial concern to safeguard and encourage the grain and shipping destinies of Rome, but there are unhappy resemblances between the warehouses (*horrea*) and the *insulae* of Ostia. The contents of the warehouses were grain and other perishables; almost 10,500,000 sacks of grain were unloaded there annually for storage and distribution during the heyday of the Roman Empire. The towpaths on either bank of the Tiber provided the avenues and means for haulers to earn three days' wages towing the lighters upstream to Rome.[157] Ostia, as compact town and market centre, came late to a more sophisticated domestic architecture. It had spent five centuries with what must seem to many of us today a stereotyped architecture of civic improvement, efficient, systematic, conformist and basically heartless. Gertrude Stein's dictum on suburbs seems as appropriate then as now: 'There is no there there.'

CHAPTER V

ITALIAN VILLAS: RURAL, SUBURBAN AND MARITIME

In the Roman villas a love of nature, the old agricultural traditions of Italy, and the fanciful luxury and refinement of hellenistic palatial architecture and pleasure grounds (paradeisoi) met.

Axel Boëthius

He to whom being at home is utter weariness often goes out from his great mansion and suddenly returns, since in truth he feels that it is in no way better out of doors. Then madly driving his colts he hastens to his country villa, pressing on as if bringing aid to a burning building; when he has reached the threshold of his villa he yawns at once, or falls heavily asleep and seeks forgetfulness, or even, in headlong haste, seeks to revisit the city.

Lucretius, *De Rerum Natura* III, 1060–7

VILLAS IN THE ROMAN DEFINITION might conform to one of several patterns and locales – rustic, suburban, pseudo-urban or maritime. The first, the country farmhouse, persisted in many guises from the beginnings of the shepherds' round thatched *capanne* to the fortified estates of the last years of the Empire. The basic agricultural function and design of the *villa rustica* are well described by Cato (234–149 BC), Varro (116–17 BC), and Vitruvius.[158] Rustic simplicity and canny thrift among the antique Romans was a favourite trope of orators and fond reflection of poets.[159] Amid the congestion and the senseless revels of the capital, the cultural hothouse and the demands of the imperial court, the regimen of farm life, of physical exercise and undisturbed sleep, of comfortable solitude amid physically attractive surroundings, were eminently desirable. Few found the idyllic wonder, the leisure and the simple quietude of Thoreau's Concord; but many sought, through financial means, to transfer positive urban values and amenities to their farm-estates or country mansions in the manner of Monroe, Madison or Thomas Jefferson.[160]

Cato the Elder's prescription for the construction of a farmhouse responds to the mounting prosperity and pretensions of the second century BC, when landed aristocrats, as proprietors of large properties (*praedia*), were ready to increase their returns by adding new tenants and leaseholders:

> If you let a contract for a new farmhouse, the builder must make all the walls as ordered from lime concrete, the pillars of squared stone, all beams that may be needed, thresholds, door posts, cross-beams, supports, stalls for the cattle for winter and summer (of the Faliscan type), a stable for horses, rooms for the slaves, three store-rooms for meats, a round table, two bronze containers, ten pigsties, a fireplace, a large door and a smaller one as the master may specify, windows, ten lattice shutters two feet high for the larger windows, six light vents, three benches, five chairs, two looms for weaving togas, a small hand-mill for grinding wheat, a laundry vat, the exterior adornments, and two olive presses.... For a farmhouse of stone and lime, the foundation shall rise a foot above ground, and the rest of the walls shall be of sun-dried brick; place the lintels and decorations that are necessary.[161]

The foundations are of concrete or masonry, the walls of concrete or adobe, indicating that *opus caementicium* had invaded farmhouse architecture at the same time that it transformed town houses and *insulae*.

Farmhouses must have abounded from earliest times in the vicinity of Rome and the major towns of Latium and Etruria; the exploitation of the Mezzogiorno certainly induced many wealthy senators to invest in new property and build estates as well in the productive south. P. Cornelius Scipio Africanus Maior, conqueror of Hannibal, acquired a coastal estate at Liternum; C. Laelius, his philosopher crony, maintained a villa at Puteoli; M. Aemilius Lepidus operated a farm at Terracina in 179; L. Aemilius Paullus, *c.* 160 BC, owned property at Velia, south of Paestum; M. Porcius Cato had farms at Casinum and Venafrum, M.

37

Terentius Varro at Casinum, Reate and Cumae (Lake Lucrinus). And these are merely a sample of property-owners of distinction in the last centuries of the Republic.[162] Population increase and pressures of various sorts on the urban population induced many to invest in less expensive rural properties which could yield a handsome return, given properly scientific and enlightened management. The army's needs, particularly during the Punic Wars and the military operations in the Hellenistic East, were unprecedented and Italian farmers must have responded with increased yields of wheat, barley, horses, mules, wool and leather. Post-war population increase and the prosperity that ensued upon the influx of booty and tribute from abroad made fresh demands on olive oil, wine and foodstuffs. One must reckon with thousands of farms and ranches over the entire face of Italy during the last centuries of the Republic. The whole basis for the leisure class in Rome, and for senators in particular, was income from property investments: senators were virtually required to be landlords. Equestrians, although their major engagement was with the world of business and commerce, were not averse to property investment either. The most rudimentary catalogue of local worthies, men of property in their native environment, would include men like Roscius of Ameria (Umbria) who owned thirteen farms worth six million sesterces; Cluentius and Oppianicus, two gentlemen of Larinum (Samnium), who managed rich estates and ranches; and Cicero and Marius, both Arpinates (Latium), who owed at least some of their standing to their productive farm properties.[163] Capitalistic farming, a lesson learned from Hellenistic kings and no doubt from the Etruscans before them, served the aspiring politician well.

The categories of farm properties were, as today, extensive and varied. Varro, who composed his prose treatise for second-century speculators and proprietors of ancestral estates, advocates the acquisition of meadows and ranches to support horses, cattle, sheep, goats, asses and mules. But grazing could equally well be supported in the hilly terrain of the central Apennines. Varro's villa at Sabine Reate was a headquarters for breeding pedigree horses;[164] others invested in game and fish preserves, or in aviaries for breeding fowl and edible birds; some included apiaries, potteries, and other 'industrial' factories in their do-mains.[165] Vergil's account, both nostalgic and reflective, of the engagements of farmers in the Po Valley near Mantua and in Campania Felix near Naples ignores the necessity for slave labour alongside free, a feature which neither Cato nor Varro omit.[166]

Until recently we were heavily dependent on literary accounts and often chance descriptions to provide a picture of the *villa rustica* of Republican days. For example, Seneca's account of the Villa of Scipio at Liternum offers intriguing suggestions con-cerning the regimen and architectural style of a country estate on the Campanian littoral:

> [The villa] is constructed of squared masonry; a wall encloses a grove; there are turrets buttressed on both sides to provide protection for the house; there is a reservoir, concealed by buildings and shrubbery, large enough to satisfy the needs of a battalion, and a cramped bath building, totally without illumination, in the old-fashioned style. . . . There are no windows, only chinks cut into the masonry to provide light and yet not weaken the structure. . . . What sort of response will be forthcoming to this? 'I certainly don't envy Scipio; a man who had such bathing habits really was living in exile.' Well, if you must know, he didn't bathe every day. Writers who have recorded the conduct of our ancestors tell us that they washed their arms and legs daily, because they dirtied these at their work, but only washed completely once a week.[167]

Scipio's estate, where the general chose to 'fade away' after he became disenchanted with the ungrateful Romans, was a total commitment, for he worked alongside his slaves in the fields. The fortified character of the property suggests that it was constructed *c.* 200 B C, before Liternum, as a Roman colony (194), assumed its coastguard function to maintain order in the environs and to safeguard the settlers against piracy.[168]

Excavation has provided no trace of Scipio's rustic mansion at marshy Liternum but elsewhere the finds of Republican farm-houses have been significant. The Villa Sambuco, near San Giovenale (Etruria), north-west of Veii, has tufa ashlar founda-tions, half-timbered walls of wooden beams and sun-dried brick,

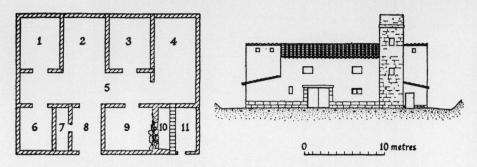

Fig. 36 left   San Giovenale. Villa Sambuco, plan. K. D. White, fig. 4, showing:
1–4 storage rooms; 5 corridor; 6 stable; 7 stairwell; 8 entrance; 9 slaves' quarters; 10
tower; 11 tool shed
Fig. 37 right   The same, reconstruction

36, 37   and a tiled roof.[169] The floors are hard tamped clay with tufa
fragments interspersed. Its late second-century BC plan conforms,
partly at least, to Cato's prescription: there are four large storage
rooms on the north side, a stable on the south-west, and a large
room, east of the southern entry, to house the slaves or villa
manager. The terrain and the provision for storage suggests that
the main produce was olives and grapes, also possibly grain. The
property was clearly not a residence but a basic structure designed
to provide good return from marketable produce. The limited
residence space, the absence of an atrium, peristyle or inner courtyard and the lack of normal domestic amenities indicate that it
was a utilitarian structure of a sort no doubt common in the
Italian scene.

Two other *villae rusticae* have been discovered at Francolise,
near Capua (Campania).[170] The Posto Villa was set in an olive-
growing region with tufa quarries adjacent. Founded on a platform of *opus quadratum* and girdled with walls of the same
bluish-grey tufa blocks, its first phase (c. 120–80 BC) provides a
basic design of a central courtyard, with porticoes or lean-tos
on three sides and the living-quarters on the north. The courtyard
well drew on cisterns carved out of the tufa rock beneath. Two
rooms with tufa foundations appear at the south-east corner,
probably quarters for the resident labourers. The porches no
doubt accommodated crops, vehicles and farm implements,
perhaps even stables for the farm animals often introduced into the
domestic context. Phase II (pre-Augustan date) features a new
north residential wing of approximately nine rooms, expansion of

the water-supply by the excavation of three large vaulted cisterns to the north of the living area, and a two-storeyed tower beside the entrance. Phase III (pre-Flavian) involved significant alterations to provide a three-room bath-suite at the north-west corner of the main wing, serviced by a *praefurnium* at the west end and with adequate drainage; the platform was further extended to enlarge the courtyard space, and two new oil-separating vats were installed with an oil press on the north-east. This villa subscribes rather closely to the Catonian requirements in its earliest phase. The second *villa rustica* at Francolise, San Rocco, also went through three building phases, of which the first (75–50 BC) was a terraced farmhouse on the atrium plan, with the working quarters on a lower terrace to the south. Phase II (50–25 BC) was 38 marked by an enlargement and redesign of the original structure with a central peristyle and a new terrace towards the north which was on a higher plane than the villa platform and ran the entire length of the new construction, incorporating a system of parallel cisterns. The excavators have detected no less than

Fig. 38 Francolise. Villa San Rocco, plan, phase II. Boëthius & Ward-Perkins, fig. 124

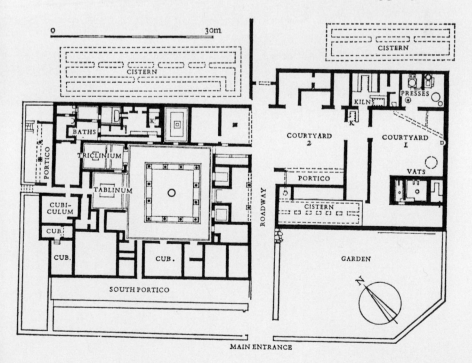

twenty-nine rooms grouped around the peristyle but which also adopt some characteristics of the extroverted 'panoramic' villas facing on the Bay of Naples. The twelve brick columns of the peristyle had stuccoed flutings. Phase III (c. AD 50) incorporated a bath-suite at the western end of the north wing of the residence, adjoining the cisterns. Three rooms adjacent to the entrance (Phase II) were converted to vats for the separation of olive oil. The villa continued to be occupied, with decreasing attention being paid to upkeep, until the mid-second century AD.

38

Recent excavations at Cosa near Ansedonia (Etruria) have yielded several sizeable villa terraces.[171] The houses seem to cluster in *insulae* and suggest comparison with the housing at Marzabotto and Vetulonia rather than with Pompeii. Maritime villas crop up along the shores of Giglio, Giannutri, Argentario and the mainland during the first and second centuries AD, but two villas are worthy of special notice. The Villa Ballantino, in the Valle d'Oro, has a concrete podium with polygonal facing and projecting round towers on the western side with two successive sets of arched dovecotes in the upper storeys. A second *villa rustica*, Le Sette Fenestre, rests on three wide terraces of coarse rubble facing north-west. The lower supports turrets with dovecotes which alternate with sturdy buttresses; the middle terrace rests on barrel-vaulted corridors comparable to those of the Villa of the Mysteries and the Villa of Diomedes at Pompeii; the uppermost terrace supports the manor house. Both are probably second-century BC villas and fairly representative of the manor architecture of the early period; both are also reminiscent of Cato's prescription and of Scipio's turreted retreat at Liternum.

The largest repertoire of *villae rusticae* clusters in the productive acreage of Campania, particularly in the region of Vesuvius. Some forty villas have been located, though somewhat casually documented, with some few examples from the second century BC, the majority from the first century AD.[172] There appears to be a fairly constant ground plan of a central farmyard, usually rectangular, with rooms grouped around it. Covered porticoes, probably refinements of earlier sheds, often run along one or more sides of the cortile. In some of the later examples the courtyard is replaced by a peristyle.

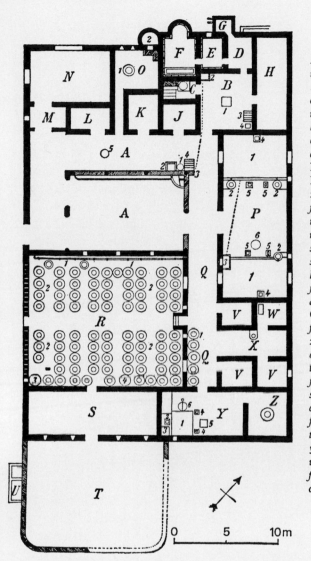

0   5   10m

One of the best preserved of the Campanian *villae rusticae* was unearthed in 1893–94 near Boscoreale, two miles north of Pompeii.[173] Villa No. 13, designed primarily to accommodate an industrial establishment, dates from the end of the Republic. The main court was colonnaded on three sides with an upper storey at the front to house the villa overseer or bailiff (*vilicus*). The kitchen, exposed to the winter sunshine for warmth, was set at the north corner of the court and opened, ominously, into a

39

large stable and, more hygienically, into a bath-suite of *apody-*
terium, *tepidarium* and *caldarium*, with a furnace room attached.[174]
Along the west side of the court the architect located a tool room,
cubicula, and a dining-room with an ante-room. The north-east
side of the court housed the wine-making equipment, presses,
vats, etc.[175] The fermentation vats occupied the largest single
floor space in the villa. Additional *cubicula* were arranged in
the area of the fermentation court, and adjacent to these were
rooms for the production of olive oil, with olive-crushers of
Vesuvian lava and a separation vat. A threshing floor completed
the industrial arrangements at the eastern extremity of the façade.
The cistern in the room of the wine-press yielded the skeleton of a
male lying beside about one thousand gold coins, costly jewellery,
and the so-called Boscoreale Silver Treasure now exhibited in the
Louvre.

Another recently excavated *villa rustica*, the Villa M. Forco
in the Ager Capenas (Campania), contains reticulate and tufa
quoins of Augustan date. The single-storey structure with earthen
floors appears to be a basic farm dwelling with a farmyard around
it; thirty yards to the west the excavators found a small Etruscan-
style tomb attached to the farm. African mosaics of much later
date help to illustrate the nature and the simple appointments of
the small farmer who inhabited this unpretentious country
dwelling.

Occasionally a *villa rustica* may recall the atrium town house
with an external portico (*cf.* Pompeii's House of Sallust) or peristyle. In fact Campanian farmhouses, mostly reburied now,
suggest that both country house and town house are, as Patroni
argued, parallel developments from a single source – the primitive
farmhouse. American excavators at Buccino in the province of
Salerno have uncovered another *villa rustica* at Vittimose, a large
third-century B C establishment with ashlar masonry remodelled
in the first century to incorporate a peristyle court.[176]

The suburban villa was another response to population pressure
and the desire for economic security. Most notable is the Pompeian Villa of the Mysteries.[177] Located outside the Herculaneum
Gate on a slope with a marvellous view of the sea, the villa rests
on a high, arched podium with subterranean vaults. Maiuri, its

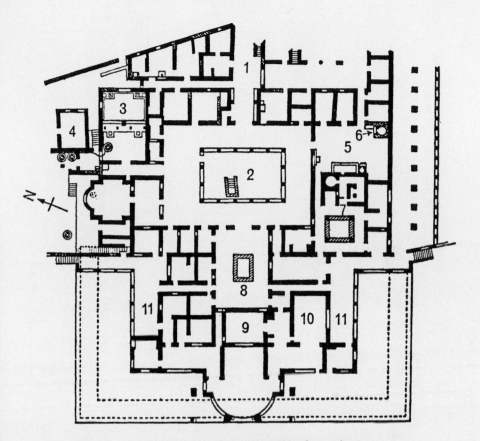

Fig. 40 Pompeii. Villa of the Mysteries, plan. K. D. White, fig. 11, showing:
1 fauces; 2 peristyle; 3 wine press; 4 wine cellar; 5 courtyard of house economy; 6
oven; 7 bathrooms; 8 atrium; 9 tablinum; 10 room of the painting of the
Dionysiac Mysteries; 11 portico

excavator, distinguished six phases of building history from *c.*
200 BC down to Flavian times. The original atrium-style building, in squared blocks of local limestone, has been identified with
the western half of the mansion, and was surrounded on three
sides by a portico. The podium, with side openings, served as a
repository for farm produce brought in from satellite farms, and
as a pleasant promenade on hot or cold days. The courtyard, and
no doubt side yards too, were contained within a wall surrounding the entire property. The doorway on the east side led into an
atrium and *tablinum*; behind these, a portico provided a view of
the coast and sea. A peristyle, a small atrium and a bath room were

40, 41

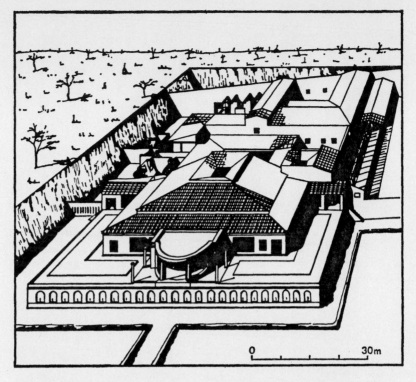

Fig. 41 Pompeii. Villa of the Mysteries, reconstruction, final phase. Maiuri, La Villa dei Misteri, *p. 56*

added *c.* 100 BC in light grey tufa construction. Paintings of Pompeian Style II were applied during Augustan times, with architectural and figure designs and including the celebrated Dionysiac frieze-painting which gives the villa its name. During the Julio-Claudian period the villa's formality and elegance yielded to more utilitarian functions: rustic quarters were appended to the north-east side, and a second floor was added above the vestibule to accommodate the resident *entrepreneur*. The three-sided portico was partly sealed by a windowed wall between the columns, and sun rooms (*solaria*), appropriate for winter siestas, were added on the south side alongside the Room of the Mysteries. Vitruvius' remarks on country estates concern a prevailing pattern: 'in town, atria are usually next to the front door, while in country seats peristyles come first, and then atria surrounded by paved colonnades opening upon palaestrae and walks.'[178] Although the Empress Livia may have resided there, there is certain epigraphical testimony to the villa's last proprietor, Lucius Istacidius Zosimus, a freedman with a Samnite-Greek cognomen and nomen, whose repairs entailed depredation in the final phases of the villa's life-span. The size of the occupancy for which the villa was designed was significant at all periods in its history. Maiuri has estimated that there were twenty-two rooms on the ground floor in Augustan times, and a total of ninety rooms just prior to the eruption.[179] The mansion endured for almost 275 years, vivid testimony to the durability of the materials and the splendid design of the building.

The Pompeian Villa of Diomedes, another example of the *villa suburbana*, shares several of the Villa of the Mysteries' features but is, overall, more attractive.[180] The plan incorporates a colonnaded atrium, the normal repertoire of rooms and apartments, a bath unit and a magnificent garden on a lower level. An apsidal room, accessible from the atrium, was furnished with three windows and served as a siesta sun-room. An open terrace ran the entire length of the portico with steps providing access to the garden below. A *quadriporticus* with pilasters and windows, blocked at a later date, faced the countryside; at both ends, facing the bay, were rooms and turrets designed as belvederes and *diaetae* (rest rooms). The subterranean *cryptoporticus* beneath the peristyle garden was illuminated by loop-holes in the walls.

The suburban Villa of the Papyri outside Herculaneum, sometimes called the Villa of the Pisones, followed much the same pattern as the Villa of the Mysteries, with a peristyle court preceding the atria and porticoes.[181] The Villa of the Papyri, so-called after the cache of carbonized papyri recovered there in 1752, although originally an atrium-style farmhouse, later incorporated an extensive peristyle with gardens and *piscinae*, and a belvedere at the end of a long promenade overlooking the sea. 42 The whole was elegantly furnished with bronze and marble sculptures to provide a perfect complement to reflective leisure and to the Epicurean tenor of life which the recovered carbonized library of Philodemus of Gardara evokes. The villa has been reasonably assigned to L. Calpurnius Piso, Julius Caesar's father-in-law and a distinguished patron of the arts during the late Republic.

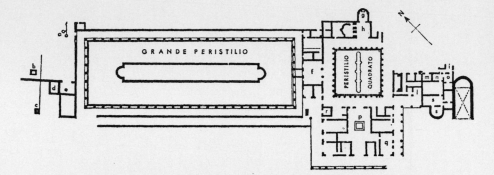

Fig. 42 Herculaneum. Suburban villa of the Papyri ('Pisones'), plan, showing:
a fountain; b room; c fountain; d room with marble floor; e sitting room; f tablinum;
g apsidal room; h salon; i bath; l library; m, n, o rooms adjacent to bath; p atrium;
q room with windows; r grain storage room; s apsidal room and salon

40   Horace's Sabine Farm, one-time property of the opulent and
munificent Maecenas, is located near the modern town of Licenza,
about ten miles north-east of Tivoli.[182] Horace's estate, the gift of
his patron in c. 33 BC after the publication of the first book of the
Satires in 35, practically guaranteed the poet against financial
worries and urban bother; it was reminiscent of his youthful
home of Venusia, and, only a day and a half's journey from Rome
(twenty-eight miles), enabled him to retreat easily and frequently.
Amidst the acreage of pasture-land, olive groves, gardens and
grazing herds Horace found inspiration for his second book of
Satires, the *Epodes* and the first three books of *Odes*, no mean
return from the benefice of his patron Maecenas. The villa is
constructed on two levels. The upper level, the house proper,
contains twelve rooms, six on the east and six on the west, a
central atrium and peristyle connecting with each other and a
43   long central corridor. Black and white mosaic floors accent
several of the rooms. The garden, accessible by three flights of
steps from the house proper, covered an area of 2,900 square
yards; it contained a central pool and was enclosed by a *quadriporticus*. The villa may have had an upper residential storey with
additional windows overlooking the Digentia river, the hill
towns of Licenza and Civitella and the landscaped garden. A
bath housing the normal *calidarium*, *tepidarium* and *frigidarium*

37 Avezzano relief, town and country houses, found in the Fucine
Lake near Alba Fucens

38 Francolise. Villa San Rocco, Phase III

39 Boscoreale. Villa rustica (No. 13), reconstruction

40 Licenza. Horace's Sabine farm, general view from west side

41 Stabiae. Villa
maritima, wall-painting.
Antiquarium, Castellam-
mare di Stabia

42 Stabiae. Villa
maritima, wall-painting

43 Capri, Damecuta. Villa maritima, Augustan, porticus with view
to medieval town, west end

44 Stabiae. Villa San Marco, peristyle garden and *piscina*

45 Stabiae. Villa San Marco, *frigidarium*

46 Pompeii. House of Marcus Lucretius Fronto, villa maritima, *tablinum* wall-painting, belvedere with people and row-boat

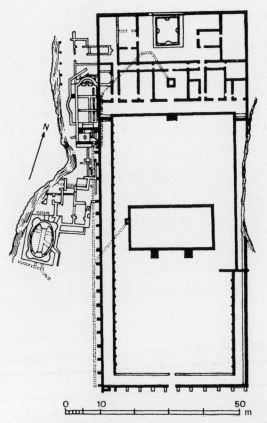

Fig. 43 Licenza. Horace's Sabine Farm, plan. G. Lugli, Horace's Sabine Farm (Rome 1931), endpaper

is an adjunct on the west side of the garden-estate, and was probably part of Maecenas' original property. Five families of free peasants (*coloni*) were tenants on Horace's estate, and eight slaves ministered to his personal needs. The poet may disclaim any magnitude for his estate (*modus non ita magnus; villula; agellus; angulus ille*), but the existing remains suggest otherwise.

Scholars have speculated often on the plan of Trimalchio's mansion in Petronius' *Satyricon*.[183] Described as an enlarged version of an earlier house, it contains four dining-rooms, twenty bedrooms, two marble porticoes and three libraries on the ground floor; upstairs are two master bedrooms and a wing for guests comprising in all some fifty rooms.[184] The front door opens into a peristyle or portico, while the atrium, *tablinum* and *alae* are located in the centre of the house. The marble portico must refer to the Hellenistic peristyle behind the house, with summer *triclinium*, landscaped garden and fountains. The entrance peristyle is Trimalchio's addition to the 'Victorian' mansion, a format shared by the Villa of the Mysteries and the Villa of Boscoreale (see p. 116), both in the Augustan design. The house pattern seems to resemble a *villa suburbana*, typical perhaps of the residences of comparably wealthy, hopefully less vulgar freedmen along the heights of Puteoli, the most likely locale for Petronius' *Graeca urbs*.

During the last century of the Republic villa architecture adopted new plans and devices to meet the tastes and the demands of the wealthy Roman *élite* and the ubiquitous *parvenu* freedmen with their seemingly limitless capital. Campania was preferred by most millionaires of the time, particularly Misenum, Baiae, Bauli, Puteoli, Lucrinus, Cumae and Naples itself.[185] The abundant mineral springs, sulphur baths and steaming *'fumarole'* which served the health centres and playgrounds at Baiae, Puteoli, Naples and Ischia exercised the same fascination in antiquity as they do today. Easy access to *pozzolana* cement, experience with innovatory architectural forms and proximity to the sea and the markets of Puteoli, Rome's major commercial harbour until supplanted by Ostia, all encouraged architects and land-speculators to a frenzy of residential building and development.[186] Strabo's contemporary comment is most enlightening:

47

> At Baiae another city has come into being, with one mansion on top of another, not inferior to Dicearchia [Puteoli] in size. But Neapolis still retains its Hellenic way of life, since those who retreat here from Rome do so for the sake of an easy retirement after a life of work from childhood, or they are individuals who yearn to live in relaxation on account of their age or the condition of their health. Romans who are captivated by this mode of living observe the number of persons who settle there to live the same kind of life, become delighted with the place of their choosing, and live out their own days there.[187]

Ataraxia, Epicurean imperturbability suggesting detachment and enlightened self-interest, co-existed with the life of total engagement, wilful disorder and licentious indulgence on the Bay of Naples; there was no single regimen along these shores at any time in the history of the area. Businessmen, financiers, politicians, clients and parasites jostled one another in the teeming streets of Naples and Puteoli, or saluted one another from their pleasure-craft on the bay. The *peregrinatio*, the seasonal sojourn in the resorts of Campania, was a time either for conspicuous living and lavish expenditure, or for *otium cum dignitate*, for quiet relaxation and decorous cultural pursuits. And amid the pleasure-seekers, the moody recluses and the profiteers there were the multitudinous poor, exiles and expatriates, slaves and outcasts, criminals and assassins. Pontiae (Ponza) and Pandateria (Ventotene), even Surrentum and Capri sometimes housed imperial exiles and prisoners, a tradition which continued into modern times on Ventotene and Procida. But throughout the long evolution of history on the Campanian shores the Italian maxim, *Vede Napoli e poi muorir* ('See Naples and die'), has reflected an abiding sentiment for these captivating shores.

Coastal estates were eagerly sought after with the advent of Hellenistic luxury to Italy after the wars of conquest abroad. The age of the elaborate town house and of the country estate quite divorced from agricultural pursuits dawned during the second century BC, and a host of luxury seaside villas (*villae maritimae*) clambered for sun-drenched space and panoramic views, especially along the Campanian littoral and the sea coast of Latium.[188]   41, 42
Cicero is our authority that wealthy Romans were anxious to buy farm properties in the *ager Campanus* so as to finance their maritime villas at Cumae (including Lucrinus) and Puteoli.[189] The Younger Pliny provides detailed, almost stupefying, descriptions of his fantastic Laurentine and Tuscan villas, one maritime and the other an elevated country mansion.[190]

The villa had become the paradigm of luxury and an habitual topic for moralists and poets who heaped contempt on the *piscinarii* who maintained ludicrously large fish-ponds, and showed an ardour for the finny tribe beyond all reason, or on property-owners who demonstrated their impatience with the land by extending the boundaries of their villas on concrete piers.[191]

Two basic architectural types emerge in the catalogue of *villae maritimae*: peristyle and *porticus*.[192] The peristyle villas, direct descendants of Hellenistic palaces, are frequently reflected in

Campanian wall-paintings. Two famous villas subscribe to this pattern, the Villa of the Mysteries, already discussed, and the Villa of Publius Fannius Synistor at Boscoreale (near Pompeii). The Villa of the Mysteries, originally an atrium-style mansion, added after 150 BC a peristyle which became the focus of the entire mansion. So too at Boscoreale, visitors entered a large central peristyle court with living rooms, private spaces, *diaetae* and *cubicula* grouped around it.[193] Varro, at the close of the Republic, laments the tendency to attach more importance to the residential than the agricultural portion of villas, and contrasts luxurious modern villas with the simplicity of the ancient estates where the prime concern was efficient agriculture. Villas had become summer residences for the wealthy, who normally left their year-round management to bailiffs. Just as prosperity assisted the evacuation during the second century, so later the Augustan peace, when Italy was finally free of brigandage and civil war, encouraged property-owners to transfer the amenities of city dwellings to the country. The town-house peristyle migrated with them to the country and to the seashore.

Fig. 44   Capri, Damecuta. Porticus Villa of Augustus. Maiuri, Capri, fig. 29

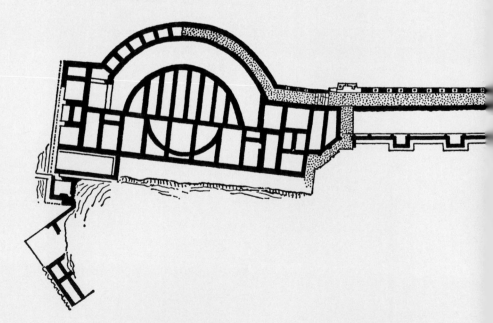

Porticus villas, according to Swoboda, evolved from a long narrow row of rooms opening on to a road or court, a primitive form still encountered in the Near East.[194] The addition of a colonnade, or *porticus*, parallel to the row of rooms, with doors opening on to the gallery, provided the basic design of the Roman *porticus* villa, and of the Hellenistic stoa as shopping centre. The *porticus* structure was particularly well adapted to the coastline, where it could accommodate several levels or simply open directly on to the shore. The Villa of Damecuta on Capri is a good example of the *porticus*-type villa by the sea.[195] Located on a   *43* plateau beneath Monte Solaro at the north-west corner of the island (uncomfortably near the modern heliport), the villa concentrated on a superb belvedere or loggia (*ambulatio*) with seating alcoves running east-west along the shore line, 492 feet above sea level. The residential area at the west end consists of a   *44* central curved projection on the seaward side with a porticoed loggia around its outer face; at the opposite end was a belvedere, surmounted today by a medieval tower, and an isolated suite of small but elegantly furnished rooms let into the cliffside and

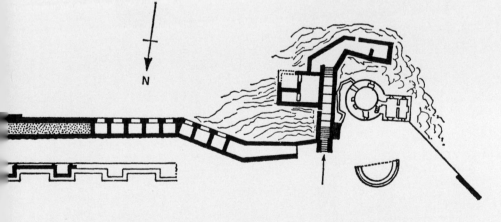

accessible only by a narrow ramp and steps. The difficulty of
48   access and the similarity of the loggia to that of the Villa Jovis
suggest that the residence may have been designed for Tiberius.
Service buildings, baths, and additional living-quarters must have
been located elsewhere on the expansive property, no doubt
splendidly landscaped and featuring domesticated and game
birds. Accessible only by sea at Punta di Gradola (= 'landing')
visitors would no doubt proceed by way of the small Villa
Gradola atop the vault of the Blue Grotto to the promontory
where the Villa di Damecuta stands.

Recent excavations at Castellammare di Stabiae (ancient
Stabiae), have yielded impressive remains of villas closely resembl-
ing the *porticus* villas familiar from Campanian wall-paintings
(many of them extracted during earlier Bourbon excavations),
and the Villa di Damecuta.[196] Architecturally the villas are of
Julio-Claudian and Flavian date, roughly AD 50 to 79. The Villa
San Marco, a fifty-room mansion on Varano's slopes, comprises
three units: a portico with spiral columns; a peristyle garden with
44; 45   a great *natatio*; and a tetrastyle atrium. Frequent finds of bricks
stamped Narcissi Augusti, along with other considerations,
suggest that the villa was designed for Narcissus, Claudius' freedman secretary, who was finally hounded to suicide in AD 54.

Fig. 45   Stabiae. Villa San Marco, plan. D'Orsi, Gli scavi archeologici di Stabiae,
pl. 22

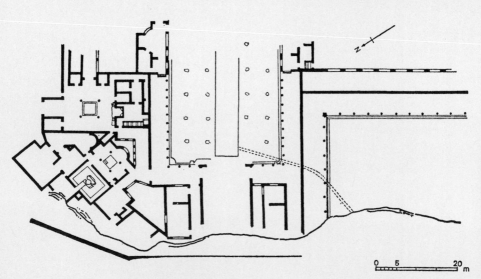

0   5   20
                          m

The upper terrace of the property exhibits a three-sided portico (*porticus triplex*), with a panoramic view of the Bay of Naples.[197] A central *porticus* with seventeen Ionic brick columns with plastered bases and fluting of helicoidal design takes the form of a loggia originally over one hundred yards long; there are two projecting side *porticus* corridors. The walls and ceilings of the *porticus* contain a veritable art gallery, constituting, in some respects, a Stoa Poikile of unique paintings. The ceiling has yielded fragments of three large-scale panels set in an elaborate 'Renaissance' framework: a planisphere of the Seasons, the apotheosis of Minerva, and Mercury. The walls of the long aisle have yielded fragmentary paintings of Apollo and Daphne, Apollo with his tripod standing on a golden candelabra, a portrait of Dionysus (a veritable Frans Hals this), a girl's portrait, a woman's head (recalling the head of the flagellated girl in the Villa of the Mysteries frieze), Pampinea, a *putto* with syrinx, a tragic female mask ('anguish'), etc. The extant short aisle features a ceiling-painting of the *quadriga* of Helios with Phaethon at the reins, and wall-paintings which include an appealing figure of Melpomene.

Steps and a ramp lead down to the western *ambulacrum* of the lower peristyle court, a *quadriporticus*, with ceiling and wall-paintings on its porticoed sides, in the adjacent *salons* (*oeci*), and in the *cubicula diurna* and *exedrae* overlooking the bay through picture windows. A great pool, probably designed for swimming rather than for exotic and ornamental fish, is located in the centre of the garden on its major axis, and measures 98 feet long by 20 feet wide. A lovely alabaster *crater* stood at the inner end of the pool. The garden, to judge by the carbonized roots, was land-scaped with shady trees and flowering bushes, and ended in a great *nymphaeum* which is decorated with large-scale painted stucco relief figures and architectural fantasies. There is a *crypto-porticus* behind with windows opening on to the outer wall. The decorations, partly removed by the Bourbons, included wall-paintings of an Amorino with a cymbal (the so-called 'Berenson putto'), two Claudian princes engaged in a sacred rite, a large-scale figure-painting of Apollo with his lyre, Iphigenia, Perseus with the head of Medusa (a marvellous forecast of Cellini's

44

bronze masterpiece in the loggia of the Piazza della Signoria in Florence) and ceiling-paintings of the rape of Europa and a flying Nike-Fortuna. Oedipus and the Sphinx (a unique painting), a delicate Nile landscape, a stupendous Medusa (from the ceiling of the connecting corridor between the two peristyles), and many smaller, less distinguished paintings have also been found.

The remainder of the capitalist Villa San Marco exhibits the normal complement of rooms and facilities, a bath complex with a tetrastyle *frigidarium* and pool, an impressive *calidarium*, kitchens, and a handsome tetrastyle atrium (entrance hall) and portal with a richly painted *lararium*, a room with marble wall panels and mosaic floor, and yet another peristyle!

45

Another great villa has been located on the hillside of Varano, at the Fondo di Marino. Discovered originally by the Bourbons and described in detail by Ruggiero as the Villa della Venditrice di Amori, it has been renamed the Villa of Ariadne by reason of a splendid mural still *in situ*. D'Orsi's new plan of the villa, an enlargement of Ruggiero's eighteenth-century version, includes a long colonnaded terrace overlooking the bay and a series of *oeci*, *cubicula* and *exedrae* opening off the terrace, some of them with picture windows. The central *triclinium* is flanked by alcoves, and has kitchen and bathing facilities behind. The end wall of the dining-room displayed a painting of the marriage of Dionysus and Ariadne ($4\frac{1}{2}$ feet by $4\frac{3}{4}$), a fragmentary Lycurgus and Ambrosia, Ganymede, Diana, and two medallion paintings, or tondi, with portraits of a young girl and a youth. A spacious *andron*, furnished with windows and flanked by two small gardens, a second room with windows, and yet another peristyle have appeared in recent excavations. All were designed to provide a panoramic view of the bay. From the *andron* a passageway, partly open, partly in the form of a tunnel, leads by a steep descent to the shore. At another level a terrace has emerged bounded by a low podium which is crenellated and supported on arches. The repertoire of paintings in this single villa is remarkably large, and always of high artistic quality. The Bourbon finds, now in the National Museum in Naples, include the Venditrice di Amori (the 'name painting'), four lovely panels of Flora, Diana, Leda and Medea, once the central decorations for a bedroom's walls, and two Nereids riding sea creatures, both socle decorations with a rococo quality. More recent finds include a youthful hero, probably Theseus, wearing a scarlet robe, part of a large-scale painting (4½ feet by 2¼), the head of an ephebe, a crouching Cupid, and a Centaur with Deianeira and Hyllus, Hercules' wife and young son. Remains of other *porticus* villas have been located off Posillipo, at Torre del Greco near Naples, at Minori on the Amalfi Drive, at Surrentum, and elsewhere.[198]

46

Sorrento and Siren Land are synonymous. Strabo's description of the coastline between Misenum and Athenaeum, the cape of Sorrento, is enlightening: 'The entire bay is adorned partly by the cities mentioned and partly by residences and gardens which continue in such an unbroken succession that they give the appearance of a single city.'[199] Augustus certainly maintained a villa on the promontory. Agrippa Postumus, brutish son of Agrippa and Julia, was exiled there in AD 7 after his removal from the villa at Boscoreale.[200] Most impressive, for the poet Statius, was the estate of Pollius Felix, his patron.[201] A *porticus* linked the seaside accommodations, a double bath-system and a shrine of Hercules, with the domestic quarters on the hilltop. Rooms were planned to enjoy different exposures with picture windows looking out towards Aenaria (Ischia), Procida, Misenum, Nesis (Nisida) and Euploia's shrine above Naples; one room, furnished with imported polychrome marbles, served as a study where the wealthy Epicurean could retreat from the sounds of the sea and the villa's personnel. This elegant villa on the south-west side of the promontory survives in sorry remains which nevertheless

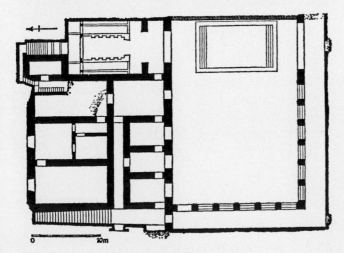

Fig. 46   Minori, Amalfi Drive, Villa Romana, Fototeca Unione

0   10m

accord with the poet's eulogy. The reticulate brickwork facing of the remains suggests that Pollius' *porticus* villa was built during the Augustan era.[202]

Multi-level villas of the *porticus* style are also known to have been part of the Neapolitan repertoire. *Porticus* houses on the southern slope of Pompeii, descending in several storeys down the hillside, probably supply the design of the villa mentioned by Philostratus, a striking Neapolitan mansion with a portico on four or five terraces enjoying a western exposure to the bay and the breezes.[203] The multi-level construction at Baiae, a vast architectural design along the slopes of the Sella di Baia, continues

47 to mystify archaeologists.[204] In many respects it recalls the terraced design of the spectacular second-century Temple of Fortuna Primigenia at Praeneste, or the hill towns of Etruria and Campania.[205] Stairways divide the great construction into sectors which communicate with seemingly separate apartments in an almost 'city' complex. The oldest structures so far identified are of Hellenistic date, the latest are assigned to the reign of Severus Alexander (AD 222–35). The presence of separate apartments, with private thermal arrangements in some sectors, suggests that the complex may be the result of local enterprise (perhaps by Sergius Orata) or of a compromise involving a number of landlords and residents. The individual 'villas', often with *porticus* or modest peristyle attached, like terraced apartments, gradually took on the aspect of a single great entity. Subsequently, if De Franciscis is correct, the entire complex became the imperial *palatium* of the Severan dynasty at Baiae.[206]

The *porticus* villas at Stabiae, Surrentum, Damecuta and elsewhere are mere tokens of the rich array that once lined the Campanian shores. Wall-paintings of seaside villas found in Pompeii and Stabiae are clearly no artist's fancy but representa-

46–48 tional art of contemporary, even local, relevance. Their peristyle gardens, sculptures, boats and landing stages, long spacious porticoes, sometimes arranged in tiers against a hillside, outbuildings and the like are now known to be part and parcel of contemporary villa styles. The curvilinear forms familiar from the wall-paintings and evidenced substantially at Val di Catena on the Adriatic[207] are refined instances of the use of concrete, particularly the

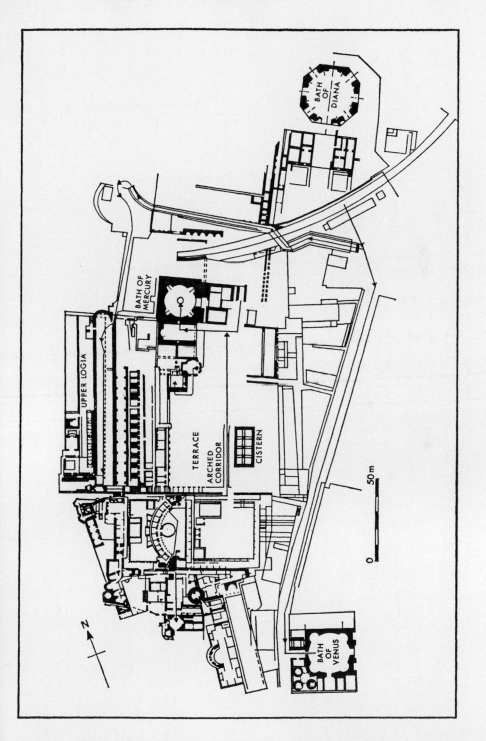

Fig. 47 Baiae. ‘The Severan Palatium’, bath buildings, apartments, plan. Maiuri,
The Phlegraean Fields, fig. 41

fast-setting hydraulic cement from Puteoli, which enabled architects to construct novel forms along jagged or sinuous coast-lines.

Peculiar to every *porticus*-style villa was the predilection for space, light, air and vistas. The *porticus* provided for all of these in a uniquely successful fashion. Cicero's allusion to Marcus Marius' picture window in his suburban villa at Pompeii is typical of the invasion of light and the 'picture window' into these summer places.[208]

Although Augustus professed a passion for Capri as a convalescent and pleasure resort, he also sought retreats elsewhere. The original residence at Prima Porta (ancient Rubra or Saxa Rubra), nine miles from Rome, was probably built between 30 and 25 BC. It occupied a large plateau overlooking the Tiber valley and was favoured by the imperial couple both because of favourable omens witnessed there and by reason of the salubrious site. Called *ad Gallinas*, its most valuable yields have been the celebrated cuirass statue of Augustus, found in 1863,[209] and the superb garden painting installed in Rome's Terme Museum in 1951–52.[210] Reminiscent of the underground apartments of the Domus Augusti on the Palatine and of the Casa dei Grifi, the Prima Porta mansion also had an underground room with plastered vaulting, forty feet long, opening onto a painted garden of six panels crowded with flowers, shrubs, birds and fruit, one of the most enchanting paintings to survive from antiquity.

49

Tiberius, the melancholy successor of Augustus, built a great palace retreat on Capri, the so-called Villa Jovis.[211] Although Augustus had shown his affection for the island by building numerous villas, Tiberius brought the number of imperial residences there to twelve, with the Villa Jovis at the apex. Augustus may have selected the site for the eyrie and started construction, but the final plan of the grandiose edifice is almost certainly the brainchild of Tiberius and his court architects. The Villa Jovis rises on the north-eastern promontory of the island, remote, defensible, and superbly located 1,095 feet above sea level. Designed as a year-round residence, the multi-level complex enjoys a magnificent panoramic view over the bay to Vesuvius and the acropolis of Cumae, to Sorrento and the Islands of the Sirens. The core of the villa, and half of its entire area, consists

48

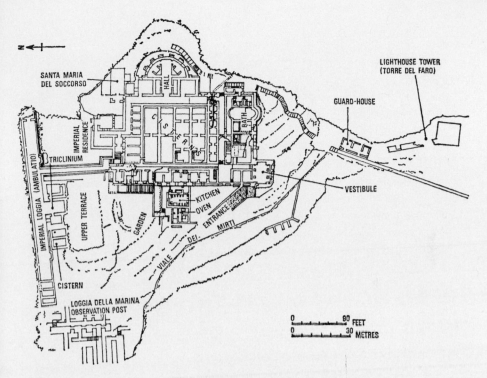

Fig. 48   Capri. Villa Jovis ('Tiberius' Villa'), plan. Fototeca Unione

of four large vaulted cisterns, each divided into three or four
compartments. Springs are totally lacking in the area and indeed
generally throughout Capri today. The baths were located on the
south side of the central cistern with an eye as well to the sun
which must have streamed through spacious windows into the
bath area. Kitchens, bakeries and store-rooms were sited beneath
the west wing of the palace, sufficiently far removed to prevent
smells from invading the imperial quarters and conveniently
adjacent to the water-supply. The entrance hall to the villa, paved
in *opus spicatum* (herring-bone pattern) opened on the south-west
side, and led through a colonnaded vestibule of four cipollino
columns into the area of the guard rooms and bath system on the
south side. The north and east sides of the villa were assigned to
private living-quarters for the emperor and his retinue of praetorian guardsmen, freedmen secretaries, and palace officials,
scholars and astrologers. The east side was occupied by a semicircular audience room (*aula*) whose central section took the form

of a long hall which was entered through a *cryptoporticus* at the west end. The rooms on either side of the long aisle, each provided with a narrow, rectangular antechamber, were probably libraries, perhaps one for Greek, the other for Latin volumes; the two rectangular alcoves looking north-east and south-west would serve as reading areas with picture windows overlooking the sea. The north side, the topmost elevation, was the area of the imperial apartments and the rooms of the praetorian guard. An extensive open-air promenade (*ambulatio*) with mural decoration, no doubt modelled after the counterpart in the Villa of Damecuta beneath Anacapri, provided a sun-terrace (*solarium*) almost a hundred yards long; two rectangular *exedrae* were designed to provide views of the northern sweep of the bay towards Ischia. The emperor's suite of rooms was on the north-west side of the villa: paved with polychrome marble, it was accessible both from the corridor which connected with the main entry and the baths, and from the service stairs that led from the kitchen area; they were also connected by means of a vaulted ramp with the terraced *ambulatio* on a lower level. An upper belvedere terrace, which today supports the church of S. Maria del Soccorso, was reserved for the emperor's private use.

44

The imperial dining area, a spacious vaulted room, opens on to the terrace loggia; its polychrome marble floor serves today as paving in the local cathedral; two additional rooms open on to the *triclinium*, one a *diaeta* for siesta accommodation, the other a more sizeable room, perhaps a winter *triclinium* or imperial apartment; small cisterns alongside provided supplementary water for the dining-room and for the parkland *nymphaea* and aviary no doubt located above. Remains of an observatory (*specularium*), catering to the emperor's addiction to astrology, rise independently on the west side of the villa. There is no discernible central axis to the villa and the private quarters of Tiberius are deliberately isolated from the central nucleus of court and cistern.

Grottoes and *nymphaea* were much in vogue during late Republican and Imperial days. The celebrated Blue Grotto on Capri was certainly a grotto-*nymphaeum* for a villa nearby.[212] Recent finds indicate that a series of sculptures, probably marine subjects, were attached to the grotto's side walls at sea level. A sloping concrete landing stage, with a brick-lined channel and traces of cutting in the wall, offer additional proof that the imperial visitors used to feast their eyes on the enchantment of the grotto from an inner landing. The Blue Grotto was simply a grander, natural version of the *nymphaea* which commonly adorned rich men's villas and domestic gardens in city and country alike. Tiberius was extremely fond of these romantic, evocative places, and one of them was the site of near tragedy. Tacitus relates that while the emperor was dining with his entourage in a cave near Formiae, the banqueters were surprised by the collapse of the grotto's roof,[213] Tiberius' life was saved by the quick intervention of Sejanus who shielded the emperor's body with his own. This grotto at Sperlonga (ancient Spelunca) finds its closest parallel in another grotto on Capri, the so-called 51; 49 Grotta dell'Arsenale, between the Piccola Marina and the Punta di Tragara. There is a comparable low wall around the rocky interior, 121 feet in diameter, and large niches are set into the end of the cave; the platform was paved with polychrome marbles and the ceiling decorated with *lacunaria*, roof-panels, lined with stucco and mosaic. The Sperlonga grotto was adapted to serve as a *nymphaeum* and banqueting hall, with marble groups illustrating episodes from epic contexts: Scylla attacking Ulysses'

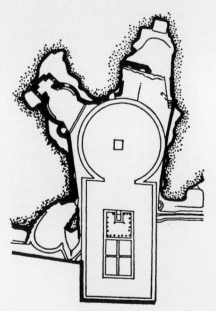

Fig. 49 Sperlonga, Villa of Tiberius, seaside grotto and piscina, plan. F. Rakob, DAI RM 71 (1964) fig. 8

companions, Polyphemus couchant and under attack (they are the largest works), the wreck of Ulysses' ship, the rape of Ganymede, the theft of the Trojan Palladium, and Menelaus with the body of Patroclus (forecast of the work in Florence's loggia). A late Republican villa adjacent to the cave completed the imperial ensemble.[214]

Caligula and Nero were notorious for their buildings, both for their number and for their virtuoso or mad-cap character. Suetonius and Pliny the Elder both suggest that Rome was virtually surrounded by the habitations of these Julio-Claudians, with their villas and gardens acquired by inheritance or assassination.[215] Some fair indication of their fantastic extravagance has emerged from the depths of Lake Nemi, seventeen miles south-east of Rome, when the sunken 'house-boats' of Caligula were discovered. Larger than some of the early Atlantic liners, they were virtually villas afloat, with every conceivable luxury installed.[216]

Nero's ventures were no less dramatic: a luxurious remodelling of his birthplace at Antium, a *porticus* villa of grandiose proportions; a scheme to link the thermal establishments of Baiae, Puteoli, Lucrinus and Avernus by a great colonnade; a canal to link Avernus with Ostia; a collapsible pleasure-craft designed to remove his irksome mother, the dowager empress Agrippina, and the like.[217] The imperial villa at Sublaqueum (Subiaco) was an enlargement of an earlier property, rendered in the design of a *villa maritima* inland. The river was dammed to create an artificial lake.[218] The Great Fire of 64 destroyed his Domus Transitoria in Rome but enabled him to fashion a replacement which would once again, as at Subiaco, compete with the logic of the setting. The resultant Domus Aurea was to be a *villa suburbana*, with another artificial lake and acres of parkland.[219] *Rus in urbe* was the imperial answer to the congestion and soul-destroying cityscape which Vulcan had tried to erase.

Nero's urban villa in the centre of Rome broke markedly with traditional methods of construction and design. Brick-faced concrete was the main constructional material, and the strait-jacketing simplicity of plan and building forms disintegrated in favour of complex designs, polygonal shapes, domical rooms and spatial effects hitherto untried on any grand scale. Nero's longing

50

47 Pompeii. Casa della Fontana Piccola, villa maritima and harbour, wall-painting from the peristyle

48 Pompeii. House of Marcus Lucretius Fronto, villa maritima, wall-painting showing colonnades, rooms and central *exedra*

49 Rome. Villa of Livia, Prima Porta, garden room mural

50 Rome. Villa Farnesina, stucco relief

51 Sperlonga. Grotto with *piscina* and sculpture >

52 Tibur (Tivoli). Hadrian's Villa, reconstruction model >

53   Sicily, Piazza Armerina. Imperial Villa, view from vestibule into garden

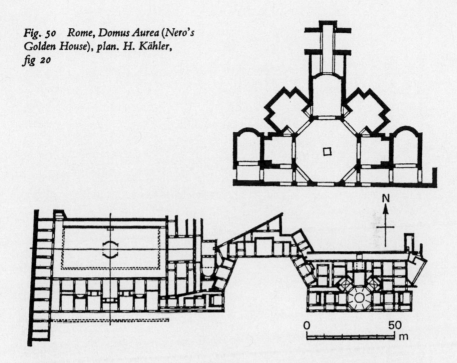

N

0   50
⊢━━━━━━━━━┤ m

for a 'contrived solitude of woods and vistas and open pastures'[220]
was dramatically satisfied by his engineer-architects, Severus and
Celer, and in an unbelievably short span of time. The design of
Nero's Golden House is colourfully related by Suetonius:

> There was an artificial lake to represent the sea, and on its
> shores buildings laid out as cities; and there were stretches of
> countryside, with fields and vineyards, pastures and woodland,
> and among them herds of domestic animals and all sorts of wild
> beasts. . . . There were dining-halls whose coffered ivory
> ceilings were set with pipes to sprinkle the guests with flowers and
> perfumes. The main dining-room was circular and it revolved
> constantly, day and night, like the universe. There were also
> seawater baths and baths of sulphur-water [from Aquae Albulae,
> near Tivoli].[221]

The artificial solitude, the exceptional *hortus*, was an expansion
and elaboration of practices long familiar in villa and domestic
architecture. Paintings found in the House of M. Lucretius Fronto

at Pompeii undoubtedly reflect the lakes, porticoes, pavilions, rustic shrines, etc., favoured by landscape gardeners (*topiarii*) in earlier days.[222] Varro's account of his villa at Casinum describes a parkland interlaced by a canal with bridges, groves, fishponds (*piscinae*) and colonnades covered with hemp netting to keep birds from escaping, a domical aviary (which defies modern restoration!), and a forest of large trees. Inside the domical roof of the aviary, supported by an inner ring of wooden columns, the morning and evening stars circled by some intriguing mechanism about the lower part of the celestial hemisphere, and a compass controlled by an outer weather-vane indicated the direction of one of the eight winds at any time of day or night![223] The stuccoes from the Villa Farnesina, now in the Terme Museum in Rome, offer another rich inventory of garden embellishments and man-made parklands, with towers, bridges, trees, spreading fields, pavilions and statues.[224] Nero's fault lay not in his ingenuity but in his selfish eccentricity: 'The Golden House shocked contemporary opinion less by its architectural pretensions than by the displacement of a crowded urban quarter to make way for a country estate in the heart of Rome.'[225] The best surviving counterparts for the villa with its spectacular gardens are the celebrated villas at Frascati, especially the Villa Aldobrandini, and the Villa Borghese in Rome.

The domestic wing of Nero's rustic *palazzo* resembles the terraced villas of Campania or the Alban Hills but with remarkable innovations: 'the deliberate interruption of the neatly rectangular plan of the main block by the incorporation of an elongated, half-hexagonal courtyard, recessed into the middle of the façade in front of the Sala della Volta Dorata, the incorporation into the middle of the west wing of an elaborate octagonal room, with central dome, and radiating vaulted chambers.' The residential sector of the Golden House on the lower slopes of the Oppian Hill, east of the Colosseum, overlooked an artificial lake (where Vespasian later located the arena of his amphitheatre); aqueducts supplied water for countless streams and cascades that tumbled down the terraced slopes like some latter-day Villa d'Este or Caserta. The vestibule stood on the site of Hadrian's later Temple of Venus and Roma, and towering over all was a gilt bronze statue of the emperor, a modern-day colossus some 120 feet high.[226]

Nero's revolution in palace architecture sparked resentment which accelerated the artist-emperor's downfall and suicide. The emperor's statement on its completion – 'Now at last I can begin to live like a human being'[227] – showed his characteristic bravura and egotistical mania. But the product of his dreams and desire, condemned, ruined and buried by his successors, nevertheless later became the inspiration for Raphael, Giulio Romano and Giovanni da Udine (their grafitti survive in the underground corridors) and the pattern for the marvellous interiors of the Villa d'Este, the Villa di Papa Giulio (Rome's Etruscan Museum), the Villa Madama, and the Villa at Caprarola.

Domitian's Albanum (sc. praedium, estate), the former property of Pompey the Great, faced on to the Via Appia by the Alban Lake.[228] The three-level structure, designed by Rabirius, Domitian's celebrated architect on the Palatine, was both impressive and ingenious in its fabric. The top terrace accommodated cisterns; the middle terrace, a tripartite design, contained a quadriporticus with a fountain set in front of a small theatre whose seats rose to the height of the top terrace, a long narrow garden with nymphaea in the central zone, and the residential quarter at the south-east. A cryptoporticus connected the lowest terrace with the palace sector, and provided quarters for the praetorian guard, stables and sunken garden after the pattern of the 'stadium' on the Palatine. The Albanum, object of envy and eulogy in the emperor's day for its elegance and refined table, covered a large tract of parkland, with terraces and promenades, waterside landing-stages, and a multitude of nymphaea and gazebos, a veritable Domus Aurea extending from Castel Gandolfo, the modern papal summer residence, to Albano and beyond the lake to the Appian highway. Domitian's other villa maritima was located at Lago di Sabaudia, near Circeo,[229] and was an adaptation of an earlier Republican villa, possibly the one to which Augustus banished the embarrassing Lepidus, fellow triumvir and Pontifex Maximus, until his death in 13 BC.[230]

Hadrian's Villa at Tibur, some twenty miles from Rome, marked the culmination of the landscape villas of Roman

Imperial date.[231] The elements derive from the tradition of Varronian villa design, from the congeries of Nero's Domus Aurea and
Domitian's Albanum, but with even grander, more diversified
52   elements infused. A mere listing of the elements provides hair-
raising evidence of the expenditure of time and architectural
resource on the project which, in all likelihood, Hadrian himself
rarely visited or enjoyed. The age-old axiality and symmetry of
Roman architectural design were forfeited once and for all in the
the baroque agglomeration of buildings and architectural forms.
Scattered over an area measuring 1000 by 500 yards, rivalling
anything devised by Severus and Celer, or even Rabirius, Hadrian's rustic estate, perhaps his personal design, jumbled palaces,
large and small, a guest hostel, basilica, pavilion, dining-rooms,
baths, a library, porticoes (including the celebrated *Poikile*),
pools, servants' quarters, a stadium, *cryptoportici*, a palaestra, a
vaulted temple of Serapis, and a complex of elongated pool and
triclinia intended to recall Alexandria's Canopus with overtones
of Antinous, his lost beloved. The urban patterns of domesticity,
extended even to country homes, had disintegrated completely.
This villa of the High Empire was 'a more or less loose and open
aggregate of seemly and separate spaces, each fashioned for the
enrichment of an individual life to the use of the particular activity
it enveloped'.[232] Spheres and cylinders were the basic design;
walls succumbed to sinuous, undulating movements that im-
parted a new life and rhythm to the buildings, and yet *utile* and
dulce, the utilitarian and the ornamental, combine with extra-
ordinary success.

The Grotte di Catullo, perhaps encompassing the villa of
Catullus, if the Valerian *gens* of Verona could claim such a breath-
taking site on Lake Garda, is a large-scale peristyle villa of the
51   second century A D.[233] The symmetrical design, still evident on
the large concrete platform, measures 590 feet long by 345 feet
wide; two rectangular blocks projected at either end, and the
northern projection supported a terrace overlooking Lake Garda
(ancient Benacus). The villa itself seems to incorporate the normal
domestic quarter facing on to a large garden court; the northern
projection probably contained a central dining area, with pergola
and flanking *diaetae*. The pattern is singularly old-fashioned in the

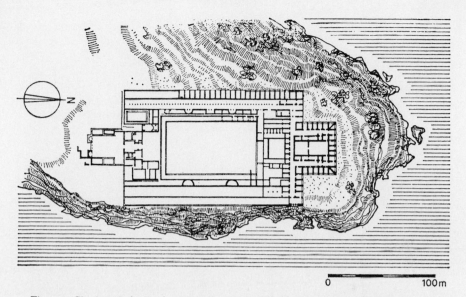

Fig. 51   Sirmione. Lake Garda, Grotte di Catullo, plan. Boëthius & Ward-Perkins, fig. 128

light of Julio-Claudian and Flavian departures, and may have served the preferences of some military or senatorial dignitary of the time, possibly even an imperial personage in its latter days.

So also the Villa of Sette Basse (AD 140–160), on the Via Latina just outside Rome, subscribes to patterns set long before; an entrance peristyle leads into a residential quarter and large garden peristyle, with an additional wing based on terraced substructures.[234]

The final villa to pass in review has been excavated recently near Piazza Armerina in central Sicily. Although scholarly opinion is divided, the villa was probably designed for the Emperor Maximian, joint Augustus with Diocletian from 286 to 305, when he abdicated and sought retirement.[235] The enormous residence, a magnified hunting lodge in the well-forested, well-watered interior of Sicily, once again abandons the age-old rigours of symmetry and axiality for the pleasant confusion of antique Italian *villae rusticae*. The components are easily identified 52 but bear little relation to one another. The triple entry opens off a horseshoe-shaped entrance court; after a sharp right turn, the visitor entered the main sector of the palace-villa, a vestibule, a peristyle garden with rooms opening on to it, a transverse corridor, 53

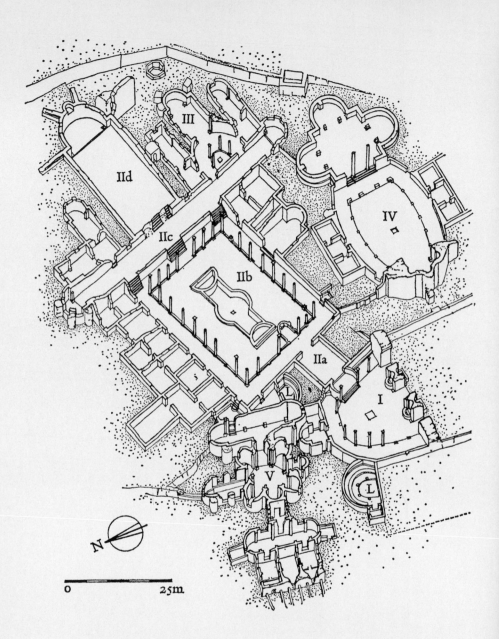

N

0   25m.

Fig. 52   *Sicily, Piazza Armerina, Imperial Villa (Maximian's?), axonometric drawing.*
Boëthius & Ward-Perkins, fig. 202, showing: I *entrance forecourt;* IIa *vestibule;*
IIb *peristyle garden, rooms;* IIc *corridor;* IId *apsidal audience hall;* III *private wing,*
bedrooms, triclinium. IV *trilobed triclinium, oval forecourt;* V *bath-suite*

and a large apsidal audience hall, reminiscent of Tiberius' Villa
Jovis. A private wing contained a semicircular cortile, two bedroom suites and a minor dining-room; the ceremonial wing, to
the south, offered a trifoliate dining-room (*triconchos*) and an oval
porticus as forecourt; a bathing complex opened off the north-west
corner of the main peristyle. The floors are entirely covered with
polychrome mosaic concentrating largely on exotic beasts –   54
ostrich, elephant, lions, etc., a veritable cavalcade of animals
destined for the amphitheatres of Italy, particularly Rome's. The
subject-matter of the mosaics and the style owe much to North
African inspiration and craftsmen, as does the villa plan itself.
The patrician mansions of North Africa, of Tunisia and Algeria,
peristyle villas with local idiosyncrasies, were starting to invade
the empire with salutary effect. The villa at Piazza Armerina
shares the Hadrianic inorganic conception, the same restless,
convoluted designs and extensions, but it also conforms to the
pomp and circumstance and ceremonial arrangements of palaces
on the Palatine and of the homes of Pompeian and Etruscan
grandees. Above all there is a new sense of introversion, of withdrawal from landscape and Nature, in favour of internal space
and preoccupation with the 'presence' of the 'almighty' ruler, the
Dominus and Deus, of passing mortality and destined divinity.
MacKendrick passes due sentence on the Sicilian retreat of Maximian, which was contemporary with Diocletian's contrasting,
castrum-like palace at Split (Yugoslavia): 'tastelessness and   73
grandeur, conspicuous waste and a daring architectural plan:
this paradoxical blend, so characteristic of the villa, explains both
what is meant by decline and why it took the Empire so long to
fall.'[236]

CHAPTER VI

ROMAN INTERIOR FURNISHING AND DECORATION

> *If the mansion of Asturicus is destroyed by fire, the matrons go dishevelled, the social élite put on mourning, the praetor adjourns his court; then we complain about the calamities of the city, and deplore its fires! While the house is still on fire, someone comes up with a gift of marble or construction materials, another offers nude gleaming statues, a third some renowned work of Euphranor or Polyclitus, or bronzes that were once the glory of ancient Asian shrines. Another will offer books and bookcases, or a bust of Minerva, or a mass of silver plate.*
>
> Juvenal, *Satires* III, 212–220

ALTHOUGH THE HOME FURNISHINGS of the major cities of Etruria and Magna Graecia were undoubtedly up-to-date imports or elaborate copies of Old World furniture and interiors, the pre-Hellenistic Roman house must have been simply, even sparsely, furnished with basic articles, modestly and conservatively designed to afford the barest amenity to the house. However, a revolution in taste and design attended the sudden entry of Rome into the main stream of Hellenistic history. Although the atrium furnishing probably remained simple and conventional, the material improved. The original dining or kitchen table (*cartibulum*), set alongside the *impluvium* between the catch-basin and the *tablinum*, assumed a more elaborate guise in marble,[237] and the patron's chair or throne (*solium*) assumed various forms with turned or rectangular legs, cut-out incisions or solid sides. Sometimes the throne was provided with armrests and a panelled back, but the form most often favoured for the formal reception had a rounded or rectangular back and solid sides culminating in

54　Sicily, Piazza Armerina. Imperial Villa, mosaic, ostrich and
antelope on ship's gangway

55 Pompeii. House of the Moralist, *triclinium*

56 Simpelveld (Leiden). Marble sarcophagus, interior relief
57 The same, different view

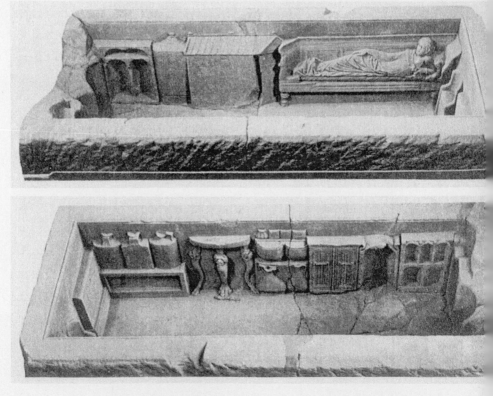

58   Herculaneum. House of the Carbonized Furniture, *cubiculum*

59   Pompeii. Villa of the Mysteries, wall-painting, Silenus, Pan and
Panisca: startled woman (side wall), Silenus with satyrs (end wall)

60   Boscoreale villa, *cubiculum*

61   The same, detail of wall-painting

62 Pompeii. House of the Vettii, red room wall-painting; Daedalus
and Pasiphaë (left); Ixion, Mercury and Juno (end wall), etc.

63 Pompeii. House of the Vettii, yellow room, wall-painting:
Hercules and serpents (left), Death of Pentheus (end wall), etc.

front in animal or monster forms.[238] The *tablinum* furnishing was more varied and accommodating. Technically a descendant of the Etruscan throne-type, the wicker-work chair of plaited straw must have been one of the most comfortable chairs in the later Imperial age. The chair with a back (*klismos*), designed for more relaxed sitting, was popular inside and out, for it was often used as a conveyance – a sort of sedan-chair – by wealthy men and women within the city's confines. Stools, folding stools, benches and footstools were the regular complement to the *tablinum* and other sitting rooms in most Roman homes, and semi-circular benches were often built into the gardens of private villas.[239] Wall cupboards and wardrobes were non-existent, but bedroom chests (*arcae vestiariae*), chests for household wares, strongboxes (*arcae*) and the like were common. Storage chests for valuables were often fixed to the floor by iron fittings and, to safeguard the contents, the wooden chests were faced with bronze or iron with ornamental hinges and bronze locks.[240] Wall shelving and wall hooks were probably common. A splendid carbonized version of a cupboard (*armarium*) was found at Herculaneum in 1935. Flanked by Corinthian columns and standing as high as a man, it served as *lararium*, cupboard and safe. Petronius refers to just such a receptacle among Trimalchio's elaborate furnishings, housing the silver Lares, a golden toilet-box (*pyxis*) containing Trimalchio's first beard, and a marble statuette of Venus.[241]

The Greeks tended to use tables for practical purposes, primarily for serving a meal in the most convenient fashion. The Romans, on the other hand, used tables and tabourets to exhibit their prized possessions. The table designs were indebted to Greek models, but, as so often happened, the Roman craftsmen enriched and elaborated the Old Country styles. Although the repertoire included round or rectangular leaf tables with three or four legs, or occasional tables with round or rectangular leaves and a single support, the most popular was the round table with three animal-shaped legs, sometimes with panther, lion or swan heads set above the legs.[242]

The commonest form of couch or divan for dining, relaxation and sleeping had turned legs, often carved from beautifully

grained woods, an elaborate headboard and sometimes a footboard as well. Pliny's remark that dining couches (*triclinia*)
reached Italy with Gnaeus Manlius after the subjugation of
Hellenistic Asia in 187 BC provides a valuable clue to the earlier
simplicity of Roman furnishing.[243] Several fine examples of
couches faced with bronze have been recovered from Pompeii
and Boscoreale, all with beautifully carved, inlaid or plated headboards. Some are inlaid with bone and ivory rather than with
bronze. Others have silver set into the bronze appliqués, and one
example, in New York, has tinted glass – red, white and yellow –
60   set into the framework. The more spectacular examples were
fashioned from gold, silver or tortoiseshell.[244] The bed-frame was
equipped with interlaced cordings of leather or rope, sometimes of
metal. Petronius provides a hilarious description of the un-
fortunate Giton clinging, Odysseus-like, to the cording which
supported the mattress above.[245] Couches were regularly supplied
with mattresses, pillows and coverlets, and on occasion, because
they were otherwise inaccessible, a step-ladder or footstool stood
alongside. In many ways the couch, with its invitation to relaxation and enjoyment, covered in fine fabrics (often dyed brilliant
colours and embroidered with gold thread) with coloured
valances hanging from the bed-frame and elaborate headboard,
was the most attractive furnishing in the home.

Chairs were not common at banquets, and the arrangement
of the three couches which furnished the *triclinium* dining-room
55   followed a Mad Hatter's formality. Since it was customary to have
three couches set at right angles to one another, with nine diners
as the ideal guest list, the 'upper' couch would normally have been
equipped with an elaborate headboard, the 'lower' couch with a
footboard, and the 'middle' couch with neither, to prevent the
carved rests from impeding the company. A variety of motifs was
used in the decoration of headboards and footboards: heads of
mules, donkeys and horses, of satyrs and maenads, and on occasion,
56, 57   swans, dogs, ducks and geese.[246] The Simpelveld marble
sarcophagus in Leiden illustrates a form of couch preferred for
relaxation and sleeping in Imperial times – a capacious daybed
with turned legs, simple headboard and footboard and a raised
side designed to be set against the wall. A carbonized version of

one of these beds was found in Herculaneum in the House of the Carbonized Furniture, with an occasional table alongside.[247] 58 Besides tables, the Romans, unlike the Greeks, also used sideboards (abaci) to display their favourite objets d'art, another furnishing imported to Rome by Gnaeus Manlius after his triumph in 187 B C.[248] The Simpelveld sarcophagus shows one in relief, with a table-like lower member and an upper zone equipped with shelving and laden with vases and boxes.

Floor-coverings in Roman residences and apartments were probably the amenity of wealthier persons able to afford animal skins (deer, wolf, bear, leopard, or lion) or rugs imported from Asia Minor. Decorative rugs were imported from the Hellenistic East and from Ptolemaic Egypt at the same time that mosaics became popular in aristocratic homes. The patterns of mosaics in the Hellenistic Greek and Roman worlds frequently reflect the geometric designs and fringes of carpets, and the popular Nilotic subject-matter may also have been borrowed from the rug-weavers' repertoire.

Houses and apartments in the Italian cities and the country towns today regularly close up during the heat of the day. There is an aversion to admitting sunlight into the interiors of houses and every conceivable device, venetian blinds, shutters, awnings, and curtains, is brought into play to fend off the rays. Literary evidence, the murals, and the actual remains do not offer any sure guide to Roman windows and their furnishings.[249] But window panes have been found on most sites of Imperial date, and sometimes earlier; they rarely exceed nine to twelve inches square. The older homes of Pompeii and Herculaneum and the bathing establishments of rustic villas usually contented themselves with slits in the masonry. When upper storeys appeared the architect could safely introduce larger windows and often directed their light ingeniously to illuminate particular sectors of rooms or wall-paintings. Ground-level windows, in Pompeii and Herculaneum, are generally iron gratings in the form of a grill, or terracotta, stone or marble blocks pierced with openings. But glass was certainly used behind the security of the garden wall (e.g., the House of the Mosaic Atrium, Herculaneum), and the House of Pansa at Pompeii yielded twenty-five panes of petra

specularis, a translucent stone used for window inserts. The panes were probably fixed with stucco into wooden frames. The use of glass advanced during the Julio-Claudian period when, for example, it served the needs of bathers at Baiae and along the salubrious shores of the Bay of Naples. Seneca comments somewhat ungratefully and probably hypocritically on the Neronian *thermae* in contrast to Scipio's dark counterpart: 'Today we call baths louse-holes if they are not designed to attract the sun all day through picture windows, unless men can bathe and acquire a suntan simultaneously, and unless they have a view over the countryside and the sea from their pools.'[250] The contemporary baths at
47 Baiae offered just such furnishings for the *jeunesse doré* and the rheumatic residents of that antique Marienbad. Glass was obviously used for small windows and to contain the heat or steam of a thermal establishment; it must also have played a major role in the elegant prospect mansions of Stabiae, Herculaneum and the Amalfitan coast.

Lighting arrangements were fairly standard throughout antiquity. Clay lamps with one or multiple nozzles provided the basic illumination. Sometimes a stand with a tapering support passed through the central tube and held the lamp aloft or the lamp was suspended by a cord or chain. Bronze lamps and candelabra were a more elegant furnishing for grander establishments.

Heating was normally provided by charcoal-heated braziers and tripods, but the warmest rooms were certainly the *culinea* and the baths where the proprietor and his family could resort to
53 smaller versions of the public baths. Almost every Campanian *domus* of distinction incorporated a private bath, and certainly the rustic and coastal villas, after Sergius Orata's experiments with hypocaustic installations in the Lucrine villas, were provided with quite handsome bathrooms.[251]

Although wall-paintings commonly survive in the houses of Herculaneum, Pompeii and Stabiae, one must also conjure up tapestries, wall-hangings, draperies and awnings in every house of middle-class status or better. Curtains (*vela*) for shelter from the sun, wind and rain were part of the everyday furnishing of atrium-style homes. During the Hellenistic period the walls of

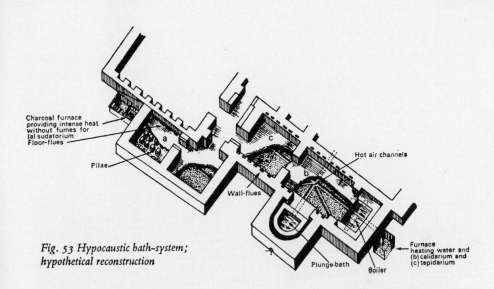

Fig. 53 *Hypocaustic bath-system;*
hypothetical reconstruction

some rooms, often dining areas, were left free of decoration to accommodate draperies which would hang from the cornice and fall neatly along the walls. Apart from the lively colour which they might impart to interiors, curtains were absolutely essential for privacy and for protection against draughts and sudden gusts in the large openings between the atrium and *tablinum*, and at the entry to the *alae* and *exedrae*. The open-air atrium also required some measure of protection against excessive heat, the searing blasts of the sirocco in August and seasonal cloud bursts. Awnings were therefore stretched under the *compluvium* opening and adjusted by means of a cord attached to a ring often inserted in an angle column, a wall-bracket or some other anchoring device. Sometimes the *compluvium* awnings were scarlet, enabling the house-owner to bathe the interior of his atrium in rosy light rather than brilliant sunshine. Peristyles were also provided with awnings between the columns so as to shield the paintings from the sun and inclement weather, and to provide a cooler and more colourful setting for *conversazione* and siesta. Windows could be closed with shutters or outside blinds.

Paved floors of beaten earth, clay or stone certainly originated with the Greeks, and similar practices were adopted by the Etruscans and Romans from time immemorial. Dining-rooms had traditionally the untidiest floors in the domicile. The Pergamene artist, Sosus, left a graphic and condemnatory picture of the filth of an unswept dining-room in a mosaic pavement.[252] Petronius no doubt reflects the continuation of these reckless dining habits in his description of the banquet of Trimalchio where, since plates were not provided, all the remnants were thrown on the floor awaiting the arrival of slaves who swept up the debris.[253] One may suppose that the several *triclinia* often incorporated into larger houses were a sheer necessity, and that the four dining-rooms of Trimalchio were probably a commonplace in the wealthier bourgeois homes. Pliny informs us that 'tesselated [i.e., mosaic] pavements had already become common and extremely popular before the Cimbrian War' (113–101 BC), as is shown by the verse of Lucilius (c. 180–102 B C): *arte pavimento atque emblemate vermiculate* – 'with paver's craft and mosaic picture-insert'.[254] *Emblema* from a technical standpoint denoted a picture translated into stone, a picture in fine tesserae (like that of Sosus mentioned above) which decorated a *triclinium* or *exedra*. Occasionally, floors were laid with an *opus spicatum*, or in Pliny's phrase 'wheat ear' tile pattern, because the bricks were laid at an angle to each other recalling the arrangement of grains in an ear of wheat.[255] Another flooring used frequently into Imperial times, called 'Greek style', is described in detail by Pliny:

> The ground is well rammed and rubble or a layer of pounded potsherds laid on it. Then charcoal is trodden into a compact mass, and on top of this is spread a mixture of coarse sand, lime and ashes to a thickness of six inches. This is carefully finished to rule and level, and has the appearance of earth. But if it is smoothed with a grindstone it will pass for a black stone floor.[256]

Vitruvius supplies comparable information on Greek-style flooring and compliments the Greeks on the drainage facilities of their flooring compound: 'at dinner parties, whatever is poured out of cups or spat from the mouth no sooner falls than it dries up, and the servants who wait there do not catch cold from that kind of floor, although they may go barefoot.'[257]

Terracotta (*opus signinum*) and charcoal-coloured lava cement flooring were long-time favourites in middle-class and proletarian housing and were, occasionally, decorated with inset chips of marble in regular, sometimes highly decorative, patterns. Herculaneum provides an almost complete spectrum of flooring techniques, from pounded earth and concrete flooring to highly elaborate mosaic and marble versions.

The House of the Bicentenary (v, 15–16) in Herculaneum has an atrium floor with simple white tesserae laid into a black mosaic ground, while the walls are painted a red-porphyry shade to provide a striking contrast and complement to the floor. The *triclinium* of the House of the Stags (iv, 21) is paved with intarsia marble tiles of different colours and shapes; one of the inner bedrooms with a red wall has a sectile marble pavement; another reception room (*oecus*) has a red-ground wall-decoration and vault and a polychrome marble flooring. The House of the Mosaic Atrium (iv, 1–2) has an eye-catching black and white chess-board mosaic in the atrium, preceded by a more elaborate, carpet-like pattern mosaic in the *fauces* made up of squares with decorative elements inset. The splendid *triclinium*, overlooking the *solarium* and the bay, is paved with marble.

The use of mosaic and marble in domestic interiors stems largely from the last century of the Republic. Pliny[258] suggests that Sulla, Lucullus, Mamurra and their like were the innovators in the use of marble for thresholds, colonnades and wall decoration, but the archaeological evidence favours its arrival during the second century BC, when a wave of philhellenism and a new acquaintance with Hellenistic interiors, palatial and bourgeois, swept over Italy with the encouragement of the Scipionic circle and other devotees.

The Pompeian House of the Faun (IV, xii, 2), though an exceptional house, does provide insight into the uses of Hellenistic luxury and elegance in a second-century Italian setting. The entrance, the *impluvium* and the *tablinum* are all paved with sectile marble, dating from the pre-Roman period. The cement floor of the first peristyle has interspersed over its surface small pieces of red, black and brown volcanic glass and pieces of limestone; the same pavement is used in the two *alae*. A cat and bird *emblema* in mosaic was set into the centre of the right *ala*, with doves in the left. The *exedra* at the right of the second peristyle has a rough

14

white pavement; the atrium is laid in lava cement. The Alexander Mosaic, discovered in 1831 on the floor of the pillared, windowed *exedra* facing on to the first peristyle garden, is now exhibited vertically in the Naples Museum.[259] Opinion differs as to whether the mosaic was imported from some Hellenistic centre or mosaic factory, or whether it was executed by a resident or commissioned artist on the spot. A border of masks, flowers and fruits embellished the threshold and a Nilotic scene accommodated to the columns of the *exedra* where the Alexander Mosaic was the major decoration. It derived, probably, from an original mural painting by Philoxenus of Eretria who painted the battle of Darius and Alexander at Issus (333 B C). A lion mosaic, probably by the same mosaicist, decorated the *oecus*; a fish mosaic graced the winter *triclinium* to the left of the *tablinum*. The so-called tiger-rider, though the beast combines traits of lion, tiger and panther, was laid on the floor of the *triclinium* at the right of the *tablinum*; a similar subject, Dionysus riding a panther, was found on Hellenistic Delos.[260] The Pompeian example is framed with ribbons, flowers and masks. There is a marvellous harmony of decoration throughout the mansion, a studied contrast between the elaborate mosaics, laid like splendid Oriental carpets in special rooms, and the elegant simplicity of the wall-decorations which are worked in stucco relief. The mosaic decoration of the House of the Faun contrasts markedly with the limited use of floor and wall mosaics elsewhere in Campania.

The *triclinium* of the House of the Neptune and Amphitrite
21   Mosaic at Herculaneum (v, 6–7) provides an unusual and exceptionally lovely example of wall-mosaic on a grand scale.[261] The house is a simple affair, combining wine shop (*taberna*) with dwelling. The size of the lot did not allow a garden or *porticus*, only a small inner court with a large fountain structure (*nymphaeum*) built into one wall. The *nymphaeum*, composed of a large vaulted niche in the centre, flanked by two smaller rectangular ones, is entirely faced with a predominantly blue mosaic representing deer-hunting scenes framed with festoons and floral motives. The inner surfaces of the niches are decorated with shells and the whole is crowned with theatrical masks and a Silenus head. The main wall of the *triclinium*, on the main axis, exhibits the mosaic

group which gives its name to the house. It is framed in shells, and overlooks the stuccoed dining couches below. The fountain in the middle of the *triclinium* is fed by the *nymphaeum*.

Pompeian-style wall-painting followed two methods: tempera and fresco. Tempera implies the application of paint to dry limestone plaster; fresco suggests the application of colours to wet plaster. Powdered marble was added to the stucco facings in the final stages. With repeated polishings the painted walls assumed a brilliance and reflecting quality which helped to illuminate and enliven the closed spaces particularly.[262] The pigments used were pure earth colours (ochre), minerals (carbonate of copper) and animal and vegetable dyes.[263] Soapy limestone and a bonding medium were added to the pigments, some of which have been recovered from Pompeii, and the finished surface of the painting was waxed to add brilliance and durability. The artists' palette included, most notably, 'Pompeian' red, blues, greens, yellows and lustrous blacks, the last reserved for rooms of special luxury and regarded as the most sumptuous shade of all. Wooden and marble panel inserts in larger wall areas were treated to the encaustic method, which most closely approximates to modern oil painting. Colours were added to heated wax and applied by means of a spatula and fine brush.

Pliny remarks that the earliest instance of applying marble veneer to brick walls occurred in the fourth-century Palace of Mausolus of Halicarnassus where white marble facing was used.[264] Cornelius Nepos is the authority for our knowledge of the first instance in Rome, assigned to Mamurra of Formiae, Caesar's engineer in Gaul and Catullus' *bête noire*. Mamurra covered whole walls of his house on the Caelian Hill with marble and, in addition, was the first to use columns of Carystus and Luna marble in his mansion.[265] Lucius Lucullus introduced black marble veneer into Roman houses *c.* 74 B C. Called Lucullan marble after its devotee, its connotation of extreme luxury in finishing persisted into later times in the use of black as the background for wall paintings.[266] The black-decorated *tablinum* of the Pompeian Villa of the Mysteries with its Egyptianizing figures and exotic motifs is a superb example. Solid, polished blocks of marble, and even marble veneer cut into the shape of blocks, were beyond the means of most 'provincial' aristocrats. But the art of imitation by the device of painting in the masonry style had already been tried in the Hellenistic world (e.g., at Delos, in the late third and early second century B C), and Italian decorators were quick to adapt the same scheme. Called Pompeian Style I (150–80 B C), the wall was first partitioned into three horizontal divisions: a dado or floorboard area, a central area with plaster cornices and mouldings, and a topmost frieze-like section.[267] The stucco was almost certainly applied to the wall in horizontal sections, thereby enabling the painter to complete the decoration of each section while the wall was still moist. The central section was designed to simulate actual structural elements in painted stucco and mouldings, at first in terms of limestone, then counterfeiting the black, red, yellow, green and violet marble blocks used in the sumptuous Hellenistic palaces and aristocratic homes of Macedonia, Alexandria, and Asia Minor. The François Tomb at Vulci offers the earliest instance of this simulated marble facing in Italy (c. 300 B C).[268] This early wall-decoration occurs in architecture of the Samnite period in Campanian cities, in the House of the Faun and the House of Sallust at Pompeii, and in the Samnite House at Herculaneum. Subsequently, decorators answered the householder's desire to enlarge the spatial effect of rooms by the use of prospect views which would help to negate the structural functions of the wall and so burst the solid limits of the enclosed, often cramped, space of bedrooms and *salons*.

The Pompeian Second Style (80 B C–A D 14) goes hand in hand with the increased use of columns in the atria and peristyles of late Republican housing. Designs were evolved which made use of painted columns, often festooned with garlands, and with piers and pilasters supporting elaborate entablatures.

Afterwards they made such progress as to represent the forms of buildings, and of columns and projecting and overhanging pediments; in their open rooms, such as *exedrae*, they depicted the façades of scenes in the tragic, comic or satyric style; and their walks, on account of the great length, they decorated with a variety of landscapes, copying the characteristics of definite spots. In these paintings there are harbours, promontories, seashores, rivers, fountains, straits, fanes, groves, mountains, flocks, shepherds; in some places there are also pictures designed in the grandstyle, with figures of the gods or detailed mythological episodes, or the battles at Troy, or the wanderings of Ulysses, with landscape backgrounds, and other subjects reproduced on similar principles from real life.[269]

The illusory world of temples, sacred enclosures, porticoes, groves and grottoes of a suggestive nature, implying sacred landscape and idyllic retreat, are as escapist as the contemporary Vergilian *Bucolics* or the pastoral landscape and country retreats of the Roman elegiac poets, Tibullus, Propertius and Ovid. These panoramic landscapes, an Italian invention, invaded almost every area of the house. One of the loveliest and most memorable to survive is a famous fresco from a house on the Esquiline Hill in Rome, the Odyssey Landscapes, discovered in 1848.[270] Behind a succession of painted scarlet pilasters, which contribute to the illusion of depth, an uninterrupted panorama-like landscape emerges; the landscape in the eight pictures which make up the sequence is vastly more important than the human actors. The painted frieze, forty-eight feet long, was originally located ten feet above the floor level. It opened like windows in the long, apparently vaulted room on to a legendary and illusionistic world, involving adventures with the Laestrygonians, Circe, the Underworld and the Sirens. The artist's palette contained relatively few colours, but he used them with consummate skill to produce effects of space and atmosphere.

The House of Livia on Rome's Palatine Hill was decorated according to the desires of the emperor, whose main concern was modesty and restraint in housing.[271] The Room of the Garlands follows the tripartite pattern cited earlier, with a middle zone of chaste white panels separated by red frames with superimposed swags of flowers, apples, plums, and grapes, and with another superimposed colonnade in a subdued grey colour. Livia's Villa at Prima Porta yielded a fantastic garden scene, fit setting for the summer *triclinium* with its vaulted roof designed like a royal pavilion looking out on to a paradise garden of firs, pines, palm trees, cypresses, fruit trees and shrubs, splendidly

49

landscaped and replete with various birds, wild and domesticated.

The Pompeian Villa of the Mysteries derives its name from the splendid large-figure (megalographic) painting in the festival hall (*stibadia*) designed for Dionysiac feastings, a kind of ritual *triclinium*.[272] The room actually formed part of a suite which comprised an adjoining bedroom with two bed-niches or alcoves, also decorated with Dionysiac themes. The great picture cycle, discovered in 1909, contains twenty-nine figures near life-size, set against a brilliant background of Pompeian red. All the figures, human and mythological, are engaged in a Dionysiac ritual of marriage preparation or initiation. The composition is intricate, but basically triadic: the rear wall, which is viewed from a wide door in the entrance wall, highlights Dionysus and Ariadne and is flanked by figures engaged in ritual acts, while the two lateral wings on the left and right walls add two side panels to the 'triptych': a lyre-playing Silenus with a startled woman, and, as its complement, a scene of ritual flagellation and a dancing Bacchant. The central and focal design is preceded by a montage of introductory and concluding compositions involving the initiate and young matron on the side and entrance walls. This unique religious painting, an Augustan frieze perhaps contemporary with the Altar of Augustan Peace, is more successful in its composition than in its execution. The variations in technique and mastery probably stem from the fact that several artists were involved with the same painting. The paintings are, in Margarete Bieber's opinion, 'testimonials of a living art and a living faith, designed for the room in which they have been found, although they use many single figures and motives from earlier Greek art'.[273] Vitruvius' acerbic comments on the vagaries and surrealistic tendencies of decorators before 14 B C (the publication date of his ten books of *De Architectura*) are especially appropriate to pictures of the late Second Style, like those of the Villa of Livia and the Farnesina:

> Those subjects which were copied from actual realities are scorned in these days of bad taste. We now have fresco paintings of monstrosities, rather than truthful representations of definite things. For instance, reeds are put in the place of

columns, fluted appendages with curly leaves and volutes, instead of pediments, candelabra supporting representations of shrines, and on top of their pediments numerous tender stalks and volutes growing up from the roots and having human figures senselessly seated upon them; sometimes stalks having only half-length figures, some with human heads, others with the heads of animals.[274]

The *cubiculum* of the Villa of Publius Fannius Synistor at Boscoreale, located about a mile distant from Pompeii, was discovered in 1900 and has been meticulously reconstructed in the Metropolitan Museum in New York.[275] Somewhat larger than   60 the normal Roman bedroom (13 feet by 4 by 20), the room quite literally bursts its confines in the depiction of illusionistic architecture, columned halls, elegant portals, streets, houses and rural landscapes. The terraced formations recall a comment by Vitruvius:

There are three kinds of scene, one called the tragic, the second the comic, and the third the satyric. Their decorations are different and unlike each other in scheme. Tragic scenes are delineated with columns, pediments, statues and other objects suited to kings; comic scenes exhibit private dwellings, with balconies and views representing rows of windows, after the manner of ordinary dwellings; satyric scenes are decorated with trees, caverns, mountains and other rustic objects, delineated in landscape style.[276]

The Boscoreale *cubiculum* painting seems to correspond strik-   61 ingly to the 'sets' described by the Augustan architect. Some have even supposed that the owner of the villa may have used this 'siesta' room as a setting for the reading of his favourite dramatic poets. But Hanfmann's assessment, which is closer to Phyllis Lehmann's brilliant study of the paintings, seems more in keeping with the 'decorum' which Vitruvius required of aristocratic house-owners: 'waking from his dreams, the owner of the Boscoreale bedroom would be greeted by the sight of vistas of regal splendor, of villas, temples, palaces, dominions of which he could dream, but which he could not afford to build.'[277]

The Third Pompeian Style of wall decoration (*c.* 15 BC–AD 50), which overlaps the Second Style, suppresses free space and is distinguished by the use of miniature Egyptianizing figures and elements. The architectural features are reduced to a minor, less forthright role, but when they are used, they appear in a more elaborate, ornamental style of columns, bands and friezes decorated with incoherent, usually minute details, all exquisitely painted; and the pictorial cycles split up into separate panel pictures. There is also a change in colour tonality from scarlets, yellow-golds and blacks to maroons, deeper golds and lavenders. The lively, recessive movement of Second Style walls is replaced by a general impression of flat areas, solid ground colour (yellow, red, green or black), separated into sizeable panels by means of slender vertical and horizontal members like tracery borders, and with small relieving panels in a contrasting shade. The style is exemplified in the Pompeian House of L.Caecilius Jucundus, the Sacerdos Amandus, and the Gilded Amorini, and the so-called Villa of Cicero.

The Fourth Style (AD 50–79, Neronian and Flavian) is a development of the Second Style with increased emphasis on the three-dimensional. Highly ornamental fantastic architecture, with stress on lineal perspective, supersedes the flatness of Style III. The earlier prevailing red and black backgrounds yield to yellow, gold and white backgrounds. Columns are often open, plaited spirals, providing very tenuous support for roofs, second storeys and balconies, the latter two provided with projecting and receding members. Small panels are frequently lodged below the larger panel pictures, usually illusionistic landscapes, seascapes, hybrid monsters or other figments of fancy. There is also a tendency to prefer Cupids in a panel or frieze setting as a complement to the large-scale mythological panels. The architectural emphasis, deep corridors and endless vistas in the Fourth Style painters' repertoire probably owed much to the Roman theatrical scene-painters. The whole is designed to impress the viewer, to deny the wall any reality, and to give a sense of spacelessness to the room. Figures, apart from the large panel inserts, fall freely and irregularly, like Epicurean atomic compounds, through space. Fixity of location is denied; there is a persistent animation, a leisurely looseness and mobility, and a sense of space everywhere throughout the design. The wall is no longer a single field, but an assortment of fields with a *pot-pourri* of subjects, heroic and *genre*, caricature, still-life and fantasy.

In his prescription for the proper aristocrat's housing, Vitruvius includes picture galleries (*pinacothecae*) which should, ideally, both have a northern exposure and open on to a peristyle for proper indirect lighting.[278] Cicero also mentions placing well-executed paintings in a 'good light', having in mind panel or easel paintings which could be set in the most appropriate spot.[279] Roman writers testify repeatedly to the mania for collecting pictures and *objets d'art* during the late Republic and during Imperial times. Old Greek Masters or Hellenistic originals in the shape of wooden panels (*pinakes*) or frescoes were sometimes removed from their original settings and transplanted to the walls of aristocratic Roman homes and public buildings.[280] The emphatic position assigned to the large panel paintings in Campanian and Roman houses is an eloquent reminder of the nature of the original picture galleries or colonnades where paintings were exhibited. One remembers that Romans, even freedmen and Levantines like Trimalchio, were proud to possess Greek masterpieces and to show off their acquired learning, since the learned man was assumed to be nearer to Heaven. Trimalchio's paintings on his atrium walls combined scenes from the *Odyssey* and *Iliad* with the gladiatorial games of Laenas, a deplorable failure of taste but a clue to the uncertain sophistication of the owner. Petronius, like many other Campanian burghers with cultural aspirations, was ready to insert reproductions of classic creations as central panels in his wall decorations, thus arranging the room as a picture gallery.[281] The House of the Vettii in Pompeii has two celebrated instances of picture galleries. One room, in addition to the three central panels, offers two smaller panels in the lower register of each wall and four in the upper, comprising twenty-one panels in all. The arrangement of the central panels, at least, is demonstrably far from casual. In fact, scholars have recently detected many instances of pictures in rooms, porticoes and the like being grouped according to their related subject-matter or a common conceptual theme.

62, 63

Programmatic painting, as it has been called, might embody religious concepts or reflect narrative relationships, and would thereby provide an intellectual unity to the decorated room.[282] Such programmes were hardly the product of journeyman house-painters. They owe their unity to patterns prescribed by painters' handbooks and to sketches of associated paintings elsewhere. In the case of mythological subject-matter painting, the life of Achilles (or Hercules) tends to find organization and unity not in the narration of successive events (as in the Odyssey Landscapes), but in the dramatic juxtaposition of events from different periods of the hero's career. This apparently deliberate combination of pictures in a single room has no precedent in Greek domestic interior design, and, in fact, becomes evident and possible in Roman paintings only with the development of the Third and Fourth Styles of decoration, when inserted pictures were easily and gracefully accommodated into the architectural framework. The favourite narrative or programmatic cycles are those which bear on the Trojan War, the life of Achilles (or Aeneas), Theban myth, the Cretan cycle (involving Dionysus and Ariadne, Theseus, the Minotaur, Daedalus and Pasiphae), a Bacchic cycle, and tragic and idyllic love themes involving Aphrodite (with Ares or Adonis) or Narcissus. Frequently, in Pompeian rooms, examples of good and bad behaviour were constrasted, as in the contemporary poetry of Vergil and Horace and their elegiac successors. The two picture galleries of the House of the Vettii provide a nice sample of the programmatic or cyclical technique. One room, to the right of the entry to the peristyle, has large panels depicting Daedalus and Icarus in the presence of Pasiphae, with the mechanical cow; the punishment of Ixion; and the discovery of Ariadne by Dionysus on Naxos. The central and left panels are clearly instances of profane love – Pasiphaë's unnatural passion for the bull and Ixion's lustful attack on Juno which condemned him to the fiery wheel. The terminal wall, on the right, foreshadows the love and apotheosis of the abandoned Ariadne as bride of Dionysus. Two unlawful passions therefore, are contrasted with Ariadne's divine bliss and fortunate love. The other room concentrates on Theban legend with: the infant Heracles' triumph over the snakes of vengeful Hera, on the left; the tragic fate of

Pentheus at the hands of the Maenads, in the central position; and finally the savage punishment of Dirce, trampled to death by a bull through the cruel contrivance of Amphion and Zethus, on the right wall. Two themes of punishment are juxtaposed with the Herculean escape from danger. Not only do the paintings find a thematic or conceptual connection within their proper confines, but there is also a responsive or balancing pattern between the two rooms, between scenes evocative of crime and punishment and scenes of heroic or divine deliverance. Both rooms face southwest on to the peristyle and are shielded from direct lighting.

The large *triclinium* of the House of the Vettii also opens on to the peristyle garden. The Pompeian red walls are divided into zones by great pillars which originally contained large panel paintings on wood or plaster. These were removed bodily from the room by citizens who returned to salvage art works and valuables after the eruption in AD 79. The panels were held in place by iron along the edges. The lower section of the wall is largely intact. The frieze above the dado consists of scenes of small-figure Cupids busy with various arts and crafts and other less onerous pursuits: the making and retailing of garlands, the jewellery trade, the operating of a cleaning and dyeing establishment (*fullonica*) and a wine shop. Elsewhere the Cupids engage in target practice, chariot races, the celebration of the Festival of Vesta and a Bacchic procession. It seems highly likely that these rich Pompeians would have shown no compunction about illustrating for their friends and company the occupations which brought them wealth and influence in Pompeii.[283] Trimalchio, Petronius' bourgeois creation, was ready to tell the story of his life and its success-pattern in conversation, in murals, and finally even in the frieze decoration of his tomb.[284] But there the comparison ends, for the paintings and decorative systems of Trimalchio's mansion at Puteoli are far removed from the Fourth Style décor of the Pompeian House of the Vettii and far closer to the Second Style with its frieze of narrative paintings with inscriptions (*cf.* the Odyssey Landscapes) and large-figure painting (*cf.* the Villa of the Mysteries). Beneath the commercial and festal panels there appear panels with groups of Psyches combined with delicate, intricately wrought scenes in connection with Apollo and Python, with Agamemnon and the stag of Artemis, with Orestes and Pylades before Thoas, and with Iphigenia in Tauris. Other Pompeian red panels in the same room contain pairs of mythical and legendary lovers: Perseus with Andromeda, Dionysus and Ariadne, Apollo and Daphne, and Poseidon and Amymone.

Such strict contrapuntal or group relationship between wall-paintings is striking and, undoubtedly, unusual in Roman interiors. One must suppose that in the majority of instances the subject-matter was dictated by the whims of the patron who sought new 'ornaments' for his grand interior. The motivation was, one may imagine, largely dictated by a desire for ostentation – to give material evidence of a cultivated and wealthy household in both private and public settings. Changes in style and in vogues for particular subjects were almost certainly dictated by the cultural policy of the capital. Certainly, the innovations in painting incorporated into Nero's Golden House must have strongly influenced the new modes of house decoration called Pompeian Style III.

The average bourgeois house of the Imperial age must have contained a wealth of gay and varied polychromy, sometimes exuberant and rich baroque visions and impressionistic landscapes, at other times more restrained and delicate in the Augustan mode. The early excavators of Pompeii and Herculaneum, with the avidity of curio seekers, used to hack paintings from their original context to enrich aristocratic collections and museums. Nowadays, the excavators have chosen to leave the walls intact and to take proper precautions (usually) for their preservation. Much of the painting discovered recently, apart from the unique finds at Stabiae,[285] has been by any standards far removed from the category of masterpieces, but it has usually an appreciable integrity and respectability in its theory of space, its prejudices about composition and its peculiar tact about subject-matter. Though often arranged or composed to accent some intellectual or allegorical point or programme, the solitary nature or gregarious profusion of associated subjects in the paintings avoids monumentality or sanctity. By their animation and declamatory nature they must have excited repeated comment or reflection from their viewers. Rarely edifying or ennobling, save in such settings as the Villa of the Mysteries and the Villa at Boscotrecase, Campanian (and Roman) paintings are an outstanding landmark in the development of Italian painting and interior decoration.

The furnishings under review were usually associated with aristocratic or wealthy bourgeois housing, and most often in the Italian towns the average plebeian member of the proletariat or the struggling poet would have counted three or four of the articles outlined as luxurious furnishing. The Roman preferred to live outdoors in the company of his gregarious fellow-citizens, in the civic centres, parks and main streets of the community. Living conditions in the larger centres cannot have been very pleasant for the plebeians. The towering *insulae* had few amenities built in and the size of the apartments, as well as their general appearance, discourage us from imagining anything approximating to present-day furnishing or decoration. The well-to-do lived graciously, and illumination, heating, and the rudimentary means of cooking made life bearable for most; but their absence would and did consign many to a grim existence in stifling *case popolare* and deplorable *pensioni*.

CHAPTER VII

EUROPEAN PROVINCES
AND BRITAIN

tu regere imperio populos, Romane, memento
(hae tibi erunt artes), pacique imponere morem,
parcere subiectis et debellare superbos.

Vergil, *Aeneid* VI, 851-3

ROME'S EMPIRE, GIGANTIC PRODUCT of reluctant annexation and ruthless aggression, stretched ultimately from the Solway Firth to the Sahara, from the Rhine and Danube to the Euphrates. Vergil's prophetic outburst which hailed the Romans as 'lords of the world, a nation wearing the toga' with guarantees of 'no bounds in space or time . . . rule without end'[286] was an accomplished reality to most Romans. Although her progress towards imperialism was neither spontaneous nor aggressive at the outset, for the Senate showed little enthusiasm for conquest because of suspicions about her ambitious generals who might seize power by force of arms, unseat the *Patres* and inherit the *patrimonium*, the process, once begun, could not be arrested. Rome's policy of intervention and defensive military action to ensure peace could hardly conceal a deep-seated will to conquest. Some of her governors, Republican and Imperial, proved to be cruel and rapacious; her tax-collectors became synonymous with sinners; but some administrators, like Cicero and Pliny the Younger, saw their offices as a commitment to safeguard and advance the security and happiness of their subjects. Self-determination in local politics and behaviour was the rule. Cities, once a prey to dissension and almost continuous warfare, knew peace; Rome's highways were safe avenues for trade and for the movement of men and ideas; the seas were freed of pirates; there was a security in Roman law promising order and humanity.

Some of the Emperors, Augustus, Trajan and Hadrian most notably, spent money lavishly and intelligently in an effort to encourage Romanization among the conquered nations. Laws and municipal charters repeatedly encouraged building projects in the provinces. Vespasian permitted anyone to annex empty lots and build on them if their owners failed to do so; Hadrian decreed that no house in any city should be torn down in order to transport building material elsewhere – a conservationist measure *par excellence.*

Literally thousands of Roman buildings, secular and religious, political and domestic, are found today on three continents – Europe, Asia and Africa. Their number increases annually thanks to aerial photography and the perseverance of foreign institutes and schools of archaeology. Time and again one marvels at the success of urbanization in unlikely zones, at the sensible and humane design of private homes and multiple dwellings. Colonial gridirons and standardized regulations notwithstanding, there emerged brilliant plans and novel accommodations which foreshadow, sometimes even overshadow, the achievements of the Industrial Revolution. Rome's Empire witnessed a Golden Age of architecture, an architecture which kept the traditional forms of the Greeks, the colonnade and the architectural ornament, but used them freshly and purposefully in countless new settings. The inherited vocabulary of forms, from Greece and Hellenistic Asia, was inescapable, but its adaptability had never been more skilfully demonstrated than in Rome's metropolitan centres and country areas. The architects of the provinces were initially, at least, Greek-speaking freedmen from the East; the interior designers, the mosaicists, the marble workers and marble sculptors, turned their talents to Roman commissions all over the Empire. Artists, architects, and sculptors were almost inevitably Greek down to the final days; the technicians, the contractors, and the masons were either Italian or provincial.[287] The Peaceable Kingdom had apparently arrived, at least in the eyes of many of Rome's provincials. MacKendrick's verdict is reasonable: 'They brought freedom from fear, and such men are no Fascists. Under them at their best Western Europe enjoyed, as never before or since, the blessings of one world.'[288] The Eastern Empire, the ultimate inheritor of the Imperial Ideal and the Christian mission, except for Judaea and parts of Mesopotamia, found the experience of Roman rule as beneficent as, certainly more solicitous and generous than, that of their earlier masters, including the Macedonian. Men of rank and education everywhere were impressed with Rome's promise of peace, her guarantees of local liberties and authority, and the continuance of economic interests in almost every sector. The conqueror, the colonizer, and the civilizer merged in Rome's image outside Italy. The stimulus of colonies, of new and renovated foundations in the provinces, of trade and caravan routes safeguarded and promoted, were counterpoise to the demand for tribute, for military service, and for obedience to the law. Rome remained Caput Mundi for centuries and many sought to live in her image.

The process of extension and consolidation of Empire in the west was gradual. After Sicily, Sardinia and Corsica, Spain became Rome's first continental province (197 BC). Although its pacification cost Rome and the Spaniards dearly, Agrippa was finally able to negotiate a durable peace in 19 BC. The territory was organized into three provinces: Baetica, Tarraconensis, and Lusitania (Portugal). Although Spain and Portugal made important contributions from their mines (silver, copper, tin, lead, and gold), and from their orchards and vineyards, and although many Italians and provincials favoured Spanish textiles, house and villa remains are scanty and, regrettably, inadequately published. Baetica, the most favoured of the Spanish provinces, has yielded only a portion of its undoubtedly major repertoire of houses and villas.

Roman France is another story. Southern Gaul, Provence today, Rome's *provincia, par excellence*, was organized as Gallia Transalpina in 121 BC. Its background of Greek colonization at Marseilles, Nice, Monaco, Antibes, Glanum, etc., and its long-standing alliance with Rome made it a desirable and productive resort for Italian immigrants. The remainder of Gaul, as far north as the English Channel and the Rhine, fell to Julius Caesar between 58 and 51 BC. Augustus took a personal interest in the reorganization of Caesar's conquests into three new provinces: Aquitania, Lugdunensis and Belgica in the north-east. All became important contributors to the Roman and Imperial economy. Gallic textiles, glass, pottery (a local Samian imitation), iron and bronze ware were staples in many Imperial homes; Gallic wines were prized as highly then as today.

MacKendrick remarks that 'Rome was eager to set up in Gaul an establishment in her own image, and the discovery by archaeologists of hundreds of Gallo-Roman villas proves how eager the Gauls were to oblige.'[289] Archaeological reconnaissance and aerial photography, particularly since 1964, enlarge the number and repertoire of rural dwellings annually. Nearly seven hundred sites with their ancient substructures have been detected by aerial photography during the past decade in the Somme; the fertile plains of Picardy alone have yielded plans of 270 villas.[290] Aerial research is both instant and complete in its 'discovery' of the buried remains: habitations, barns, agricultural outbuildings and sometimes even outlying farm-buildings, ponds, quarries and foundries reveal their ghostly outlines inside surrounding walls or ditches. Philology has made its contribution as well by locating an impressive number of Gallo-Roman properties by simply associating place-names ending in -ac or -at in the south, and with -e and -y in the north, with the Latin suffix -acum or -acus appended to a property owner's name for fiscal purposes. Properties with the Pauli-acus denomination appear today as Pauilhac in Aquitaine, Pauliat in Auvergne, and as Pouille or Pouilly in the north.[291]

More conventional archaeological methods have also yielded important information about house patterns and life-styles in the towns of Provence, most notably at Glanum (Bouches-du-Rhône) and Vasio (Bouches-du-Rhône). Glanum (modern St Rémy) lies 54 miles north of Marseilles and 15 miles northeast of Arles (Arelate).[292] Founded by Greeks from Marseilles during the sixth or fifth century BC, Glanum was a prosperous Hellenistic emporium during the third century BC and the impress of Hellenistic house-forms survived into Roman times. Today the awesome Mausoleum of the Julii and the monumental arch vie for attention with the remains of several impressive private houses.

The House of Sulla, replaced by the Agrippan basilica c. 20 BC, lies on the south-east side of a main street of Glanum. Its six small rooms have walls decorated in Pompeian Style II and

54

64

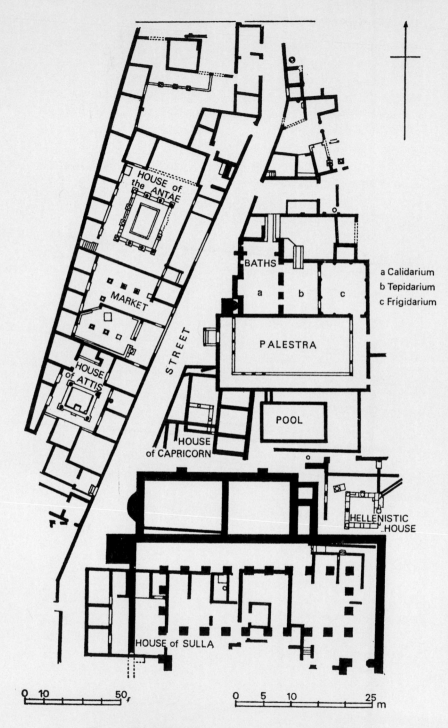

HOUSE of
the ANTAE

MARKET

HOUSE
of ATTIS

BATHS

a   b   c

a Calidarium
b Tepidarium
c Frigidarium

PALESTRA

STREET

POOL

HOUSE
of CAPRICORN

HELLENISTIC
HOUSE

HOUSE of SULLA

0 10   50ₓ

0   5   10   25
                   m

Fig. 54   Saint Rémy (Glanum), street plan, houses and bath

opus signinum floors with white marble cubes inset in a lozenge pattern. The proprietor's name, a curious irony in a community occupied by Marian troops during the Cimbrian War (101 BC), appears in a geometric-style threshold mosaic; a wall graffito refers to the consulship of Gaius Sosius in 32 BC. Three other buildings attract attention on the block opposite. The House of Attis (Maison d'Atys), a Hellenistic Delian-style dwelling, is named after the priest-lover of Cybele. He is the subject of a decorative relief found in the *impluvium* court off the vestibule. Four substantial columns with Ionic bases hedge the *impluvium* which, following the Hellenistic and Campanian practice, supplied the house cistern. After the building was completed, an altar was incorporated into the *impluvium* court and two rooms were floored in black and polychrome mosaic. Another relief in the same house depicted the Fortuna or Tyche of Glanum with Mercury alongside. Immediately adjacent to the House of Attis is a sanctuary designed to accommodate the Dendrofori (Branch-bearers) of Glanum, a religious *collegium* dedicated to the service of the Magna Mater (Cybele). The House of Attis was in all likelihood, therefore, the residence of the priestesses of Cybele. Even more impressive than the House of Sulla or the Attis House is the Maison des Antes which lies beyond the collegial sanctuary and an adjoining market building. A vestibule leads into a rectangular atrium court with an *impluvium* (27 × 20 feet) and a peristyle of twelve fluted limestone columns with Ionic capitals. Large reception rooms which are accessible from the court, painted walls, pebble mosaic paving, an *exedra* with *antae* crowned with Corinthian capitals, and a stable annex, recall comparable opulence in Delian dwellings, the House of the Dolphins, the House of Dionysus, and the Maison de la Colline, but the atrium-cum-peristyle house complexes at Pompeii are equally relevant. Drains led excess water from the north-east corner of the *impluvium* and from the house latrine into a street sewer; a stairway led to an upper storey overlooking the peristyle court. The town twice fell to German attack, to the Cimbri at the end of the second century BC, and *c.* AD 270.

Vasio (Vaison-la-Romaine) by the river Ouvèze, lies 16 miles north-east of Orange (Arausio).[293] Originally an Augustan foundation *c.* 20 BC, Vasio was meant to supersede the Gallic *oppidum* on the opposite river bank. The new-style capital of the Vocontii, organized along colonial grid-lines and built on an impressive scale, offered colonnaded streets with shops, a fountain house, baths, theatre, a public portico and park. Long narrow properties, found also at Vicus Belgica on the Tongres–Cologne road, and at Verulamium, Silchester and elsewhere in Britain,[294] suggest that many of the burghers of Vasio gained desirable and costly street-frontage by resorting to strip-housing and one-room *tabernae*, a pattern familiar at Ostia and Rome and generally throughout the Empire in built-up centres. Although trades-people and the lower-income segment of the citizenry might seek accommodation in strip-houses, perhaps even *pensione*-style dwellings, the more affluent favoured layouts similar to those at Pompeii and Herculaneum. Vasio's most celebrated sons, certainly Sextus Afranius Burrus, a patron of the town and tutor to Nero, and possibly Tacitus, Rome's greatest historian, could have found suitable housing in any of the mansions so far unearthed. Tacitus' equestrian father, likely procurator of Gallia Belgica and officer with the Rhine armies (AD 46–58), would certainly have had the means for comfortable retirement.

55   Vasio's House of the Silver Bust includes a handsome portico with shops in its east façade and faces on to a stepped pavement. Behind lies an appealing reception area which leads into a Corinthian-style atrium with twelve columns. From the atrium there is a pleasant vista through the *tablinum* into a small peristyle garden with *piscina* and well-head. Beyond the *tablinum* to the north-west there is a second peristyle garden, a larger trapezoidal design, with a bath-suite adjoining. The bedrooms lie to the north of the atrium on the second storey. Alongside the main entry is a service corridor which communicates with the 'back hall' and a kitchen garden on the right. The silver bust which provides a name for the mansion was discovered under roof debris in 1924 and is a relic of the ultimate catastrophe which overwhelmed the house during the raids of the third century AD. The House of the Dolphin, to the west of the House of the Silver Bust, was discovered during the excavations of 1949–54 and appears to be

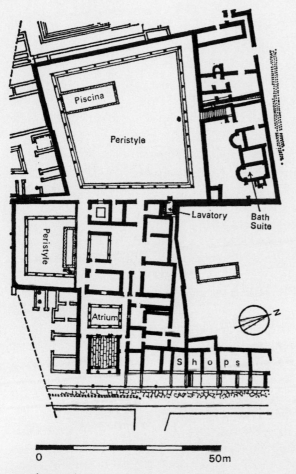

Fig. 55 Vaison-la-Romaine (Vasio), House of the Silver Bust, plan. Boëthius & Ward-Perkins, fig. 136

Piscina

Peristyle

Peristyle

Atrium

Lavatory

Bath Suite

S h o p s

0   50m

another rich man's house with similar elements: two colonnaded peristyles, one with *piscina* and *exedra*, a mosaic floor, a bath-suite with hypocaustic installations, latrines, and an atrium-*impluvium-tablinum* complex. Finally, in the Puymin quarter of this provincial Pompeii, Sautel unearthed the House of the Messii, so-called from a dedication to Messia Alpina found in the remains. Once again, the early Imperial architect designed another peristyle mansion with *piscina*, mosaic floors, frescoed walls and latrine; a bath-suite was added subsequently. In summary, the town houses of Glanum and Vasio, under the Roman dispensation, owe as much to Campanian and Italic house plans as to Delian prototypes, if not more. The Hellenistic influence pervaded both Provence and Campania and the architects, possibly from the eastern Mediterranean, must have been conscious of indebtedness and influence from both continents. The atrium-style mansion is decidedly Italic.

Benoit discovered a superior town house of terraced design at Aquae Sextiae (Aix-en-Provence). The mansion contains a large inner peristyle and a small colonnaded atrium at the entrance. The layout, common to Delos and Cyrenaica, but usually designated Rhodian, involves two peristyle areas, one on a higher level than the other. Overseas parallels at Aquae Sextiae, and at Vasio and Glanum, suggest that wealthier townsfolk employed Greek architects to design their houses according to modes which were popular in Italy and elsewhere.

Alesia (Alise-Sainte-Reine, Côte d'Or),[295] capital of the Mandubii, saw Gallic national resistance to Rome under Vercingetorix broken by Julius Caesar in 51 BC. Excavations have produced remains of private houses which combine both Celtic and Roman elements under one roof: deep storage cellars (Celtic) and sturdy stone walls with narrow windows (Roman), both proof against the inclement weather. Town-house remains elsewhere in France are abundant but hardly ever as revealing or impressive as those of Glanum and Vasio.

Country houses, which Caesar calls *aedificia*, are plentiful throughout the rich agricultural terrain of France and the Low Countries. Even before Caesar's conquest, Romans had to live and farm in Transalpine Gaul. But with law and order secured, emigrants to France and the Low Countries soon approached the numbers of expatriates and colonists in Spain, Greece and Asia. Long before the advent of Roman arms, Celtic landholders with means had resorted to corridor-style housing, rectangular buildings with a front corridor, sometimes adapted as a porticoed verandah, often with one or more rooms projecting from the ends. The corridor-villa, familiar in Germany, France and England and obviously part of a basic repertoire of house-plans, was probably native to the continent and exported across the Channel.

Recent aerial research in Picardy and Artois, already noticed, has done much to clarify the typology of rural dwellings in the wheat-bearing country of the Somme. Judging by the photographs there is a surprising consistency in the villa designs, large or small. The main building, normally of the elongated corridor-house design, usually faces east on to a rectangular courtyard which connects through a low wall with a second, more expansive courtyard. Out-buildings often appear in two ranks on either side of the outer courtyard. The entire estate is normally contained within a rectangular frame of wall or of mound and ditch combined. Deviations from the basic axiality and symmetry of the design are noticeably rare but there are instances of trapezoidal farmyards or courts.

The Anthée villa, near Namur (Belgium),[296] a corridor-style construction, is highly reminiscent of recently detected villa sites in Picardy and Artois. It dominates the inner core of a larger domain of 30 acres wherein the inner court is separated from the larger main enclosure by a gateway, not unlike the pattern suggested by the Trier mural. The tenant buildings in the larger enclosure offered accommodation and service areas (forge, pottery kilns, etc.) for the upkeep of the farm. The buildings were destroyed during the barbarian raids of 275-6 and never rebuilt.   68

Smaller villas are usually restricted to a single courtyard and single main house; larger properties have the manor house occupying the pride of place with service and administrative buildings ranged along the sides of the outer court. The manager's or bailiff's lodging sometimes adjoins the main house, at other times it dominates the lateral constructions of the outer court. The bailiff's house, though reduced in scale, is often identical with that of the laird, sometimes it adopts a much less elaborate design. Tripartite aisled-houses or barns, detected in the aerial photographs, are more familiar in Romano-British archaeology, but were probably indigenous to Northern Europe. They might serve as the residences of the *vilicus* (or *maior*) and his dependants; they could also house farm-hands, draught animals, even valuable equipment employed on the estate.

Aerial photography in northern France and Picardy suggests that there was a remarkable consistency in the layout of Gallo-Roman estates. 'There is almost always a small square structure which breaks, towards the middle, the low wall separating the two courtyards. In the same way one finds two or three small buildings grouped together outside the walls or the enclosure ditches, and still further away, set back some hundreds of yards from the main building, a little chalky mound.'[297] Such uniformity of design and structure probably indicates that a master plan was involved in the development of particular areas of the Roman province.

Whether part of the early consolidation period, or products of the Late Empire, the rural estates of Picardy, manned by hundreds of slaves, must have adhered to a busy agricultural-industrial schedule concentrating on wheat and sheep-raising during the spring and winter, and on wool production, possibly even iron-working, during the long winters. Agache is convinced that the capacious cellars found on the larger estates, with light and air admitted through the stone blocks, were factories for the processing of wool and weaving.

Average-size villas in northern France measure anything from 400 to 800 feet in length; more commodious, luxurious manor houses anything from 800 to 1,150 feet. Isolation was an inescapable factor in northern living. Even 'elementary' farms, with modest house and barn-byre, rarely appear in clusters of more than two or three in any given area, after the pattern of contemporary farm houses in the American and Canadian mid-west.

Two Gallo-Roman villas, excavated in recent years at Chiragan and Montmaurin, offer rich insights into the life-style of provincial millionaires near the Pyrenees. One of these, Chiragan (Haute-Garonne)[298] on the borders of Gallia Narbonensis, near Martres-Tolosanes, flanks the Roman highway between Toulouse (Tolosa) and Dax. The original villa, a peristyle mansion of Augustan date, was enlarged in Trajanic times by the addition of a garden court bordered by *cryptoportici* which led to a small hexagonal summer-house overlooking the River Garonne. Another *cryptoporticus*, east of the peristyle, gave access to the workmen's cottages which were neatly disposed in rows at some distance from the main house. The original Augustan bath-suite yielded to a more elegant replacement. The third phase of the villa's history, from *c*. AD 150–200, was the period of its greatest splendour and fulfilment. The architect used Pyrenees marble from the St Béat quarries to build the new fountain court, together with two miniature 'dower houses' near the baths and the Trajan court, and a whole new quarter

56

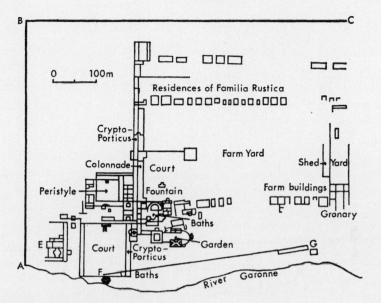

0 ___100m

Residences of Familia Rustica

Crypto-
Porticus

Colonnade

Court

Farm Yard

Shed → Yard

Peristyle

Fountain

Farm buildings

Granary

E

Court

Crypto-
Porticus

Baths

Garden

G

A

F. Baths

River Garonne

Fig. 56   Chiragan (Haute Garonne), villa, plan. P. MacKendrick, Roman France, fig. 5.7

south-east of the baths. The new wing provided an apsidal *triclinium*, similar to the dining-room at Lullingstone Roman Villa (Kent), an atrium, yet another enclosed green space with an *exedra*, and a second summer-house. A gallery of selected imperial portraits, from Augustus to Septimius Severus, unearthed in a fifth-century deposit on the property, probably indicates that the second- and/or third-century proprietor was either an imperial official or a singularly patriotic individual with exceptional means. The final phase of Chiragan's history during the fourth century highlights the agricultural side. Four sets of buildings extend from the Trajanic *cryptoporticus*: a series of stalls capable of housing thirty yoke of oxen; twenty residences for the rustic *familia*, capable of housing about a hundred families with their working equipment; eleven workshops largely devoted to weaving; and a fourth set of buildings, set at right angles to the others and parallel with the *cryptoporticus* with barns and sheds facing on to a three-sided barnyard. Careful measurement and computation suggest that the villa, enclosed within a 40-acre tract, covered seven and a half acres, that the entire estate

65

probably covered about 2,400 acres, and that the workers must
have numbered something in excess of 350, a figure which is
compatible with the residential quarters here described. The villa
succumbed to Vandal attack in 408; the successor village,
Martres-Tolosanes, less than a mile away, drew on Chiragan's
ruins for its building materials.

Chiragan is the second-largest villa to be excavated in France;
Montmaurin (Haute-Garonne), only 20 miles west, is the largest.[299] Like Chiragan, certainly in its final phase, Montmaurin
was the centre of an extensive domain (3,750 acres). The broad
alluvial terrace where the villa once stood lies alongside the
River Save. The Nébouzan district, wherein the estate lies,
probably derives its name from Nepotianum which suggests that
the proprietor of the villa's final years may have been named
Nepotianus. The name Nebozanum appears in a medieval charter
of 1342. Because the lay-outs of Chiragan and Montmaurin are
closely similar, and because Chiragan antedates Montmaurin
by only a short interval, one may reasonably conjecture that
both proprietors, certainly in the final years and possibly at the
outset, sought counsel and design from the same architectural
source.

Montmaurin's earliest design as *villa rustica* dates from Neronian
times (*c.* AD 50). The residence was laid out symmetrically around
a large central court and faced south-west towards a series of
farm buildings neatly arranged in rows. Inside the villa enclosure
was a large rectangular farmyard surrounded by stables, workshops, storerooms and the like. This first estate flourished until
the end of the second century when the villa and the enclosure
were bowled over by a disastrous flood. The early third century,
a time of prosperity generally throughout France if not in Britain, was unexceptional for Montmaurin. The property's second
phase dawned *c.* AD 250. Although excavation has revealed
that the subsidiary buildings, outside the central court and alongside the large farmyard, were not reconstructed, Fouet argues that
the *fundus* was in fact reorganized to cope more efficiently with
its extensive domains. Farm-hands, Fouet believes, were replaced by tenant *coloni* who lived on farms which were quite
removed from the main house. Although they owed labour and

payment in produce to the master, they undoubtedly enjoyed a greater degree of independence than their predecessors. The main property, under the direct surveillance of the manor house, had a large farmyard on its west side and housing for the farm-hands, a forge, storage buildings, etc. The life-span of the enhanced villa was abruptly and drastically curtailed by the barbarian destruction of 276. But the greatest period was still to come. The ultimate villa (Phase III) covered 10 acres and con-tained almost two hundred rooms! A long carriage-road led to the great entrance court, a D-shaped portico (175 feet wide and 70 feet deep), which contained a hexagonal Gallic shrine and altar, one of several pagan shrines in the villa's environs. Beyond the entrance portico lie the peristyle (6,458 square feet) with waiting-rooms on the south side, two dining-rooms, one for summer and a heated one for winter, and other unspecified rooms, all decorated with colourfully painted walls (AD 325). Another peristyle lies beyond with apsidal garden spaces on both sides and a summer-house at the rear. Aquaria and marble veneer, possibly even murals, enlivened the setting and added a note of regal elegance. A bath system, furnished with cipollino marble columns with Tuscan capitals, was arranged alongside the first peristyle court. Adjacent to the baths were the stables, forge, and dormitory housing for the farm-hands and their dependants. The finds made at the villa, colourful mosaics in formal non-figured patterns, fragmentary sculptures, locally produced and imported Spanish pottery, millefiori glass, coins and lamps, all befit a wealthy proprietor who was doubtless engaged in a large-scale provisioning enterprise, serene and prosperous on his self-sufficient estate, warm in winter (with almost a dozen heated rooms in the plan), cool in summer amid open courts, gardens and summer-house. The marble used so lavishly in the colonnades, doorways, wall veneers and flooring came from the Pyrenean quarries of St Béat, a luxury shared by Chiragan as well. Fire caused heavy damage to the villa c. 350–375 and, although the château and the Gallic shrine were repaired, there was a decline in the appearance and in the maintenance of the estate. The earlier fire was presage of the ultimate fate of Montmaurin which, like Chiragan, lay directly in the path of the Vandals as they followed their invasion route to Spain, and the great country house was reduced to a smouldering ruin in the early fifth century.

Lugdunum Convenarum (St-Bertrand-de-Comminges) near by was a prosperous transit point in Trajanic times between Toulouse and the west and between Spain and Gallia Narbonensis.[300] But customs duties were only part of a larger and richer revenue from mines, marble quarries, agriculture and hotels. Lugdunum Convenarum was an early centre of Romanization in the area, a major Augustan community when Chiragan and Montmaurin were first built. One may suppose that their first builders were either ambitious Italians with ready cash and an eye for agricultural profit, or wealthy Gallic aristocrats who adapted their ancestral estates to new pattern of Italian agronomy and rural management. Whichever be true, Lugdunum Convenarum undoubtedly played a major role in their genesis and their development just as the villas, when ruinous and deserted, played their role in the genesis of later settlements near by.

Finally, we look to a number of the Gallic intelligentsia of the fifth century for yet another eye-witness account of a rich man's estate. Sidonius Apollinaris, the celebrated Lyonnaise writer and Bishop of the Arverni (c. 469), has left a tantalizing account of his villa estate of Avitacum which is usually located, but not yet discovered, on the shores of Lac d'Aydat (Puy-de-Dôme) about 12 miles south-west from Clermont-Ferrand. The mansion no doubt formed a substantial part of his wife's dowry. Sidonius' description, more rhapsodic than precise, suggests a mansion facing north-south with a bath-suite on the south-west and superbly planned quarters for the men and the women of the establishment, located with proper respect for appealing vistas. 'On leaving the *piscina* one comes across the front of the ladies' dining-room; joined on to this, with only a barrack partition between them is the household storeroom (*cella penaria*), next to which is the weaving-room (*textrinum*). On the east a portico overlooks the lake; it is supported on round composite pillars rather than by a pretentious array of monolithic columns. . . . From this dining-room we pass on to a living-room (*diaeta*) or small dining-room (*cenatiuncula*), all of which lies open to the lake and to which almost the whole lake lies open. In this room are a semicircular dining-couch (*stibadium*) and a glittering side-board (*abacus*), and on to the floor or platform on which they stand is a gentle ascent from the portico by steps which are not made either short or narrow. . . . When you have finished your meal a drawing-room (*deversorium*) will offer you welcome, one which is truly a summer room because it is not in the least sun-baked, for, as it is open to the north only, it admits daylight but not sunshine; before you reach it there is a narrow ante-chamber (*consistorium*), where the somnolence of the ushers (*cubicularii*) has room to doze rather than to sleep.'[301]

Sidonius' account of his pride and joy by the lake reveals traits and amenities found on the great estates at Montmaurin and Chiragan, at Bignor and Lullingstone in England, and in the Roman castles of the Rhine.

Patterns of living and housing in Gallia Belgica, in spite of a daunting climate and indomitable neighbours across the Rhine, varied little from those elsewhere in Europe. Villa properties of considerable scale and opulence started with the first century AD and became more numerous and even more elegant during the second and third centuries. But, however impressive and palatial the design, country houses were never entirely divorced from agriculture or some other profitable activity. Tenant farmers and slaves supplied the work-force until the end.

Belgic huts of timber with wattle and daub and drystone cottages with thatched roofs remained the basic repertoire. The farm-house at Mayen,[302] 25 miles west of Koblenz (Confluentia) followed a pattern familiar in the British experience. From a mere Celtic hut at the outset it was transformed, after the advent of the Augustan legions, into a stone-walled corridor-villa with a single living room, a portico with protecting wings and a basement. Heating was provided by a hearth in the central room throughout most of its history. The storage pit of the earlier period was replaced by a silo in later times.

As in France and Britain, the change-over to 'Roman-style' living was neither instant nor widespread. Many farmers of modest means remained content with the corridor-villa, a monotonous but malleable form, throughout the period of

occupation. Some sought better, more spacious, more interesting lay-outs at Pillig, for example, near Mayen, and at Bollen-
66   dorff,[303] beside the River Sauer, where the corridor-villa included
a cellar with barrel vaults and, during the second century, a
modest bath-suite with hypocausts. Another 'ancestral' home,
at Weitersbach,[304] was improved by a portico enclosing three
sides of a front courtyard, a bath-suite, and rooms with hypocaustic heating.

Ausonius (c. 310–393) provides an account of fourth-century
villas along the River Moselle which is almost breathless with
admiration and awe: 'This one stands high upon a mass of
natural rock, this rests upon the verge of the jutting bank, this
stands back and claims the river for its own, making it a prisoner
in an enfolding bay. Yon occupies a hill whose bulk looms high
above the stream, claiming free prospect o'er tilth, o'er waste,
and the rich outlook enjoys the lands about as though its own.
Nay and another, though it rests its foot low down in the well-
watered meadows, makes up the natural advantage of a mountain's height rearing its threatening steep until the soaring roof
breaks in upon the aether, displaying, like Memphian Pharos, its
lofty tower. This has for its own the catching of fish imprisoned
in the fenced flood between the sunny grass-grown rocks; this,
perched upon the ridge's topmost crest, looks down with prospect
just bedimmed in haze upon the stream which slides below. What
need to make mention of their courts set beside verdant meadows,
of their trim roofs resting upon countless pillars? What of their
baths, contrived low down on the verge of the bank, which
smoke when Vulcan, drawn by the glowing flue, pants forth his
flames and whirls them up through the channelled walls, rol-
ling in masses the imprisoned smoke before the scorching blast!
I myself have seen some, exhausted by the intense heat of the
baths, scorn the pools and cold plunge-baths, preferring to
enjoy running water, and, straightway refreshed by the river,
buffet the cool stream, threshing it with their stroke. But, if a
stranger were to arrive here from the shores of Cumae, he would
47   believe that Euboean Baiae had bestowed on this region a
miniature copy of its own delights: so great is the charm of its
refinement and distinction, while its pleasures breed no excess.'[303]

Ausonius was tutor to the later Emperor Gratian (367–383) in the court of Valentinian (364–375) at Trier (Augusta Treverorum), an official capital of the Empire from Diocletian to the late fourth century, and an eye-witness to the pavilions and pleasure domes along the Moselle. His verse account (c. 370) of a journey from Bingen to Trier is as sensitive to the smiling pastoral scenery as to the lordly mansions along the river. The luxury villa at   57 Nennig,[306] 25 miles south of Trier, near the Luxembourg border, is typical of the terraced riverside villas extolled by the poet. The main building, a corridor-plan dwelling with an impressive façade more than 150 feet long, has porticoes on both sides. To the north lies a suite of rooms facing on to a peristyle court with a fountain, and beyond these, to the west, lie the workrooms of the manor house. A guest house (south) was linked with the baths by a long *cryptoporticus* (836 feet long) lined with statuary. The baths, reminiscent of Ausonius' steam baths, have a pool measuring 700 square feet, seven rooms, five of them apsidal, three with hypocaustic heating. The architect guaranteed privacy and insurance against fire by locating the baths at some distance from the main building. The two-storeyed mansion with its pleasurable porticoes and landscaped garden, fountains and

Fig. 57   Nennig. Villa, 3rd century AD, elevation and plan. Boëthius & Ward-Perkins, fig. 139

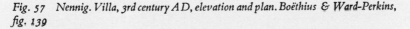

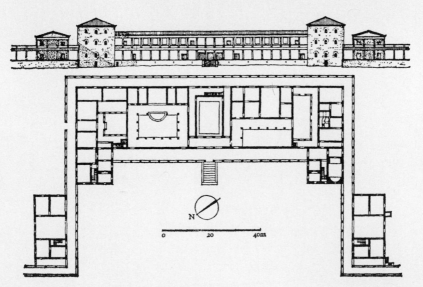

vistas, recalls dream houses in Pompeian murals, the remote forebears of this provincial mansion. The interior decorations include a celebrated mosaic of the late second century consisting of eight octagonal medallions and one square insert, all depicting gladiatorial scenes and including entr'acte entertainment provided by a horn and a water-organ.[307] The living rooms were decorated with fresco paintings of Amazons, wild animals, floral and geometric patterns. A large-scale mausoleum, south-west of

69   the baths, comparable to the grander version at Lullingstone (Kent), completes the design of the riverside mansion. It continued to be occupied into Late Imperial times.

One of the most scientifically excavated of the German villas,

58   and one of the best reported, lies 3 miles west of the Claudian colony of Cologne (Colonia Agrippinensis) at Müngersdorf.[308] The main headquarters for the 10-acre walled estate, with verandahs terminating in towers, had twenty-nine rooms; the baths were partly furnished with Belgian marble veneer and provided with flush toilets. The interior decoration of the building includes mosaic paving and Pompeian Fourth Style painting. The house, which was never destroyed, had a life-span of three to four

Fig. 58 Köln-Müngersdorf. Villa, 3rd century AD, elevation and plan. Boëthius & Ward-Perkins, fig. 138

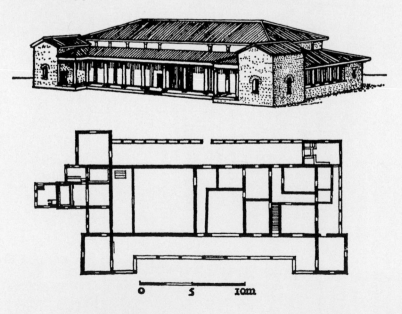

0   5   10m

centuries. Wittlich, 11 miles north-west of Bernkastel, is the site of another riverside mansion with a two-storeyed façade and a bath facility.[309]

Konz (Contionacum),[310] superbly located at the confluence of the Saar and Moselle, is yet another magnified version of a corridor-style villa (275 × 125 feet), with porticoes on both the north and south sides and projecting wings on both sides of the long central section forming an L-shaped lay-out. The external 59 walls were decorated with motifs in green and yellow and with red garlands against a white ground; the interior had a black and white *opus sectile* floor in the apsidal audience- or throne-chamber. This spacious property was either a summer palace built originally for Constantine or Valentinian, or the residence of some Gallic millionaire whose estate might conceivably house the Imperial family as required.

The villa at Pfalzel (Palatiolum)[311] stands on a low eminence overlooking the surrounding farmland. The three-storey estate is concentrated about a central court, with projections at the four 60 corners and in the middle of each side. The main entrance (west) had windows only at the second and third storey. The interior

Fig. 59 Konz (Contionacum). Villa, plan. Wightman, p. 166

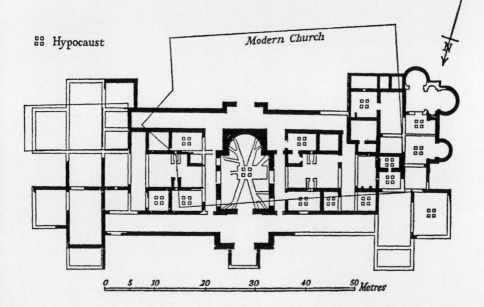

██ Hypocaust   Modern Church   N

0   5   10   20   30   40   50 Metres

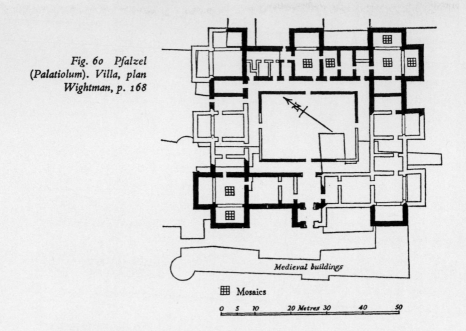

Fig. 60 Pfalzel (Palatiolum). Villa, plan Wightman, p. 168

Medieval buildings

⊞ Mosaics

0   5   10   20 Metres 30   40   50

rooms had *opus sectile* floors and mosaic decorations on the arches of the house doors and windows. The second-floor exterior windows were small but the third-floor fenestration, between the turrets, favoured a more expansive arched design. The final phase of the villa's history, during the time of Julian (361–363) or Valentinian (364–375), was marked by large-scale expansion; a building of comparable plan and scale rose to the west of the

61 original property. The manor house at Weilerbüsch, near Fliessem,[312] 20 miles north of Trier, began its life as a corridor-house with projecting wings at front and rear, a twenty-room mansion with a bath-suite set within an enclosure and with subsidiary buildings lining the main access to the villa. The villa was later vastly enlarged to incorporate another suite of rooms along the north side and a second bath-suite. The courtyard and gardens of the renovated mansion were enclosed within walls and the south side of the house was redesigned to provide apsidal sun-porches about the large courtyard. Mosaic floors and another pavilion at the north-west corner completed the make-up of this seventy-room mansion. Almost certainly an imperial property, the 36-acre estate may even have served as a stud farm.

During the excavations for an air-raid shelter near the celebrated cathedral of Cologne, remains were found of a peristyle

64 Saint-Rémy (Glanum). Courtyard house

65 Montmaurin (Haute-Garonne). Villa, model

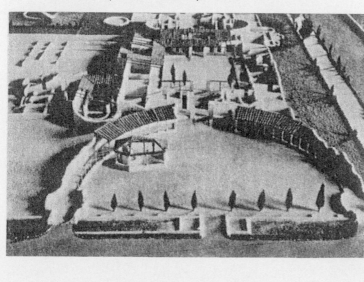

66   Pillig (near Mayen). Villa and farmyard foundations, air view

67   Ditchley, Oxon. Roman villa and its dependencies, foundations, air view

68 Trier wall-painting, villa and peasants

69   Lullingstone, Kent. Villa with temple mausoleum and circular
temple

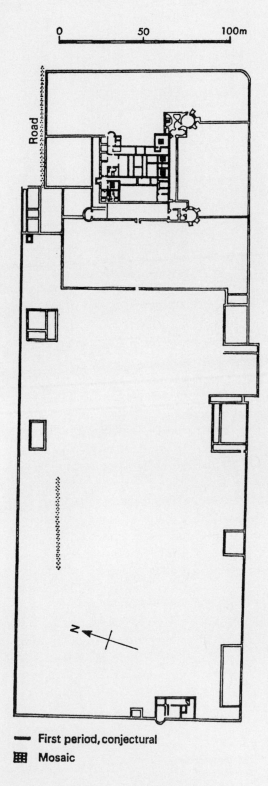

0   50   100m

Road

*Fig. 61   Weilerbüsch, near
Fliessem. Villa, plan.
Wightman, p. 144*

N

— First period, conjectural

⊞ Mosaic

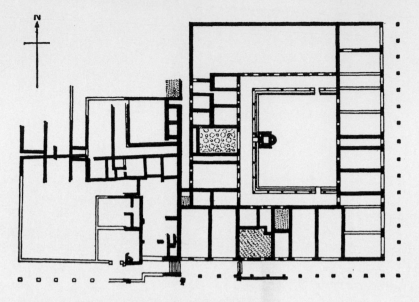

Fig. 62   Cologne. Peristyle house, near the cathedral, plan

62   house which probably housed a wealthy grain merchant who chose to live near the commerical harbour. The original house was oriented north–south with a *triclinium* at the south end and with a peristyle garden and fountain. Entry to the riverside mansion was from the south into the peristyle garden; the dining-room, a two-storeyed banqueting hall with clerestory lighting, was floored with polychrome mosaic medallions, twenty-seven of them, with depictions of the myth of Dionysus, the Seasons, birds and fruit.[313] The east wing containing the *triclinium* and the west both faced on to the garden; a verandah provided a direct view of the Rhine. Remodelling and reconversion of the east wing *c.* 260 produced a grain warehouse (*horreum*) of impressive scale, about 55 feet wide and 17 feet long, a facility which was directly accessible from the river after the pattern of Ostian and Roman storage and shipping offices.

68   A wall-painting found near the Basilica of Trier illustrates our notions of country life in the northern provinces.[314] The painting has been interpreted as representing the façade of a porticoed villa with projecting wings and a landscaped garden behind. But one is perhaps better justified in interpreting the portico with three columns and the two-storeyed gable ends as the entry to the

inner courtyard of an estate which raised fruit and shade trees judging by the impressionistic versions in the background. More peasants, wearing hooded shoulder capes, in the foreground, occur in the reliefs of the 75-foot grave monument of the Secundinii, wealthy cloth merchants at Igel, between Rheims and Trier.[315] The tenant farmers there are pictured in the act of offering their lord and master gifts or rent in kind including fur or skins; a four-wheeled wagon, drawn by mules, with corded bales of cloth or woollen goods, leaves the *villa rustica* bound for market through an arched gateway. The Simpelveld sarcophagus (*c.* AD 150), now in the Leiden Museum, has a sculptured interior with 'snapshots' of the house interior: a wickerwork basket chair, a wardrobe, a sideboard laden with demijohns, a table with lion's-foot legs, shelves laden with wine pitchers, etc., a cupboard with panelled doors, and household shrines.[316] The Neumagen (Noviomagus) funerary reliefs, found 25 miles south of Trier in 1878, now displayed in the Trier Rheinisches Landesmuseum, offer additional scenes of villa life: the payment of rents, the mistress having her hair washed and set with four maids in attendance, and youngsters at school. The pupils, like the mistress, are seated in high-backed cane chairs.[317]

56, 57

Overlooking the Ahr Valley at Blankenheim,[318] 30 miles south-west of Bonn, are the remains of another sizeable villa. Constructed originally *c.* AD 100, the villa, probably headquarters of a wine-producing estate, had twenty rooms, a bath suite, and a 100-foot verandah. After fire destroyed the original villa *c.* 150, another was constructed about a century later. The original foundations were altered: the projecting wings were discarded entirely and a 200-foot verandah was built. Entry was no longer from the west but from the south; the room capacity was doubled and hypocaustic installations became more common throughout the house; the bath-suite, part of the earliest complex, was improved by the addition of a furnace-room, and the toilet was flushed by run-off water from the baths. The villa's career came to an abrupt end during the reign of the Emperor Magnentius (AD 350–353).

Midway between Trier and Otrang, at Welschbillig,[319] are the remains of a villa of Imperial date, perhaps a stud farm or hunting preserve, by and large the product of *c*. 260. The manor house lies within an enormous walled property. The most notable feature of the estate is the *piscina*, 190 feet long and 60 feet wide, large enough for a mock naval engagement (*naumachia*). Like the pool of the Villa of the Papyri in suburban Herculaneum, this was bordered with one hundred and twelve sculptural likenesses of Greeks, Romans and barbarians of distinction. Inscriptional evidence indicates that troops were involved in the construction work, perhaps the cavalry contingent whose horses were raised in the grassy environs of the villa.

The Imperial Court at Trier added much to the celebrity and prosperity of the area. Trier's finest hour came with Constantine (306–337) whose parents, Constantius Chlorus (293–305) and Saint Helena, had once resided there. The Imperial City meant to rival Rome with its forum, basilica, baths, circus and palace, and, judging by Ausonius, emperors and their courtiers could find more tranquillity in the grandiose villas by the Moselle than in those by the Tiber: 'the roofs of country-houses, perched high upon the overhanging river banks, the hillsides green with vines, and the pleasant stream of Moselle gliding below with subdued murmuring'.[320]

Although subjected by Julius Caesar to invasion in 55 BC and short-term occupation in 54, Britain's formal entry into the Roman Empire was delayed until the time of Claudius who invaded and made a province of Britain in AD 43.[321] The Roman forces landed at Richborough (Rutupiae); Claudius joined his legions after the preliminary advances and Colchester (Camulodunum) became the capital of the new province. The legions marched west, north and north-west and by AD 47 the Fosse Way, from Lincoln (Lindum) to south Devon, became the first Roman frontier. Client rulers were patronized and protected, Cogidubnus in the west, in his regal house at Fishbourne near Chichester, Prasutagus, ruler of the Iceni in the north-east, and Cartimandua of the Brigantes further north. A serious upheaval came in AD 61 with the revolt of Boudicca (Boadicea), the liberationist widow of Prasutagus. Colchester was sacked, London was abandoned and the Ninth Legion was defeated. By reason of its remote position *vis-à-vis* the Mediterranean world,

63

Fig. 63   Fishbourne (Sussex). Palace villa of Cogidubnus, isometric drawing by David Neal, Cunliffe, fig. 30

Britain played no major role in the annals of the Empire until the third and fourth centuries A.D.

The conspiracy of silence in the literary testimonia is compensated, fortunately, by the rich array of archaeological data. Ground exploration and aerial photography provide the incentive and signposts for the recovery of endless numbers of towns, camps, and country estates.[322] Verulamium and the cantonal capitals of Wroxeter and Silchester, together with Caistor-by-Norwich, are almost entirely visible from the air. Wroxeter, the fourth-largest town in Britain in area, offers some 70 acres of town plan, all discernible in the crop patterns when viewed from above.

Celtic Britain, before the Roman conquest and during the Iron Age, shared many of the features of rural Gaul and the Rhineland: a rural society living in isolated farmsteads and rude dwellings of wood or stone often with grain storage-pits as complement.[323] The turf-roofed hovels, cottages and thatched-roof dwellings of the tribal Celtic society were unlikely harbingers of the manor houses and mansions of Imperial times. These native homes, often clustering in ill-defined communities, recur throughout the Fenlands and Wessex in the Sussex Downs, and in the Thames Valley and Severn areas.

Romanization introduced new farming techniques which were less costly in effort and far more productive, and brought about salutary improvements in the sordid, unsanitary arrangements of British living. Ancestral huts of wood or stone, rectangular and round, with man and beast enjoying the same roof, were superseded by rectangular cottages with wooden floors, painted plaster and window glass after the pattern of the houses and *tabernae* in the ascendant colonial towns in the province. The Romano-British farmer, with his new-found but hard-earned means, sought to imitate the amenities and the life-style of the European townsman by building cottages which combined structural solidity with efficiency and comfort. But there was no helter-skelter rush towards things Roman. Many Britons retained their primitive ways, following the old pastoral dictates, particularly in the hinterland territories of Wales and in the south-west. The Iron Age died slowly outside the confines of Roman occupation.

Slavery was no novelty in Roman Britain; it had been characteristic of the Celtic tribal system. So the pattern of seigniorial estates and villa management, with the resident laird or bailiff, and with vassals and tenants supplying the task-force, came easily. By the fourth century AD, the great period of villa expansion in Britain, the staff and tenants (*coloni*) were attached to the land like medieval serfs, and on an inherited basis, paying their rent in kind or cash, and providing maintenance work and labour on the manorial properties.

Tangible evidence of adaptation to Roman standards and modes of living appear in the countless sherds of Samian ware and coin finds. The British farmer found solace for conquest in his newly acquired implements and tools: a more efficient plough which enabled him to cope with larger, more productive fields, and, from ordnance, the iron-tipped spade, rake and scythe, together with chisels, draw-knives, spoke-shaves and the carpenter's plane.[324] To safeguard their grain during a wet harvest season, farmers with means provided themselves with insulated corn-dryers with double floors and underground flues. Roman hydraulics brought improved methods of irrigation and water-supplies, with wells that might lie 200 feet deep. Flocks and herds were never better nourished than during Roman times. New crops, fruit trees, flowers and apiculture were introduced; cattle and horse-breeding techniques advanced and many of the wealthier farmers managed sheep and cattle ranches of unusual size in Somerset and the Cotswolds.[325]

The noteworthy pre-Roman farm at Little Woodbury,[326] south-west of Salisbury, is a 3-acre estate set within a wooden palisade. There are two huts within the enclosure, both circular, with diameters of 30 and 50 feet, with timber uprights and wattle or plank walling. Pit silos large enough to store seventy bushels of grain a year indicate that the cultivable area was probably between 15 and 20 acres with additional land set aside for seed corn or left fallow. Bone remains indicate that the owner kept small herds of cattle and some sheep; dogs tended the sheep and protected the flocks. The autarky of the estate was further fortified by a pottery and iron foundry.

Three- and four-roomed cottages were an early elaboration of the basic form. Gradually, certainly by Neronian times, rectangular, timber-framed corridor-type dwellings became part of the builder's repertoire. A projecting wing (or wings) at one end (or both) of the front corridor provided the basis for new symmetry in design; the entrance was normally central. The end rooms offered additional, semi-private accommodation and verandahs, a break with the pattern of 'motel' cubicles opening off the controlling corridor. The new-style farm-house marked no revolutionary departure from past schemes and modes of living. Frere remarks that the villas 'can be seen as a new system growing up beside, and out of, the old. On the one hand, they clearly continue the tradition of the old isolated Celtic farmstead, but on the other, they exhibit new features in their quick adoption of Roman techniques and in their capacity to exploit new opportunities.'[327] Inspired by the standards of town life and drawing on magnified fortunes, the villa-owner occasionally created a duplicate version of his corridor-house in the rear. The tripartite design of the corridor-villa, with four or more rooms behind the main stone corridor, with timber posts and roof supports, was characteristic not only of first-century Britain but also of continental housing in general. Built on stone and rubble foundations, with plastered surfaces inside and out, the two-storey version of the corridor-villa resembled an embryonic Tudor-style mansion.

The farm-house at Lockleys, Welwyn (Herts), excavated in 1937 and recently reappraised by Graham Webster, surmounts the disputable remains of two Belgic huts of the first century AD.[328] The first timber-frame corridor-house (70 feet × 25) with five rooms was a product of the post-conquest era (AD 60–150). The second house on the site followed much the same pattern (AD 150–300) and was destroyed by fire. The final construction (c. 340), which rose at the south end of the site, broke completely with previous arrangements and was occupied until the last quarter of the fourth century.

The Park Street House (Herts)[329] gives indications of a long building history, from the earliest round or oval Belgic hut, then a rectangular stone-built dwelling (26 feet long × 10–12 feet broad), to a third phase which was almost identical in plan and construction with the Lockleys villa except for the absence of a verandah. The winged-corridor form appears in the second-century rebuilding which included a channelled hypocaust in one room designed for drying corn. The house was completely and finally rebuilt in the early fourth century.

67 The Ditchley House,[330] north-west of Woodstock, Oxfordshire, marks advances over both the Lockleys and Park Street houses. The original dwelling, a product of Flavian times, was a rectangular timber design but it was superseded during the early second century by a winged corridor-villa set within a rectangular ditched enclosure. The basic plan is comparable to that of Lockleys, save for the two rooms at either end. A corridor was later added in the rear with one end partitioned to provide a small kitchen, pantry and larder. Although water was undoubtedly plentiful, there is no evidence of a bath-suite in the reconditioned house. A large barn, 70 feet wide × 280 feet long, was divided into a nave and aisles by timber posts and served as

the slave dormitory and storage area. The site and its buildings were deserted for almost a century before it was reoccupied and rebuilt *c.* 300 with stone verandahs adding an air of elegance on both façades, and a second storey. The absentee landlord no doubt visited the house occasionally, but the bailiff was in permanent residence. During its fourth-century phase, the barnhouse was superseded by a large granary, 36 feet square, which could store the produce of the 500–1,000-acre farm. The farmhands were *coloni* whose task was to provide the proprietor with labour and payment in kind from the grain fields, orchards and vegetable gardens which made up the estate.

The Ditchley House, with its subsidiary structures, its pride of place and modern amenities, is a comparatively modest but typical version of the corridor-villa found throughout Britain, at Mansfield Woodhouse and Norton Disney in Nottinghamshire, at Brading on the Isle of Wight, at Llantwit-Major in Glamorgan, in Staffordshire and elsewhere.[331]

Only a few areas of England were devoid of villas or towns during the Roman occupation, most notably in southern Britain, Salisbury Plain, Cranborne Chase and the Fen Basin.[332] Even so, the presence of farmsteads, peasant villages, and in the Fenlands, of drainage dykes and canals, serve notice that men did live there, perhaps as tenants under Imperial sufferance on terrain which had been confiscated after uprisings.

Elsewhere the evidence is abundant for a new way of life in the country towns and districts. Certainly, the presence of the Roman legions made new demands on grain-growing and animal-raising. The British response to the Army's need for grain, meat, salt, leather, pottery, ironware and the like, was spirited and the rewards were liberal. Certainly the remodelling and alterations at Park Street, at Lockleys near Verulamium, and at Ditchley after the mid-first century, required expertise and capital not hitherto available. Seneca's notorious loans no doubt provided some of the wherewithal; so too did the continental tradesmen who emigrated from Gaul and Italy in search of greener fields, built homes in the towns and branched out to work the land.

Town-dwelling Romans and aristocratic Britons, the decurional and merchant class, were the likeliest owners of the largest farms. They drew their livelihood from their estates and left their occupancy, probably, to the villa manager, tenants and slave *contubernales*, with perhaps younger sons, family misfits or needy relatives in residence as token proprietors. Frere speculates that 'though some of the villa-owners may have been speculators from other provinces or their agents, and others retired centurions from the garrison, the vast majority were the wealthier members of native British *civitates*. The very simplicity and slow development of the majority of early villas make this clear.'[333]

Certainly not all British farms were Romanized, even architecturally; many adhered conservatively and without malice to the Iron Age patterns. The revolution attendant upon the Roman occupation was neither sudden nor accelerated. Most of the archaeological evidence available today suggests that the process of change and assimilation took a long time. Near-by garrison towns and flourishing urban communities no doubt provided the best incentive to new-style living. Tradesmen, the military, enlightened governors and, occasionally, royal visitors were frequently the best champions and promoters of Romanization. M. Trebellius Maximus, Britain's governor from 63 to 69, was worthy predecessor of the paragon Agricola (78–84); both sought to curb the excesses and cruelty often associated with Roman occupation by advocating civic life and cultural synthesis. The appearance of town houses in the earliest phases of Roman Canterbury and Colchester (Camulodunum), the country houses at Lockleys and Park Street, timber-framed houses on flint-and-mortar foundations, are in marked contrast to Iron Age houses of earlier times.

Refinements came to the fore most splendidly during the second century. By then civic squares and public baths, basilicas and temples, paved streets, abundant water supplies and ample drainage facilities, and a measure of security, became the accepted norm of garrison towns and revitalized British centres. Agricola, father-in-law of the Roman historian Tacitus, and subject of his eulogistic biography, mounted a spirited campaign to infuse new culture, to convert hard-nosed army officers into reputable townsmen. Upon retirement from the army, many of them must have invested their savings in suburban properties.

Town life in Britain differed very little in fact from patterns elsewhere in the western provinces. Roman colonial sites would normally adopt the grid plan and centuriation scheme of the homeland. Evidence, apart from Silchester, St Albans (Verulamium), Colchester (Camulodunum) and Wroxeter, and more recently Bath, is undeniably limited but we are probably justified in assuming that the town streets would contain *domus*-style architecture and *tabernae*. First- and second-century house plans at Verulamium are usually rectangular (50–65 feet long, 25–30 feet wide) set at right angles to the streets; the earliest Silchester houses average about 80 × 40 feet. Verulamium's residences frequently contain five or six rooms with one room often floored in yellow concrete, sometimes in *opus signinum*, the rest in clay. After the mid-second century and a catastrophic fire (*c.* 155), private houses at Verulamium attained greater size and more durability, partly no doubt to insure against another holocaust. Flint and mortar appeared in the foundations and lower walls; tiled roofs, murals, mosaics and tessellated pavements were a sign of the new prosperity. 'A Romano-British town-house type had been evolved. Each building seems to have stood in its own grounds, often at the corner of an *insula*, and was L-shaped, or of courtyard plan, consisting of anything from ten to thirty rooms connected by a corridor.'[334] The houses at Silchester were even more pretentious, and of an earlier date: the corridor-verandah might grace three of the four sides and the timber-frame house rested on flint foundations. We are probably safe in assuming that residences in the towns favoured the strip-housing design, that they were long, narrow rectangular buildings, commonly about 50 × 25 feet, with a shop at the front and with living-quarters behind or above. This type of housing responded to the pressure of urban population and the high cost of building lots, particularly in the commercial zones of the community, as buildings today conform to the dictates of traffic and economy.

Shops (*tabernae*) from earliest times were usually of clay applied to a timber framework or simple adobe. They are known best among the military *vici* in the frontier areas.[335] Many of the town houses opened their façades for business on the street, like the houses with shops at Pompeii, Herculaneum and Ostia.

Excavated settlements in Roman Britain are still few in number: Silchester, Caerwent, Colchester, Verulamium, Caistor-by-Norwich, Wroxeter, and Bath, the last two only partially uncovered. Silchester,[336] which has been completely excavated, was a town of some 2,500 to 4,000 persons. After AD 45 the Old Town could display a forum, basilica, public baths, several temples and houses after the Roman plan. Town-planning as such was virtually non-existent in the early community; Hadrian's royal visit no doubt inspired the City Fathers to adopt a regular street system and this entailed the replacement or remodelling of earlier structures. The Antonine city covered an area of 100 acres and its fortifications still survive to the height of 15 feet. The rebuilt baths (c. 350) indicate that urban needs had not declined by then.

Roman Colchester,[337] founded c. AD 50, was the earliest city to be established in the British Isles. The Roman colony numbered 15,000 persons and covered 180 acres. The grid street pattern provided 400 insulae. The temple of the Imperial Cult, built under Claudius, was rebuilt after the Boudiccan sack of AD 61 and Colchester no doubt remained the cultural and religious capital of the province through the Roman occupation. Londinium[338] evidences few traces of the Roman period when the city, like Rome itself, enjoyed Roman protection and favour by reason of its location at the strategic crossing point of the Thames. First as trading centre, then as prosperous communications centre, Londinium gradually attracted the government offices away from Camulodunum. Large (pop. 45,000) and prosperous, London's status was enhanced by the construction of the Governor's Palace at Cripplegate Fort. Continuous occupation and rebuilding have reduced the odds of recovering much besides enigmatic fragments of Roman London; even the destruction of World War II did not enable the archaeologist to recover very much.

Bath (Aquae Sulis),[339] a major therapeutic centre and focus of an important pewter and stone-quarrying industry, was also a bustling market centre, acting as collection depot for grain from the farms of Salisbury Plain. Thirty villas have been discovered within a 10-mile radius of Bath along with remains of some

houses and a hostel within the city. During the late third and
early fourth centuries there was a building boom inside the city
walls, often on virgin sites, suggesting that the villa-owners,
but perhaps not their stewards who remained on the farms,
sought the security of the city's defences.

Noblest of the early country mansions of Roman Britain is the
splendid Flavian palace at Fishbourne,[340] near Chichester, in
Sussex. After accidental discovery in 1960, subsequent excavations, most ably conducted by Barry Cunliffe, produced evidence
of several building phases. The earliest timber building probably
served as a military installation during the invasion period.

64

*Fig. 64   Fishbourne (Sussex). Palace Villa and garden of Cogidubnus in relation to the
modern village's plan. Cunliffe, fig. 31*

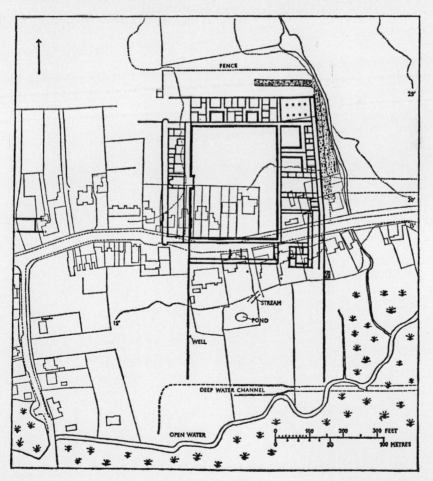
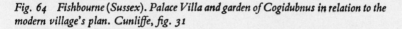

Thereafter, the property entered upon its civilian phase (AD 75) with a stone-built luxurious establishment founded on a platform of clay and stones and covering an area of two acres. The plan was impressive: a large colonnaded courtyard, about 200 feet square, with additional courtyards on the north and east sides, both designed as formal gardens. The central room of the complex, on the higher western range, was approached by a flight of steps from the main court; it evidently served as the audience chamber. This grand establishment was clearly meant to accommodate a person or persons of high rank, probably best identified with Cogidubnus, native client king and faithful servant of Rome who was ennobled by the senatorial rank of *legatus Augusti*. Throughout, the mansion is a masterpiece of decoration: walls of marble veneer from Carrara and Skyros; *opus sectile* floors, and floors of black-and-white mosaic. But most notable is the marvellously landscaped formal garden furnished with paths, hedges, fountains and basins, in a style
49   strikingly reminiscent of the murals of Livia's summer *triclinium* at Prima Porta outside Rome.[341] The plan is familiar, a winged corridor-house; but the portico which is the connecting unit dominates two other colonnaded courts where the living and entertaining quarters were located. The east wing contains the entrance hall and bath-house and the two larger peristyle courts; the west wing has an audience-chamber at the centre and dominates the whole design. Like some Oxford or Cambridge college, this great villa has become the showpiece of Roman Britain, a *pièce de résistance*, a vivid testimonial to the sophistication and high-style of the *ultimi Britanni* who found favour with Rome. Its inspiration was Italian; its design, with the courtyard in front of the hall and main salons, was British-Continental; the construction methods and the landscaped gardens are Rome's contribution to provincial fashion. After several remodellings and adaptations, the villa was eventually destroyed by fire.

'We might, therefore, be justified in regarding a villa as a place in the country belonging to someone who was, in feeling if not actually in origin, a town-dweller. His motives for engaging in agriculture might vary, from the hard economic to the Vergilian romantic, but his house would still be, in its

appointments, *urbs in rure*. The owner would remain at heart a
citizen.'[342] Lullingstone Roman Villa in Kent[343] is a splendid   65
instance of Rivet's definition. Set on an embankment overlooking
the River Darenth, the earliest property consisted of a rather
simple establishment with flint and mortar walls, built no doubt
by some convert to Agricola's programme of Romanization.   69
The house was drastically remodelled *c.* 180 so as to accommodate a bath-suite, a loggia alongside the river, mosaic floors and
painted plaster. The owner, probably from the Mediterranean,
sought to glamorize his modest six-room house with some
modern décor. But as in Campania, where villa properties
changed hands abruptly during political upheavals, the Lullingstone villa-owner no doubt fell foul of the procurator,
Sextus Clodius Albinus, and had to evacuate his riverside retreat.
For almost a century it remained unoccupied. The house was
restored *c.* 280–290, probably by a wealthy farmer who foresaw
rich returns from the broad farmlands in the area and from the
extensive woodlands and pasturage for cattle and horses. But
the fourth-century phase was clearly the apogee of its history.
Remodelled inside and out, the villa assumed the air of a proud
manor house with the dining and reception halls at the centre,

Fig. 65   Lullingstone (Kent). Villa, AD 330–80, plan. Meates, fig. 3

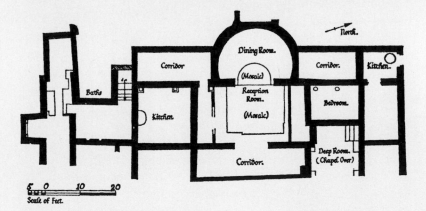

both decorated with polychrome mosaic floors and lighted by windows in the south wall. The bath building, rebuilt *c.* 280, lay at the south end of the mansion; the so-called Deep Room, once devoted to a cult of Water Goddesses, became the sealed repository for two senatorial marble busts, property of the original builder, awesome relics of an earlier dispensation. Some time later, *c.* 350, the owner converted the chambers above the Deep Room into a house-church or chapel-complex. One room, with a frieze of six Christians engaged in prayer, served as the chapel; the antechapel or narthex lay outside. Mystery attaches to the owners and the uses of the chapel. One may perhaps suppose that the villa was used by its owners largely as a summer residence; but the bailiff and retainers must have lived there all the year round, accommodating members of the Christian community in the chapel or house-church, a practical substitute for the basilica provided in towns and cities.

The Lullingstone appointments were luxurious. The reception hall leading to the dining-room had a mosaic floor with a central panel depicting Bellerophon, mounted on Pegasus, delivering the death thrust to Chimaera; the corners were embellished with seasonal deities, with Spring as a young girl with a swallow

70   perched on her shoulder. Beyond lay the apsidal dining-room, with a red tessellated floor. The diner's attention would focus on Europa's abduction by Jupiter in the guise of a bull, with a couplet above alluding to Vergil's *Aeneid*. These main rooms were illuminated by small windows set into the south wall. The baths, linked with the house by a mosaic-floored corridor, provided the normal arrangements and hypocaustic heating. There are no rooms in the single-storey house which were clearly designed as bedrooms, save for a small room where two coin hoards were discovered; the owners probably used the dining couches and the *triclinium* as the master bedroom! The kitchen lay in the north-west corner of the villa. Behind the villa, on a second higher terrace, excavations have revealed traces of two religious buildings, a small circular temple of the second century, later dismantled, and a sizeable mausoleum built to accommodate the lead coffins of two young people, a man and a woman, beneath

69   the square tomb-chamber. The central room entered from the

70 Lullingstone, Kent. Villa, interior rooms, including apsidal
dining-room, view from balcony

71 Llantwit-Major (Glamorgan). Villa and farmyard

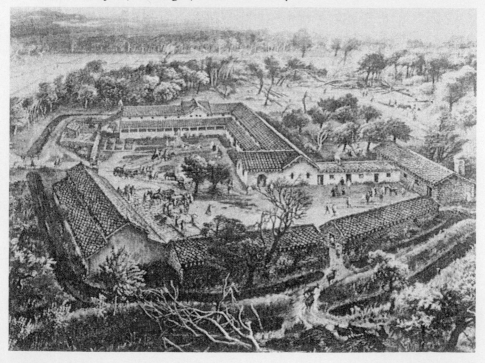

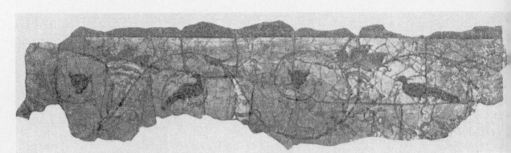

72 St Albans (Verulamium). Peopled scroll mural with pheasants
and panther masks from Blue House Hill

73 Yugoslavia, Split (Spalato). Palace of Diocletian, model

74 Masada, Israel. Air view of Herod's Palace, villa on three
terraces

75 Praeneste. Barberini mosaic, Nile scene in Roman Egypt

76 Carthage. Villa of Squire Julius, mosaic

south had an ambulatory and vault of tufa blocks. With the advent of Christianity, the mausoleum was allowed to deteriorate. After 380 the baths were filled in, the barn became a garage and stable for a short time, and by 400 the declining villa, with the Christian chapel still active, was set afire by barbarians. Alan Sorrell's drawing reminds one forcefully of an Elizabethan farm-house, a long low bungalow with a network of wooden beams and stuccoed walls and terracotta roof tiles, proud property of wealthy landowners who could combine otium and Christian service in the loveliest of settings.

Another country house, at Llantwit-Major, Glamorganshire,[344]   71; 66

Fig. 66   Llantwit-Major (Glamorgan). Villa and dependencies, plan. Nash Williams, fig. 20

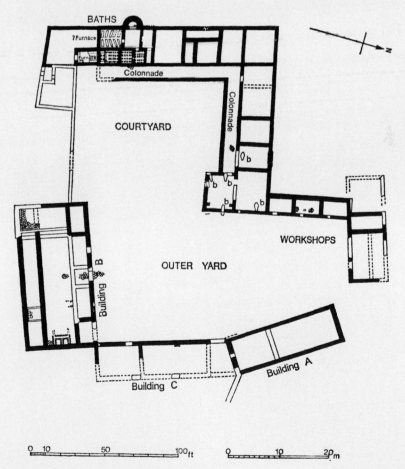

between the forts at Cardiff and Neath, had a fine view to the Bristol Channel less than two miles away. The buildings, excavated between 1938 and 1948, cover an area about 250 feet square. The original timber buildings (c. 180) were superseded by stone constructions (c. 300). They gathered around two courtyards in a rather haphazard fashion, no doubt as a consequence of periodic alteration and reconstruction. The manor house had painted plaster walls, some mosaic floors, and a self-contained bath-suite at the west end of the L-shaped plan. An aisled-house (or basilican-barn) provided accommodation for the farm-hands, the animals and the workshops. When the family occupying the house withdrew c. 350, the servants and hired hands continued to occupy the aisled-house while the main house gradually disintegrated. The baths had a long life in their remodelled fourth-century form but eventually became an iron foundry. The entire property was deserted by c. AD 400.

The aisled-house, found at Llantwit-Major and Ditchley, was probably of Germanic origin although it appears most often in Britain, notably around the Humber and Fens.[345] The earliest example of the aisled-house in England was discovered at Ening (Suffolk) where the original second-century timber building was later rebuilt, partly in stone. Normally two rows of supports divided the interior into a nave and two side aisles. Although designed to provide rooms for the staff, for vehicles, food, draught-animals and agricultural implements, the building could also serve a social function. Landlord and tenants could celebrate and communicate in a building which finds its closest analogy in the medieval hall.

During late Flavian and Antonine times Romano-British farmhouses tended to be simplified versions of the country mansions of Italy, with central heating, mosaic floors and painted walls in the minority of cases. After the third century, a time of turmoil, of dislocation and economic strain, the British economy revived and new standards of living are manifested in the rural houses of England. This twilight prosperity of Britain, exceptional within the Empire, was a direct consequence of the greater stability of the island's fortunes. While Gaul was rent asunder by peasant revolts during the third and fourth centuries, perhaps inducing nervous landowners to invest their native capital in Britain, and while Emperors passed in sudden, drastic succession, Britain's autarky survived the time of strain. The noblemen of England did not forsake the land or renounce their concern for their tenants and when peace and order were restored the country was able to evidence its prosperity freely and expansively. While barbarian marauders and raiders came perilously close to her frontiers and coastal ports, Britain embarked on a vast programme of construction, or repair, embellishment and enlargement with a great burst of extravagance. Capital was plentiful and the Last Hurrah in Roman Britain was hearty and sustained.

During this final period of revival, there was renewed emphasis on creature comforts and delights: hypocausts were no longer confined to one room; mosaic pavements, geometric or figured, and bath-suites were *de rigueur* during this final flowering when Romano-British villas acquired a scale and standard of comfort comparable to Georgian country houses of another age. Layouts remained constant, ranges of buildings clustering around one or more courtyards; but the economic aspect of the country estates never diminished: the pleasure dome never superseded the idea of productive estates. Bignor,[346] for example, in Sussex, has natural boundaries which imply an arable area of almost 2,000 acres along with strips of forest, downs and alluvial marshland for grazing; a single barn on the property could store fodder for fifty-five head of cattle which could be accommodated in the side aisles. Woodchester[347] (Gloucestershire) is a fourth-century seigniorial estate located on high ground with a commodious manor house and farm buildings which are segregated from the main house in a lower court. The situation, near extensive downs, suggests that the landowner raised sheep. The house has a large central dining-room in the main block and heated wings set symmetrically around a large garden court in the style of Fishbourne; the outer court, entered by a triple gateway, has two buildings of the barn-dwelling type joined together. The *triclinium* had a floor mosaic with circular design 25 feet in diameter. The landowner was either a large-scale sheep-rancher or a magnate from near-by Cirencester (Corinnium Dubonnorum) who maintained the Woodchester villa as a luxury-retreat or gentleman's farm.

Life along the walls, in the garrison posts and forts has become an open book as a result of aerial photography and ground detection.[348] Housesteads, on Hadrian's Wall, covered an area at least twice as large as its protective fort. The settlements which clustered around the forts, here as along the *limes* of Germany, are inclined to be rather unsystematic, random developments along the roads which lead to the forts. The buildings are often high-timbered structures, with long narrow *tabernae*, cabarets, and workshops which catered to the needs of the legionaries and their dependants. Trajan's column shows typical settlements outside the walls of forts in the Danubian zone. Chesters (Cilurnum), another shopkeepers' town, has a *vicus* or village development outside the south gate.

Manor houses like Lullingstone survived until the end of the fourth century.[349] By that time, with the withdrawal of Roman arms, and the collapse of the central government, the roads, aqueducts, drains, etc., fell into disrepair and disuse. The Saxons moved into a disintegrating society where the corridor-villas and aisled-houses were fast diminishing; desertion and fire and sword had taken a heavy toll. One may speculate whether or not the Saxons, whose social organization was based on the Great Hall, would have occupied some of the aisled-houses; but perhaps by then, hopelessly isolated, and with their economic and social functions spent, there were none left worth occupying.

British archaeology has not only determined the location and plan of innumerable town houses and villas but has also shed much light on the material background, the sheer mechanics of maintaining a dwelling in Roman times, and not only in Britain but also throughout Western Europe.[350] Life in the insular province does not appear to have differed very significantly from the Gallic or even Italian mode, except that it had a lower profile.

Building materials were fairly constant everywhere. British builders, always masters of clay and timber, with the assistance or counsel of legionary architects, were able to raise two-storeyed city and country mansions with ease.[351] Flint sleeper walls served to elevate the wooden frame some two to three feet above the ground and so reduced the danger of wood-rot. Walls were often 2 feet thick, with quoins of brick or tile, sometimes even carefully dressed stone; occasionally they reveal bonding courses of tile after the Roman style. Thresholds were normally of wood or mortar, but occasionally tile or brick would provide a more durable version. Entrance doors might measure up to 9 or 10 feet in width; internal doors, although here the evidence is somewhat scanty, were anything from 3 to 6 feet wide. Doors were usually massive oak constructions, studded with nails and bronze adornments; they turned on pivots or sometimes leather hinges, and were safeguarded usually with cross bars or locks and keys. Windows, with square or rounded heads, were normally well above street level. The climate of Britain and north-western Europe made window-glass a necessity; the panes, often greenish and semi-transparent, were set into wooden or metallic frames and usually measured about 12 × 8 inches.[352]

Roofs were either thatched, than which no material was more close-fitting, shingled, turf-constructed or tiled. The tiles, one inch thick, were usually rectangular, 16 × 12 inches, and were provided with flanged sides; rounded imbrex tiles covered the joints between the rows of tiles; gable-ends were often decorated with some sort of ornament or finial in either stone or clay.

To judge by the Italian survivals, ceilings were usually plastered, sometimes barrel-vaulted. Where timber was abundant, house-owners may have preferred beams and plank roofing. Romano-British walls were plastered and painted from earliest times and often in garish combinations of primary colours with striped and mottled marble patterns. The interior walls just as frequently seem directly indebted to patterns and vogues of interior decoration at Pompeii, Stabiae, Rome and elsewhere. Several unusual wall designs have been discovered at Verulamium in the remains of a second-century town house:[353] portions of a red ground wall with painted panels containing two candelabra with delicate foliage or spiral decoration and in the centre a blue dove on a perch; a ceiling painting from the same corridor using wheat-ears as a lattice work against a purple ground; and from another corridor, a large sheet of plaster (12 feet long × 5 feet high) with   72 a beautiful peopled scroll design. Against a yellow ground the artist designed a scroll of green and black acanthus leaves and stalks, with interest centring upon alternating pheasants and panther masks with bright highlights; scarlet acanthus buds, visible here in profile, recur elsewhere in Verulamium, and at Cirencester and Dorchester. The Verulamium murals are probably the work of resident interior decorators, immigrants from the Mediterranean, who combined forces with local artists. House-owners, on the eve of applying the first murals or of redecorating, might consult pattern books, as modern householders consult wallpaper collections, to select their favourite subject-matter for motifs. The Verulamium walls actually have reasonably close parallels in Pompeii, in the House of the Tragic Poet and the House of the Second Mosaic Fountain.

The second-century Lullingstone villa had cream walls stippled in red, blue and yellow. The basement room retains traces of three water nymphs in a wall niche, and white walls with a dado of rectangles and lozenges, panels and orange date palms with scarlet fruit. But even more eye-catching are the six Christian figures on the house-chapel walls: all are brightly arrayed and festooned with pearls and are half life-size. The Chi-Rho monogram in red on a white ground appears twice within a brightly coloured wreath; two birds, perched precariously on the ends of ribbons, are intent upon scarlet berries falling from the wreath.[354] The villa at Llantwit-Major underwent two periods of decoration: the first favoured the polychrome incrustation technique of Pompeian Style I; the second preferred crimson and dark blue flecks against a light-blue ground. The catalogue of murals from Romano-British sites contains few surprises.

Although stucco work undoubtedly complemented murals in wealthier British homes, only a modest amount of evidence has been found, certainly nothing to compete with the fine material in the Trier Landesmuseum. However, a Roman house at Gorhambury, excavated between 1955 and 1960, has yielded fragments of a painted cornice and some stucco mouldings from a figured frieze, no doubt grace-notes for a barrel-vaulted room.[355]

Floors in the earlier town houses, and regularly in the country homes, were of clay or chalk or rammed gravel; opus signinum tiles and tesserae appear in second-century town houses and in more affluent country homes; wooden floors, a constant fire hazard and liable to rot, were restricted to ground-level rooms, often in *tabernae*. Mosaic floors, geometric and figured, black-and-white and polychrome, have turned up in rich array. Most splendid and best known are the pavements at Lullingstone, Low Ham and Hinton St Mary.[356]

The Lullingstone mosaics (*supra*) vie for popular interest with the splendid series of Dido and Aeneas scenes from the *frigidarium* of a bath-suite at Low Ham (now in the Castle Museum, Taunton). At Hinton St Mary (Dorset) a large pavement features a bust of Christ at the centre with the Chi-Rho monogram behind his head, the tree of life, hunting scenes, rosettes and pomegranates, and Bellerophon combating the Chimaera, an allegory no doubt of the Christian triumph over evil and death. Mosaic floors from a chapel (?) at Frampton (Dorset), probably the work of the Hinton St Mary mosaicists, depict Neptune with the Chi-Rho monogram. The finest mosaics, whether Christian or pagan in association, derive from the properties, house-chapels and bath-suites of wealthy landowners. At least two conclusions may be drawn: that Christianity in Roman Britain was practised chiefly by the richer landowners; and that the subject matter and compositional schemes, which are often closely paralleled by examples in Gaul and North Africa, derived from pattern books which provided common inspiration for artists, maybe even book illustrators, throughout the Empire.

The larger houses of Roman Britain and of Europe generally contained a minimum of ten or twelve rooms. Heating was a perennial problem. Uusally, where funds were available, house-owners had recourse to hypocaustic or 'radiant' heating in at least one room outside the bath-suite. Otherwise they resorted to braziers with lighted wood-charcoal or tiled open hearths. Wall fireplaces are rare. Boon's capsule description of the hypocaustic system common in Silchester is helpful: 'a cavity is constructed below the floor and connected to a furnace in an outside wall at foundation level. The heat and gases generated here circulated under the floor, warmed it, and passed up small chimney-flues embedded in the walls. The flues were made of box-shaped tiles cramped to the walls and covered by a plastic rendering. How the flues terminated is uncertain, but it seems possible that they were led at right angles through the walls to debouch under the broad eaves of the roof.'[357] Fuel for the furnace must have been fairly abundant: oak, willow, hazel, alder, any kind of combustible debris. Farms with no hypocaustic heating must have resorted to the kitchen as family parlour. Sometimes heated rooms rested directly on solid masonry with criss-crossing heating channels. The Saalburg experiment to determine the efficacy of the system indicated that a room (17 × 15 feet), resting on floor pillars (*suspensurae*), with an eight-inch floor and wall tubes, could be maintained at a constant temperature of 73°F, after firing with charcoal over a day and a half and stoking twice daily.[358] Townsfolk without interior heating in their homes could frequent the public baths, the most democratic of Roman institutions despite Tacitus' strictures (*Agricola*, 21) on their debilitating effects.

Interior lighting during daytime hours came from upper windows (a requirement of corridor-villas), from doorways, and from 'picture-windows' opening on to interior courtyards and peristyle gardens. Otherwise, the darkness could be relieved, if not dispelled, by pottery oil lamps and candles, single or multiple in arrangement.

Water was normally available from district fountains in the cantonal towns and communities, from wells or branch aqueducts in the countryside. Lincoln (Lindum) brought water in from a spring over a mile away, pumping it through a pipe-line sealed in concrete to resist rupture into a reservoir alongside the town wall.[359] Verulamium and Caerwent used distribution pipes of hollowed timber with iron collar joints every four to seven feet. Water could be brought into the homes by clay, lead or even wooden pipes. Although internal plumbing in lower-class homes and on modest farms would be non-existent, middle-class homes and more affluent farms certainly used surplus water to flush their drains; no doubt city-dwellers were permitted to open their sluices at established hours daily. Wroxeter (Viroconium Cornoviorum) had an overflow duct running alongside the main street which provided water to flush the house drains near by. Every major street at Lincoln had stone-constructed sewers to receive the waste from private houses and shops. Refuse and garbage were burnt or dumped into pits within the house block or property.

Interior decoration, stucco-work, painted plaster and mosaic floors might impart an air of elegance and refinement to life in Britain, and in the European provinces generally, but the actual furnishings of the average *domus* or *villa rustica* were probably meagre and pretty uncomfortable.[360] Wooden chairs, stools and benches, wickerwork furniture and cushions were basic; wooden couches, with lathe-turned legs, about a foot high, served as settees, *triclinium* couches, and day-beds; *cubiculum* beds were normally fitted with a headboard and footboard, and were usually upholstered and covered with leather; mattresses, pillows, and blankets made them reasonably comfortable, certainly preferable to the floor during inclement weather. Woven stuffs, brightly coloured coverings, furs and woollen rugs and hangings would add colour and warmth to the interiors. The often riotous colours on interior walls were yet another response to the need for warmth indoors. Imported red glazed Samian ware, local ceramics, Gaulish and Rhenish pewter and silver decorated and brightened side-boards and dining tables.[361]

While Augustus was reorganizing Gaul, his stepsons, Tiberius and Drusus, set about subjugating the Alpine territories as a protective measure against invaders and as safeguard for com-munications with the west, north and east. Raetia-Vindelicia and Noricum were incorporated into the empire in 15 BC. Illyricum on the Dalmatian coast was organized as an Imperial province in 11 BC, as was Pannonia, roughly the territory of modern Hungary, a year or two later.

The defeat of Quinctilius Varus, commander of the Rhine legions, in the Barenau–Wiehengebirge area in AD 9, was a setback for Augustus' imperial designs against the Germans.[362] Arminius, a one-time auxiliary in the Roman army, liberation leader of the Cherusci and other militant Germans, gave Augustus serious misgivings about further aggression in the north. Legionary commands had to be stationed along the west bank of the Rhine; Pannonia needed three legions to protect its Danubian frontier; Illyricum required two. Colonies like Augusta Vindelicorum

(Augsburg), and military bases, like Castra Regina (Regensburg) were planted in the newly organized territories. The Celtic and Illyrian natives, like the Britons overseas, were organized into cantonal communities (*civitates*) which had a strong appeal for Italian immigrants. Aquileia at the head of the Adriatic became the commercial bridge for Noric and Rhaetian merchandise and for world imports into the Alpine region. The iron ores of Styria and Noric steel were in demand in Imperial times.

The Dalmatian coastline had been a favourite resort of Italian traders and immigrants from late Republican times and a major objective of Augustan arms.[363] Salona, Iader and Narona were virtually Italian cities transplanted to congenial and productive terrain. Although mining and recruitment for the auxiliary forces were Rome's main interests in the area, the military establishments along the Save and Drave river valleys became the nucleus for many of the great cities of later time: Emona (Ljubljana), Siscia (Sisak) and Srimska Mitrovica (Sirmium), one of the Tetrarchic capitals of Diocletian's reorganized Empire, were all originally Roman military colonies.

Unfortunately, the remains of Roman domestic architecture in the Danubian provinces and the Balkans have, at least until recently, been sadly neglected. The frontier communities of Aquincum, near Budapest, and Carnuntum, 25 miles from Vienna, are notable exceptions; so too are the villas of Pannonia (Hungary) which were admirably described and documented by by Mrs B. Thomas.[364] Generally speaking, residential layouts in Noricum (Austria), Pannonia and Moesia on the lower Danube are heavily indebted to Italic patterns and to the defensive style of 'castrum' architecture which became a characteristic of these restive areas. The Italic plan is neither unexpected nor unreasonable by virtue of comparable climatic and topographical conditions. The influx of Italian traders and legionaries virtually determined the course of development. Dacia (Romania), Trajan's celebrated conquest across the Danube (AD 101–106), retains its Romance tongue in a Baltic environment but evidences little of architectural moment for this study. However, the resurgence of archaeology in Romania gives promise of renewed activity and more scientific documentation for the future.[365]

The Pannonian villas are concentrated largely in the lake country of Balaton and Neusiedel, in the Leitha valley, and in the territories bounded by the Drave and Danube or the Drave and Save rivers.[366] The Lake Neusiedel villas, mostly retirement homes for veterans of the wars with the Marcomanni at the close of the second century, are heavily indebted to Italian peristyle- and porticus-villa plans. Elsewhere the homes of wealthy aristo- crats, of equestrian landlords and merchant princes, show the influence of Rome's Asiatic provinces, the source, no doubt, of much of their wealth and sometimes their native habitat. Notable examples of first- and second-century villas in Pannonia are visible at Baláca, Tac-Fövenypuszta, and Eisenstadt-Gölbe- säcken. Hungarian archaeologists have also unearthed impressive mansions along the *limes* – the defensive line and highway – planted, for security reasons in the vicinity of *castella*, particularly at Brigetio and Aquincum. All were, interestingly enough, the properties of Syrians who served in the Imperial legions. Atrium- style houses have also appeared in urban contexts, at Eisenstadt and at Gyulafirátót-Pogánytelek.

Native farmers and land-holders, following the pattern else- where in Western Europe, wavered between acceptance and outright rejection of Roman domestic forms and methods of construction. However, between AD 150 and 200, the corridor- villa, almost certainly imported from the Rhine valley, made significant inroads into Pannonia and Noricum. The repertoire, rich in variants wherever it appeared, is similar to that of Western Europe and North Africa. The element of insecurity, an in- escapable fact of provincial life during the third century and later, induced isolated land-holders, often tenant farmers, to seek compensating succour from the proprietors of large estates in their environs. The fortified estate at Sümeg, near Lake Balaton, is a walled construction with four turrets. It faces on to a large courtyard furnished with service and residential buildings, some with hypocaustic heating! The main house, two storeys high on the north, east and south sides, is typical of the grand- style villas elsewhere during the Late Empire. Another, at Hosszúhetény, near modern Pécs, responds in similar fashion to the invasion menace of the Tetrarchic era. This splendid mansion, of apsidal design with sturdy house-walls, faces on to a large open courtyard to which access is gained through a turreted portal. Here, as elsewhere, the local peasantry placed their hopes for safety and protection in perilous times. Of the hundred or more villas in Hungary, none is more impressive than Parndorf between the Danube and Lake Neusiedel.[367] Although garish colours, inside and out, make the villa something of an artistic nightmare, the 30-acre extent of the property, the sheer size of the villa, with thirty-four rooms, all heated, and its long history, a span of over two centuries, make it a memorable site. Carnuntum, 10 miles north, was undoubtedly the market town for the produce of the Parndorf estate. The Roman villa at Katsch (Chatissa)[368] in Upper Styria (Noricum) is a corridor-villa with the canonical courtyard, farm buildings and service sheds; it fell to the Marcomanni, Marcus Aurelius' foes, after AD 160.

Civilians resident in Aquincum (Hungary)[369] and Carnuntum[370] (Austria) lived in weather-resistant stone and timber houses, almost invariably single-storeyed. The corridor-type house, with an expansive timber verandah, was the favoured form among the middle class and city gentry. Patterns of accommodation, probably the daily regimen, were incontestably Roman: 'window-glass, painted wall-plaster and moulded stucco, an occasional floor mosaic, and regularly one room with central heating'.[371]

The early second-century Governor's Palace at Aquincum (near Budapest) had contemporary rounded towers built into the walls of its main façade. The impressive courtyard provided residential and bathing accommodations on the north side, storage and workrooms on the south, and a small temple for the Imperial cult in the centre. The corridor-style mansion, dominating the court on its east side, housed the state rooms, a central audience-chamber, and balanced suites with radiant heating and plumbing. The Legate's residence at Aquincum is similar to those at Dura-Europos and Sirmium and foreshadows the palace of Diocletian at Split.

The strategic importance of Pannonia increased during the reign of Constantine and resulted in the construction of a number of Imperial residences in this notably Christian sector. The reign of Valentinian (364–375) was a prelude to new invasions and large-scale devastation throughout most of Pannonia except for Sopianae, north of the River Save. When Attila became master of the province, his palace which surmounted Roman ruins provided inspiration for later barbaric rulers, brutes like Arpad and Kuzsan, to seek at least temporary accommodation in abandoned villas in the same province.

The province of Illyricum offers important remains of urban and rural domestic architecture, the most notable, of course, being the palace of Diocletian at Split, but Doclea, near the Albanian frontier, also has an impressive town-house opposite the forum and second-century basilica. The rectangular mansion (98 × 75 feet) is organized round a central court; it has twenty rooms, a bath-suite with hypocaustic installations and a *laconicum* (dry-heat room), and several religious structures. The house has been assigned on reasonable grounds to the Flavii, a wealthy family responsible for the construction of the forum.

City residences near Salona were conditioned by the colonial grid which was largely obliterated during Christian times. To judge by their outline, the wealthier citizens lived in rectangular atrium-style houses with up-to-date amenities: bathing facilities, mosaic floors, wall-plaster, radiant heating and occasionally private water lines drawing on the municipal reservoirs. More town houses, ranging from the first to the fourth century in date, have been unearthed at Zadar (Iader), Asseria, and Domavia. Handsome *villae rusticae* have been found at Dretwlj, Tastovčići (the Papian estate), and Strupnić; Ljušina, near Bosanska Krupa, has a large-scale mansion of twenty or so rooms, including an apsidal chamber, all grouped round the three sides of an open courtyard.

Diocletian's 'dream palace' was a geometrical design, as four-square and schematic as his reconstructed Empire. His radical reform of the Empire, a division into East and West, and his system of four rulers, two Augusti and two Caesares, was a bureaucratic solution to the growing problem of army commands, Imperial succession and inflation. The edicts and measures required by the reorganization are hardly germane to our study but the effects had weighed heavily on provincial life during the

73

fourth and fifth centuries. Land-holding remained largely the prerogative of the wealthy during the Tetrarchic Period: the senatorial class and newly-rich members of the goverment bureaux held vast estates; the local magnates, the decurional class, still based their wealth and prestige on their property holdings; the Church gradually accumulated large estates as well; but the small-farmer class vanished under the wave of taxation and imperial encroachment along with their private holdings. Large estates, throughout the Empire, most obviously in North Africa, Germany, France and even Italy, continued to support free tenants and *coloni*, hired hands who as a consequence of Diocletian's census were virtually serfs, unable to leave the land except under special conditions.

Diocletian's reform brought into being four new western capitals: Trier (Augusta Treverorum), Milan (Mediolanum), Ravenna, and Sirmium; the eastern capital was established first at Nicomedia (Izmit), later at Byzantium, renamed Constantinople by his Christian successor. The two Augusti, Diocletian and Maximian, abdicated in 305. Although both were Illyrian-born, Maximian probably made his retirement home in Sicily while Diocletian chose to 'fade away' in his fortress-palace at Split.[372]

53

The palace, remarkably preserved in its modern context, combines the features of a *porticus*-villa with those of the commandant's quarters in a military establishment.[373] The building materials accentuate the massive scale and defensive character of the palace: limestone masonry, concrete domes and marble columns. The plan of the walled estate departs perceptibly from rigid regularity: the south side, overlooking the sea, measures 600 feet, the north side 575 feet, and the east and west sides, 720 feet. Square and octagonal towers accentuated the fortress-like character of the architectural design. The main gates, which were located on the two long sides and on the north (Porta Aurea), admitted visitors to axial colonnaded streets which crossed at the centre. The Imperial quarters were perched on the south side to take full advantage of the marvellous sea view. The southern complex contained an Imperial mausoleum replete with four antique Egyptian sphinxes, and on the opposite

67

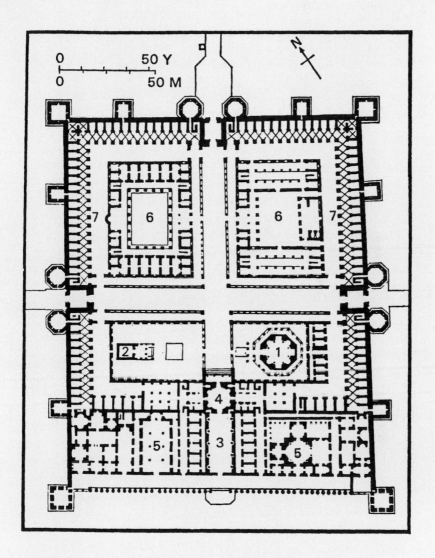

Fig. 67 *Yugoslavia, Split (Spalato). Palace of Diocletian, plan. W. F. and R. K.*
Swan (Hellenic) Ltd., showing: 1 *emperor's mausoleum;* 2 *temple;* 3 *great hall;*
4 *domed vestibule,* 5 *emperor's apartments;* 6 *residential blocks;* 7 *quarters for the guards*

(western) side, a Temple of Jupiter (now a Baptistery) and two rotundas of indeterminate use. A gallery with a rhythmic arcade and columnar screen and three small loggias crowned the southern walls. The seaward side offered no major access to the palace, only a modest landing. The terraced apartments contained an audience-chamber on the north–south axis with a corridor-gallery behind. Two large halls rose on either side of the central suite, a basilical audience hall on the west, and a domed banqueting hall on the east. Private apartments and a bath-suite lay beyond the larger facilities and completed the palace design.

This marriage of villa and *castrum* was no isolated phenomenon. The commandant's quarters, originally a leather tent at the centre of the *castrum*, had gradually yielded to more suitably accommodating designs in wood and stone. The amenities befitting the Legate's rank, here the Imperial presence, were richly provided: hypocaustic heating, mosaics and wall-paintings, banqueting and reception halls, and slave quarters.

Comparable, but less grandiose forms appear in the palace of the Severan Dux Ripae at Dura-Europos, the Governor's Praetorium at Cologne (Colonia Agrippinensis), Pfalzel near Trier, and the pre-Constantinian palace in Trier itself, at Volubilis in Mauretania Tingitana, Vetera (Xanten) on the Rhine, Aquincum and Carnuntum, where Marcus Aurelius had his headquarters from 171 to 173, and at Philippopolis (Sheba) in southern Syria. The Governor's Palace at Philippopolis, where Philip the Arab (244–249) was born, has often been advanced as a parallel, even as a model for Diocletian's version at Split. A much more likely precedent and model exists in Diocletian's palace at Antioch, a grandiose construction blossoming within the fortress of Valerian (253–259) on the island opposite the Asiatic megalopolis.[374]

Architectural historians have detected a tidy combination of western and eastern, particularly Syrian, elements in the Dalmatian palace. The architects – perhaps Zotikos was one – showed their preference for Hellenistic over Italic forms in the splendid ceremonial design of the palace; their more immediate precedents lay in the Antonine Age and their inheritors among the Byzantines. The projecting towers recall the villa forms of earlier, as well as contemporary, villa designs; the octagonal mausoleum with its circular interior, the arches of the water-front gallery, which recall the Porta Nigra at Trier, and the apsidal audience hall, are all familiar elements in Western architecture. But the details of the gates and columns are manifestly Syrian inasmuch as they recall the Temple of Dionysus at Baalbek (Lebanon). Diocletian's palace, Robert Adams' resort for eighteenth-century architectural elements and designs, combines elements of two worlds in a dramatic and harmonious fashion, and Diocletian died there in 315 with greater serenity than many who preceded and followed after him.

CHAPTER VIII

EASTERN PROVINCES AND NORTH AFRICA

FROM TIME IMMEMORIAL, the patterns of housing and town planning in the Eastern Mediterranean and Aegean Turkey had affected and controlled other parts of the Mediterranean world, near and far. Just as Mycenaean palaces probably owed some measure of inspiration to the *megara* of Asiatic rulers, so also temple forms and the earliest orders are Oriental in their inspiration and earliest uses. Etruscan town plans at Marzabotto and Orvieto, even the *Etrusca disciplina* so basic to Etruscan religion and cult practice, owe much to the styles of organized living which evolved in Asia Minor, styles which were exported to the west by historical personalities like Hippodamus of Miletus and by countless others who remain nameless. Axiality and symmetry, hallmarks of Etruscan and Roman civic centres and religious sanctuaries and equally of their house plans, derive from a medley of elements – native Italic, Villanovan, and undoubtedly Eastern Mediterranean. The designs of Hellenistic domestic architecture, peristyle-houses and palaces, are the visible embodiments of Eastern forms. Their transfer and importation to Italy by successful commanders and aspiring commercial magnates are reflected in the city mansions of Pompeii and Herculaneum and in the public buildings of Republican Rome. And the influence did not cease with the Republic because infusions from Hellenistic Egypt, from Antioch and Seleucia, from Pergamum, Cos, Rhodes, and Ephesus appear repeatedly in monuments of the first century BC and in the grandiose fora of Vespasian and Trajan in later times. It is not incidental that the names of Roman architects so frequently betray Oriental origins.[375]

Rome's Eastern Empire was initially an outgrowth of the Punic Wars. Although her earlier relations with the federal leagues and Macedonian rulers were charged with humanity and a genuine desire for peaceful relations without imperial obligations, the role of liberator of the Greeks from the demands of the Macedonian monarchy eventually led Rome to organize Macedonia as a province in 146. Antiochus III of Syria shared the same treatment as Macedonia and with the break-up of the royal families, the heirs to Alexander's conquests and imperial arrangements, Rome soon became mistress of a considerable empire: Asia, the Pergamene kingdom of the Attalids, in 133, and Cilicia in c. 100 BC; and after the wars with Mithradates, self-styled and enormously successful champion of the Asiatics against Roman rule, there were Bithynia-Pontus, Cilicia and Syria, all acquired and expertly organized by Pompey in 63. Cyprus was added to Cilicia in 58. Defensive and aggressive imperialism became confused; Rome's meddlings in international politics eventually yielded an Eastern empire rich in resources, expert and persistent in industry and commerce, and the centre and birthplace of popular religious cults. From the time of the conquest, and even before, there was a constant stream of natives from the Eastern Mediterranean to the West, émigrés who came as sailors, traders, businessmen and (less freely) soldiers to seek their fortunes and find new homes in chillier but more secure lands of opportunity.

Roman Greece, including Macedonia and Achaea (27 BC), the peninsular territory of the Peloponnese, played only a modest imperial role in comparison with the wealthier provinces of the East.[376] Although Athens remained an educational and tourist haven and Greek exports of marble, honey and wine were avidly sought after in the Western empire, the general impression is that Greece had become a sequestered, reasonably cultured backwater. There is a strikingly meagre record of housing in Greek and Roman times. Apart from Corinth,[377] an important administrative centre, pleasure resort and emporium, Philippi in the north, and some areas of western Greece and the Peloponnese, the number of excavated and adequately published Roman houses and villas is amazingly small, given the proximity of Greece to Italy and the Eastern provinces and the reasonably good conditions for agriculture. Serious study of the surface remains is desperately needed along with a careful compilation and examination of earlier finds.

In Aegean Turkey, for example at Priene,[378] a city exceptional for its Hellenistic town houses, and at Miletus,[379] wealthier citizens could rebuild existing older houses or update their interiors merely by uniting two houses into one. The *megaron* plan, characteristic of Priene's houses, could easily be transformed into a peristyle plan by such a marriage. And there would ensue the advantages of better light and air circulation. In addition, consonant with the Eastern traditions, it would be possible to isolate the male apartments from the wing reserved for the women and children.

Termessos, some 20 miles north-west of Antalya on the southern coast of Turkey, enjoyed special favour during the Roman period as 'friends and allies' of the Roman people, entitled to 'formulate their own laws'. The so-called Founder's House on the site has an impressive front door, ennobled with Doric pillars, on its west façade which leads into an *impluviate* atrium reception area similar to those encountered in Delian and Campanian house plans. To the east of Antalya excavators have found impressive evidence of Roman building at Side[380] during the second and third centuries. Two peristyle houses, both products of the late Hellenistic period, continued in use under Roman rule, one in conjunction with streetside shops. Both houses were abandoned during the fourth century but were reactivated during the fifth and sixth centuries when Side became the centre of a diocese.

Undoubtedly the most exciting Roman house finds in Asia Minor appear at Ephesus. This ancient planned city, 'metropolis' of Asia (i.e. Ionia), prospered mightily under Rome during the first and second centuries. Ephesus regained her earlier commercial prosperity and controlled the banking affairs of all of western Anatolia. Although the pioneer excavations were those of the British architect, J. T. Wood, in 1869, followed by those of D. G. Hogarth for the British Museum, the major recovery of the celebrated site since 1895 is owing to the persistence and expertise of the Austrian Archaeological Institute, most recently to Franz Miltner, Fritz Eichler and Hermann Vetters.[381] Two remarkable *insulae* have been unearthed of late on the slopes of Mount Koressos (Bülbüldãg) opposite the Temple of Hadrian.[382] The blocks are separated by a stepped passageway more than 9 feet wide which starts at street level and mounts the terraced hillside. Beneath the steps the civil engineers of Ephesus designed a vaulted drainage channel, almost 6 feet high, to service the apartment blocks. The same paving covered the clay piping which conveyed water, diverted through branch pipes, into the apartments at every level. Both *insulae* were built during the first century AD but underwent numerous rebuildings down to the seventh century. The eastern block, which conforms to three levels, is of a trapezoidal design, 48 yards wide and 82 yards deep, with a streetside 60 yards wide. The ground floor of the *insula*, facing on to the Street of the Kuretes, offers twelve rectangular vaulted shops, one of them a *thermopolium*. The masking colonnade is decorated with mosaic paving of the fifth

68

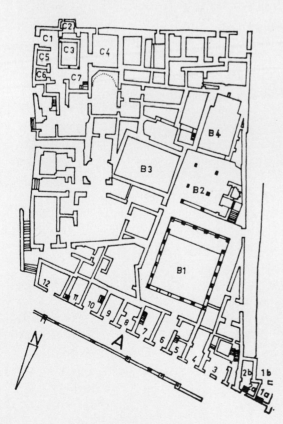

Fig. 68 *Ephesus, slopes of Bülbüldãg, eastern insula, plan. Akurgal, fig. 169*

century AD. A long corridor, opening off the stepped passageway or alley, provides access to the cross-vaulted rooms above the shops. Rectangular windows in the ceiling of the corridor provided light and ventilation for these interior rooms which were obviously the *cenacula* or *pergulae* of the working class, modest garrets which were once thought to be peculiar to Roman *tabernae* and apartment buildings, but which are now revealed as patterns of metropolitan accommodation in Asia Minor, certainly as early as the first century AD and no doubt earlier.[383] One may reasonably suppose that the *taberna-pergula* pattern, accepted into the Roman architectural repertoire in Hellenistic times, found its inspiration in the bazaars and skyscrapers of cities on the Eastern Aegean. The merging of commercial interests with domestic arrangements, a style which has become deeply ingrained in European multiple-storey housing, undoubtedly derives from the East.

Largest and most impressive of the several house components of the *insula* is a two-storeyed mansion (B 1–14) on the second terrace, rising above the barrel- and cross-vaulting of the *tabernae* one and half storeys below. The original house was restored after an earthquake during the first century and underwent even more serious renovations during the reign of Diocletian (*c.* AD 300) when the whole interior was faced with coloured marble revetments and a fountain was installed in the southern part of the peristyle. The entrance vestibule, off the alleyway, led into a peristyle (B 1) with twenty-four blue marble Ionic columns (73 × 62 feet). Off the peristyle corridor and up a flight of stairs is a large room (B 2) with a ceiling supported by four columns, undoubtedly the *oecus* of the patrician establishment. Off the *oecus* lies the dining-room (B 3), identified as the *cenatorium equestre*, 'baronial dining hall', with a fountain installed during the Severan period. The décor and appointments in both the peristyle and the dining-room suggest that the house-owner was a wealthy, influential citizen of Ephesus in Severan times. A portrait of the Emperor Commodus (180–192) and a Carrara portrait-herm of a *grande dome* of the Severan royal house (193–235) share the limelight with classicizing double-herms and copies of Boëthius' sentimental groups of children with a pet bird or hare. The dining-room, originally accessible from the *oecus* and from the southern rooms, was closed off when the walls were redecorated *c.* 300 in a style recalling Second Pompeian but with a heightened baroque emphasis. The closest parallels for this style of decoration are found in the Imperial Palace at Thessalonica and in the Basilica of Junius Bassus at Rome. At the same time the peristyle was modernized with *opus sectile* marble paving and new capitals which are similar to those in the Constantinian Baths at Trier. The room to the south of the *oecus*, originally a barrel-vaulted chamber, later groin-vaulted, has been identified as a private basilica catering to the needs of the owner. The remainder of the *insula*, on its eastern side, at the second and third levels, accommodated smaller middle-class units (C 1-7) which opened off the alley to the east.

The second Ephesian block, the larger one, like its eastern 69 neighbour, conforms to the same terrace levels and water system. Five units, all dating from the first century AD, but repeatedly remodelled, cluster within the great complex. The south-eastern corner of the block is occupied by a peristyle unit (A 1-16) with twelve rooms on the ground floor and a second storey. The apartment underwent alterations during the second century which both enlarged and modernized the interior. The entrance vestibule (*prothyron*) (A 1) appears at the third terrace level at the foot of a flight of steps leading from the alley. The vestibule led directly into the peristyle, a pleasant open-air zone which was richly decorated with frescoed walls and an ornamental mosaic floor and fountain. A second-century pastoral scene replaced the original figured mural. The rooms off the peristyle were also richly decorated with frescoes of floral groupings and *erotes* (A 10, 11), and with mosaic floors and wall paintings (A 3). The high-ceilinged salon (A 3) east of the peristyle was a veritable art gallery of subject-matter murals inspired by Euripides and Menander, with depictions of the struggle of Hercules and Achelous for Deianeira (*c.* AD 175-200). Three barrel-vaulted rooms (A 4-6) with fourth-century frescoes lie above the peri-style-pinacotheca level, one of them probably a summer *triclinium* with a view over the peristyle. A bathroom with hypocaustic installations (A 8) and an adjoining kitchen (A 13) complete

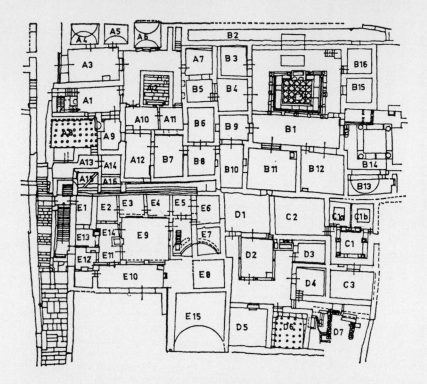

Fig. 69 Ephesus, slopes of Bülbüldäg, western insula, plan. Akurgal, fig. 170

the arrangements of this luxury apartment. Another two-
storeyed peristyle unit (B 1–16) lies in the south-west corner of
the *insula*. The peristyle (B 1) with its Corinthian colonnade and
frescoed walls provided access, light and ventilation for at least
seven rooms (B 3, 4, 9 (10), 11, 12, 15, 16), many of them decorated with floor mosaics (B 3–8), others (B 9, 10) with wall
frescoes of the Nine Muses. Several rooms (B 12–16) are decorated with late fourth- or early fifth-century murals commissioned after the destructive earthquake of 358 or 368. The
spacious kitchen (B 14) has a central basin with four columns.
The north-west corner of the block contains another peristyle
house (C 1–3) with fresco paintings of Apollo with the Nine
Muses and Sappho from the period of Diocletian (C 2), and a
late-style floor mosaic (C 3). The peristyle (C 1) has a figured
floor mosaic dating from the third century surmounting an
earlier geometric design. Another peristyle unit (D 1–7) had

frescoed portraits of the philosophers Cheilon and Socrates in the peristyle (D 1) dating from *c.* AD 100–150. A bathroom (D 6) with hypocaustic arrangements lies on the ground level north of the peristyle court and its fountain installations. A fifth unit (E 1–15), another two-storey design, lies in the north-east corner of the *insula* with entry from the stepped alley. The apartment began as a peristyle *domus* but, during a period of alterations, the open space was roofed over (E 9) for use as a large hall. A ground-level room (E 15) of apsidal design with barrel-vaulting no doubt served as a private basilica after the second century. The first-century frescoes of the peristyle walls (E 9) featured a series of philosophers set within framed panels against a red background. An excellent likeness of Socrates discovered *in situ* is now in the Selçuk Museum.[384]

Strabo, writing in Augustan times (*c.* 25 BC), states that the citizenry of Babylon in his time responded to the pressure of population by building multiple-storey vaulted houses, and that multi-level housing was also to be encountered at Tyre and Aradus.[385] Ephesus offers yet another, even more decisive antecedent for the Roman *insulae* in its apartment blocks containing several units of peristyle design and with shops along the street. Rome undoubtedly contributed heavily to the development of the *insula* – garden courts, common stair-wells and more elaborate stores – but the pattern was Eastern and the transfer to Italy owed everything to the immigration of persons and ideas to the West.

After the death of Herod the Great in 4 BC and the banishment of his successor, Archelaus, to Gallic Vienne in AD 6, Augustus recognized Judaea as a province of the Roman Empire. The country was riddled with dissension and class divisions. The wealthy landowners saw Rome as guarantor of their social position and their bank accounts; the Sadducees and Pharisees formed a theocratic society bound to collide with emperor-worship; the Zealots, the national extremists, and the antipathy between Jew and Gentile gave no promise of lasting peace for the Roman administration. Pontius Pilate, enmeshed in circumstances no man could have foretold or obviated, was probably more enlightened than many who made up the exasperated, disillusioned and corrupt company of senior administrators in Judaea. Concessions were made on both sides, but the smouldering resentment flared up in AD 66. Hopes for peace and reconciliation were dispelled when the extremists and fanatics gained control. Vespasian laid siege to Jerusalem in 68, but the death of Nero and the confusion of the next year or so interrupted the Roman campaign. Titus, Vespasian's son and heir, finally reduced the city and destroyed the temple in May of 70. The final reduction of Judaea came in 73 with the fall of Masada. The Arch of Titus in the Roman Forum, raised piously by Titus' brother, Domitian, in AD 82, offers a pictorial record in stone of Titus' triumphal procession in Rome in the early summer of 71 after the capture of Jerusalem and the despoiling of the Temple.

Herod's palace-villa at Masada, excavated recently by Yigael Yadin, has aroused considerable interest and acclaim for a number of reasons, principally for its inspirational value to the new nation of Israel and for its architectural merits.[386] The ruins today, which are distributed over three terraces, subscribe faithfully to the eyewitness account of Josephus, the Jewish historian of the conquest.[387] The uppermost terrace supports the so-called Northern Palace, a nine-room residence of unexpectedly modest design and furnishing, a public bath-building, a semicircular colonnaded terrace, storerooms and cisterns. The restrictions of the terrain imposed great obstacles upon the construction engineers who managed, nevertheless, to design a residence which would conform not only to the exigencies and marvels of the site but also to the demands for security. The upper terrace is also the only spot on Masada where even a modicum of shade or refuge can be found against the searing sun and the rabid south wind. The middle terrace, 60 to 70 feet below, supports a circular pavilion with a covered portico behind. On the lowest terrace, 40 to 50 feet below, a windowless belvedere provided the ultimate resort for sequestered relaxation with a gorgeous view of the valley. Herod's engineers countered the challenge of the narrow limits of this lowermost terrace by constructing an artificial platform on the lip of the abyss, a man-made foundation which rested on supporting walls sometimes 80 feet high. The *diaeta* or belvedere partly recalls forms used conventionally in

74

Campanian villas by the sea, particularly in the Augustan villa at Damecuta and in the great *aula* of Tiberius' Villa Jovis on Capri. *44, 48*

A larger palace rises at the western edge of the Masada rock, close to the ramp which the Romans finally succeeded in constructing at the close of the protracted siege. This second palace provides residential quarters on the south-east, service areas on the north, storerooms, reception areas, and a throne-room. The mosaic floors resemble geometric versions on Delos, with motifs of olive branches, pomegranates, fig and vine leaves, etc. Ward-Perkins remarks that 'this was a late Hellenistic architecture with strong Italian overtones – just what one would have expected from a patron of Herod's known tastes and upbringing'.[388] No one can visit this awesome site without experiencing mixed emotions, sympathy for the courageous resistance and suicidal courage of the Jewish extremists, respect for the methodical Roman siege tactics, and admiration for the engineering virtuosity of the palace builders. The Herodian villa at Wadi Qelt, outside Jericho,[389] matches Cogidubnus' palace at Fishbourne (Sussex) in scale and richness of decoration, but no palace in the Roman Empire can match Herod's palace at Masada.

Houses of much simpler dimension have been found throughout Syria.[390] The village houses of Taqle, for instance, offer a basic one-room module, sometimes partitioned by walls or columns, more often, no doubt, with curtains and movable screens, and with a tendency to open up along one side, usually the south. Man and beast in all likelihood shared the same roof. When triply divided these simple *liwan* forms are strikingly similar to the tripartite arrangements of Etruscan tombs and houses, ancestors of the *atrium-tablinum-alae* arrangements of Roman dwellings. Other house forms have been unearthed at Banaqfur (first century AD) and at Benabil (second century AD) where double porticoes served as façade for two-storeyed dwellings, sometimes with a courtyard in front for storage buildings and workshops. Often, throughout Asia Minor, landed estates would include a tower of two or three storeys to enable the landlord to keep an eye on his property and fieldworkers and to provide additional storage and housing space. During the third and fourth centuries country houses, mounted on hills, sought maximum security behind walled enclosures.

Excavations at Antioch, at Seleucia-Pieria, the port of Antioch, and throughout north-west Syria, reveal a preference for single-storey peristyle houses during the late second and third centuries.[391] The *triclinium*, main focus of the axial design, often appears at the end of a colonnaded courtyard in a manner not unlike the lovely House of Cupid and Psyche at Ostia, or on an infinitely more modest scale, an Arabic Alhambra. The mosaic floors of Antioch also offer fine testimony to the verdict of Ammianus Marcellinus on Antioch as *orientis apicem pulcrum*, 'fair crown of the Orient'.[392] Houses of every description and class, from modest establishment to mansion, added colour and interest to their interiors by locating mosaics adroitly throughout the house plan.[393] The House of the Boat of Psyche, at Daphne, is a fairly standard suburban villa of the second or third centuries. The entrance colonnade was flanked by five ornamental niches containing pools of water lined with mosaics; the *triclinium* and three additional rooms had mosaic pavements. Nearly every house in Antioch or the suburbs contained geometric, floral, or figured pavements, some of them copies of Old Masters, other highlighting episodes from classical literature and mythology, some of them clearly allegorical. Unlike carpets or rugs, which might be used as complements for ceremonial uses or to lessen the winter's chill, they supplied a permanent flooring which would be cool in summertime, easily swabbed and brightened by the use of water in a number of settings, in *piscinae*, reflecting pools and fountains. Throughout southern Syria, at Petra, Jerash (Gerasa), Bostra, and Antioch, builders frequently introduced rooms roofed with transverse arches into the rectangular house design to provide greater height and coolness for the interior. Habitats with two storeys often resorted to external stone staircases in the manner of modern Aegean architecture.

Septimius Severus, an African from Lepcis Magna and one-time governor of Pannonia, was proclaimed emperor in AD 193.[394] His wars to consolidate his power cost the Empire dearly: Antioch was captured and looted and lost its primacy in Syria to Laodicea, and ancient Byzantium was levelled. Septimius remembered Trajan's conquests in the East, his extension of the Empire to include Dacia, Armenia and Mesopotamia as provinces but shrugged off remembrance of Trajan's failure to contain the Parthians for longer than his lifetime. However, Septimius was able to recapture Ctesiphon (Trajan's prize in 116) and declared Mesopotamia a Roman province once more, with two legions as garrison. After Septimius Severus' death at York (Eburacum), his son, Caracalla (211–217), launched another Parthian War, but was murdered near Carrhae by the prefect of the praetorian guard, Macrinus, the first equestrian emperor (217–218). Elagabalus (218–222), Macrinus' unlikely successor – a thirteen-year-old Syrian priest of Baal was something of a novelty as emperor – was soon replaced by his cousin, Alexander Severus (222–235). The Severan dynasty, in power for almost forty years, sought to maintain Septimius' conquests in the East, conquests which were richly signalized in the triple arch at the west end of the Forum Romanum.

Housing in the Middle East, along the frontier territory of the Tigris and Euphrates river valleys, shows nothing distinctive before the advent of Roman arms, particularly those of the Severan emperors. The basic adobe house adhered to the flat roof which provided a cool dormitory space during the hottest season, and favoured a heterogeneous cluster of rooms around a central court where draught animals and camels might be stabled at nightfall. One may find their counterparts today outside any Iranian or Syrian desert community.[395]

The Yale University excavations at Dura-Europos on the Euphrates unearthed something far more splendid, the remains of a third-century palace, built under Elagabalus or Alexander Severus, probably the former.[396] Here the Emperor's Legate, the   70 Dux Ripae, like the Governor at Aquincum on the Danube, enjoyed the optimum of European amenities amid alien surroundings. The corridor-villa with two rather abbreviated wings overlooking the river provided the Commandant with splendid isolation and the most sophisticated appointments in living accommodation, an apsidal dining-room and bath-suite. A large peristyle court behind the residential quarter accommodated the palace staff, reception rooms and the cavalry. A second peristyle

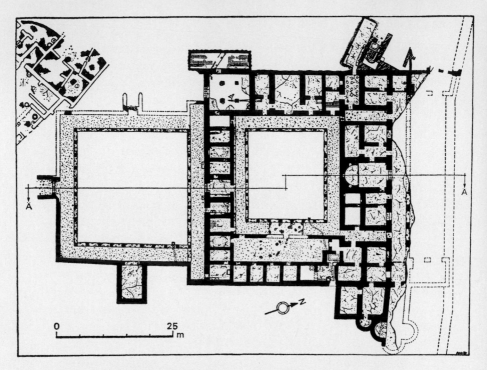

*Fig. 70 Dura-Europos (Syria). Palace of the Dux Ripae, plan. A. H. Detweiler,
M. I. Rostovtzeff, fig. 7*

which was entered through an impressive portal framed the
'basilical' hall where ceremonial activities and diplomatic recep-
tions could be held. Flat roofs of the practical hereditary design
provided a no-nonsense aspect to the building's silhouette, but
the plaster ceilings inside, laid on a rush framework, might curve
to provide a pseudo-vaulting. The headquarters of the River-
Bank Legate differed only slightly from the 'praetorium' architecture of far-distant rivers, the Rhine, the Moselle, the Danube,
and no doubt the Thames.

The Roman buildings of North Africa are among the most
spectacular in the entire Roman world: the *kaisareion* at Cyrene,
the market and forums of Lepcis Magna, the stupendous theatres
of Sabratha and Lepcis, the forums of Timgad and Cuicul, the
hunting baths and the basilica at Lepcis, the monuments of
Thuburbo Maius and Thugga, the amphitheatres at El Djem
and Carthage, are undeniably splendid. There are literally thousands of Romano-African houses too, most of them alike except

in size and opulence, but as in mainland Greece and Spain, only a small percentage of this multitude has been excavated and a far smaller percentage of that total has been published.[397]

Vergil's vignette of Dido's Carthage rising like some colonial capital amidst mud-brick buildings (*Aeneid* 1, 421–9) was more than a literary commonplace, it was symptomatic of Caesarian Africa and of the future face of Roman North Africa.[398] Cato's war-cry, *Delenda est Carthago*, was inspiration in part for Rome's final capture of the Punic capital and the organization of its territory as the first African province in 146 BC. Annexation and acquisition followed fitfully thereafter: Cyrenaica (74 BC), Egypt (30 BC), and Mauretania Tingitana and Caesariensis (AD 44). The Emperors retained a tight control over Egypt because it was the ultimate granary for Rome. Africa profited enormously, and contributed greatly, under Trajan and the Severan Emperors. Provincial Africa not only provided candidates for the Imperial purple, she also gave Rome writers like Apuleius and St Augustine. Monumental civic centres and commemorative arches were the pattern of the military colonies and commercial capitals, but amid the marble and brick splendour of the Roman cities and the elegant country homes, the mud-brick constructions of the natives lingered on in the kasbahs and 'habitat' sectors of the metropolitan centres and in the countryside. Materials notwithstanding, builders became expert at fashioning barrel-vaults and saucer domes of reeds and clay, practical and economical insurance against the oppressive winds and heat of the littoral and interior zones.

The decay of the building materials combined with the passage of time and continuous habitation have erased anything of significance which might have lasted from Phoenician times into the Roman era. Most regretted perhaps are the houses of Ptole- 75 maic Egypt which flicker fitfully in Nilotic murals and mosaics, nowhere more impressively than in the rich tapestry of the Barberini Nile Mosaic at Palestrina (Italy). The mosaic was lodged in the great Sanctuary of Fortuna Primigenia at Praeneste during the large-scale remodelling of the site by Sulla and his lieutenant Varro Lucullus *c*. 80–75 BC. The 'aerial' perspective of the Nile in flood offers a rich menagerie of human and animal

life in a panoramic view.[399] Several types of construction are
introduced: a colonnaded building with a large awning; a
truncated portico with groups of soldiers assembled for a banquet;
a tower house, shepherd's stable, sacred shrines, an enclosure with
two more Egyptian towers, and other less discernible forms.
Tower houses (*pyrgoi*) recur often enough in Nilotic murals and
mosaics to warrant the belief that they were a common house-
form. The construction material is invariably mud brick with
some modest decoration at the roof level and only a modicum
of timber and stone. Excavations at Sicilian Motya revealed that
Phoenician-Carthaginian architects favoured a comparable skyscraper design with wooden superstructures founded on stone
basements.[400] Mud skyscrapers up to seven storeys high remain
part of the architectural scene in Southern Arabia and Tunisia
even today.

Papyri and literary texts provide additional clues, often
extremely tenuous, about other types of dwelling, the methods
and materials of construction, decoration and conveniences, but
the visible remains are scanty and in a metropolis like Alexandria
no doubt beyond recovery. Only pitiful remnants of Graeco-
Roman Philadelphia and Arsinoë have survived, partly owing
to inept recovery and preservation of earlier finds.[401] The
feverish pursuit of papyri at Tebtunis, for example, often
deterred archaeologists from undertaking the proper examination and publication of houses found at the site. Upper Egypt,
particularly at Tell Edfu (Apollinopolis Magna), had homes with
deeply recessed entrances for protection against sand and oppressive
heat, two-storeyed dwellings with external staircases which
admitted light and air only through ceiling apertures. Rural
homes favoured either a truncated pyramidal design with a low
parapet wall on the roof for security's sake or the tower design
already mentioned.

Along the Egyptian coastline and in the busy port towns of
Ptolemaic and Roman Africa, we must conjure with conglom-
erations of dockyard buildings, a confusion of warehouses,
retail shops and taverns, branch offices and hotels and rooming-
houses which catered to the needs and desires of the port officers,
shipping agents, businessmen, sailors, and stevedores who made

their living there. At Ptolemais (Cyrenaica), where Roman town-house and villa architecture introduced a note of splendour, the perennial mud-brick forms persisted in one- and two-storeyed houses, possibly even in apartment blocks after the patterns cited for Tyre and Aradus.

Interior cities like Volubilis, a Roman *municipium* in Mauretania almost directly opposite Gibraltar, have yielded some very attractive town houses.[402] The House of the Venus Mosaic on the Decumanus Inferior, the aristocratic quarter by the aqueduct, has a double and single set of doors on the north side opening into a square vestibule. Three steps down lies the colonnaded atrium with an ornamental *piscina* or *euripus* distinctly reminiscent of the House of the Corinthian Atrium at Herculaneum. The main room of the house (26 × 33 feet) lies on the main axis behind the colonnaded atrium with three bays at the entrance. The mosaic floor depicts Venus with the Three Graces and Eros with an inscription at the north-east corner supplying the name of the house-owner VINCENTIUS ENICESAS (Vincentius you have won). Bedrooms and other unidentifiable rooms opened off the atrium court. The south-west corner of the mansion is given over to a second court (*atriolum*) with an elaborate *nymphaeum* and some large rooms; the north-west corner, in the rear, contains the bath-suite. At least two other houses, the House West of the Governor's Palace and the House of the Two Old Presses, exhibit the same elements: colonnaded atrium, three-bayed *tablinum* or *oecus*, and a second court. The House West of the Governor's Palace and the House of the Beasts have a north portico which extends the width of the house. Inscriptional evidence indicates that the colonnaded Governor's mansion on the Decumanus Maximus was rebuilt by M. Ulpius Victor, procurator of the city under Gordian III (238–244). The dimensions (230 × 230 feet), the street portico, the Corinthian atrium, spacious *tablinum* and two additional atriums, the use of polychrome *opus sectile* floor panels, the bath-suite and the vast number of small rooms indicate that it served a double function as private residence and government office. Volubilis provides a good cross-section of second- and third-century housing, ranging from the Governor's Palace and rich men's mansions to more modest workmen's housing – two-room mud-brick affairs, with kitchen, dining-room and parlour combined in the front, and bedroom behind with curtain dividers, a plain style of living which still abides throughout North Africa and the Near East.

The dispute over the origins of the Volubilis-type house, particularly with respect to the mansions in the north-east sector, resolves into two schools of thought: one, favoured by Charles-Picard and Étienne, regards the houses of North Africa as basically Greek and not Roman, as directly influenced by Hellenistic houses which suited the climatic conditions of North Africa; the other, championed by Thouvenot and Graham, finds comparable examples and likely patterns for the North African houses in the developed atrium-style houses of Ostia (The House of the Columns, The House Near the Round Temple).[403] Patrician and middle-class homes of North Africa, although they deviate frequently from any strict axial design, almost invariably favour the pattern of *fauces*-colonnaded atrium-*tablinum*. The colonnaded atrium was a novelty during the first century AD, a modernism which overseas colonists might readily prefer in their new settings. Certainly the plan found favour in Julio-Claudian and Flavian Pompeii and Herculaneum, and by the second century Ostia had absorbed the peristyle atrium into its standard repertoire, finding satisfaction, no doubt, in the freer circulation of air, the chance to use floor mosaics and wall-paintings in an open-air setting, the appealing prospect from the entrance hall into the interior spaces, and the enviable location for the main room of the house facing directly on to the atrium court and pool. Graham's verdict is convincing: 'the North African house owed its origin not to the adopting and adapting by the Phoenicians of a Greek house type, but rather to the direct importation by colonists from Italy of the atrium house type in the form current there in the first and second centuries of our era'.[404]

Elsewhere, at Ptolemais (Cyrenaica), Italian, American and British excavators have exposed two remarkable houses dating from the first century AD: a villa and a palatial town house. Houses at Ptolemais generally had to conform to a grid pattern which provided for house blocks 164 feet wide, considerably larger than the 142 foot width common elsewhere.

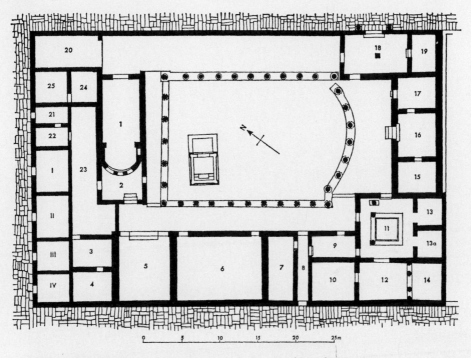

Fig. 71 Ptolemais (Libya). Villa, diagrammatic plan. Kraehling, fig. 43

The aforementioned villa shares its block with two other   71
houses.⁴⁰⁵ The construction materials, dressed stone socle and
mud-brick walls faced with stucco, are characteristic throughout North Africa and the Near East; porticoes, door frames and
second-storey window frames are of stone. The flat roof, again
following standard procedures, contained poles, brush and mud;
floors were either covered with mosaic or *opus sectile* marble.
The house is dominated by an open peristyle court which one
entered from the north-east corner through an impressive
vestibule two steps below the street level. Secondary entrances
led through a long narrow corridor (8) to the kitchen (7) on
the west side, and from the north-east corner to the service
area. The living-quarters and dining-rooms (5, 6) lay along the
west and south sides of the peristyle court; shops (I–IV) opened
on to the street on the north side. The south-west corner of the
house has a self-contained suite of rooms (9–14) for the villa
owner with access to the women's quarters upstairs. The male
apartment offered a small peristyle court with an *impluvium*, an

oecus (12) and private dining-room (14) and a bedroom (10). The layout of this master-suite adheres to the atrium-house pattern with central *tablinum* (*oecus*) and two *alae* (10, 14). The southern colonnade was curved to provide a decorative foreground for three rooms (15–17) at the south end of the house. The unfluted Ionic columns were plastered and painted and supported an entablature with architrave and Doric frieze and a simple cornice with lion-head waterspouts. The house-owner was probably a wealthy African who chose to build his country house in an urban context, to crowd a naturally expansive design into a city block. The east side fails to conform to the west where the rooms face on to the peristyle garden. The curving portico recalls similar versions in Pompeian wall-paintings of maritime villas.

The Palazzo delle Colonne at Ptolemais[406] is an urban *domus* which, like the villa, had to conform to the demands of a heavily populated community where building lots were limited and expensive. Space limitations and the natural slope of the lot forced the architect to provide rooms on two storeys. The Palazzo, like the villa, dates to Julio-Claudian or Flavian times, and is expertly designed for public and private life. The main peristyle court, two storeys high, has two major rooms opening on to it. At the south end there is another atrium-style court with adjoining rooms which no doubt served the family's needs;

72, 73

Fig. 72   Ptolemais (Libya). Palazzo delle Colonne, plan. Pesce, infra., pl. XI

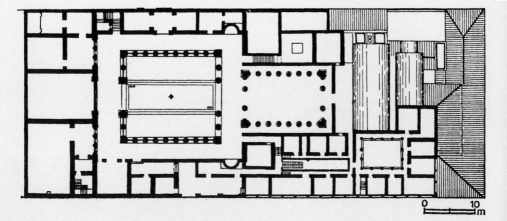

Fig. 73   Ptolemais (Libya). Palazzo delle Colonne, axonometric view. Pesce, 'Palazzo delle Colonne' in Tolemaidi di Cirenaica *(Rome 1950), pl. IX*

at the north end there is a colonnaded rectangular hall with heart-shaped angle columns designed to meet the business or official demands of the property owner. The colonnaded *oecus* appears elsewhere in the Villa of Herod at Jericho and in the great reception hall of Domitian's Palatine Palace. The archaeologists are convinced that women were quartered separately here and elsewhere in the larger houses of Ptolemais, leaving the *oecus* free for male use rather like the *diwan* of the Oriental house. The Palazzo certainly shares many features with the Villa: shops and bath facilities at the north end; two-storey construction, with the advantages of less street noise and better ventilation; peristyle courts and modern bath-suites; but the furnishings and scale of the Palazzo, which contains almost one hundred rooms, far surpass the simpler somewhat rudimentary décor and amenities of the Villa.

The House of Jason Magnus at Cyrene[407] covers two *insulae* of the city plan. Unlike the Roman villa at Ptolemais and the more elegant Palazzo, the Flavian mansion at Cyrene is the result of a merger of two earlier homes, a rich man's house on the west, and, across a side street, a less pretentious dwelling on the east. By the second century AD the composite residence was completed. The western wing of the house rises around a central quadrangle with a Rhodian-style portico on all sides; three of the colonnades supported an upper storey; the southern colonnade rose above the others in response to the high ceilings of the main rooms. The decoration throughout is elegant: a mosaic corridor in the peristyle court and polychrome *opus sectile* marble tiles within a mosaic border for the banqueting hall; a colossal statue of Hercules in the entrance hall and statues of the Nine Muses in the portico. Two of the mosaic floors featured Amphitrite on a sea-horse, one with the Four Seasons in the spandrels; another in the north wing depicted Theseus killing the Minotaur in a geometrical labyrinth with Ariadne holding the thread's end at the entrance; her supporting remark – EPAGATHE (Good Luck) – was set in mosaic above her. To the west there is a detached Temple or Shrine of Hermes. The mosaic in front of the altar records a dedication to Hermes by Januarius, a slave of Ti. Jason Magnus during the reign of Commodus

(180–192), and the excavators have assigned the name of Jason Magnus to the neighbouring mansion.

Timgad (Thamugadi)[408] was a Roman colony founded *c.* 100 by Trajan's Third Augustan Legion about 100 miles from the Mediterranean on a 3,500 foot plateau overlooking an important military highway. Designed to keep watch over restive mountaineers and to promote the Romanization of the district, the colony offered residential *insulae* 70 feet square, each capable of containing at least two houses. The single-storey houses mostly faced on 15 foot-wide streets which were paved with blue and white limestone. Limestone and mortared stonework, a departure from the normal stone foundation and mudbrick construction, were normal throughout the walled community and in the suburbs. Several of the houses are worthy of notice. The House of M. Plotius Faustus Sertius lies at the south-west corner of the city near the wall. It has two courts, both equipped with pools, a complex ensemble of rooms and two bath-suites. Reception rooms, offices and private quarters suggest that the house, accessible from four sides, served as both residence and office building. The House of the Piscina (65 × 164 feet), near the Arch of Trajan, combines two *insulae*. The southern section, which is best preserved, has a series of rooms opening on to a peristyle court with a blue granite pool and pink marble columns; the bath-suite was located in the eastern wing; the *oecus*, south of the peristyle, had an exceptionally lovely floral mosaic, a masterpiece of pink acanthus patterns, almost certainly the petrified version of contemporary floor rugs or embroidery.

Elsewhere in North Africa, Roman houses rarely attain the scale or the character of the aforementioned. Two are worthy of notice, however: the House of the Muses at Althiburos (Tunisia),[409] a second-century residence in a spacious setting, and the surf-side house at Tipasa,[410] a terraced villa overlooking the sea with shops and a streetside portico included in its fabric. Excavations at Utica (Carthage),[411] Uthina (Tunisia),[412] El Djem,[413] Cuicul (Djemila), Lepcis Magna,[414] and Sabratha (Libya) offer additional examples of town houses but make few departures rom the designs already described. Most of the African town

74

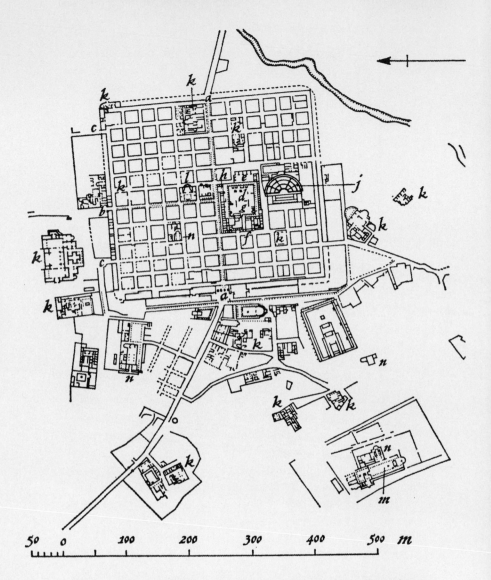

Fig. 74 Timgad (Thamugadi). Plan of the Trajanic colony. Grant, fig. 6, showing:
a *two main gates*; b *a north gate* c *two posterns*; d *the forum*; e *town-hall*; f *curia*;
g *temple*; h *public lavatory*; j *theatre*; k *bath-buildings*; l *library*; m *Donatist cathedral*;
and n *4th-century Christian churches*

houses favour shadowy downstairs apartments behind street colonnades, sometimes with *tabernae* in their façades; some favoured a sunken peristyle and subterranean rooms for coolness.[415] A second storey and balcony often projected over the street colonnade. Some, certainly not all, featured elegant dining and reception rooms with attractive mosaic 'carpets'.

The mosaics of North Africa, pride of the museums at Tunis (Bardo, El Alaoui), Timgad, Djemila, Cherchel, Constantine, Lambèse and Philippeville, are somewhat lacking in artistic sophistication but they do have a forthright quality about them and they certainly constitute one of the richest sources of contemporary views of life and manners in the African provinces. Several of them feature rich men's homes set amid lovely parklands or spreading farmlands. The fourth-century mosaic of Squire Julius,[416] found at Carthage (14 × 18 feet) is a three-tiered polychrome design; in the upper register her Ladyship 76 sits in the park alongside a poultry yard while behind her a shepherd *colonus* herds sheep and goats with the aid of a dog and a woman brings a kid to her mistress; a round hut of reeds rises in the background. At the top left, winter chores balance the summer activities of the top right: a man carrying two live ducks and a woman with a basket of black olives bring their offerings as well to her Ladyship. The central register is dominated by the villa of Julius which lies within a park. Two towers rise from the corners and there is a centrally located arched entrance in the massive lower wall of the villa which leads into a courtyard. A colonnaded loggia appears at the second-storey level. Behind the villa façade, perhaps within the courtyard, lie the bath-suite with domical roofs and an unidentifiable structure. A hunting scene is depicted on either side of the villa with His Lordship on his mount following his beater and keeper of the hounds. The lowest register portrays the Mistress standing in front of her chair in a springtime setting; her puppy, a servant girl with necklace and toilet box, and two *coloni*, one with a basket of flowers, the other with three fish, complete the charming vignette. The autumnal segment, at lower right, portrays the Master seated grandly in his orchard while one *colonus* advances with two cranes and a roll inscribed Ju(lio) dom(ino) and another, coming from the vineyard in the rear, carries a basket of grapes and a live hare.

Three semicircular tableaux on display in the Bardo Museum provide additional insights into fourth-century living. Each mosaic (17 feet in diameter and 10¾ feet high) has a different theme: (a) the mansion in its parkland setting with ducks and geese in the foreground; (b) an elongated structure with a horse tethered at the gate with an olive orchard and vineyard behind and a shepherdess engaged in spinning in the foreground; (c) a vineyard and trees with a pool of water in the foreground and two pavilions with a farm in the centre. Richmond commented with insight on the spinning shepherdess of the second tri-folium panel: 'Such women are not romantic figures in Dresden or Meissen china: their spare time in the fields is occupied in picking and spinning the wool left by the flocks on bushes or any object that would catch it, and they would be expected to return at the end of day with so much thread to their credit.'⁴¹⁷

The Tabarka (Thabraea) mosaic (Bardo Museum) comes from a villa some 80 miles west of Tunis. Although the perspective is somewhat confusing and the shorthand depiction of familiar elements is often ambiguous, nevertheless the general design

75

Fig. 75   Tabarka (Thabraea). Mosaic, villa estate. Musée du Bardo, Tunis. Drawing by Jan Wisher after Nash Williams

and meaning are clear. The interior courtyard, with a one-sided portico, shows arches springing from the columns and massive towers rising at the corners. Between the towers are five windows inset, no doubt, with small panes of opaque glass after the style of Diocletian's palaces at Antioch and Split.

The Tabarka mosaic is a pertinent illustration of the grandiose residences of country squires and Imperial agents which were characteristic of Africa and the Empire generally during Late Imperial times. They responded reasonably well to climatic conditions and present perils. Certainly in North Africa, the traditional porticoes were eminently well designed to take advantage of the sun's rays in winter and to provide shade during torrid summer days. Second-storey apartments and loggias set well above ground level, even the towers sometimes, offered attractive and well-ventilated living and dormitory space.

The North African mosaics also offer priceless information on the regimen and manifold engagements of country properties. Distant heirs to Carthaginian and Hellenistic entrepreneurial expertise, these African estates enjoyed a remarkably close economy in Late Imperial times. Agriculture, viticulture and arboriculture, horse-raising, sheep- and goat-ranching, and hunting all contributed to the villa's prosperity; its maintenance rested with the *coloni* whose contributions in produce and labour were indispensable.

The walled estates in the mosaics, with their large doors and somewhat parenthetic watchtowers, are hardly illustrations of the   76 fortified villas which are known to be characteristic of the last days of the Empire.[418] The mosaics are more likely representative of the courtyard villas of the third and fourth centuries which archaeologists have unearthed not only in Africa but generally throughout Europe. The late villas of Libya and Algeria usually had courtyards with workrooms, storerooms and stables, foundries and ovens, capable of sustaining an embattled property for a reasonable length of time. During peaceful periods the hired hands and fieldworkers lived in wooden huts outside the villa's enclosure. 'Blockhouse' towers flanking the main entrance of the fortified villa, particularly the rounded form, were a direct legacy from the *castrum* and the heavily defended entry, often

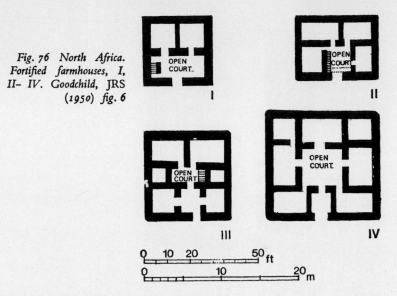

I

II

III

IV

0 10 20   50 ft

0   10   20 m

77 comprising several successive gates, and courtyard, probably reflect modifications to the military forts (*castella*) of the later period when the military barracks, stables and workshops, once central to the ground plan, were removed and planted against the walls to make them more accessible during siege, leaving open areas at the centre to accommodate refugees from the countryside. Monasteries were equally indebted to the *castellum*. Goodchild remarks of Cyrenaica, where a reasonable number of these fortified villas and military *castella* have been found, that 'from the fifth century onward the whole province had become a Limes . . . it is almost impossible to distinguish in more densely inhabited areas, between the fort and the fortified farm.'[419]

To some degree the history of the *villa rustica* had come full circle, from the turreted villa of Scipio Africanus at marshy Liternum, already a residential fossil in Seneca's time, to the towered estates of North Africa and the Empire generally. The tower to be sure was no stranger to villa design.[420] Mosaics, murals and literature all testify to its presence on country and seaside properties for centuries. But the earlier versions were probably both a status feature and a convenience to enable the owner-manager to observe his properties from a high level. But by Severan times in North Africa, and by the mid-fourth cen-

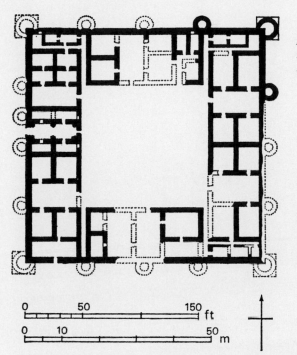

Fig. 77   el-Kastal (Arabia).
Roman auxiliary fort, plan.
R. Macmullen, Ill. F.

0   50   150
|_____| ft

0   10   50
|_____| m

tury in the East, the skyscraper element had become a factor in
siege resistance, a sturdy complement to the stockades, earth-
works, moats and other defence equipment of the walled estates.

The passage from the fortified villa to the fortified medieval
mansion almost certainly began during the final troubles of the
Roman Empire. And yet men continued to enjoy the fruits of
civilized life, to find years of happiness, sometimes even a measure
of monastic peace and productive leisure as the clouds gathered.
Radiant heating, abundant water supplies, shadowy arcades,
garden courts with spacious pools and fountains, dining and
reception halls resplendent with mosaics and wall paintings,
were the outward and comfortable symbols of civilization amid
a disintegrating world.

NOTES

ABBREVIATIONS

ABSA	*Annual of the British School at Athens*	*MAAR*	*Memoirs of the American Academy at Rome*
AJA	*American Journal of Archaeology*	*Mel. Rom.*	*Mélanges d'archéologie et d'histoire de l'école française de Rome*
AJP	*American Journal of Philology*	*Mon. Ant.*	*Monumenti Antichi*
AM	*Mitteilungen des Deutschen archäologischen Instituts, Athenäischer Abteilung*	*NH*	Pliny, *Naturalis Historia*
		NS	*Notizie degli scavi di antichità*
BCH	*Bulletin de correspondance hellénique*	*NS*	New Series
BdA	*Bolletino d'Arte*	*PBA*	*Proceedings of the British Academy*
Bull. Comm.	*Bulletino della Commissione archeologica comunale in Roma*	*PBSR*	*Papers of the British School at Rome*
CAH	*Cambridge Ancient History* (Cambridge 1923–39)	*RAAN*	*Rendiconti della Accademia di archeologia, lettere e belle arti di Napoli*
Camp. Rom.	*Campania Romana: Studi e materiali editi a cura della sezione Campana degli Studi Romani*, vol. I (Rome 1938)	*RE*	A. Pauly, *et al.*, eds, *Real-Encyclopädie der classischen Altertums-wissenschaft*
CQ	*Classical Quarterly*	*Rend. Linc.*	*Rendiconti dell'Accademia dei Lincei*
DH	Dionysius of Halicarnassus	*Rend. Pont.*	*Rendiconti della Pontificia Academia romana di archeologia*
HSCP	*Harvard Studies in Classical Philology*	*RIL*	*Rendiconti dell'Istituto Lombardo. Classe di Lettere, Scienze morali e storiche*
ILN	*Illustrated London News*		
Itinerari	*Itinerari dei Musei e Monumenti d'Italia* (Libreria dello Stato, Rome)	*RM*	*Mitteilungen des Deutschen archäologischen Instituts, Römische Abteilung*
JDAI	*Jahrbuch des Deutschen archäologischen Instituts*	Rostovtzeff, SEHRE[2]	M. Rostovtzeff, *A Social and Economic History of the Roman Empire* (2nd ed. Oxford 1957)
JHS	*Journal of Hellenic Studies*		
JRS	*Journal of Roman Studies*	*St. Etr.*	*Studi Etrusci*

FOREWORD

1 Bertha Carr Rider, *Ancient Greek Houses* (Cambridge 1916); reprint, Chicago, 1964.

2 Consult D.M.Robinson, *et al.*, *Excavations at Olynthus* (Baltimore 1929–46), especially Vol. VIII, *The Hellenic House* (by D.M. Robinson and J.W.Graham), Vols. X (contents and equipment of Olynthian houses), and XII; J.W. Graham, 'The Greek House and the Roman House', *Phoenix* XX (1966), 3–24; Rodney Young, 'An Industrial District of Ancient Athens', *Hesperia* XX (1951), 135–288; H.A. Thompson, *Hesperia* XXVIII (1959), 98–103; for recent work on Delian houses and earlier bibliography consult R.E.Wycherley, *How the Greeks Built Cities* (London 1962), Chapter VII, 185ff.

3 Consult Dorothy B.Thompson, *Archaeology* XIII (1960), 234–40; *id.*, *The Athenian Shopping Center: The Athenian Agora* (Princeton 1971), fig. 20 and text; *AJA* LXXIII (1969), 341ff. (Mikion's establishment).

4 *Cf.* A.Kriesis, 'Tradition in Evolution: the Persistence of the Classical Greek House', *Architectural Review* (June, 1949), 267ff.

5 The superbly exhibited Roman material in the Trier Landesmuseum, and the skilful reconstruction of the Roman House at Augst (Augustodunum) are exemplary undertakings, suitable models for comparable undertakings in North Africa, where villas abound with mosaic floors intact, and France, where Roman seigniorial mansions could compete with any château on the Loire for tourist and scholarly attention. The newly opened museum built alongside the south transept of the Cathedral of Cologne incorporates the third-century Dionysus mosaic and the three-storey high tomb of Poblicius. The J. Paul Getty Museum in Malibu, California, recreates the design of the Villa of the Papyri at Herculaneum.

6 On Roman architects in Italy consult W.L.MacDonald, *The Architecture of the Roman Empire. I: An Introductory Study* (New Haven, Conn. 1965), *passim;* in the provinces, Ramsay MacMullen, 'Roman Imperial Building in the Provinces', *HSCP* 64 (1959), 207ff.

7 *Cf.* C.C.Van Essen, L'Architecture dans l'Énéide de Virgile', *Mnemosyne* 7 (1939), 225–36.

8 Vergil, *Aeneid* VI, 853 (Anchises to Aeneas).

CHAPTER I

9 On origins, consult, *inter alios:* J.B.Ward-Perkins, 'The Problem of Etruscan Origins', *HSCP*, 1959, 1–26; G. Säflund, *Historia*, 1957, 10–22 (equating 'the Villanovans' with Etruscan immigrants); H. Hencken, *Tarquinia and Etruscan Origins* (London 1968); H. H. Scullard, The *Etruscan Cities and Rome* (London 1967); M. Pallottino,

Etruscologia (Milan 1968) and *Le Origine degli Etruschi* (Rome 1947).

10 Herodotus I, 94.

11 DH I, 20 f.

12 E.H.Richardson, *The Etruscans* (Chicago 1964), 1–9.

13 Vitruvius IV, 7; consult L. Polacco, *Tuscanicae dispositiones. Problemi di architettura dell'Italia protoro-*

mana (Padua 1952).

14 On rock-cut chamber tombs in general, consult M. Demus-Quatember, *Etruskische Grabarchitektur* (Baden-Baden 1958).

15 For Caere, consult B. Pace *et al.*, 'Caere: Scavi di Raniero Mengarelli', *Mon. Ant.*, 1955, *passim*; for funeral pavilions, see R. Ross Holloway, *AJA*, 1965, 341–7, and Richardson, *op. cit.* (note 12), 116, 198. For the ancient testimony see Strabo V, 2, 5; Vitruvius II, 10, 2; DH I, 37, 4.

16 *Cf.* E. Gjerstad, *The Swedish Cyprus Expedition* IV, 2 (Stockholm 1948), 232 ff.

17 Consult J. B. Ward-Perkins, 'Veii: The historical Topography of the Ancient City', *PBSR*, 1961; *NS*, 1922, 379–85, fig. 3; A. de Agostino, *Veio: I Ruderi, Le Terrecotte* (M. P. I. Guide), 108.

18 *Cf.* F. E. Brown, 'New Soundings in the Regia; the Evidence for the Early Republic', *Entretiens sur l'antiquité classique*, 1967, 45–60 (rectangular huts with curved corners).

19 See G. Becatti and F. Magi, *Tarquinii* III–IV: *Le pitture degli Augure e del Pulcinella* (Rome 1955), *passim*.

20 Varro, *De Lingua Latina* V, 161. The word *aethre* (= atrium?) appears on the Zagreb mummy-wrapping in an obscure context.

21 Vitruvius VI, 3, 1: 'In the Tuscan [*cavaedium*], the girders that cross the breadth of the atrium have cross-beams on them, and valleys sloping in and running from the angles of the walls to the angles formed by the beams, and the rainwater falls down along the rafters to the roof-opening [*compluvium*] in the middle.' The central hall and reception area of the town house was ascribed to the Etruscans by Vitruvius (VI, 3, 1) and Varro (*De Lingua Latina* 5, 161). For speculation on the origins of the atrium in upper-class Etruscan mansions, *cf.* Boëthius

and Ward-Perkins, *op. cit.*, (note 29), 152; Maiuri, *NS*, 1930, 381 ff., 1942, 404 ff., 1944–45, 130 ff., for Oriental inspiration *cf.* E. Gjerstad, *op. cit.* (note 16), 232 ff,; L. Crema, *L'Architettura romana* (Turin 1959), 105 ff.

22 G. Patroni, *Rend. Linc.*, 1902, 467–507.

23 *Phoenix*, 1966, 7.

24 E. Brizio, 'Relazione degli scavi eseguiti a Marzabotto presso Bologna', *Mon. Ant.*, 1891, cols. 249–442. G. A. Mansuelli, 'La casa Etrusca di Marzabotto', *RM*, 1963, 44–62; *id.*, *ILN*, 13 Oct. 1962, 557; Mansuelli and R. Scarani, *L'Emilia prima dei Romani* (Milan 1961).

25 The colonial city's life-span was limited. Founded at a time when the Etruscans were extending their power northward into Aemilia, it was destroyed little more than a century later by the invading Gauls and never resettled.

26 Servius, on Vergil, *Aeneid* I, 730, specifies that the atrium was used for cooking and derived its name (black room) from the smoke stains: *ibi etiam culina erat, unde et atrium dictum est; atrium enim erat e fumo.*

27 See *NS*, 1922, 382, fig. 3, and F. E. Brown, 'Cosa I: History and Topography', *MAAR*, 1961, 7–113.

28 *Cf.* A. von Gerkan and F. Messerschmidt, 'Das Grab der Volumnier bei Perugia', *NS*, 1931, 475–505; Boëthius and Ward-Perkins, *op. cit.*, 67 ff., fig. 38 (section and plan).

29 A. Boëthius and J. B. Ward-Perkins, *Etruscan and Roman Architecture* (London 1970), 63 ff.

30 *Cf.* Demus-Quatember, *op. cit.* (note 14), *passim*: G. Rosi, 'Sepulchral Architecture as Illustrated by the Rock Façades of Central Italy', *JRS*, 1925, 1–59; *cf.* also M. Bizarri, *La Necropoli di Crocefisso del Tufo in Orvieto*, I, II (Florence 1962–66).

31 Consult N. Alfieri and P. E.

Arias, *Spina* (Florence 1958); also
Aifieri, 'The Etruscans of the Po and
the Discovery of Spina', *Italy's Life*,
1957, 91–104.
32 Livy X, 4; consult C. Laviosa,
St. Etr., 1960, 310–37; 1961, 31–45.
33 On Etruscan furnishings in general consult G. M. A. Richter, *The*

*Furniture of the Greeks, Etruscans and
Romans* (London 1966), 85–96, figs.
427–75.
34 Richter, *op. cit.*, figs. 427–9.
35 Consult S. de Marinis, *La Tipologia del bianchetto nell'arte etrusca arcaica* (Rome 1961).

CHAPTER II

36 See M. Grant, *Cities of Vesuvius*,
(London 1971), 26ff.
37 Pliny, *Epistles* VI, 16, and 20
(extracts).
38 Vitruvius VI, 3.
39 Pliny, *NH* XXXVI, 6–7, *cf.* the
House of the Wooden Partition at
Herculaneum (III, 11–12); see A.
Maiuri, *Ercolano*, 207 ff.; *id.*, *Herculaneum*[5] (Rome 1959), 31 f.; Crema
op. cit., 115 f.
40 G. Patroni, *Rend. Accad. Linc.*,
1936, 1937; P. Grimal, *Les Jardins
romains* (Paris 1953), ch. 7.
41 Consult E. T. Salmon, *Samnium
and the Samnites* (Cambridge 1967).
The Oscan word for house, *triibom*
(cf. Latin *trabem*, beam) might suggest
that Samnite (and Italic) houses were of
wooden construction appropriate to a
peasant society. For archaeological
confirmation see F. von Duhn, *Italische
Gräberkunde* I (Heidelberg 1924–39),
541 f.; for the Oscan term see E. Vetter,
Glotta 29, 1924, 215.
42 Cicero, *Paradoxa* V, 2, 38.
43 Pompeian buildings are assigned
three numbers: the first Roman
numeral refers to the region, the second
(lower case) to the block, and the Arabic
numeral to the house number within
the block; buildings in Herculaneum
carry two numbers, for the block and
for the house. Ostian buildings follow
the Pompeian pattern and the numbers
refer to the regionary map in G.
Calza, G. Becatti *et al.*, *Scavi di Ostia*,

vol. 1 (Rome 1953).
44 For the House of the Surgeon, cf.
A. Mau, (tr. F. W. Kelsey), *Pompeii:
Its Life and Art* (New York 1899),
280–2; Maiuri, *Pompeii*[14] (Rome
(1970), 38; A. Maiuri, *NS*, 1930, 391
f.; Crema, *op. cit.*, 105, 108; E.
Gjerstad, *Gnomon*, 1954, 135 f.;
Salmon, *op. cit.*, 140, notes, 1, 2.
45 Vitruvius VI, 3. See also Maiuri,
NS, 1930, 381 ff.; 1942, 404 ff.;
1944–45, 130 ff. *Cava aedium* (sometimes *cavaedium*) is Vitruvius' term
for the house type derived, according
to his view, from the Etruscans.
46 Vitruvius, VI, 5, 1.
47 *Cf.* Mau, *op. cit.*, 283–7; Maiuri,
Pompeii[14] (Rome 1970), 98 f. For
recent excavations in the House of
Sallust consult A. Laidlaw and J. Packer,
AJA, 1971, 206 f.
48 Consult F. Noack and K.
Lehmann-Hartleben, *Baugeschichtliche
Untersuchungen am Stadtrand vom Pompeji* (Berlin and Leipzig 1936); Crema,
op. cit., 112, fig. 101.
49 Cato, *De Agricultura* XXXVIII,
3, 'lime and an aggregate of stone and
brick set in concrete'.
50 Consult G. Lugli, *La Tecnica
edilizia romana* (Rome 1957), *passim*.
51 Vitruvius II, 8, 1. *Opus incertum*
signifies *opus caementicium* with a
facing of asymmetrical blocks, a
concrete masonry style in use from the
second century B C
52 Vitruvius II, 7.

53 *Cf.* Mau, *op. cit.*, 301–8 (with plan); Maiuri, *op. cit.*, 51 f.; Vitruvius VI, 3, 1 (tetrastyle atrium).

54 Vitruvius VI, 7, 3. L. Richardson, Jr, 'Pompeii: The Casa dei Dioscuri and Its Painters', *MAAR*, 1955, 63–5, 110, argues that the House of the Dioscuri contains the only Cyzicene Atrium in Pompeii. *Cf.* Crema, *op. cit.*, 116, fig. 109.

55 Mau, *op. cit.*, 349; Maiuri, *op. cit.*, 37; Maiuri, *NS*, 1944–45, 142 f.; W. F. Jashemski, 'The Flower Industry at Pompeii', *Archaeology*, 1963, 112–21; esp., 114, pl. 5.

56 *Cf.* Mau., *op. cit.*, 288–97; Maiuri, *op. cit.*, 42 ff.; A. W. van Buren, *AJA*, 1963, 401 f., for phases of reconstruction.

57 See A. Maiuri and R. Pane, *La Casa di Loreio Tiburtino e la Villa di Diomede in Pompei* (Rome 1947).

58 For the peristyle addition consult Boëthius and Ward-Perkins, *op. cit.* (note 29), 74, 155 f.

59 *Cf.* Cicero, *Ad Quintum Fratrem* III, 1, 2 and 5; P. Grimal, *op. cit.* (note 40), *passim*; and Jashemski, *op. cit.* (note 55).

60 See Richardson, *op. cit.* (note 54).

61 Other Pompeian examples have been detected in the atrium of the House of Epidius Rufus (IX, i, 20), a cleaners' and dyers' establishment (VI, viii, 21), and the *atriolum* of the bath in the House of Menander (VI, vii, 21).

62 Keys survived in the peristyle and *atriolum* of the House of the Vettii (VI, xv, 1–2), and in the peristyle and latrine of the House of the Silver Wedding (V, ii).

63 Vitruvius VI, 3, 10.

64 Mau, *op. cit.*, 309–12; Maiuri, *op. cit.* (note 47), 56; *cf.* Richardson, *op. cit.*, 7–18, for treatment of Corinthian atria.

65 A. Maiuri, *Herculaneum⁵* (Rome

1959), 40 f.

66 A. Maiuri, *Ercolano (Nuovi Scavi)* (Rome 1959), 280–302; *op. cit.* (note 65), 26 ff. See also A. Maiuri, *Studies in honor of D. M. Robinson* I, 423–9 (*Oecus Aegyptius*).

67 Maiuri, *op. cit.* (note 47), 77. Twelve paintings of the Pompeian forum removed from the house during the excavations of 1755–7 are now in the Museo Nazionale, Naples.

68 *Cf.* A. Maiuri, *La Casa del Menandro e il suo tesoro di argenteria* (2 vols. Rome 1933); K. D. White, *Roman Farming* (London 1970), 435 f.

69 Maiuri, *op. cit.* (note 65), 42 f.

70 Mau, *op. cit.*, 313–20; Maiuri, *op. cit.* (note 47), 34 f.

71 Mau, *op. cit.*, 321–40; Maiuri, *op. cit.*, 44–8.

72 Maiuri, *op. cit.*, 49 f.

73 Maiuri, *op. cit.* (note 65), 63 ff.; for the Corinthian banqueting hall see Vitruvius VI, 3, 8–10.

74 Maiuri, *op. cit.* (note 66), 302–22; *op. cit.* (note 65), 59 ff.

75 Petronius houses his freedman millionaire, Trimalchio, in an enlarged and refurbished Augustan house which contains four dining-rooms, twenty bedrooms, two marble porticoes, three libraries, and, upstairs, two master suites and a wing for guests. The 'Porte Sublime' led into a great portico or peristyle; the atrium lay beyond in a restricted area. The fictional portico, perhaps a Neronian affectation (?), publicized Trimalchio's career in a series of allegorical, megalographic wall-paintings. For discussion, see G. Bagnani, *AJP*, 1954, 16–39; P. W. Harsh, 'The Origins of the Insula at Ostia', *MAAR*, 1935, 49–50; and A. Maiuri, *La Cena di Trimalchione* (Naples 1945), 243–5.

76 *Cf.* Seneca, *Epistles* XC, 25, for use of window glass.

77 Diodorus V, 40. See also Vitruvius VI, 3, 7; VI, 5, 2–3; V, 9, 5 (colon-

nades and walks); P. Grimal, *op. cit.*
(note 40), *passim*; Crema, *op. cit.*
(note 21), 113 f.

78 V. J. Bruno, 'A Town House at
Cosa', *Archaeology*, 1970, 232–41.

CHAPTER III

79 *Aeneid* VIII, 306–69.
80 *Aeneid* VIII, 347 f. (Capitol);
VIII, 455 f. (Evander).
81 *Aeneid* VIII, 652–4.
82 *Cf.* P. L. MacKendrick, *The Mute
Stones Speak* (London 1962), 62–74,
and figs. The Hut of Romulus measures
16 ft. 1 in. by 11 ft. 10 in.
83 *Aeneid* VIII, 654; *cf.* Vitruvius
II, 15 (Capitoline).
84 *Cf.* F. E. Brown, 'The Regia',
MAAR, 1935; *id.*, *Entretiens sur l'antiquité classique*, 1967, 45–60.
85 A. Boëthius, *The Golden House of
Nero* (Michigan 1960), 10 ff.
86 Plutarch, *Poplicola* X, 2–4; *cf.*
DH V, 19. 1–2; Cicero, *De Hatrus-
picum Responsis*, XVI; Livy II, 7.
87 Plutarch, *Poplicola*, 20.
88 Livy XLIV, 16, 10. For later
survivals *cf.* Suetonius, *Nero*,
XXXVIII.
89 *Cf.* G. Lugli, *La tecnica edilizia
romana con particolare riguardo a Roma
e Lazio* (2 vols. Rome 1957); A.
Boëthius, 'Vitruvius and the Roman
Architecture of His Age', *Svenska
instituet i Rome Skrifter*, 1939, 114–43.
90 *Cf.* B. Tamm, *Auditorium and
Palatium. A Study of Assembly-rooms
in Roman Palaces during the First
Century B.C. and the First Century
A.D.* (Stockholm, 1963), esp. 34 ff.
91 *NH* XXXVI, 4–8.
92 *NH* XXXVI, 48–50.
93 *NH* XXXVI, 109–10.
94 Cornelius Nepos, *Atticus* XIII,
1–2, 5; Plutarch, *Lucullus*, XXXIX.
95 *Cf.* G. E. Rizzo, *Le Pitture della
'Casa dei Grifi' con note topografiche
di A. Bartoli* (Rome 1936); Boëthius
and Ward-Perkins, *op. cit.* (note 29),

157, fig. 82 (terrace house of General
Championnet, Pompeii); A. W. van
Buren, *Rend. Pont.* 3, 1940, 57–61.
96 *Cf.* Noack and Lehmann-Hartle-
ben, *op. cit.* (note 48).
97 G. M. Hanfmann, *Roman Art*
(Greenwich, Conn. 1964), 224, pl. V.
The paintings are in the Antiquario del
Palatino; the mosaic floor is *in situ*.
98 Domus Augusti (Liviae): E. Nash,
Pictorial Dictionary of Ancient Rome I
(London 1961), 310–15, and bibliography; B. Tamm, *op. cit.*, 44 ff.;
G. M. Hanfmann, *op. cit.*, 229, pl. VII
(colour, garland room), and bibliography. For new paintings in an
upstairs vaulted *cubiculum*, consult P.
Romanelli and G. Carettoni, 'Nuove
Pitture del Palatino', *BdA*, 1955, 208 ff.
99 Vitruvius VI, 3, 8; the rooms
may also be Suetonius' *conclavia sine
marmore ullo* designed for meetings and
banquets.
100 Suetonius, *Augustus*, LXXII, 1.
101 Suetonius, *Augustus* XLV; Cassius Dio LVII, 11. For the Augustan
domus consult O. E. Richmond, 'The
Augustan Palatium', *JRS* IV (1914)
193–226, who speculates that the
terraced mansion beneath the monumental approach to the Temple had
once been the short-term property of
Marc Antony, presented to Agrippa
and Messalla in 31 and burned in 29.
Certainly the scale of the mansion
with its bath-system and splendid
view over the Circus Maximus would
befit Antony's life-style and interests.
See more recently, G. Carettoni, 'I
Problemi della zona Augustea del
Palatino alle luce dei recenti scavi', *Rend.
Pontif. Accad.* XXXIX, 55–75; *Illus-*

trated *London News* 6790 (Sept. 20, 1969), 6792 (Oct. 4, 1969); and Nevio Degrassi, 'La Dimora di Augusto sul Palatino e la base di Sorrento', *Rend. Pontif. Accad.* XXXIX (1966–67), 76–116.
102 Vitruvius VI, 5, 2.
103 Domus Tiberiana: consult Nash, *op. cit.*, 365–74, and bibliography. Caligula extended the palace to the north-west and incorporated the Temple of Castor.
104 *Cf.* Boëthius, *op. cit.* (note 85), 94–128.
105 Suetonius, *Nero*, XXXI; Seneca, *Epistles* LXXXVI, 6; C, 6; Statius, *Silvae* I, 3, 36–7; I, 5, 42–3. Consult Nash, *op. cit.*, 375–9, with bibliography.
106 Consult Nash, *op. cit.*, 316–38, and bibliography; H. Kähler, *The Art of Rome and Her Empire* (New York 1963), 115–20; Boëthius and Ward-Perkins, *op. cit.* (note 29), 230–5, 251–3.
107 Dio Cassius LXV, 10, 4.
108 Suetonius, *Domitian*, XIV, 4; for phengites, see Pliny, *NH* XXXVI, 163.

109 F. E. Brown, *Roman Architecture* (New York 1961), 40.
110 *Cf.* G. Becatti, 'Casa ostiensi del tardo impero', *BdA*, 1948, 102–28, 197–224. For *House of Fortuna Annonaria*, *ibid.*, 23–5, fig. 22; Boëthius and Ward-Perkins, *op. cit.*, 335, fig. 130A (plan of fourth-century remodelling); R. Meiggs, *Roman Ostia* (Oxford 1960) 254.
111 *House of the Tempio Rotondo*: Meiggs, *op. cit.*, 255, fig. 17, pl. 13a; Becatti, *op. cit.*
112 *Cf.* Meiggs, *op. cit.*, 83–97, *contra* G. Calza and G. Becatti, *Ostia*[4] (Rome 1961) 10.
113 *Domus of Cupid and Psyche*: *cf.* J. E. Packer, *AJA*, 1967, 123–31; Boëthius and Ward-Perkins, *op. cit.*, 334–6, fig. 130: cf. the villa of Desenzano (fourth century AD), for similarities, in E. Ghislanzoni, *La Villa romana in Desenzano* (Milan 1962). Ward-Perkins finds the closest parallels to these late Ostian houses in contemporary houses in Syria, as revealed by excavations at Antioch.
114 M. Wheeler, *Roman Art and Architecture* (London 1964), 133.

CHAPTER IV

115 Boëthius and Ward-Perkins, *op. cit.*, 285, describe the *taberna* in its developed Roman form as 'a tall, deep, barrel-vaulted chamber, open in front almost to its full width . . . closed by means of a series of sliding panels . . . with a wooden mezzanine [inside], for storage or lodging, accessible by wooden steps and lit by a small window over the door'. Varro, *De Lingua Latina*, V, 162, indicates that *cenacula* originally meant upstairs dining-rooms, but later included upstairs apartments. For evidence of early Rome *cf.* Livy XLIV, 16, 10; Scipio's

atrium-house, Livy XXXIX 44, 7. For the Pompeian forum consult J. Russell, *Phoenix* XXII, 1968, 306 ff.
116 *Cf.* G. Lugli, *Anxur Terracina* (Rome 1926), Terracina alta, Zona III, no. 6, fig. 17 (*cf.* Boëthius and Ward-Perkins, *op. cit.*, fig. 67); Boëthius, *op. cit.* (note 85), 137 ff.
117 *Cf.* Boëthius and Ward-Perkins, *op. cit.*, 119 f., fig. 68; J. E. Packer, *MAAR* XXXI, 1971, 52 f.
118 *Cf.* above, p. 51.
119 The House of Fabius Amandio at Pompeii (I, vii, 2–3) provides another *pensione*.

120 Maiuri, *op. cit.* (note 66), 407–16; Packer, *op. cit.*, 55–6.

121 Vitruvius II, 8, 20.

122 Meiggs, *op. cit.* (note 110), 237.

123 *Cf.* J.E.Packer, 'Roman Ostia: Architectural Structure and Decoration', *AJA*, 1965, 172 f.: 'the word would appear to mean only a large dwelling in which smaller units are rented out. Accordingly, an *insula* meant either a large building covering an entire block or only a small part of another structure. The term was used rather with a legalistic than an architectural connotation.'

124 Strabo XVI, 1, 5 (Babylon); 2, 23 (Tyre); 2, 13 (Aradus); for insulae at Ephesus, *see infra*, pp. 213ff.

125 *Cf.* J.J.S.Whitaker, *Motya, a Phoenician colony in Sicily* (London 1921), 17.

126 *Cf.* W.Phillips, *Quatban and Sheba* (London 1955), 46, 60; Boëthius, *op. cit.* (note 85), 145, note 20; G.C. Picard, *Daily Life in Carthage* (New York 1961), 48.

127 Boëthius, *op. cit.*, 146 ff.

128 G.Lugli, *La Tecnica edilizia romana* (2 vols. Rome 1957), *passim*; 'L'Opus Caementicium in Vitruvio', *Studi minori di topografia antica*, 1965, 33–40.

129 Pliny, *NH* XXXVI, 109.

130 Juvenal, *Satires* XI, 12–13; Tacitus, *Annals*, XV, 46; Juvenal, *Satires* III, 223–5; Strabo V, 3, 7; Pliny, *NH* XXXVI, 24, 106; 54, 176; Martial, *Epigrams*, 117, 7 f., etc.

131 Strabo V, 3, 7.

132 Juvenal, *Satires* III, 193–202.

133 Livy XXI, 62 (218 BC).

134 Strabo V, 3, 7 (ordinances); Forum Augustum (2 BC), *cf.* Boëthius and Ward-Perkins, *op. cit.* (note 29), 190 ff.; P.Zanker, *Forum Augustum* (Tübingen 1968).

135 Vitruvius II, 8, 20.

136 Seneca, *De Consolatione ad Marciam* XXII, 3; *De Beneficiis* IV, 6, 2;

Epistles XC, 10; *Controversiae* II, 1, 11; *De Ira* III, 35, 4–5; *De Tranquillitate Animi* XI, 7.

137 Tacitus, *Annals* XV, 43. Augustus' edict relating to the height of *insulae*, apparently ignored by many architects, was revised to require that no *insula* should exceed 70 feet; Trajan later reduced the height to 60 feet (Aurelius Victor, *Epitome* 13, 3).

138 Cicero, *De Officiis* III, 66; Pliny, *NH* XXXVI, 55, 176; Plutarch, *Crassus*, II; Vitruvius II, 8, 17.

139 Vitruvius II, 8, 17 (revised). *Cf.* Boëthius and Ward-Perkins, *op. cit.*, 118, note 5.

140 Pliny, *NH* XXXVI, 55, 176; Tacitus, *Histories* III, 71; Vitruvius II, 8, 17.

141 Strabo V, 3, 7; Suetonius, *Augustus*, LXXXIX.

142 For the Aracoeli *insula cf.* Boëthius, *op. cit.* (note 85), 137 ff., fig. 73; Nash, *op. cit.* (note 98), I, 506 f., figs. 623 f.; constructed of brick, travertine and concrete, it probably housed between 40 and 50 residents. For the Via Biberatica shop-apartments consult Nash, *op. cit.*, II, 149–58, and W.MacDonald, *The Architecture of the Roman Empire* (New Haven and London 1965), 75 ff.

143 Aulus Gellius, *Noctes Atticae*, 15, 1, 2 (mid-second century AD).

144 Herodian VII, 12, 5–6 (third century AD); Symmachus, *Epistles* VI, 37, records the collapse of a tenement into Trajan's Forum (fourth century AD).

145 For Ostian history and building consult Meiggs, *op. cit.* (note 110), Calza and Becatti, *op. cit.* (note 112); Packer, *op. cit.* (note 117), *passim.*

146 Hermansen, *Phoenix*, 1970, 342 ff., argues that housewives used balconies (and upstairs windows) to conduct business dealings with street vendors and as a landing to lift foodstuffs, water, wine, etc. by a rope attached to a basket or net.

147 *Cf.* Boëthius, *op. cit.* (note 85), 158 ff. with figs.

148 T. Kleberg, *Hôtels, restaurants et cabarets dans l'antiquité romaine* (Uppsala 1957); G. Girri, *La Taberna nel quadro urbanistico e sociale di Ostia* (Rome 1956).

149 Petronius, *Satyricon*, XCV.

150 Consult Calza and Becatti, *op. cit.*

151 *Cf.* Calza *NS*, 1923, 183–5; Packer, *op. cit.*, 152–5; for terrace roofs. *cf.* Seneca, *Epistles* CXXII, 8.

152 *Cf.* R. Calza and E. Nash, *Ostia* (Rome 1959), 27–8, fig. 16; Harsh, *op. cit.* (note 75), 20, 25–7; Packer, *op. cit*, 122–34. The plan recurs on a magnified scale in the *Casa a Giardino* (III, ix, 1–26); *cf.* Calza and Becatti,

op. cit., IV, 113–33.

153 *Cf.* Calza and Nash, *op. cit.*, 36–7; Packer, *op. cit.*, 166–71.

154 *Cf.* Calza and Nash, *op. cit.*, 29; B. F. Maj, 'La Casa delle Volte Dipinte: Contributo alla edilizia privata imperiale', *BdA*, 1960, 45–65.

155 Population figures are notoriously imprecise. For Rome, A. von Gerkan, *RM*, 1940, 165 ff., suggests 700,000 in Imperial times; Meiggs calculated Ostia's maximum population at 50–60,000 (*op. cit.*, 532–4); Calza estimated 36,000; Packer, more conservatively but plausibly, estimates a maximum of 20,000.

156 Juvenal, *Satires* III, 62.

157 Consult G. Rickman, *Roman Granaries and Store Buildings* (Cambridge 1971), *passim*.

CHAPTER V

158 Cato, *De Agricultura*; Varro, *De Re Rustica* I, 13; III, 5, 8–17 (villa at Casinum); Vitruvius VI, 6, 1–7; Pliny, *NH* XXXVI, 111 f.; Columella, *De Re Rustica* I, 6, 1, encourages a triple villa complex: *villa urbana, villa rustica,* and *villa fructuaria* (productive farm).

159 For puritanism and thrift, *cf.* Horace, *Satires, Odes* (*passim*); Juvenal, *Satires* (*passim*); Seneca, *Epistles* (*passim*), etc.

160 Consult K. Lehmann, *Thomas Jefferson, American Humanist* (New York 1947).

161 Cato, *De Agricultura*, XIV; *cf.* Vitruvius VI, 6, 1–7.

162 For refs. consult T. Frank, *An Economic Survey of Ancient Rome* I and V (Baltimore 1933 and 1940), 208 f.

163 For refs. consult Frank, *op. cit.*, 295 f.

164 Varro, *De Re Rustica* II, 6, 5; I, 20, 3; *cf.* Frank, *op. cit.*, 367.

165 *Cf.* Frank, *op. cit.*, 367 ff. Varro's

aunt raised an average of 5,000 thrushes annually at her villa near Cures in Sabinum for a profit of 60,000 sesterces, 'twice as much as a farm of 200 iugera [130 acres] provides' (Varro *De Re Rustica* III, 2, 14).

166 Consult L. P. Wilkinson, *The Georgics of Vergil: A Critical Survey* (Cambridge 1969); A. G. McKay, *Vergil's Italy* (Greenwich, Conn., 1970), K. D. White, *op. cit.* (note 68), 39–41.

167 Seneca, *Epistles* LXXXVI.

168 *Cf.* J. H. D'Arms, *Romans on the Bay of Naples* (Cambridge, Mass., 1970), 1 ff.

169 *Cf.* V. H. Poulsen, *San Giovenale* (Malmö 1960), 313–20 (second century B C).

170 *Cf.* P. von Blankenhagen, M. A. Cotton and J. B. Ward-Perkins, 'Two Roman Villas at Francolise, Prov. Caserta, etc.', *PBSR*, 1965, 55–69, and figs.

171 F. E. Brown, 'Cosa I: History

and Topography, *MAAR*, 1951, 89; id., *St. Etr.*, 1927, 447–9; id., *NS*, 1927, 204–10; F. Castagnoli, *MAAR*, 1956, 164 f.
172 *Cf.* R. G. Carrington, 'Studies in the Campanian Villae Rusticae', *JRS*, 1931, 110 ff.; 'Some Ancient Italian Country Houses', *Antiquity*, 1933, 261–80; Rostovtzeff, *SEHRE*², 551–3, note 26 (thirty-six Campanian estates); K. D. White, *op. cit.*, 415–45.
173 *Cf.* Mau, *op. cit.* (note 44), 361–6 and plan IV; K. D. White, *op. cit.*, 422–6; for silver treasure *cf.* H. de Villefosse, 'Le trésor de Boscoreale', *Monuments Piot*, 1899, 7–279, pls. 1–36.
174 For the proper location of the kitchen, Vitruvius VI, 6, 1; for kitchens and utensils *cf.* B. Fowler and E. Rosenbaum, *Apicius: The Roman Cookery Book* (London 1958), ch. IV, 29–40.
175 For arrangements *cf.* Pliny, *NH* XIV, 21, 136.
176 *Cf.* AJA, 1970, 148.
177 Consult A. Maiuri, *La Villa dei Misteri*² (2 vols. Rome 1947); Boëthius and Ward-Perkins, *op. cit.*, note 29), 159 f., 319 fig. 123); K. D. White, *op. cit.*, 438 f.; on the north-east wing for agricultural processing (AD 14–63).
178 Vitruvius VI, 5, 3
179 Maiuri, *op. cit.* (note 177), 42.
180 For Villa of Diomedes *cf.* Maiuri, *Pompeii*⁶ (Rome 1953), 81 ff., fig. 15; Mau, *op. cit.*, 355–60.
181 Consult D. Mustilli, 'La villa pseudourbana ercolanese', *RAAN NS* 1956, 77–97; cf. D'Arms, *op. cit.*, 173 f., H. Bloch, *AJA*, 1940, 490 ff.
182 *Cf.* G. Lugli (tr. G. Bagnani), *Horace's Sabine Farm* (Rome 1930); Francesco Dioniso, 'Le ville di Orazio: La villa rurale del "Digentia" e la villa signorile di "Tibur" ', Società di Villa d'Este, *Atti e Memorie* (Tivoli), 1966. See also M. Neuerburg, 'The Other Villas of Tivoli, *Archaeology*, 1968, 288–97.

183 *Cf.* G. Bagnani, 'The House of Trimalchio', *AJP*, 1954, 16–39; id., 'And passing rich . . .', *Studies in Honour of Gilbert Norwood* (Toronto 1952), 218–23; Harsh, *op. cit.* (note 152), 49–50; Maiuri, *op. cit.* (note 75), 184 On seasonal dining-rooms see Vitruvius VI, 4, 1–2; VI, 7, 3. For dining *al fresco* consult P. Soprano, 'I Triclini all'aperto di Pompei', in *Pompeiana, raccolta di Studi per il secondo centenario degli scavi di Pompei* (Rome 1950), 288–310.
185 Consult D'Arms, *op. cit.*, passim.
186 *Cf.* Münzer, S.V. 'C. Sergius Orata', *RE* 2 A, 1713–14; Pliny, *NH* ᵀX, 168; Valerius Maximus IX, 1, 1; D'Arms, *op. cit.*, 18 ff.
187 Strabo V, 4, 7.
188 *Cf.* C. Gatti, 'Le ville maritime italiche e africane', *RIL*, 1957, 285–305.
189 Cicero, *De Lege Agraria* II, 78.
190 Pliny, *Epistles* II, 17; V, 6; see especially H. H. Tanzer, *The Villas of Pliny the Younger* (New York 1924), 7–26; A. N. Sherwin-White, *The Letters of Pliny* (Oxford 1960), 186 ff., 321 ff.; A. W. van Buren, *Rend. Pont.* (1943–44), 165–92 (Laurentine Villa); for the estates at Como, Pliny, *Epistles* IX, 7.
191 Contemporary criticism includes: Cicero, *De Legibus* II, 1; Sallust, *Catilina*, 12; Horace, *Odes* II, 15, 10 f.; Horace, *Odes* III, 1, 33 ff., III, 24; Strabo V, 2, 5 (Persian influence) and Horace, *Odes* I, 38; Propertius III, 2, 8 ff.; Pliny, *NH* XXXV, 26; Pliny, *NH* XXXIV, 34; see also D'Arms, *op. cit.*, 40 ff.
192 Consult K. M. Swoboda, *Römische und romanische Paläste* (Vienna, 1924); Boëthius, *op. cit.*, 94–102; H. Drerup, 'Die römische villa', *Marburger Winckelmann-Programm*, 1959, 1–77; M. Rostovtzeff, 'Pompeianische Landschaften und römische Villen', *JDAI*, 1904, 103–26; 'Die hellenistisch-römische Architekturlandschaft', *RM*,

1911, 1–160. For the problem of nomenclature of *porticus* and peristyle consult A. Maiuri, *La Parola del Passato* I (1946), 306–22.

193 Consult P. W. Lehmann, *Roman Wall Paintings from Boscoreale* (Cambridge, Mass., 1953).

194 *Cf.* note 192.

195 *Cf.* A. Maiuri, *Capri (Itinerari,* 93) (Rome 1958), 60–9; *cf.* also A. Maiuri, 'La villa augustea di "Palazzo a Mare" a Capri', *Camp. Rom.* I, 115–41.

196 For ancient testimony, *cf.* Pliny, *NH* III, 70; *id., Epistles* VI, 16 (Villa of Pomponius); F. di Capua, 'Contributi all'Epigrafia e alla Storia della Antica Stabia', *RAAN* NS 1938, 83–124; L. D'Orsi, *Gli Scavi Archeologici di Stabia*² (Milan 1965); *id., Come Ritrovai l'Antica Stabia*² (Milan 1962); O. Elia, *Pitture di Stabia* (Naples 1957); *ibid., Napoli Nobilissima* II, 2 (1962) 43–51 (Villa San Marco).

197 Varro, De Re Rustica I, 13, 3.

198 Consult, *inter alios:* R. T. Günther, *Pausilypon: The Imperial Villa Near Naples* (Oxford 1913), 145–62; L. Breglia, 'Avanzi di una villa romana a Torre del Greco', *Camp. Rom.* I, 91–8; A. Schiavo, 'La villa romana di Minori', *Palladio,* 1939, 129–33; A. Maiuri, *RAAN* NS, 1954, 89 ff.; P. Mingazzini and F. Pfister, 'Surrentum', in *Forma Italiae, Regio* I, vol. 2 (Florence 1946), 100–60 (nos. 20–37, with map I); P. Dubois, *Pouzzoles Antique* (Paris 1907), 355–66 (Puteoli); D'Arms, *op. cit.,* 129 ff.

199 Strabo V, 5, 8.

200 Suetonius, *Augustus* LXV, 1 (AD 6); *cf.* D'Arms, *op. cit.,* 75 f.

201 Statius, *Silvae* II, 2.

202 Consult D'Arms, *op. cit.,* 220 ff. For the site *cf.* Mingazzini and Pfister, *op. cit.,* 54–70.

203 Philostratus, *Imagines* I, praef. 4; *cf.* Noack and Lehmann, *op. cit.* (note 48).

204 Consult A. Maiuri, *Campi Flegrei (Itinerari,* 32)⁴ (Rome 1963), 72–86; A. de Franciscis, 'Underwater Discoveries Around the Bay of Naples', *Archaeology,* 1967, 212–14; see also R. F. Paget, 'The "Great Antrum" at Baiae: a Preliminary Report', *PBSR* NS, 1967, 102–12; C. G. Hardie, *PBSR,* 1969, 14–33; D'Arms, *op. cit.,* 109 ff.

205 *Cf.* Boëthius and Ward-Perkins, *op. cit.* (note 29), 140 ff., figs, 77, 78, 79.

206 *Cf.* note 204.

207 *Cf.* Boëthius and Ward-Perkins, *op. cit.,* 322 f., note 15, fig. 125.

208 Cicero, *Ad Familiares* VII, 1, 1.

209 *Cf.* H. Kähler, *Die Augustusstatue von Primaporta* (Cologne 1959); the introductory pages examine the villa site, especially the terrace garden on the south-east side of the complex; see also J. M. C. Toynbee, *Gnomon,* 1963, 510–13, and H. Ingholt, *Archaeology,* 1969, 176–87, 304–18, who regards the statue as copy of an original erected in the court of the Sanctuary of Athena in Pergamum *c.* 19 BC.

210 Consult M. M. Gabriel, *Livia's Garden Room at Prima Porta* (New York 1955). For ancient refs. to the villa see Pliny, *NH* XV, 40, 136–7; Suetonius, *Galba,* I.

211 Tacitus, *Annals* IV, 67, 5; Suetonius, *Tiberius,* LXV, 2. Consult A. Maiuri, 'Il palazzo di Tiberio detto "villa Iovis" a Capri', *Atti del III Congresso Nazionale di Studi Romani* 1933, 156–71; *id., Capri* (Rome 1958); D'Arms, *op. cit.,* 86–9.

212 *Cf.* de Franciscis, *loc. cit.* (note 204), 215 f.

213 Tacitus, *Annals* IV, 59 (AD 26).

214 *Cf.* G. Jacopi, *L'Antro di Tiberio a Sperlonga* (Rome 1963); B. Conticello, 'Restoring the Polyphemus from Sperlonga', *Archaeology,* 1969, 204–7; Mackendrick, *op. cit.* (note 82), 173–8; F. Fasolo, 'Architettura classiche a Mare', *Quaderni,* 1956, 1–6.

215 *Cf.* Boëthius and Ward-Perkins, *op. cit.*, 204–8; 211–16.

216 *Cf.* G. Ucelli, *Le navi di Nemi* (Rome 1940); MacKendrick, *op. cit.*, 178 ff.

217 Antiate villa: M. E. Blake, *Roman Construction in Italy from Tiberius through the Flavians* (Washington 1959), 40 f.; Baian *opera*: Suetonius, *Nero*, 31, 3; Avernus-Ostia canal: Suetonius, *loc. cit.*, Tacitus, *Annals* XV, 41, 2; Agrippina's vessel: Suetonius, *Nero*, 34.

218 Blake, *op. cit.*, 41–2; cf. Tacitus, *Annals* XIV, 22 (A D 60).

219 *Cf.* J. B. Ward-Perkins, 'Nero's Golden House', *Antiquity*, 1956, 209–19; Boëthius, *op. cit.* (note 85), 94–128; W. L. MacDonald, *op. cit.* (note 142), 20–46 (Nero's palaces).

220 Tacitus, *Annals* XV, 42; *cf.* Martial XII, 57, 21 (*rus in urbe*).

221 Suetonius, *Nero*, XXXI; *cf.* Varro's aviary at Casinum, Varro, *De Re Rustica* IV, 5, 9, and A. W. van Buren, *JRS*, 1919, 59–66.

222 *Cf.* M. Rostovtzeff, *JDAI*, 1904, 103–22; *RM*, 1911, 1–185.

223 Varro, *De Re Rustica*, IV, 5, 9 (Casinum).

224 Farnesina stuccoes: cf. G. Lugli, *Mél. Rom.*, 1938, 5–17 (Augustan Villa Suburbana, 'Farnesina'); H. G. Beyen, *Studia Vollgraf* (Amsterdam 1948), 3–21, the town house of M. Vipsanius Agrippa and Augustus' daughter Julia (19–12 B C); E. L. Wadsworth, 'Stucco reliefs of the First and Second Centuries still Extant in Rome', *MAAR*, 1924, 9–102, pls. 1–49.

225 J. B. Ward-Perkins, *The Italian Element in Late Roman and Early Mediaeval Architecture* (London 1947), 6.

226 J. B. Ward-Perkins, *Antiquity*, 1956, 217.

227 Suetonius, *Nero*, XXXI, 2.

228 Dio Cassius LXV, 9, 4; cf. R. V. D. Magoffin, 'The Alban Villa of Domitian', *AJA*, 1910, 79 ff.; G. Lugli, *Bull. Comm.*, 1917, 29–78; 1918, 3–68; 1919, 153–205; 1920, 3–69; G. Lugli, *NS*, 1946, 60–83 (Pompey's villa); MacDonald, *op. cit.*, 47–74.

229 *Cf.* G. Lugli, *Forma Italiae, Regio* I, vol. I, 2, 65–76, map 3; G. Jacopi, *NS*, 1936, 21–50.

230 Suetonius, *Augustus*, XVI, 4.

231 *Cf.* H. Kähler, *Hadrian und seine Villa bei Tivoli* (Berlin 1950); S. Aurigemma, *Villa adriana*³ (Tivoli 1955); E. Clark, *Rome and a Villa* (New York, 1952), 141–94; R. Vighi (tr. J. B. Ward-Perkins), *Villa Adriana* (Rome 1959).

232 Brown, *op. cit.* (note 109), 42.

233 Boëthius and Ward-Perkins, *op. cit.*, 330 ff., fig. 128.

234 *Cf.* T. Ashby, *PBSR*, 1907, 97–112; N. Lupu, *Ephemeris Dacoromana*, 1937, 117–88; H. Bloch, *I Bolli laterizi e la storia edilizia romana* (Rome 1947), 256–68.

235 *Cf.* G. V. Gentili, *The Imperial Villa of Piazza Armerina* (*Itinerari*, 87) (Rome 1956), who argues in favour of Maximianus as owner; Azevedo favours Nicomachus Flavianus, a scholarly recluse; Ragona argues for Claudius Mamertinus. A. Carandini, *Ricerche sullo stile e la cronologia dei mosaici della Villa di Piazza Armerina* (Rome 1964), implies that the *dominus* may have been a millionaire supplier of animals for Roman entertainment, perhaps during the early fifth century. See also B. Pace, *I mosaici di Piazza Armerina* (Rome 1955); H. P. l'Orange and E. Dyggve, *Symbolae Osloenses*, 1952, 114–28; G. V. Gentili, *La Villa Erculia di Piazza Armerina: i mosaici figurati* (Milan 1959); and N. Neuerberg, 'Some Considerations on the Architecture of the Imperial Villa at Piazza Armerina', *Marsyas*, 1959, 22–9.

236 MacKendrick, *op. cit.*, 340.

CHAPTER VI

237 *Cf.* Varro, *De Lingua Latina* V, 125.

238 Richter, *op. cit.* (note 33), 98 ff.

239 Richter, *op. cit.*, 102 ff.

240 Richter, *op. cit.*, 114.

241 Richter, *op. cit.*, 115 ff.; Maiuri, *Ercolano* (*Itinerari*, 53) (Rome 1936), 41, pls. XXIII, fig. 42; Petronius, *Satyricon*, 29.

242 Richter, *op. cit.*, 110 ff.

243 Pliny, *NH* XXXIV, 14.

244 Richter, *op. cit.*, 105 ff.; D.K. Hill, 'Ivory Ornaments of Hellenistic Couches', *Hesperia*, 1963, 295 ff.

245 Petronius, *Satyricon*, 97.

246 Richter, *op. cit.*, 107 f.; D.K. Hill, *Journal of the Walters Art Gallery*, Baltimore, 1952–53, 49–61 (first-century B C bronze couch).

247 Maiuri, *Ercolano*, 41 f.

248 Pliny, *NH* XXXVI, 8, 14; Richter, *op. cit.*, 116

249 *Cf.* R. Herbig, 'Fensterstudien an antiken Wohnbauten', *RM*, 1929; V. Spinazzola, *Pompei alla luce degli scavi nuovi di Via dell'Abbondanza*, 1910–23 (3 vols. Rome 1953), ch. 3: 'Fenestre e problemi della luce'; G. Webster, 'Roman Windows and Grilles', *Antiquity*, 1959, 10–14 (with figs.).

250 Seneca, *Epistles* LXXXVI (Scipio's villa at Liternum).

251 Maiuri instances, *inter alia*, baths built over the ovens in the House of the Cryptoporticus, Pompeii, and the House of Menander, Pompeii (*NS*, 1933, 220, 270).

252 Pliny, *NH* XXXVI, 60, 184; cf. K. Jex-Blake and E. Sellers, *The Elder Pliny's Chapters on the History of Art* (London 1896), 224; G.E. Rizzo, *La Pittura Ellenistico-Romana* (Milan 1929), 42.

253 Petronius, *Satyricon*, 34.

254 Pliny, *NH* XXXVI, 61, 185.

255 Pliny, *NH* XXXVI, 62, 187.

256 Pliny, *NH* XXXVI, 63, 188.

257 Vitruvius VII, 4, 5.

258 Pliny, *NH* XXXVI, 7, 48–50; 64, 189.

259 Consult B. Andreae, *Das Alexandermosaik* (Bremen 1959).

260 *Cf.* R. V. Schoder, *Masterpieces of Greek Art* (1960) pl. 75 (colour). *cit.* (note 84), pl. 75.

261 For illustration see G. M. Hanfmann, *op. cit.* (note 97), pl. 20; *cf.* also A. Maiuri, *Ercolano* I, 393–403, figs. 330 ff.

262 Vitruvius VI, 3, 5–11.

263 Vitruvius VII, 7–14; Pliny, *NH* XXXV, 30–49.

264 Pliny, *NH* XXXVI, 6, 47.

265 Pliny, *NH* XXXVI, 7, 48.,

266 Pliny, *NH* XXXVI, 8, 49–50.

267 *Cf.* Vitruvius VII, 5, 1. On the styles consult A. Maiuri, *Roman Painting* (Geneva 1953), *passim*.

268 *Cf.* H. H. Scullard, *The Etruscan Cities and Rome* (London 1967), 122f.

269 Vitruvius VII, 5, 2.

270 *Cf.* M. H. Swindler, *Ancient Painting* (New Haven, Conn., 1929), 328, 338 f., fig. 529, 542; A. Maiuri, *Roman Painting*, 33 ff.; *cf.* W. J. T. Peters, *op. cit.*, 27–32; P. H. von Blanckenhagen, *RM LXX*, 1963, 100–46; A. Gallina, *Le Pitture con paesaggi dell' Odissea dall' Esquilino* (Rome 1964).

271 *Cf.* G. E. Rizzo, *Monumenti della pittura antica*, sez. III, fasc. 3, 'La casa di Livia' (Rome 1936); for decoration of the newly identified House of Augustus, *cf.* O. E. Richmond, *JRS* IV (1914), 193–226; G. Carettoni, 'I Problemi della zona Augustea del Palatino alle luce dei recenti scavi', *Rend. Pontif. Accad.* XXXIX (1966–7), 55–75; *ibid.*, *ILN* 6790 (Sept. 20, 1969) (plates).

272 Cf. M. M. Gabriel, *op. cit.* (note 210); see also above, pp. 124.

273 M. Bieber, *AJA*, 1959, 101; cf. A. Maiuri, *La Villa dei Misteri²* (Rome, 1947), *id.*, *Roman Painting* (Geneva, 1953), 51, 59 f.; M. Cooke, *JRS* III, 1913, 167 ff.; M. Bieber, *JDAI*, 1928 (1929), 298–330; J. M. C. Toynbee, *JRS* XIX, 1929, 67–87; G. Zuntz, *PBA* XLIX, 1963, 177–201; A. M. G. Little, *Roman Perspective Painting and the Ancient Stage* (Kennebank, Maine, 1971); *id.*, *A Roman Bridal Drama at the Villa of the Mysteries* (Kennebank, Maine, 1972).

274 Vitruvius VII, 5, 3.

275 Cf. B. F. Cook, 'The Boscoreale Cubiculum: A New Installation', *Bulletin of the Metropolitan Museum of Art*, 1964, 166–83; Lehmann, *op. cit.* (note 193), 189 ff. (bibliography); see above, pp. 116.

276 Vitruvius V, 6, 9.

277 Hanfmann, *op. cit.* (note 97), 226, and pl. VI.

278 Vitruvius VI, 5, 2; cf. A. W. van Buren, *MAAR*, 1938, 70–81.

279 Cicero, *Brutus*, 261.

280 Vitruvius VII, 3, 10; Pliny, *NH* XXXV, 49, 173.

281 Cf. G. Bagnani, (*op. cit.*, note 183); 'And passing rich . . .' (*op. cit.*, note 183).

282 On programmatic painting consult K. Lehmann, 'The Imagines of the Elder Philostratus', *Art Bulletin*, 1941, 16–44; *id.*, 'A Roman Poet Visits a Museum', *Hesperia*, 1945, 159–69; C. Schefold, *Pompejanische Malerei: Sinn und Ideengeschichte* (Basel 1952); *id.*, *Vergessenes Pompeji* (Munich 1962); M. L. Thompson, *Programmatic Painting in Pompeii: The Meaningful Combination of Mythological Pictures in Room Decoration* (Unpublished dissertation, New York University, 1960).

283 Cf. Schefold, *op. cit.*, 139 ff.; M. Borda, *La pittura romana* (Milan 1958), 78 ff.; 87 ff.; H. Kähler, *op. cit.* (note 106), 106–9.

284 Petronius, *Satyricon*, XXIX (murals); LXXI (tomb reliefs).

285 Cf. Elia, *Pitture di Stabia* (Naples, 1957).

CHAPTER VII

286 *Aeneid* I, 282, 278–9.

287 Consult Ramsay MacMullen, 'Roman Imperial Building in the Provinces', *HSCP* 64 (1959), 207–35 *passim*.

288 Paul MacKendrick, *The Roman Mind at Work* (Princeton 1958), 28.

289 MacKendrick, *Roman France*, 128.

290 R. Agache, 'Aerial Reconnaissance in Picardie', *Antiquity* XXXVIII (1964), 113–19; R. Agache, R. Chevallier, General G. Schmiedt, *Études d' archéologie aérienne.* (Paris 1966), esp. Agache, 'Recherches aériennes de l'habitat gallo-romain en Picardie', 75–88.

291 For details consult M. H. d'Arbois de Jubainville, *Recherches sur l'origine de la propriété foncière et des noms de lieux habités en France* (Paris 1890).

292 H. Rolland, 'Fouilles de Glanum', *Gallia, Supplément* I (1946); XI (1958); F. Chamoux, 'Les Antiques de St.-Rémy-de-Provence', *Phoibos* VI–VII (1951–3, publ. 1955), 97–111; P. MacKendrick, *Roman France*, 21–8 (air view, plate 1.10).

293 J. Sautel, *Vaison dans l'antiquité*, 3 vols., with supplements. Avignon-Lyon, 1927–42; *id.*, *Vaison dans l'antiquité: sites, histoire et monuments de Vaison-la-Romaine* (Lyon 1955);

MacKendrick, *op. cit.*, 105–14 (air view, plate 4.9); R. Syme, *Tacitus*, Vol. II (Oxford 1958), 622 ff.; Pierre Pellerin, *En ressuscitant Vaison-la-Romaine* (Paris, 1962). P. A. Février, *JRS* LXIII (1973) 1–28, espec. 24–25 (Maison du Dauphine).

294 *Cf.* J. Soyer, 'Découverte d'emplacement d'habitat gallo-romain dans la plaine d'Aix', *Revue archéologique de Narbonnaise I* (1968), 201–18.

295 Consult Joël Le Gall, *Alésia, archéologie et histoire* (Paris 1963); MacKendrick, *op. cit.*, 45–56 (plan, fig. 2.10).

296 *Cf.* R. De Maeyer, *De Romeinsche Villa's in Belgie* (Antwerp 1937), 77–83.

297 Agache, *Antiquity* XXXVIII (1964), 118.

298 L. Joulin, 'Les établissements gallo-romains de la plaine de Martres-Tolosanes', *Mém. Ac. Inscr.* I, série 11 (1901) (= Chiragan); MacKendrick, *op. cit.*, 131–4 (plan, fig. 5.3).

299 *Cf.* H.-P. Eydoux, 'La fasteuse ville de Montmaurin', *Monuments et trésors de la Gaule* (1958), 220–52; Georges Fouet, 'La villa gallo-romaine de Montmaurin (Haute Garonne)', *Gallia*, Suppl. XX (1969); MacKendrick, *op. cit.*, 134–40 (air view, plate 5.5; model, plate 5.7).

300 *Cf.* H.-P. Eydoux, 'La Resurrection de Lugdunum Convenarum', *Lumières sur la Gaule* (1960), 157–89; B. Sapène, *St.-Bertrand-de-Cominges (Lugdunum Convenarum), centre touristique de l'art et d'histoire* (Toulouse 1954).

301 Sidonius (Apollinaris), *Poems and Letters.* Transl. W. B. Anderson. 2 vols., Cambridge, Mass., 1936; quotation, Vol. I, *Epistle* II, 2.

302 E. Oelmann, 'Ein Gallorömischer Bauernhof bei Mayen', *Bonner Jahrbücher* CXXXIII (1928), 51–140; *id.*, 'Zu den Rekonstruktionen des Hauptgebäudes im gallorömischen Bauernhof bei Mayen', *op. cit.*, 141–52; E. M. Wightman, *Roman Trier and the Treviri* (London 1970), 139.

303 P. Steiner, 'Die römische Villa von Bollendorf', *Trierer Jahresberichte* XII (1923), 1–59.

304 *Cf. Trierer Zeitschrift* XXIV–XXVI (1956–8), Jahresberichte, 511–26; Wightman, *op. cit.*, 139–41 (plan, fig. 13).

305 *Decimus Magnus Ausonius.* Transl. H. G. Evelyn White. Cambridge, Mass., 1919; quot., *Mosella* 321–48; F. Marx, 'Ausonius' Lied von der Mosel', *Rh. Mus.* LXXX (1931), 368–92.

306 H. Mylius, 'Die Rekonstruktion der römischen Villen Nennig und Fliessem', *Bonner Jahrbücher* CXXIX (1924), 109–20; Wightman, *op. cit.*, 145–7 (plan, fig. 16); P. MacKendrick, *Romans on the Rhine* (New York 1970), 147–51 (grounds and plan, 148; mosaic, 151).

307 A pipe organ with an air-pressure system regulated by water was found in the garrison town of Aquincum (Hungary). *Cf.* Werner Walcker-Mayer, *Die römische Orgel von Aquincum* (Stuttgart 1970); MacKendrick, *op. cit.*, 202–4 (plate, model).

308 P. Fremersdorf, *Die römische Gutshof Köln-Müngersdorf* (Berlin 1933); H. Schmitz, 'Die wirtschaftliche Bedeutung des römischen Gutshofes in Köln-Müngersdorf', *Bonner Jahrbücher* CXXXIX (1934), 80–93; MacKendrick, *op. cit.*, 55–8 (model, 57); Wightman, *op. cit.*, 153–4, 156, 185.

309 *Cf. Trierer Zeitschrift* XVI–XVII (1941–2), Jahresberichte, 229–35; MacKendrick, *op. cit.*, 145–7 (reconstr. drawing).

310 *Cf.* E. Gose, 'Die Kaiserliche Sommerresidenz in Konz, Landkreis Saarburg', *Germania* XXXIX (1961), 204–6; Wightman, *op. cit.*, 165–8 (plan, fig. 19); MacKendrick, *op. cit.*, 243–4.

311 F. Kutzbach, 'Das ältere Hoch-schloss in Pfalzel bei Trier', *Germania* XIX (1935), 40–53; J. Steinhausen, 'Palatiolum und Venatius Fortunatus', in *Aus Mittelalter und Neuzeit, Fest-schrift G. Kallen* (Bonn 1957), 303–15; Wightman, *op. cit.*, 168–9 (plan, fig. 20).

312 *Cf.* note 306, Mylius, *op. cit.* 120–8; MacKendrick, *op. cit.*, 144 (plan, model, 146); Wightman, *op. cit.*, 143–5 (plan, fig. 15).

313 Franz Fremersdorf, *Das römische Haus mit dem Dionysos-Mosaik vor dem Südportal des Kölner Domes* (Berlin 1956); *id.*, *Dionysos-Mosaik in dem römischen Haus vor dem Südportal des Kölner Domes* (Cologne 1957); O. Doppelfeld, 'Das Dionysos-Mosaik am Dom zu Köln', *Schriftenreihe der archäologischen Gesellschaft Köln* VIII, 3 (1967).

314 Wightman, *op. cit.*, 145 (plate 6b).

315 F. Drexel, 'Die Bilder der Igeler Saüle', *Römische Mitteilungen* XXXVIII (1920), 83–142; H. Dragendorff, E. Krüger, *Das Grabmal von Igel* (Trier, 1924) MacKendrick, *op. cit.*, 239–44 (ills).

316 *Cf.* MacKendrick, *op. cit.*, 190–1 (ills).

317 *Cf.* W. von Massow, *Die Grab-mäler von Neumagen* (Berlin 1932), 132 ff., with reconstrs.; Wightman, *op. cit.*, plates 14a, 14b, 16c, 17a; MacKendrick, *op. cit.*, 234–9 (ills).

318 F. Oertel, 'Die römische villa bei Blankenheim in der Eifel', *Bonner Jahrbücher* CXXIII (1916), 210–25; MacKendrick, *op. cit.*, 143–4 (illustr. model, Phases I and III).

319 H. Koethe, 'Die Hermen von Wellschbillig', *Jahrb. d. deutsch. Arch. Inst.* L (1935), 198–237; Wightman, *op. cit.*, 169–70 (plates 13a 13b); MacKendrick, *op. cit.*, 151–3 (pool, reconstr. drawing).

320 *Cf.* note 305: *Mosella* 20–2 (transl. H. G. Evelyn White).

321 *Cf.* C. E. Stevens, 'Britain be-tween the Invasions', in *Aspects of Archaeology in Britain and Beyond* (W. F. Grimes, ed.) (London 1951), 332–44.

322 *Cf.* J. K. St Joseph, 'The Contri-bution of Aerial Photography', in *The Civitas Capitals of Roman Britain* (J. S. Wacher, ed.) (Leicester 1966), 21–30 (Plate I, Wroxeter, Salop.; II. Silchester, Hampshire).

323 *Cf.* H. W. Bowen, 'The Celtic Background', in *The Roman Villa in Britain* (A. L. F. Rivet, ed.) (London 1969), 1–48.

324 Consult K. D. White, *Roman Farming* (London, 1970).

325 *Cf.* S. Applebaum, 'Agriculture in Roman Britain', *Agricultural History Review* VI (1958), 68–86.

326 Consult A. L. F. Rivet, *Town and Country in Roman Britain* (London 1966), 37–40 (plan, 109) (Little Wood-bury, Wilts.).

327 Sheppard Frere, *Britannia: a history of Roman Britain* (London 1967), 265.

328 *Cf.* J. B. Ward-Perkins, *Antiquar-ies Journal* XVIII (1938), 339–76; *id.*, *Antiquity* XIV (1940), 317 ff.; and Graham Webster's reappraisal in *The Roman Villa in Britain* (ed. A. L. F. Rivet), 243–6.

329 *Cf. Arch. J.* CII (1945), 21–110; CXVIII (1961), 100–35.

330 *Cf.* A. L. F. Rivet, *Town and Coun-try in Roman Britain*, 111–12 (air view, Watts Wells, Ditchley); J. Liversidge, *Britain in the Roman Empire* (London 1967), 108 (plan of excavation).

331 *Cf.* W. H. Manning, 'The Villas in Roman Britain', *Antiquity* XXXVI (1962), 56 ff.; Sir Ian Richmond, 'The Plans of Roman Villas in Britain', in *The Roman Villa in Britain* (A. L. F. Rivet, ed.), 49–70; Rivet, *Town and Country, passim.*

332 Consult C. F. C. Hawkes, 'Bri-tons, Romans and Saxons around Salisbury and in Cranborne Chase', *Arch. J.* CIV (1948), 27–81.

333 Frere, *op. cit.*, 265.

334 Frere, *op. cit.*, 247–8.

335 Consult Sir Ian Richmond, 'Industry in Roman Britain', in J. S. Wacher (ed.) *The Civitas Capitals of Roman Britain*, 76–86; Peter Solway, *The Frontier Peoples of Roman Britain* (Cambridge 1967), 167 ff.; Liversidge, *op. cit.*, 68 ff.; Sheppard Frere, and others, *Verulamium Excavations*, Vol. I (Oxford 1972), describes a long series of stone shops on the *cardo maximus* with frontal colonnade or portico (*c.* A D 275).

336 George C. Boon, *Roman Silchester: The Archaeology of a Romano-British Town* (London 1957): Chapter VI, Houses (134–52); Chapter VII, Homes (157–73).

337 Consult M. R. Hull, *Roman Colchester* (Oxford 1958).

338 Consult R. Merrifield, *The Roman City of London* (London 1965); J. Liversidge, *op. cit.*, 102–13; W. F. Grimes, *The Excavation of Roman and Mediaeval London* (London 1967).

339 Consult Barry Cunliffe, *Roman Bath* (Society of Antiquaries Research Report, London 1969); *id.*, *Roman Bath Discovered* (London 1971).

340 Consult Barry Cunliffe, *Excavations at Fishbourne, 1961–1969*. Vol. I. The Site. Vol. II. The Finds. The Society of Antiquaries, London 1971; *id.*, *Fishbourne. A Roman Palace and its Garden* (London 1971).

341 *Cf.* M. M. Gabriel, *Livia's Garden Room at Prima Porta* (New York 1955).

342 Rivet, *Town and Country in Roman Britain*, 105.

343 Consult G. W. Meates, *Lullingstone Roman Villa* (London 1955); *id.*, *Lullingstone Roman Villa* (Ministry of Works Guide) (London 1963; reprinted 1966).

344 *Cf.* V. E. Nash Williams, 'The Roman Villa at Llantwit-Major in Glamorgan', *Archaeologica Cambrensis* CII (1953), 89–163; and reappraisal by Graham Webster in A. L. F Rivet (ed.), *The Roman Villa in Britain*, 238–43.

345 *Cf.* J. T. Smith, 'Romano-British Aisled Houses', *Arch. J.* CXX (1963), 1–30; Frere, *op. cit.*, 270 ff. (barn dwelling/basilican villa).

346 *Cf.* S. E. Winbolt and G. Herbert, *The Roman Villa at Bignor, Sussex* (Guidebook. Chichester, n.d.).

347 Consult S. Lysons, *An Account of Roman Antiquities discovered at Woodchester in the County of Gloucester* (1797); *Transactions Bristol and Gloucester Archaeological Society* XLVIII (1927), 75–96; LXXIV (1956), 172–5.

348 The shop-residence in Britain was a Continental rather than a direct Roman legacy. 'It lasted thenceforward until modern times, when it still survives as in the old family business. It is the direct antithesis of the multiple store: not large-scale industry engaged in mass-production of stocks of standard goods, but a small concern producing individual requirements, goods specifically ordered, such as might be commissioned on one market-day and ready on the next.' Sir Ian Richmond, *The Civitas Capitals of Roman Britain* (ed. J. S. Wacher) 76. Consult also Lino Rossi, *Trajan's Column and the Dacian Wars* (London 1971) (plates) for two-storey shops in Romania; Peter Salway, *op. cit.*, 167 ff. (houses and shops in British *vici*).

349 *Cf.* S. Frere, 'The End of Towns in Roman Britain', in J. S. Wacher (ed.), *The Civitas Capitals of Roman Britain*.

350 For social and economic aspects consult A. L. F. Rivet in his *The Roman Villa in Britain*, 173–216; for critical assessment of villa research consult Graham Webster, 'The Future of Villa Studies', *The Roman Villa in Britain* (A. L. F. Rivet, ed.), 217–49.

351 Consult George C. Boon, *Roman Silchester*; A. Birley, *Life in Roman Britain* (London 1964); L. Liversidge,

Britain in the Roman Empire. These compendia provide additional details and examples on every aspect of home life in Roman Britain.

352 D. Harden, 'Domestic Window Glass, Roman, Saxon and Mediaeval', in E. M. Jope (ed.) *Studies in Building History* (London 1961), 44–52; Graham Webster, 'Roman Windows and Grilles', *Antiquity* XXIII (1959), 10–14.

353 Consult J. Liversidge, 'Wall-paintings from Verulamium', *British Museum Quarterly* XXXV (1971), 87–93; *id.*, *Britain in the Roman Empire*, 84–101; *id.*, 'Furniture and Interior Decoration', in *The Roman Villa in Britain* (A. L. F. Rivet, ed.), 127–72; and as background for the Verulamium scroll painting, J. M. C. Toynbee and J. B. Ward-Perkins, 'Peopled Scrolls: a Hellenistic motif in Imperial Art', *PBSR* XVIII (1950).

354 *Cf.* K. S. Painter, 'Villas and Christianity in Roman Britain', *British Museum Quarterly* XXXV (1971), 156–75.

355 Consult I. Antony, 'The Roman Building at Gorhambury', *St. Albans Architectural and Archaeological Society Transactions* (1961), 21–30. For additional stuccoes at Bignor Villa and Fishbourne, consult the reports (*supra*).

356 For Christian mosaics consult J. M. C. Toynbee, *Art in Britain under the Romans* (Oxford 1964), 228 ff.; *id.*, *The Christian Roman Mosaic, Hinton St. Mary, Dorset*, Dorset Monographs III, Dorset Natural History and Archaeological Society, 1964; K. S. Painter, 'The Roman Site at Hinton St. Mary', *British Museum Quarterly* XXXII (1967), 15–31; D. J. Smith, 'The Mosaic Pavement', in *The Roman Villa in Britain* (A. L. F. Rivet, ed.), 71–125.

357 Boon, *Roman Silchester*, 102; see also 101–14 for detailed account of

hypocaustic systems at Silchester; also Liversidge, *Britain in the Roman Empire*, 41–50; G. De Angelis D'Ossat, *Tecnica costruttiva e impianti delle terme* (Mostra della Romanità: Civiltà romana, No. 23, Rome 1940); R. J. Forbes, *Studies in Ancient Technology*, Vol. V: Heat and Heating, Refrigeration, Light (2nd edn, 1966).

358 For the reconstructed hypocaust and the experiment in the frontier fort of Saalburg, 20 miles NE. of Mainz, consult Fritz Kretzschmer, 'Hypokausten', *Saalburg Jahrbuch* XII (1953), 7–41.

359 For the Lincoln aqueduct and pump *cf.* F. Thompson, *Roman Lincoln, 1945–54* (Lincoln 1955); Liversidge, *op. cit.*, 50–7 (drainage, water-supply); G. C. Boon, *Roman Silchester* 159–60 force pump for well-water, fig. 31); Frere, *op. cit.*, 245 f. (Verulamium sewer, etc.).

360 Consult J. Liversidge, *Furniture in Roman Britain* (London 1955); and 'Furniture and Interior Decoration', in *The Roman Villa in Britain* (A. L. F. Rivet, ed.), 127–72.

361 Consult K. Jackson, *Language and History in Early Britain* (Edinburgh 1953) for a list of Latin words which survived into Brittonic languages along with the article or concept, e.g. plumbum, stagnum, columna, cuneus, fenestra, maceria, parietem, porta, postis, scala, transtrum, vitrum, cera, flamma, focus, fontana, puteus and taberna; and J. W. Brailsford, *The Mildenhall Treasure: a Handbook*. 2nd edn (London 1955), a fourth-century silver service specifically Christian in character.

362 *Cf.* C. M. Wells, *The German Policy of Augustus* (Oxford 1972), 240 f. Varus was related to Augustus by marriage with Claudia Pulchra and to Agrippa by an earlier marriage.

363 *Cf.* J. J. Wilkes, 'The Military Achievement of Augustus in Europe,

with special reference to Illyricum',
*University of Birmingham Historical
Journal* X (1965), 1–27.
364 E.B.Thomas, *Römische Villen
in Pannonien* (Budapest 1964).
365 H. Daicoviciu, *Dacii* (Budapest
1965); Lino Rossi, *Trajan's Column
and the Dacian Wars* (London 1971).
366 Consult A. Boëthius and J.B.
Ward-Perkins, *Etruscan and Roman
Architecture* (Harmondsworth 1970),
363 ff.; P. MacKendrick, *Romans on
the Rhine* (London 1970), 140 ff.
367 *Cf.* MacKendrick, *op. cit.*, 141–2
(plan, p. 142).
368 *Cf.* MacKendrick, *op. cit.*, 140–1
(plan 5.8).
369 Consult J. Szilagyi, *Aquincum*
(Berlin 1956).
370 Consult E. Swoboda, *Carnuntum:
seine Geschichte und seine Denkmäler*
(Römische Forschungen in Nieder-
österreich), 4th edn (Graz and Cologne
1964).
371 L. Septimius Severus, governor
of Upper Pannonia, member of a

Punic family and native of Lepcis
Magna, was proclaimed Emperor by
his troops at Carnuntum in 198.
372 The present place-name, Split
or Spalato, has usually been derived
from palatium (*cf.* Pfalzel), but J.J.
Wilkes (*Dalmatia*, 388) properly associ-
ates the name with the late Roman
geographical place-name, Aspalathus,
after a thorny plant which yielded an
essence for perfume and scented oils
(*cf.* Pliny, *NH* 13, 18, etc.).
373 Consult E. Hebrard, J. Zeiller,
Le Palais de Dioclétien (1912); K. M.
Swoboda, *Römische und romanische
Paläste*, 148 ff.; T. and J. Marasovic,
Diocletian Palace (Zagreb 1968);
Boëthius and Ward-Perkins, *op. cit.*,
524–9 (figs. 200, 201); L. Crema,
L'Archittetura romana, 612–19 (figs. 775,
810–13, 824); Wilkes, *Dalmatia* 387 ff.
374 Boëthius and Ward-Perkins,
op. cit., 528; *cf.* G. Downey, 'The
Palace of Diocletian at Antioch',
Annales archéologiques de Syrie III
(1953). 106 ff.

CHAPTER VIII

375 Ramsay MacMullen, *HSCP* 64
(1959), 207–35.
376 J. A. O. Larsen, 'Roman Greece'
in Tenney Frank, *Economic Survey of
Ancient Rome* IV.
377 *Cf.* H. S. Robinson, *The Urban
Development of Ancient Corinth*. American School of Classical Studies in
Athens, 1965.
378 Th. Wiegand, H. Schrader,
Priene. (Berlin 1904); P. MacKendrick,
The Greek Stones Speak, s.v. Priene,
and bibliography.
379 Consult Gerhard Kleiner, *Das
römische Miletos* (Wiesbaden 1970);
MacKendrick, *op. cit.*, s.v. Ephesus,
and bibliography.
380 *Cf.* Arif Müfid Mansel, *Die*

Ruinen von Side (Berlin 1963).
381 *Cf.* Franz Miltner, *Ephesus* (Vienna
1958); Josef Keil, *Führer durch Ephesus*
(Vienna 1964); MacKendrick, *op. cit.*,
s.v. Ephesus, with bibliography; Hakki
Gültekin, *A Guide to Ephesus* (Izmir
1965); W. Alzinger, *Ein Rundgang
durch die Ruinen* (Berlin/Vienna 1972).
382 Hermann Vetters, *ILN* 244 (16
May 1964), 766–8; (23 May 1964),
822–5; *id.; Österreich. Akad. der
Wissenschaften* (Wien) Anzeiger *CIX*
(1972) 83–102; ; *id.*, 'Zum Stockbau in
Ephesos', *Mélanges Mansel* (Ankara
1973), 69–92.
383 *Cf. Acts of the Apostles*, I, 13
(upper chamber or storey: *hyperōon*).
Homer (*Iliad* II, 514; XVI, 184;

Odyssey I, 362) uses *hyperōon* for the upper part of the house reserved for women; Antiphon, I, 14, for a spare room; Aristophanes, *Knights* 1001, for an attic or garret. The Last Supper was enacted in an upper room which was probably the meeting place of the disciples after the Resurrection.

384 *Cf.* frigidarium fresco, Villa San Marco (Villa of Narcissus) at Stabiae; the wall-painting, first century A D, depicts the same figure from another angle.

385 *Cf.* Strabo XVI, 1, 5 (Babylon); XVI, 2, 23 (Tyre); XVI, 2, 13 (Aradus). Pomponius Mela II, 7, 6, refers to the Aradus highrise buildings.

386 Consult Yigael Yadin, *Masada: Herod's Fortress and the Zealots' Last Stand* (London 1966).

387 (Flavius) Josephus. *The Jewish War*, transl. H. St J. Thackeray (Cambridge, Mass. Vols. II and III, 1961, 1968). The palace and the siege by Flavius Silva, the governor, are described in Book VII (Volume III) 252, 280–303 (description and history of the palace); 304–406 (siege and capture of Masada).

388 Boëthius and Ward-Perkins, *op. cit.*, 416.

389 *Cf.* J. A. Pritchard, 'The Excavation at Herodian Jericho, 1951', *Annual of the American Schools of Oriental Research* XXXII–XXXIII, 1–13, with plates. The first-century B C villa contains a bath-suite; Aristobulus, brother of Miriamne, was probably drowned there.

390 *Cf.* Boëthius and Ward-Perkins, *op. cit.*, s.v. Syria; G. Tchalenko, *Villages antiques de la Syrie du Nord.* 3 vols (Paris 1953–8).

391 Consult R. Stillwell, *Antioch-on-the-Orontes* III (Princeton 1941), 1 ff.; id., 'Houses of Antioch', *Dumbarton Oaks Papers* XV (1961), 45–57; Glanville Downey, *Ancient Antioch* (Princeton 1963), s.v. houses.

392 Ammianus Marcellinus, XXII, 9, 14.

393 Doro Levi, *Antioch Mosaic Pavements*, 2 vols (Princeton 1947).

394 The remains of a villa of the Septimii, property of the father or brother of Septimius Severus, were explored in 1869–70 near Baccano, 27 miles north from Rome. For details, consult G. Becatti, E. Fabricotti, A. Gallina, *et al.*, *Mosaici Antichi in Italia: Regione Settima. Baccano: Villa Romana* (Rome 1970).

395 Adobe brick was favoured by ancient house-builders throughout Asia and Africa for a number of reasons: it was inexpensive to make and demanded no skilled labour; it was fireproof and resilient to seismic shocks (*cf.* modern Turkey and Iran); it was soundproof in an urban setting and offered reasonable insulation against heat and cold. A coating of stucco or clay, in bright colours or earthy hues, guaranteed against weathering.

396 For general décor and cult associations, consult M. I. Rostovtzeff, *Dura-Europos and its Art* (Oxford 1938).

397 On 19 May 1972, the Tunisian Government through UNESCO invited participation in a large-scale archaeological campaign 'Pour Sauver Carthage'. The ancient city has never been systematically excavated and the Punic, Roman and Byzantine remains are imperilled by the urban sprawl of modern Tunis.

398 *Cf.* A. Deman, 'Virgile et la colonisation romaine en Afrique du Nord', in *Hommages à Albert Grenier* (ed. M. Renard) (Collection Latomus, Vol. LVIII. Pt. 1 (3). (Brussels 1962), 514–26.

399 Consult Eva Schmidt, *Studien zum Barberinischen Mosaik in Palestrina* (Strasburg 1929), 38–42; G. Gullini, *I Mosaici di Palestrina* (Rome 1956); G. M. Hanfmann, *Roman Art* (Greenwich, Conn. 1964), colour plate XXVI, with commentary and bibliography.

400 *Cf.* J. J. S. Whitaker, *Motya, a Phoenician Colony in Sicily* (London 1921), 17.

401 Consult Maria Nowicka, *La Maison privée dans l'Égypte ptolemaïque* (Warsaw/Cracow 1969), with 101 figs.

402 Consult Raymond Thouvenot, *Volubilis* (Paris 1949): Palace of Gordian, 47-8; House of the Venus Mosaic, 54-6; *id.*, *Les Maisons de Volubilis: le palais dit de Gordien et la maison á la mosaïque de Vénus* (Publications du Service des Antiquités du Maroc, XII), Rabat 1958; Robert Étienne, *Le Quartier nord-est de Volubilis* (Paris 1960).

403 J. W. Graham, 'The Greek House and the Roman House', *Phoenix* XX (1966), 20-4.

404 Graham, *op. cit.*, 23.

405 Carl H. Kraeling, *et al. Ptolemais, City of the Libyan Pentapolis* (Chicago 1962).

406 G. Pesce. *Il Palazzo delle Colonne in Tolemaide* (Rome 1959).

407 P. Mingazzini. *L'Insula di Giasone Magno a Cirene* (Rome 1966); Richard Goodchild, *Cyrene and Apollonia, a historical guide* (London 1959); *id.*, *Kyrene und Apollonia* (Zurich 1971).

408 Consult E. Boeswillwald, R. Cagnat, A. Ballu, *Timgad, une cité africaine sous l'empire romain* (Paris 1905); H. F. Pfeiffer, *MAAR* (1931), 157-65 (restoration); C. Courtois, *Timgad; antique Thamugadi* (Algiers, Service des Antiquités 1951); Suzanne Germain, *Les mosaïques de Timgad: étude descriptive et analytique* (Paris 1969).

409 *Cf.* A. Merlin, *Forums et maisons d'Althiburos* (Notes et documents, VI) (1913), 39-45; Boëthius and Ward-Perkins, *op. cit.*, 185.

410 *Cf.* Boëthius and Ward-Perkins, *op. cit.*, 185 (plan); J. Baradez, 'Les Fouilles de Tipasa', *Libyca* II (1954), 89 ff.

411 A. Lézine, 'House of the Figured Capitals', *Karthago* VII (1956), 3-53; *id.*, *Carthage-Utique. Études d'Architecture et d'Urbanisme* (Paris 1969) (2nd-century *insulae*, houses, shops).

412 *Cf.* P. Gauckler, 'House of the Laberii', in *Monuments et Mémoires Piot* III (1896), 177-299.

413 *Cf.* L. Foucher, *La Maison de la procession dionysiaque à El-Jem* (Paris 1963).

414 Giacomo Guidi, 'La Villa del Nilo', *Africa Italiana* V (1933), 1-56 (2nd-century villa at Lepcis Magna).

415 For example, at Bulla Regia (Hamman Daradji).

416 *Cf.* Alfred Merlin, 'La Mosaïque du Seigneur Julius à Carthage', *Bulletin du Comité Archéologique des Travaux historiques et scientifiques* XXXVIII (1921), 95-114; G. Charles-Picard, 'Mosaïques africaines du IIIe siècle après J. C.', *Revue Archéologique* II (1960), 171 ff.; Thérèse Précheur-Canonge, *La vie rurale en Afrique romain d'après les mosaïques* (Paris 1962).

417 Richmond, *Civitas Capitals of Roman Britain* (ed. J. S. Wacher), 82.

418 Consult Ramsay MacMullen, *Soldier and Civilian in the Later Roman Empire* (Cambridge, Mass. 1963); P. Brown, 'Christianity and Local Culture in Late Roman Africa', *JRS* LVIII (1968), 49-86. Towers constructed to supervise ranches or at the corners of country mansions may be a legacy from the period of Carthaginian suzerainty. *Cf.* Vergil, *Aeneid* IV, 585: regina e *speculis* ut primam albescere lucem/ vidit et aequatis classem procedere velis (586).

419 *JRS* XLIII (1953), 73.

420 *Cf.* P. Grimal, 'Les Maisons à tour hellénistiques et romaines', *Mélanges d'archéologie et d'histoire de l'École française de Rome* LVI (1939), 28 ff.

BIBLIOGRAPHY

GENERAL REFERENCE WORKS

Anderson, W.J., *Architecture of Greece and Rome* (London 1927)

Blake, M., *Ancient Roman Construction in Italy from the Prehistoric Period to Augustus* (Washington 1947)
  Roman Construction in Italy from Tiberius through the Flavians (Washington 1959)

Boëthius, A., and Ward-Perkins, J.B., *Etruscan and Roman Architecture* (Harmondsworth 1970)

Brown, F.E., *Roman Architecture* (New York 1961)

Crema, L., *L'Architettura romana* (*Enciclopedia Classica*, III, vol. 12, I) (Turin 1959)

Etruscan Culture, Land and People. (Archaeological Research and Studies conducted in San Giovenale and its environs by members of the Swedish Institute in Rome) (New York and Malmö 1962)

Fyfe, H., *Hellenistic Architecture* (London 1936)

Graham, J.W., 'The Greek and the Roman House', *Phoenix* XX, 1966, 3–31

Grimal, P., *Les Jardins romains à la fin de la république et aux deux premiers siècles de l'empire* (Bibliothèque des Écoles françaises d'Athènes et de Rome, CLV) (Paris 1943)

Lawrence, A.W., *Greek Architecture* (Harmondsworth 1957)

Lugli, G., *La Tecnica edilizia romana con particolare riguardo a Roma e Lazio* (2 vols. Rome 1957)

Macdonald, W.L., *The Architecture of the Roman Empire* I: *An Introductory Study* (New Haven, Conn., 1965)

Mansuelli, G.A., *Le ville nel mondo romano* (Milan 1958)

Martin, R., *L'urbanisme dans la Grèce antique* (Paris 1954)

Nash, E., *Pictorial Dictionary of Ancient Rome*[2] (2 vols. London 1968)

Plommer, H., *Ancient and Classical Architecture* (London 1956)

Robertson, D.S., *A Handbook of Greek and Roman Architecture*[2] (Cambridge 1954)

Scranton, R.L., *Greek Architecture* (New York 1962)

Vitruvius, *De Architectura libri X.* Transl. M.H. Morgan (Cambridge 1914)

Wheeler, R.E.M., *Roman Art and Architecture* (London 1964)

Wycherley, R.E., *How the Greeks Built Cities*[2] (London 1962)

CHAPTER I

Åkerström, A., Studien über die etruskischen Gräber (*Acta Instituti Romani Regni Sueciae*, III) (1934)

Banti, L., *Il Mondo degli Etruschi* (Rome 1960)

Boëthius, A., and Ward-Perkins, J.B., *Etruscan and Roman Architecture* (London 1970), Part I, ch. 3, Etruscan Architecture, 25–83

Demus-Quatember, M., *Etruskische Grabarchitektur* (Baden-Baden 1958)
Dennis, G., *The Cities and Cemeteries of Etruria* (London 1883)
Ducati, P., *Etruria antica* (Turin 1927)
Durm, J. W., *(Die) Baukunst der Etrusker und Römer* (Stuttgart 1905)
Heurgon, J., *La Vie Quotidienne chez les Étrusques* (Paris 1961)
Mansuelli, G. A., *Etruria and Early Rome* (London 1966)
Pallottino, M., *Etruscologia*[6] (Milan 1968);
    Le Origine degli Etruschi (Rome 1947)
Pareti, L., *La tomba Regolini-Galassi* (Rome 1947)
Richardson, E. H., *The Etruscans* (Chicago 1964)
Scullard, H. H., *The Etruscan Cities and Rome* (London 1967)
Wolstenholme, G. E. W., and O'Connor, C. M., eds, *Ciba Foundation Symposium on Medical Biology and Etruscan Origins* (London 1959).
    Etruscan Culture, Land and People (Archaeological Research and Studies conducted in San Giovenale and its environs by members of the Swedish Institute in Rome, (New York and Malmö 1962)

CHAPTER II

Boëthius, A., and Ward-Perkins, J. B., *Etruscan and Roman Architecture* (Harmondsworth 1970), 118 ff., 152 ff., 312 ff.
Brion, M., *Pompeii and Herculaneum: The Glory and the Grief* (New York 1961)
Brown, F. E., 'Cosa I, History and Topography', *MAAR* XX, 1951, 5–114
    Richardson, E. M., and Richardson, L., Jr, 'Cosa II: The Temples of the Arx', *MAAR* XXVI, 1960
Carrington, R. C., *Pompeii* (Oxford 1936)
Catalano, V., *Storia di Ercolano* (Naples 1953)
Corti, E., *The Destruction and Resurrection of Pompeii and Herculaneum* (London 1951)
Crema, L., *L'Architettura romana* (*Enciclopedia Classica*, III, vol. 12, I) (Turin 1959)
D'Arms, J. H., *Romans on the Bay of Naples* (Cambridge, Mass. 1970)
Deiss, J. J., *Herculaneum, Italy's Buried Treasure* (New York 1966)
Della Corte, M., *Case ed abitanti di Pompeii*[2] (Pompeii 1954)
Étienne, R., *La Vie quotidienne à Pompéi* (Paris 1966)
Grant, M., *Cities of Vesuvius: Pompeii and Herculaneum* (London 1972)
Grimal, P., *Les Jardins romains à la fin de la République et aux deux premiers siècles de l'Empire: Essai sur le naturalisme romain* (Bibliothèque des écoles françaises d'Athènes et de Rome, CLV) (Paris 1943)
Lugli, G., *La Tecnica edilizia romana con particolare riguardo a Roma e Lazio* (2 vols. Rome 1957)
MacKendrick, P. L., *The Mute Stones Speak* (London 1962)
Maiuri, A., *Ercolano: I Nuovi Scavi* (1927–1958) (Rome 1959)
    Herculaneum[5] (*Itinerari*, 53) (Rome 1959)
    Herculaneum and the Villa of the Papyri (Novara 1963)
    Pompeii[14] (*Itinerari*, 3) (Rome 1970)
    Pompei ed Ercolano: Fra Case e Abitanti (Milan 1959)
    L'Ultima Fase edilizia di Pompei (Instituto di Studi Romani)

Sezione Campana. Italia romana: Campania romana, II) (Rome 1942)

Mau, A., tr. Kelsey, F. W., *Pompeii: Its Life and Art* (New York 1899)

Polacco, L., *Tuscanicae dispositiones. Problemi di architettura dell' Italia protoromana* (Università di Padova. Pubblicazioni della facoltà di lettere e filosofia, XXVII) (Padua 1952)

Spano, G., *La Campania Felice nelle età piu remote. Pompei dalle origini alle fase ellenistica* (Rome 1941)

Spinazzola, V., *Pompei alla luce degli scavi nuovi di Via dell'Abbondanza* (Anni 1910–1923) (Rome 1953)

van Buren, A. W., *A Companion to the Study of Pompeii and Herculaneum* (Rome 1938)
s.v. 'Pompeii', in *RE* XXI (1952), cols. 1999–2038

von Duhn, F. K., *Italische Gräberkunde umgearbeitet und ergänzt von F. Messerschmidt* (Bibliothek der klassischen Altertumwissenschaften, II) (Heidelberg 1924–39)

Warsher, T., *Codex Topographicus Pompeianus* (37 vols. Rome, 1936)

CHAPTER III

Becatti, G., 'Casa Ostiensi del Tardo Impero, *BdA*, 1948, 102–28; 197–224

Blake, M. E., *Roman Construction in Italy from Tiberius through the Flavians* (Washington 1947), 115–123 (Domitian's palace)

von Blanckenhagen, P. H., *Flavische Architektur und ihre Dekoration* (Berlin 1940)

Boëthius, A., 'Vitruvius and the Roman Architecture of his Age', *Dragma* . . . *M. P. Nilsson* (Lund 1939), 114–43
'The Neronian Nova Urbs', *Corolla Archeologica*, 1932
'Remarks on the Development of Domestic Architecture in Rome', *AJA*, 1934, 158 ff.

Brown, F. E., *Roman Architecture* (New York 1961)

Carettoni, G., *et al.*, *La Pianta marmorea di Roma* I (Rome 1961)

Gatti, G., 'Caratteristiche edilizie di un quartiere di Roma antica', *Saggi in onore* . . . *V. Fasolo* (Rome 1961), 49–66

Grant, M., *The Roman Forum* (London 1972)

Harsh, P. W., 'Origins of the *Insulae* at Ostia', *MAAR*, 1935, 9 ff.

Kähler, H., *The Art of Rome and Her Empire* (New York 1963)

Lugli, G., *Roma antica* (Rome 1946), 509–17 (Palace of Domitian)
Capitolium, 1947, 41–50 (pre-Neronian Rome)

MacDonald, W. L., *The Architecture of the Roman Empire* I: *An Introductory Study* (New Haven, Conn. 1965), ch. 3.

Meiggs, R., *Roman Ostia* (Oxford 1960)

Packer, J. E., 'The Insulae of Imperial Ostia' (unpublished dissertation, Rome and Berkeley 1964)
'The *Insulae* of Imperial Ostia', *MAAR*, 1971, esp. 65–79

Robathan, D. M., 'Housing Conditions in Ancient Rome', *Classical Outlook*, 1953, 33–5

Wataghin-Cantino, G., *La Domus Augustana: personalità e problemi dell'architettura flavia* (Turin 1966)

CHAPTER IV

Becatti, G., *Scavi di Ostia: I mosaici e i pavimenti marmorei* (Rome 1961)

Blake, M.E., *Roman Construction in Italy from Tiberius through the Flavians* (Washington 1959)

Boëthius, A., 'Remarks on the Development of Domestic Architecture in Rome', *AJA* XXIV, 1934, 158–70
   The Golden House of Nero (Michigan 1960), 129–85
   Town Architecture in Ostia (Göteberg 1951)
   and Ward-Perkins, J.B., *Etruscan and Roman Architecture* (Harmondsworth 1970)

Buttafava, C., *Elementi architettonici ostiensi* (Milan 1963)

Calza, G., 'Le botteghe in Roma antica', *Capitolium* XIV, 1939, 221–30

Calza, G., Becatti, G., et al., *Scavi di Ostia*, vols I–IV (Rome 1953–61)

Calza, G., and Nash, E., *Ostia* (Rome 1959)

Carcopino, J., *Daily Life in Ancient Rome* (New Haven, Conn. 1940)

Dudley, D.R., *Urbs Roma* (London 1967)

Germano, P., *La casa celimontana dei SS. Martiri Giovanni e Paolo* (Rome 1894)

Harsh, P.W., 'The Origins of the *Insula* at Ostia', *MAAR* XII, 1935

Mackendrick, P.L., *The Mute Stones Speak* (New York 1960), 251–65

Maiuri, A., *Ercolano, i nuovi scavi*, I, II (Rome 1958)

Meiggs, R., *Imperial Ostia* (Oxford 1960)

Packer, J.E., 'Roman Ostia: Architectural Structure and Decoration', *AJA*, 1965, 172 ff.
   The Insulae of Imperial Ostia (PhD dissertation, Berkeley 1964)
   'The *Insulae* of Imperial Ostia', *MAAR*, 1971

Robathan, D.M., 'Housing Conditions in Ancient Rome', *Classical Outlook*, 1930, 33–5

Squarciapino, M.F., 'Piccolo Corpus dei Mattoni Scolpiti Ostiensi', *Bull. Comm.*, 1956–58, 183–204

van Aken, A., 'The Cortile in Roman Imperial Insula-Architecture', *Svenska Institut i Rom*, Skrifter XV, 1950, 112–28

Ward-Perkins, J.B., 'The Italian Element in Late Roman and Early Mediaeval Architecture', *PBA*, 1951, 163–94

Wilson, F.H., 'Studies in the Social and Economic History of Ostia, *PBSR*, 1935, 41–68; 1938, 152–63

CHAPTER V

Balsdon, J.P.V.D., *Life and Leisure in Ancient Rome* (London 1969)

Billiard, R., *L'Agriculture dans l'antiquité d'après les Géorgiques de Virgile* (Paris 1928)

Blake, M.E., *Roman Construction in Italy from Tiberius through the Flavians* (Washington 1959)

Boëthius, A., *The Golden House of Nero* (Michigan 1962)
  and Ward-Perkins, J.B., *Etruscan and Roman Architecture* (Harmondsworth 1970)
Brehaut, E., *Cato the Censor on Farming* (translation and commentary) (New York 1933)
Crova, B., *Edilizia e tecnica rurale di Roma antica* (Milan 1942)
D'Arms, J.H., *Romans on the Bay of Naples* (Cambridge, Mass. 1970)
della Corte, M., *Case ed abitanti di Pompei*,[3] ed. P. Soprano (Naples 1965)
Dubois, C., *Pouzzoles Antique. Bibliothèque des Écoles Françaises d'Athènes et de Rome*, fasc. 98 (Paris 1907)
Étienne, R., *La vie quotidienne à Pompéi* (Paris 1966)
Frank, T., *An Economic Survey of Ancient Rome*, vol. I (Baltimore 1933); vol. V (Baltimore 1940)
Grimal, P., *Les Jardins romains à la fin de la république et aux deux premiers siècles de l'empire. Bibliothèque des Écoles françaises d'Athènes et de Rome, CLV* (Paris 1943)
Heitland, W.E., *Agricola, A Study in Ancient Agriculture from the Point of View of Labour* (Cambridge 1921)
Maiuri, A., *La Casa del Menandro* (Rome 1932), 186 ff., figs. 87–98
  La Villa dei Misteri[2] (2 vols. Rome 1947)
Mansuelli, G., *Le ville nel mondo romano* (Milan 1958)
Mau, A., tr. Kelsey, F.W., *Pompeii, Its Life and Art* (New York 1899)
McKay, A.G., *Ancient Campania I: Cumae and the Phlegraean Fields* (Hamilton, Canada 1972); *Ancient Campania II: Naples and Coastal Campania* (Hamilton, Canada 1972)
Rostovtzeff, M., *The Social and Economic History of the Roman Empire*[2] (Oxford 1957)
Swoboda, K.M., *Römische und romanische Paläste* (Vienna 1924)
Tanzer, H.H., *The Villas of Pliny the Younger* (New York 1924)
Toynbee, A.J., *Hannibal's Legacy*, I, II (Oxford 1965)
van Buren, A.W., s.v. 'Villa,' *RE* 2 XVI (Halbbd. (1958), 2142–59
White, K.D., *Roman Farming* (London 1970)

CHAPTER VI

Becatti, G., *Arte e gusto negli scrittori latini* (Florence 1951)
Beyen, H.G., *Die pompejanische Wanddekoration vom 2. bis zum 4. Stil* (The Hague 1938)
Borda, M., *La Pittura romana* (Milan 1958)
Calabi-Limentani, I., *Studi sulla società romana: il lavoro artistico* (Milan 1958) (patronage and artistic standards)
Curtius, L., *Die Wandmalerei Pompejis* (Leipzig 1929)
Dawson, C.M., *Romano-Campanian Mythological Landscape Painting* (New Haven, Conn. 1944)
Felletti Maj, B.M., 'La Casa a l'Arredamento', *Mostra della Romanità, Civiltà Romana*, No. 15 (Rome 1940)

Liversidge, J., *Furniture in Roman Britain* (London 1935)

Maiuri, A., *Roman Painting* (Geneva 1953)

Mau, A., tr. Kelsey, F. W., *Pompeii: Its Life and Art* (New York 1899).

Peters, W. J. T., *Landscape in Romano-Campanian Mural Painting* (Gröningen 1963)

Richter, G. M. A., *The Furniture of the Greeks, Etruscans and Romans* (London 1966), 97–121

Schefold, K., *Die Wände Pompejis* (Berlin 1957)

von Blanckenhagen, P. H., and Alexander, C., 'The Paintings from Boscotrecase', *RM*, VI Ergäzungsheft (Heidelberg 1962)

Warsher, T., *Codex Topographicus Pompeianus* (Rome 1936)

CHAPTERS VII AND VIII

GENERAL

Badian, F., *Roman Imperialism in the Late Republic* (Oxford 1968)

Balsdon, J. P. V. D., *Rome, The Story of an Empire* (New York 1972)

Brown, Peter, *The World of Late Antiquity* (London 1971)

Charlesworth, M. P., *The Rome Empire* (London 1951)

Frank, Tenney, *An Economic Survey of Ancient Rome*, 5 vols (Baltimore 1933–40). Vol. II, Roman Egypt to the reign of Diocletian; III, Britain, Spain, Sicily, Gaul; IV, Africa, Syria, Greece.

Grant, Michael, *The World of Rome* (London 1960)

MacMullen, Ramsay, *Soldier and Civilian in the Later Roman Empire* (Cambridge, Mass. 1963)

Mattingly, H., *Roman Imperial Civilization* (London 1957)

Mommsen, Th., *The Provinces of the Roman Empire* (London 1886); also (for Western provinces only) ed., T. R. S. Broughton (Chicago 1968)

Millar, Fergus, *et al.*, *The Roman Empire and its Neighbours* (London 1967)

Petit, P., *La Paix romaine* (Paris 1967)

Rostovtzeff, M. I., *The Social and Economic History of the Roman Empire*[2] (rev. by P. M. Fraser, Oxford 1957)

Walbank, F. W., *The Awful Revolution, The Decline of the Roman Empire in the West* (Liverpool 1969)

CHAPTER VII

HISPANIA

Almagro, M., *Ampurias, Guia de los excavaciones* (Barcelona 1951)

MacKendrick, Paul, *The Iberian Stones Speak: Archaeology in Spain and Portugal* (New York 1969)

Sutherland, C. H. V., *The Romans in Spain. 217 B.C.–A.D. 117* (London 1939)

Syme, Sir Ronald, *Colonial élites: Rome, Spain, and the Americas* (Oxford 1958)

Thouvenot, R., *Essai sur la province romaine de Bétique* (Paris 1940), Chapter X, 528–40
Wiseman, F. J., *Roman Spain: an Introduction to the Roman Antiquities of Spain and Portugal* (London 1956).

GALLIA NARBONENSIS, GALLIA AQUITANIA, GALLIA LUGDUNENSIS
Benoit, F., *Recherches sur l'hellénisation du Midi de la Gaule* (Aix 1965)
Brogan, Olwen K., *Roman Gaul* (London 1953)
Dion, R., *Histoire de la vigne et du vin en France* (Paris 1959)
Donnadieu, A., *La Pompéi de la Provence: Fréjus* (Paris 1927)
Duval, P.-M., *La vie quotidienne en Gaule pendant la paix romaine* (Paris 1952)
Gauckler, P., *et al.*, *Inventaire des mosaïques de la Gaule et de l'Afrique* (Paris 1909–15)
Grenier, A., *Manuel d'archéologie gallo-romaine*, 4 vols (Paris 1931–60)
Grenier, A., 'La Gaule romaine', in Tenney Frank, *Economic Survey of Ancient Rome* III (Baltimore 1937), 379–664
Harmand, L., *L'Occident romain* (Paris 1960)
Hatt, J.-J., *Histoire de la Gaule romaine²* (Paris 1966)
MacKendrick, Paul, *Roman France* (New York 1972)
Maeyer, R. De, *De Overblijfselen der Romeinsche Villa's in Belgie* (Antwerp 1940)
     De Romeinsche Villa's in Belgie (Antwerp, 1937)
Pobé, Marcel (Jean Roubier, photographs), *The Art of Roman Gaul* (London 1961)
Powell, T. G. E., *The Celts* (London 1958)
Stern, H., *Receuil Général des Mosaïques de la Gaule* (Paris 1957, 1960, 1963)

GALLIA BELGICA
Breuer, J., *La Belgique romaine* (Brussels 1946)
Chadwick, N. K., *Poetry and Letters in Early Christian Gaul* (London 1955)
Cuppers, F., *Frühchristliche Zeugnisse im Einzugsgebiet am Rhein und Mosel*, W. Reusch, ed. (Trier 1965), 152–62
Holmes, T. Rice, *Caesar's Conquest of Gaul²* (Oxford 1911)
Jones, A. H. M., *Later Roman Empire* (Oxford 1964)
Koethe, H., 'Die Bäder römischer villen im Trierer Bezirk', *Berichte der Römisch-Germanischen Kommission* XXX (1940), 43–131
MacKendrick, Paul, *Romans on the Rhine* (New York 1970)
Oelmann, E., 'Gallo-Römische Strassensiedlungen und Kleinhausbauten', *Bonner Jahrbücher* CXXVIII (1923), 77–97
Parlasca, K., *Die Römische Mosaïken in Deutschland* (Römisch-Germanische Forschungen, Vol. XXIII) (Berlin 1959)
Petrikovitz, H. von., *Das römische Rheinland* (Cologne 1960)
Schindler, R., *Landesmuseum Trier, Führer durch die vorgeschichtlicher und römische Abteilung* (Trier 1970)
Schönberger, H., 'The Roman Frontier in Germany: an Archaeological Survey', *JRS* LIX (1969), 144–97
Stähelin, Felix, *Die Schweiz in römischer Zeit³* (Basel 1948)
Steiner, P., *Römisch Landhaüser im Trierer Bezirk* (Berlin 1923)
     Das römische Landgut bei Fliessem. Guidebook (1939)

Swoboda, K. M., *Römische und romanische Paläste*[2] (Vienna 1924)
Ternes, C. M., 'Les Villas romaines de Grand-Duché de Luxembourg', *Helinium* VII (1967) 121–43
Thompson, E. A., *The Early Germans* (Oxford 1965)
Wells, C. M., *The German Policy of Augustus. An Examination of the Archaeological Evidence* (Oxford 1972)
Wightman, Edith M., *Roman Trier and the Treveri* (London 1970)

BRITANNIA

Birley, A., *Life in Roman Britain* (London 1964)
Birley, E., *Roman Britain and the Roman Army* (Kendal 1953)
Blair, Peter Hunter, *Roman Britain and Early England: 55 BC–AD 871* (London 1963)
Bonser, W., *A Romano-British Bibliography* (Oxford 1964)
Boon, George C., *Isca: the Roman Legionary Fortress at Caerleon, Mon.* (Cardiff 1972)
   Roman Silchester: The Archaeology of a Romano-British Town (London 1957)
Burn, A. R., *Agricola and Roman Britain* (London 1953)
Corder, P., *The Roman Town and Villa at Great Casterton, Rutland,* i–iii (Nottingham 1951, 1954, 1961)
Dudley, D. R. and Webster, G., *The Rebellion of Boudicca* (London 1962)
Frere, S. S., *Roman Canterbury*[3] (1962)
   Britannia: a history of Roman Britain (London 1967)
Jackson, Kenneth, *Language and History in Early Britain* (Edinburgh 1953)
Liversidge, Joan, *Britain in the Roman Empire* (London 1968)
MacMullen, Ramsay, 'Rural Romanization', *Phoenix* XXII (1968), 337–41
Richmond, I. A., *Roman Britain* (Pelican History of England 1). (Harmondsworth 1955)
   'The Roman Villa at Chedworth', *Gloucestershire Archaeological Society* LXXVIII (1959), 5–23
   'Roman Britain', *JRS* L (1960)
Rivet, A. L. F., *Town and Country in Roman Britain* (London 1958)
   (ed.) *The Roman Villa in Britain* (London 1969)
(*Corneli*) *Taciti De Vita Agricolae*, ed. R. M. Ogilvie, Sir Ian Richmond (Oxford 1967)
Toynbee, J. M. C., *Art in Britain under the Romans* (Oxford 1964)
Wacher, J. S. (ed.), *The Civitas Capitals of Roman Britain* (Leicester 1966)
Wheeler, R. E. M. and T. V., *Verulamium: a Belgic and two Roman Cities* (Society of Antiquaries Research Report, XI) (Oxford 1936)
White, K. D., *Agricultural Implements of the Roman World* (London 1967)
   Roman Farming (London 1970)

NORICUM, PANNONIA AND DALMATIA

Alföldi, G., *Noricum.* Translation from German by A. Birley (London 1973)
Wells, C. M., *The German Policy of Augustus. An Examination of the Archaeological Evidence* (Oxford 1972)
Wilkes, J. J., *Dalmatia* (London 1969)

CHAPTER VIII

ASIA AND THE EASTERN PROVINCES

Akurgal, Ekrem, *Ancient Civilizations and Ruins of Turkey* (Istanbul 1973)

Bean, George E., *Aegean Turkey: an archaeological guide* (London 1966)
   Turkey's Southern Shore: an archaeological guide (London 1968)
   Turkey Beyond the Maeander: an archaeological guide (London 1971)

Colledge, M. A. R., *The Parthians* (London 1967)

Cook, John, *Ionia and the East* (London 1962)

Downey, G. A., *A History of Antioch in Syria* (Princeton 1961)

Jones, A. H. M., *The Cities of the Eastern Roman Provinces*[2] (Oxford 1971)

Kraehling, Carl H., *Gerasa, City of the Decapolis* (New Haven, Conn. 1938)

Lawrence, A. W., *Greek Architecture* (Harmondsworth 1957)

Lepper, F. A., *Trajan's Parthian War* (Oxford 1948)

MacKendrick, P., *The Greek Stones Speak* (New York 1962)

Magie, David, *Roman Rule in Asia Minor to the end of the Third Century after Christ*
   2 vols (Princeton 1950)

Martin, Roland, *L'Urbanisme dans la Grèce antique* (Paris 1956)

Rosenbaum, E., *et al. A Survey of Coastal Cities in Western Cilicia* (Ankara 1967)

Rostovtzeff, M. I., Bellinger, A. R., *et al.*, *The Excavations at Dura-Europos,
   conducted by Yale University and the French Academy of Inscriptions and Letters*.
   Final Report, 1943–

Rostovtzeff, M. I., *Caravan Cities* (Oxford 1932)
   The Social and Economic History of the Roman Empire[2], rev. by P. M. Fraser
   (Oxford 1957)

Thouvenot, R., *Les Ruines de Dougga* (Tunis 1958)

Warmington, B. H., *The North African Provinces from Diocletian to the Vandal
   Conquest* (Cambridge 1954)

THE AFRICAN PROVINCES: EGYPT, CYRENAICA, AFRICA PROCONSULARIS AND
MAURETANIA

Aurigemma, Salvatore, *L'Italia in Africa. Le scoperte archeologiche* (1911–43):
   Tripolitania: Vol. I, 1–2 (Rome 1960–2). Publ. by Comitato per la documen-
   tazione dell'opera dell'Italia in Africa
   I Mosaici di Zliten (Rome-Milan 1926)

Baradez, J., *Fossatum Africae. Recherches aériennes sur l'organisation des confins
   sahariens à l'époque romaine* (Paris 1949)

Bell, H. I., *Egypt from Alexander the Great to the Arab Conquest* (Oxford 1948)

Benoit, F., *L'Afrique mediterránéenne* (Paris 1931)

Bianchi-Bandinelli, R., *Leptis Magna* (Rome 1963)
   Rome, The Late Empire. Roman Art, AD 200–400, transl. Peter Green (London
   1971)

Birley, A., *Septimius Severus. The African Emperor* (London 1971)

Broughton, T. R. S., *The Romanisation of Africa Proconsularis* (Baltimore 1929)

Butler, H. C., *Ancient Architecture in Syria* (Princeton Univ. Archaeol. Exped.
   II B) (Leyden 1909)

Charles-Picard, G., *La Civilisation de l'Afrique Romaine* (Paris 1959)
'Africo-romani centri', *Enciclopedia Universale dell'Arte* I, col. 147 ff. (Venice-Rome 1959)
Di Vita, A., *Sabratha* (Basle 1969)
Floriani-Squarciapino, M., *Leptis Magna* (Basle 1966)
Gatti, C., 'Le ville maritime italiche e africane', *RIL* XCI (1957), 285–305
Germain, Suzanne, *Les mosaïques de Timgad: étude descriptive et analytique* (Paris 1969)
Gsell, Stephane, *Les monuments antiques de l'Algérie* (Paris 1901)
Haynes, D. E. L., *An Archaeological and Historical Guide to the pre-Islamic Antiquities of Tripolitania*[2] (Tripoli 1955)
Johnson, A. C., *Egypt and the Roman Empire* (The Jerome Lectures ser. 2) (Ann Arbor 1951)
Leschi, L., *Djémila: antique Cuicul.* (Algiers 1953)
Lézine, A., *Carthage-Utique: Études d'Architecture et d'Urbanisme* (Paris 1968)
Luckhard, Fritz, *Das privathaus im ptolemäischen und römischen Ägypten* (Bonn 1914)
Romanelli, P., *Storia delle province romane dell'Africa* (Studi pubblicati dall' Istituto Italiano per la Storia antica, XIV) (Rome 1959)

ARCHITECTURAL GLOSSARY

Note: Many of the more technical terms are discussed in the text.

ala Side passages, later wings, to right and left at far end of the atrium, perhaps originally waiting rooms, *cf.* 'aisle'.

ambulatio Terrace for promenade and exercise.

andron Room reserved for men, particularly for dining.

anta Pilaster terminating the lateral walls of a temple *cella*, usually responding to a column. Two columns set between two *antae* are described as *in antis*.

apodyterium Changing room of a bath building.

ashlar Regular masonry of squared stones laid in horizontal courses with vertical joints.

atriolum Small atrium, hall or antechamber.

atrium Entrance hall of a Roman Etruscan-style house between the entrance passage (*fauces*) and *tablinum* in the middle of the far end. The central part of the roof (*compluvium*, 'rain-collector') sloped inwards to a central *impluvium* (catch basin) to supply the cisterns beneath.

balneum, *balineum* Public or private bath building of ordinary scale; distinct from *thermae*, the great public baths.

basilica An oblong rectangular building with central nave and two side aisles lit by a clerestory; for commercial and legal use.

biclinium Technically a dining couch for two persons, but also used of a dining-room with two couches rather than the usual three (*triclinium*).

caementa Irregular pieces of stone or brick used as aggregate in Roman concrete. *Cf. opus caementicium.*

cal(i)darium The hot room, or steam room, of a Roman bath.

cardo Roman surveying term for north-south streets.

caseggiato Ital. a multiple dwelling apartment house.

cava aedium (*cavaedium*) Term for basic Italic house types used by Vitruvius: (1) *tuscanicum*, of Etruscan derivation; (2) tetrastyle, with columns at each angle of the *compluvium*; (3) Corinthian, with additional intermediate columns; (4) *displuviatum*, with roof sloping downwards and outwards on all four sides; (5) *testudinatum*, with a ridge roof.

cenaculum Originally denoted dining-room, later an upper storey, garret

columbarium Dovecote.

compluvium Open central portion of roof of Roman atrium, above *impluvium*.

conclavium Oblong, closed room for dining or sleeping.

cortile A courtyard incorporated within an apartment block or commercial building admitting light and air to interior rooms and providing a concourse for business and domestic functions. (Ital.)

cryptoporticus Underground vaulted corridor, often with oblique lighting through the vault or side-wall.

cubiculum Bedroom.

dado Lower part of a wall when decorated as continuous plinth or wainscot.

decumanus Roman surveying term for east-west streets. *Decumanus maximus* implies the main street.

diaeta Living-room.

distyle Consisting of two columns.

dolium Large earthenware storage jar.

domus Residence or house of a single family.

euripus Narrow channel, water basin in peristyle garden.

exedra Semicircular or rectangular recess; sometimes semicircular stone or marble bench.

fauces Entrance hall to an atrium, and passage between atrium and peristyle.

frigidarium Cold room of a Roman bath.

hexastyle Consisting of six columns.

horreum (pl. -a) Grain storage warehouse.

hortus Garden, park, orchard.

hypocaust Floor with space beneath for circulation of hot air.

impluvium Shallow water-tank in Roman atria to catch rainwater falling through *compluvium*.

insula Apartment house, tenement suite, or *pensione* unit in converted *domus*. Used also to denote a city block.

lararium Space reserved for the tutelary deities (*Lares*); a shrine located in the Roman house interior or garden.

megaron Main hall of a Mycenaean palace, later of a Greek house.

natatio Swimming pool of a public bath or garden.

nymphaeum Once a cave with running water sacred to nymphs (*cf.* lymph); later an artificial grotto or public fountain.

octastyle Consisting of eight columns.

oecus (Greek, *oikos*). Main room or unit of a Greek house, successor to Greek *megaron*. Vitruvius applies *oecus* to dining halls; tetrastyle, Corinthian, Egyptian and Cyzicene.

opus caementicium Roman concrete masonry of undressed stones (*caementa*) laid in lime, sand, often *pozzolana* mortar.

opus craticium Inexpensive Roman wall construction involving wooden framework or latticework containing *opus incertum*, hasty mortar work and stucco facing. Used primarily in cheaper housing and jerry-built apartment buildings, it lacked stability and was highly inflammable.

opus incertum Facing of irregularly shaped small blocks in *opus caementicium* from second century BC.

opus latericium Masonry of crude brick.

opus reticulatum Successor to *opus incertum* with facing of network of small squared blocks laid in diagonal lines. *Cf.* Lat. *reticulum*, 'net'.

opus sectile Paving or wall veneer of coloured marble tiles.

opus signinum Concrete floor with inserted fragments of terracotta, stone or marble.

opus spicatum Brick flooring laid in grain ear or herring-bone pattern.

opus vittatum Facing combining small tufa or stone blocks alternating with brick courses.

orthostate The lowest course of the interior shrine wall of a Greek temple or any 'upright' stone slab used to form the lower zone of a wall.

oscillum Originally a little image of the face, a diminutive circular mask of Dionysus (Bacchus) hung from trees to be moved by the wind; later used of marble discs often hung between the columns of peristyles or porticoes with complementary subjects or subject-matter on the two sides, e.g. satyr and nymph, Bacchus and Maenad, etc.

palaestra Exercise ground used for, wrestling, boxing, ball-games, etc.

peperino Volcanic stone (tufa) from Alban Hills, south-east of Rome.

pergula A projection in front of a house, used as a shop, booth, or stall.

peristyle Inner, colonnaded garden court of Pompeian and Hellenistic homes.

pinacotheca Picture gallery.

piscina Pool (lit. fish-pool). Used of plunge pools in baths and swimming pools in a palaestra, or of fish tanks in private gardens.

pozzolana (sc. *pulvis Puteolanus*) Volcanic sand from central Italy, found particularly at ancient Puteoli (mod. Pozzuoli) in Campania; its quick-drying properties assisted experiments in domical architecture and underwater constructions.

quadriporticus Enclosed courtyard with porticoes on all four sides.

revetment Terracotta or marble facing applied to walls.

ridge pole Beam along edge of roof.

socle Lower part of a wall.

stoa Greek equivalent of Latin *porticus*; used frequently of multiple colonnades, sometimes two-storeyed shopping centres, lawcourts, public galleries.

taberna Rectangular room, often vaulted, opening off the street; normally applied to shops, workshops or poor man's housing.

tablinum (Orig. *tabulinum*.) Central room at far end of atrium, originally the master bedroom, later record depository (*tabulum*, 'record, archival material'), and reception room.

tepidarium Warm room of a Roman bath.

testudinate Implies a ridge roof.

tetrastyle Consisting of four columns, often at corners of *impluvium*.

thermae Large public baths, distinct from *balnea*.

thermopolium Place where warm drinks and food were sold, restaurant.

triclinium Originally a dining-room with three banqueting couches (*klinai*); later the principal reception room, successor to atrium-*tablinum* complex.

triconchos Room of trefoil or three-lobed design.

tufa Principal building stone of Latium and Campania, volcanic stone.

velum, *velarium* Awning stretched over a forum, theatre, amphitheatre, or atrium for protection against sun.

vestibulum Entrance from street to *fauces* of a house.

viridarium Plantation of trees, pleasure garden.

xystus Landscaped Roman garder planted with groves of plane trees and flower beds.

LIST OF ILLUSTRATIONS

PLATES

1 Rome, Palatine Antiquarium Hut of Villanovan period, reconstruction.

2 Villanovan hut urn. Museo Nazionale di Villa Giulia, Rome

3 Veii. Temple of Minerva, model. Istituto di Etruscologia, Rome

4 Caere (Cerveteri). Tomb of the Capitals, interior

5 Caere (Cerveteri). Tomb of the Shields and Chairs

6 Tarquinii. Tomb of the Augurs, interior. Ny Carlsberg Glyptotek, Copenhagen

7 Marzabotto. Etruscan house foundations

8 Perugia. Tomb of the Volumnii

9 San Giovenale. Etruscan terrace houses

10 Etruscan funeral urn, house design, short side. Museo Archeologico, Florence

11 The same, long side

12 Caere (Cerveteri). Tomb of the Painted Stuccoes, interior

13 Chiusi. Etruscan ash urn, house design. Staatliche Museen zu Berlin

14 Herculaneum. Air view of the excavations: House of the Mosaic Atrium and garden right centre

15 Pompeii. House of the Silver Wedding, dining alcove (*oecus*)

16 Pompeii. House of the Dioscuri, atrium and peristyle

17 Herculaneum. House of the Wooden Partition, atrium, *impluvium*, *tablinum* and garden

18 Pompeii. Villa of Julia Felix, garden

19 Herculaneum. Samnite house, atrium and balcony

20 Pompeii. House of Menander, atrium, *tablinum* and peristyle garden

21 Herculaneum. House of the Neptune and Amphitrite Mosaic, atrium, *impluvium*, *tablinum* and mosaic

22   Pompeii. House of the Vettii, garden

23   Cosa. SUNY House, view from the north-east

24   Ostia. House of Cupid and Psyche, view to *nymphaeum*

25   Rome, Palatine Hill. House of Livia, wall-paintings

26   Rome, Palatine Hill. Domus Flavia (or Augustana), model of Domitian's palace. Museo della Civiltà Romana, Rome

27   Rome. Market of Trajan, Via Biberatica, shops and upper rooms

28   Herculaneum. Casa a Graticcio, streetside façade

29   Herculaneum. Casa a Graticcio, second storey, axonometric plan

30   Ostia. Air view of the excavations looking north-west

31   Ostia. Casa dei Dipinti, garden court, reconstruction

32   Ostia. Caseggiato di Diana, courtyard

33   Ostia. Caseggiato di Diana, south façade along Via di Diana

34   Ostia. Caseggiato di Diana, axonometric plan

35   Ostia. Casa delle Volte Dipinte, reconstruction

36   Ostia. *Insulae*, reconstruction model. Museo della Civiltà Romana, Rome

37   Avezzano relief, town and country houses. Museo Torlonia, Avezzano

38   Francolise. Villa San Rocco, Phase III

39   Boscoreale. Villa rustica (No. 13), reconstruction. Museo della Civiltà Romana, Rome

40   Licenza. Horace's Sabine farm

41   Stabiae. Villa maritima, wall-painting. Antiquarium, Castellammare di Stabia

42   Stabiae. Villa maritima, wall-painting. Museo Nazionale, Naples

43   Capri, Damecuta. Villa maritima, Augustan

44   Stabiae, Villa San Marco, peristyle garden and *piscina*

45   Stabiae. Villa San Marco, *frigidarium*

46   Pompeii. House of Marcus Lucretius Fronto, villa maritima, wall-painting. Museo Nazionale, Naples

47   Pompeii. Casa della Fontana Piccola, villa maritima and harbour, wall-painting

48   Pompeii. House of Marcus Lucretius Fronto, villa maritima, wall-painting. Museo Nazionale, Naples

49   Rome. Villa of Livia, Prima Porta, garden room mural. Museo Nazionale delle Terme, Rome

50   Rome. Villa Farnesina, stucco relief. Museo Nazionale delle Terme, Rome

51   Sperlonga. Grotto with *piscina* and sculpture

52   Tibur (Tivoli). Hadrian's Villa, reconstruction model. Museo della Civiltà Romana, Rome

53   Sicily, Piazza Armerina. Imperial Villa, view from vestibule into garden

54   Sicily, Piazza Armerina. Imperial Villa, floor mosaic

55   Pompeii. House of the Moralist, *triclinium*

56   Simpelveld (Leiden). Marble sarcophagus, interior relief. Rijksmuseum te Leiden

57   The same, from a different angle

58   Herculaneum. House of the Carbonized Furniture, *cubiculum*

59   Pompeii. Villa of the Mysteries, wall-painting

60   Boscoreale villa, *cubiculum*. Metropolitan Museum of Art, New York. Rogers Fund, 1903

61   The same, detail of wall-painting

62   Pompeii. House of the Vettii, red room, wall-painting

63   Pompeii. House of the Vettii, yellow room, wall-painting

64   Saint-Rémy (Glanum). Courtyard house

65   Montmaurin (Haute-Garonne). Villa, model

66   Pillig (near Mayen). Villa and farmyard foundations, air view

67   Ditchley, Oxon. Roman villa and its dependencies, foundations, air view

68   Trier wall-painting. Landesmuseum, Trier.

69   Lullingstone, Kent. Villa, c. AD 360 with temple mausoleum and circular temple

70   Lullingstone, Kent. Villa, interior rooms

71   Llantwit-Major (Glamorgan). Villa and farmyard

72   St Albans (Verulamium). Peopled scroll mural. British Museum, London

73 Split (Spalato) Yugoslavia. Palace of Diocletian, model. Museo della Civiltà
    Romana, Rome

74 Masada, Israel. Air view of Herod's palace

75 Praeneste. Barberini mosaic

76 Carthage. Villa of Squire Julius, mosaic. Bardo Museum, Tunis

FIGURES

1   Cosa. Capitolium, plan

2   Regia, Forum Romanum, plan

3   Domus Italica, prototype plan (Patroni)

4   Domus Italica, prototype reconstruction (Patroni)

5   Marzabotto. House plans, *insulae* Regio IV

6   Domus Italica, plan (Luckenbach)

7   Domus Italica, reconstruction (Luckenbach)

8   Pompeii. House of Pansa, atrium house, plan

9   Pompeii, House of the Silver Wedding, atrium house, tetrastyle, floor plan

10 Pompeii. House of the Labyrinth, atrium house, Corinthian *oecus*, plan

11 Pompeii. House of the Surgeon, plan

12 Pompeii. House of Sallust, plan

13 Pompeii. House of Pansa, cross-section and plan

14 Pompeii. House of the Faun, plan

15 Pompeii. House of Marcus Loreius Tiburtinus, section and view

16 Herculaneum. Samnite House, schematic plan

17 Herculaneum. House of the Mosaic Atrium and House of the Stags, plans

18 Herculaneum. House of the Mosaic·Atrium, *oecus Aegyptius*, cross-section

19 Herculaneum. House of the Mosaic Atrium, garden and *cubicula*, recon-
    struction

20 Herculaneum. House of the Mosaic Atrium and House of the Stags, south
    façade, over city wall, reconstruction

21   Pompeii. House of the Vettii, plan

22   Pompeii. House of the Vettii, reconstruction

23   Cosa. SUNY House

24   Rome, Palatine Hill. House of Livia, plan

25a Rome, Palatine Hill. House of Augustus

25b The same, general plan

26   Rome, Palatine Hill. Domus Flavia (or Augustana), Domitian's Palace. Solid colour indicates buildings at the upper level now in whole or part upstanding.

27   Ostia. House of the Round Temple

28   Ostia. *Insula* façade, ground floor *thermopolium*, reconstruction

29   Ostia. *Casette tipo*, plan *c*. AD 117–38

30   Ostia. Garden house, *c*. AD 117–38, plan

31   Ostia. *Insulae*, cross-section and reconstruction

32   Ostia. Caseggiato del Larario, plan

33   Ostia. Caseggiato di Diana, first floor, plan

34   The same, *piano nobile*

35   Ostia. Casa delle Volte Dipinte, plan

36   San Giovenale. Villa Sambuco, plan

37   The same, reconstruction

38   Francolise. Villa San Rocco, plan, phase II

39   Boscoreale, near. Villa rustica (No. 13)

40   Pompeii. Villa of the Mysteries, plan

41   Pompeii, Villa of the Mysteries, reconstruction, final phase

42   Herculaneum. Suburban villa of the Papyri ('Pisones') plan

43   Licenza. Horace's Sabine Farm, plan

44   Capri, Damecuta. Porticus Villa of Augustus

45   Stabiae, Villa San Marco, plan. D'Orsi

46   Minori, Amalfi Drive. Villa Romana

47 Baiae. 'The Severan Palatium', bath buildings, apartments, plan

48 Capri. Villa Jovis ('Tiberius' villa'), plan

49 Sperlonga. Villa of Tiberius, seaside grotto and piscina, plan

50 Rome. Domus Aurea (Nero's Golden House), plan

51 Sirmione, Lake Garda. Grotte di Catullo, plan

52 Sicily, Piazza Armerina. Imperial Villa (Maximian's?), axonometric drawing

53 Hypocaustic bath-system, hypothetical reconstruction

54 Saint-Rémy (Glanum) street plan, houses and baths

55 Vaison la Romaine (Vasio), House of the Silver Bust, plan

56 Chiragan (Haute Garonne), villa, plan

57 Nennig. Villa, 3rd century AD, plan

58 Köln-Müngersdorf. Villa, 3rd century AD, elevation and plan

59 Konz (Contionacum). Villa, plan

60 Pfalzel (Palatiolum), Villa, plan

61 Weilerbüsch, near Fliessem. Villa, plan

62 Cologne. Peristyle house, near the cathedral, plan

63 Fishbourne (Sussex). Palace villa of Cogidubnus, isometric drawing

64 Fishbourne (Sussex). Palace villa and garden of Cogidubnus in relation to the modern village's plan

65 Lullingstone (Kent). Villa AD 330–80, plan

66 Llantwit-Major (Glamorgan). Villa and dependencies, plan

67 Yugoslavia. Split (Spalato). Palace of Diocletian, plan

68 Ephesus, slopes of Bülbüldăg, eastern *insula*, plan

69 Ephesus, slopes of Bülbüldăg, western *insula*, plan

70 Dura-Europos (Syria). Palace of the Dux Ripae, plan

71 Ptolemais (Libya). Villa, diagrammatic plan

72 Ptolemais (Libya). Palazzo delle Colonne, plan

73 Ptolemais (Libya). Palazzo delle Colonne, axonometric view

74   Timgad (Thamugadi). Plan of the Trajanic colony

75   Tabarka (Thabraea). Mosaic, villa estate

76   North Africa, fortified farmhouse, I, II–IV

77   el-Kastal (Arabia). Roman auxiliary fort, plan

Bibliographical references may be found in full in the bibliography.

SOURCES OF ILLUSTRATIONS

PLATES

Alinari, Florence: 42; Anderson, Rome: 25, 49, 59, 62, 63: Ashmolean Museum, Oxford: 68; Ediz. Vincenzo Carcavallo, Naples: 17; Crown Copyright (Alan Sorrell): 67, 70; Felbermeyer, 3, 39; Fototeca Unione: 20, 14, 15, 16, 19, 20, 22, 23, 24, 28; 29, 31, 32, 33, 34, 35, 38, 40, 43, 44, 45, 46, 47, 48, 51, 53, 54, 73; Landesmuseum, Bonn: 66; Landesmuseum, Trier: 68; Libero D'Orsi: 41; Mansell Collection: 5, 8, 18, 37, 58; Oscar Savio: 36; R. Schoder, S.J.: 76; Edwin Smith: 55; Soprintendenza alle Antichità, Florence: 10; Verulamium Excavation Committee: 72; Villani, Bologna: 7; J. B. Ward-Perkins: 64; Y. Yadin: 74.

Plans redrawn by Gillian March and Sarah Lillywhite.

INDEX

Numbers preceded by the letter 'n' refer to notes. Notes are indexed only when they contain information other than bibliographical, to which there is no obvious reference in the text. Only those authors are included in the index whose names occur in the text.

Achaea, 211
ad Gallinas, 124
Adams, Robert, 209
adobe, 101, 221, n395
advertisements for rental units,
    82
aedificia, 164
aerial photography, 24, 159,
    164–5, 181, 196
Africa, North, 222–37
Agache, R., 165
Agricola, Cn. Julius, 186, 191
agricultural implements, 182
Agrippa, M. Vipsanius, 158,
    nn101, 224
Agrippa Postumus, 121; House
    of, *see* Rome
Agrippina, 128
aisled houses, 165, 184–5, 194,
    195, 196
Aix-en-Provence, *see* Aquae
    Sextiae
Alba Longa, 64
Alban Lake (Lacus Albanus),
    131
Alban stone, 72
Albano, *see* Albanum
Albanum (villa), 131
Albinus, Sex. Clodius, 191
Alesia (Alise-Sainte-Reine), 164
Alpine territories, 201
Althiburos (Tunisia), House of
    the Muses, 231
Ameria, 102
Ammianus Marcellinus, 220
andron, 69, 120
Ansedonia, *see* Cosa
Antae, House of the, *see*
    Glanum
Antinous, 132
Antioch (Syria), 208, 220,
    n113

Antium (Anzio), Villa, 128
Antony, M., Palatine house,
    n101
apartment blocks, apartments,
    see insula
Apollinopolis, Magna, *see* Tell
    Edfu
Apollo Palatinus, temple of, 69,
    70, 71
Apuleius, 223
Aqua Serino (Campania), 61
Aquae Sextiae, town houses,
    164
Aquae Sulis, *see* Bath
Aquileia, 202
Aquincum (Hungary), 202,
    203, 204, 208, n307
Aquitania (Gaul), 158
Arabia, Southern, 224
Aradus, 217
Ara Pacis Augustae (Rome), 69
architects: Tamphilus, 68;
    Severus and Celer, 73, 74;
    Hadrian, 131–2; provincial,
    157; Zotikos, 208; oriental
    names, 210, n6
Ariadne, Villa of, *see* Stabiae
Aristobulus, n389
Arminius, 201
Arretium (Arezzo), 29
Arsinoë (Egypt), 224
art galleries, 32, 41, 61, 73, 151
ash urns (hut design), 12–13,
    pl. 2
Asia Minor (Turkey, Aegean
    Greece), 11, 15, 26, 34–5, 41,
    46, 47, 61, 66, 68, 80, 117,
    138, 139, 144, 145, 146, 157,
    164, 210–11, 217, 219–20
Aspalathus (= Split), n372
Asseria (Illyricum), 205
Asturicus, 136

Athens, Greek houses, 6
Atria (= Adria), 16
atrium (atria), Tomb of Capitals
    (Caere), 14; derivation, 16;
    prototypes, 16–22; Vitruvius
    on, 16–17; Tuscan, 17; im-
    pluviate, 18; testudinate, 18;
    Etruscan innovation, 21–2;
    court, 32; tetrastyle, 35;
    Corinthian, 35, 225; scale,
    73; conversion to *insula*, 81;
    country and city, 110; pro-
    tective measures, 141; colon-
    naded, 225; African use,
    226; nn21, 26
Atticus, T. Pomponius, villa, 68
Attila, 205
Attis, House of, *see* Glanum
Auden, W. H., 7
Augsburg, 202
Augst (Basel, Augusta Raurica),
    6, n5
Augurs, Tomb of the, *see*
    Caere
Augusta Treverorum, *see* Trier
Augusta Vindelicorum, *see*
    Augsburg
Augustus (Octavian), 69; fire
    regulations, 86; civic respons-
    ibility, 98; Gaul, 158; Ger-
    many, 201; Capri villas, 124;
    House of, *see* Rome; Villa
    of, *see* Prima Porta
Aulus Gellius, 89
Ausonius, Moselle villas, 172–
    3, 180
Austria, *see* Noricum
Avitacum, villa, 170–1
awnings, 141
Aydat, Lac d', *see* Avitacum

Baalbek (Lebanon), 209

Babylon, high-rise housing, 217
Baccano (Italy), villa, n394
Baiae (Campania), 114, 122, 140, 172, fig. 47
Baláca (Hungary), 203
Balaton, Lake (Hungary), 203
balconies, 91, 96, n146
Banaqfur (Syria), 219
Barberini Mosaic, 223–4, pl. 75
Bardo Museum (Tunis), mosaics, 234
Barenau-Wiehengebirge, 201
barns, see aisled houses
Bath (Somerset), 188
bath-suites: public, 80–1, 95, 140, 200; private, 42, 95, 105, 108, 112, 120, 125, 140, 172, 199–200
beds (and couches), Etruscan, 26, 27; 201, pls 58, 60
Belgic Gaul, see Gallia Belgica
Benabil (Syria), 219
Benacus, Lacus, see Lake Garda
Benoit, F., 164
Berlin Museum, Chiusi house urn, 24, pl. 13
Bicentenary, House of the, see Herculaneum
Bieda, 23
Bignor (Sussex), villa, 195
Blankenheim, villa, 179
Blera, see Bieda
blocks, see insulae
Blue Grotto, see Capri
boarding houses, see insulae
Boëthius, A., categories of insulae, 91, 100; evolution of insulae, 84
Bollendorff, corridor villa, 172
Boon, G. C., hypocaustic system, 199–200
Boscoreale (Herculaneum), cubiculum reconstruction, 6, 149, pls 60, 61; villa rustica No. 13, 107–8, pl. 39, fig. 39; villa of M. Fannius Synistor, 116, 149; villa of Agrippa Postumus, 121
Boscotrecase (Campania), villa, 155
Bostra, 220
Boudicca (Boadicea), 180
Bourbon excavations, 118
Brading (Isle of Wight), villa, 185

Brigetio (Hungary), limes mansions, 203
Britain, 180–201; invasion, conquest, 180; Romanization, 182–3; aerial photography, 181, 196; Celtic, Iron Age dwellings, 181–2; areas devoid of Roman occupation, 185; supplies to legions, 185; estate owners, 185–6; town life, 187; house-plans, 187; tabernae, 187; fourth-century revival, 194–5; villas, 195; Roman evacuation, Saxon arrival, 196
Brizio, E., 19, 21
Brown, F., 65, 76, n109
Bruno, V., 63
Buccino (Salerno), villa rustica, 108
building materials, Etruscan, 12, 14, 20; tufa, 40–1; Roman, 66–7; brick, 87–8, 89–90; Cato on, 101; pozzolana, 40, 67, 114, 123, 124; provincial, 166, 169, 183, 184, 196–7, 204, 227
Burrus, Sextus Afranius, 162
Byzantium, 206, 220

Caelian Hill (Rome), 145
Caere (Cerveteri), tombs: of the Capitals, 14, pl. 4; of the Augurs, 16; of the Painted Stuccoes (Reliefs), 27–9, pl. 12; of the Shields and Chairs (degli Scudi e delle Sedie), 25, pl. 5; banqueters' sarcophagus, 26
Caerwent, Monmouthshire (Venta Silurum), water pipes, 200
Caesar, C. Julius, 111, 158
Caistor-by-Norwich, Norfolk (Venta Icenorum), 181
Caetronius, House of, see Pompeii
Caligula (Gaius), 75, 128, n103
Calvus, C. Licinius Macer, house, 72
Calza, R., 91
Campania, housing, 34–5, 60–61, n75; villae rusticae, 106; attractions, 114, 115; porticus villas, 122, 124, 197

Camulodunum (Colchester, Essex), 180, 186
Canterbury, Kent (Durovernum Cantiocorum), town houses, 186
capanne, 12
capitalist farming, 102–3
Capitals, Tomb of the, see Caere
Capri, 31; Villa Jovis, 73, 75, 118, 124–6, 135, 219, fig. 48; Blue Grotto, 118, 126–7; Villa of Damecuta, 117–18, 126, 219, pl. 43, fig. 44; Villa Gradola, 118
Carbonized Furniture, House of the, see Herculaneum
carbonized remains, 31, 111, pl. 58
Carettoni, G., 71
Carnuntum (Austria), 202, 204, 208, n371
carpets, 139
Carrara (Luna), marble, 68, 145
Carthage, mosaics, 233–4, n397, pl. 76
cartibulum, 37, 136
Carystus marble, 68, 145
Caserta, 130
Casinum, Varro's estate, 101, 102, 130
Castel d'Asso, 23
Castel Gandolfo, see Alba Longa
castella (forts), 203, 236, fig. 77
Castellammare di Stabia, see Stabiae
Castor, Temple of (Rome), 76, n103
Castra Regina, see Regensburg
castrum, 208, 235
catalogues (Roman), 77, 83
Cato, M. Porcius (De Agricultura), 40, 100, 101, n49; and Villa Sambuco, 103, 104
Catullus, 67, 132
Catulus, Q. Lutatius, 67, 68
Cavum aedium (cavaedium), Varro on, 16–17; tuscanicum 37, n45; testudinatum, 37; displuviatum, 37–8
Celer, architect, 73, 129
ceilings, 197, 222
cellars, Gallic, 165
Celts, housing, 164

cenacula, 48, 80, 256, n383
Cerveteri, *see* Caere
chairs, Etruscan, 25–6; Roman, 136–7; provincial, 179, 201
Charles-Picard, G., 226
Chatissa, *see* Katsch
Cherusci, 201
chests, Etruscan, 26–7; Roman, 137
Chichester, *see* Fishbourne
Chiragan, villa, 166–70, fig. 56
Chiusi (Clusium), ash urn, 24, pl. 13
Christianity, Herculaneum 'cross', 81; mosaics, 192–3, 198–9; 204
Cicero, M. Tullius, 36, 47, 67, 102, 115, 124, 151, 156; Villa of, *see* Pompeii
Circeii, *see* Circeo
Circeo, Domitian's villa, 131
Cirencester, Gloucestershire (Corinnium), 195, 198
cisterns, 20, 22, 49, 82, 104, 105, 108, 124–5
civitas, civitates, 202
Claudius, Emperor, 29
Claudius Mamertinus, n235
cliens, clientes, client, 32, 66, 73
Clivus Palatinus (Rome), 75
Clodia, 67
Clodius, P., 67
Cluentius, 102
Clusium, displuviate manor house, ash urn, 24
Cogidubnus, Ti. Claudius, 190
Colchester, Essex, *see* Camulodunum
Cologne (Colonia Agrippinensis), peristyle house, 176, 178, 208, fig. 62
Colonne, Palazzo delle, *see* Ptolemais
Columella, n158
Columns, House of the, *see* Ostia
compluvium, origins, 17, 22
concrete, use of, 101
Constantine, Emperor, 175
Constantinople, 206
constructional details, Britain, houses, villas, etc., 197–9
Contionacum, *see* Konz
Corinnium Dubonnorum, *see* Cirencester

Corinth, 211
corn dryers, 182
corridor villas, houses, 165, 183–4, 185
Cosa, *atrium publicum*, 22–3; history, excavations, 61–2; SUNY house, 62–3, pl. 23, fig. 23; *villae rusticae*, 107; houses, *insulae*, 106
Cotswolds, ranches, 183
couches, divans, Etruscan, 26; Roman, 137–8; provincial, 201; pls 56, 57
Crassus, L. Licinius, 67, 68
Crassus, M. Licinius (triumvir), 87
Cryptoporticus, House of the, *see* Pompeii
cubiculum, Boscoreale, 6, 149, pls 60, 61
Cuicul (Djemila), 231
Cumae, 12, 172
Cunliffe, B., 189
Cupid and Psyche, House of, *see* Ostia
Cures (Sabinum), villa, n165
Curiosum Urbis Romae Regionum XIV, 77, 83
curtains, draperies, 49, 140–1
Cyrene (Cyrenaica), House of Jason Magnus, 230–1
Cyzicene *oecus*, 53, n54

Dacia, 202, n348
Dalmatian Coast, 202
Damecuta, Villa of, *see* Capri
Danubian territory, 196, 201, 202, 203, 204
Daphne (Antioch), House of Boat of Psyches, 220
De Agricultura, *see* Cato
De Architectura, *see* Vitruvius
De Modo Aedificiorum, 88
De Re Rustica, *see* Varro
decumanus, 20
de Franciscis, A., 122
Delos, 144, 161, 219
Desenzano (Italy), n113
Diana, House of, *see* Ostia
Diocletian, 133, 135, 205–9
Diodorus Siculus, 11, 61
Diomedes, Villa of, *see* Pompeii
Dionysiac Mysteries, 148, pl. 59
Dionysius of Halicarnassus, 11, 12, 14

Dioscuri, Domus of the, *see* Ostia
Dioscuri, House of the, *see* Pompeii
Dipinti, Casa dei, *see* Ostia
Ditchley House, Oxfordshire, villa, 184–5, aisled house, 184–5, pl, 67
Djemila, *see* Cuicul
Doclea (Illyricum), town house, 205
Dolphin, House of the, *see* Vasio
Domavia (Illyricum), 205
Domitian, Domus Flavia, 73, 230; Lago di Sabaudia villa, 131
domus, town house: 77, 83; Domus Italica, 17–18, 22, 34, 35; figs. 3, 4, 6, 7; Roman, 30–63, pl. 37; Vitruvius on, 32; axiality, 34; *tablinum*, 33–4; vistas, 34; *andron*, 34; *triclinia*, 34; *cubicula*, 34; *ala*, 34; formal design, 66–7; patriarchal form, 80; Romano-British, 187
Domus Augustana, *see* Domus Flavia
Domus Aurea (Rome), 73, 74, 75, 128–31, 154, fig. 50
Domus Flavia, 68–9, 73, 74–7, 131
Domus Tiberiana, 73, 74, 75, n103
Domus Transitoria, 73, 75, 128
doors, 32, 34, 49, 66, 90, 197, pl. 17
Dorchester, Oxfordshire, 198
D'Orsi, L., 120
dovecotes (*columbaria*), 106
drains, 20, 50, 65, roof 93–4, 142, 161, 200, 213
Drave, River, 202, 203
Dretwlj (Illyricum), 205
Drusus, 201
Dura-Europos (Syria), Palace of Dux Ripae, 204, 208, 221–2, fig. 70

Egypt, Ptolemaic, 223; Tell Edfu, 224
Eisenstadt-Gölbesäcken (Hungary), 203
Elagabalus, Emperor, 221
El Djem (Tunisia), 231

Emona, see Ljubljana
Ening, Suffolk, aisled house, 194
Ephesus (Turkey), *insulae*, 212–17, figs. 68, 69
Epidius Rufus, House of, see Pompeii
Esquiline Hill (Rome), 72, 73, 147
Étienne, R., 226
Etruscans, origins, 11, 12, 13, n9; temples, 13–14; carpentry, 14; doors, 16; Hellenistic housing, 23; cinerary urns, 24, pls 10, 11, 12, 13; displuviate house, 24; furnishings, 25–9; daily life, 28–9
Etrusca disciplina, 210
Evander, 64

Farnese, Cardinal Alessandro, 73
Faun, House of the, see Pompeii
Fenlands, Celtic homes, 182; settlements, 185
fires, causes, 86; protective measures, 86, 91
Fishbourne, Chichester, Sussex (Noviomagus Regnensium), 189–90, fig. 64
Fliessem, see Weilerbüsch
Florence, Etruscan urn, palace design, 24, pls 10, 11
flooring, 142–3, 198–9
Fortuna Annonaria, House of, see Ostia
Fortuna Primigenia, Temple of, Praeneste (Palestrina), 223–4
Frampton, Dorset, Christian mosaic, 199
furnishings, Etruscan, 25–9; Samnite, 36; Roman, 136–40; Gallic, 179; British, 201
Forma Urbis Romae (Marble Plan), 67, 77, 88, 96, 99
Fouet, G., 168
France, see Gaul
Francolise (Campania), Posto Villa, 104–5; San Rocco Villa, 105–6, pl. 38, fig. 38
Frascati (Tusculum), 130
Frere, S. S., 183, 186, 187
Fronto, Lucretius, House of, see Pompeii
furnishings, Etruscan 25–9; Samnite, 36; Roman, 136–40; Gallic, 179; British, 201

Gadara, 111
galleries, see art galleries
Gallia Belgica, 158, 162, 171–80; Belgic huts, 171; Romanization, 171–2; Italian and Delian influence, 163
Garda, Lake (Lago di), 132–3, fig. 51
gardeners, 53, 58
gardens, landscaping, 44–5, 46, 47, 61, 97, 129–30; Britain, 190; painting, 124, 147, pl. 49
Gaul, Roman, town houses, 159–64; villas, 164–70; corridor-style villas, 165; estates, general design, 165–6; aerial photography, 159, 164–5
Gerasa, see Jerash
Germany, see Gallia Belgica
Getty, J. Paul, museum, n5
Gilded Amorini, House of the, see Pompeii
Glanum, House of Sulla, 159, 161; House of Attis (Maison d'Atys), 161; House of the Antae (Maison des Antes), 161; pl. 64, fig. 54
Golden House, see Domus Aurea
Goodchild, R., fortified villas, 236
Gorhambury House, stucco work, 198
Graham, J. W., 18, 22, 226
granaries, see horrea
Graticcio, Casa a, see Herculaneum
Greece (Roman), 211
Griffins, House of the, see Rome
Grotta dell'Arsenale (Capri), 127
Grotte di Catullo (Sirmione), 132
Grotto of Tiberius, see Sperlonga
Gyulafirátót-Pogánytelek (Hungary), 203

Hadrian, Emperor, 77
Hadrian's Wall, 196
Hadrian's Villa, see Tibur
Hanfmann, G. M., 69, 149

heating, 140; hypocaustic, 199–200, fig. 53
Hellenistic house plans, 210
Hellenistic (Eastern) influences, 40
Herculaneum (Ercolano), 30, 32–3, 80; Houses: of the Bicentenary, 81, 143; of the Carbonized Furniture, 139, pl. 58; Casa a Graticcio (of the Trellis), 82–3, pls 28, 29; of the Mosaic Atrium, 51, 53, 61, 139, 143, pl. 14, figs 17, 18, 19, 20; of the Neptune and Amphitrite Mosaic, 55, 144–5, pl. 21; of the Wooden Partition, 49, pl. 17; Samnite House, 23, 51, 81, 146, pl. 19, fig. 16; of the Stags, 60, 143, figs 17, 20; of the Telephus Relief, 59; Insula Orientalis, 81; Villa of the Papyri, 31, 111, 180, n5, fig. 42; house and block numbers, n43
Hermansen, G., nn 146, 148
Herod the Great, 217, 218, 219
Herodian, 89
Herodotus, 11, 28
Heurgon, J., 28
Hinton St Mary, Dorset, 199
Hippodamus, 6–7, 15, 20, 210
Holloway, R., 14
Horace, 29, 112–13, pl. 40, fig. 43
horrea, 99, 178, n157
Hortensius Hortalus, Q., 67, 69, 72
horticulture, see gardeners, gardens
Hosszúhetény (Hungary), turreted mansion, 203–4
hotels, taverns, 94, n148
house boats (Lake Nemi), 128
houses, *passim*
Housesteads, Northumberland (Vercovicium), 196
Hungary, see Pannonia
hut urns, 12, 13, 64, pl. 2
hypocaustic heating, 199–200, fig. 53

Iader (Yugoslavia), 202, 205
Igel (Trier), 179
Illyricum, 201, 205–9

Imperialism, general, 8, 156-8; western, 158-9; eastern, 157-8, 210-11
impluvium, 17, 46, 61
insula, insulae, origins, 83, 84, 213-17; definition, 83, n123; ox incident, Rome, 86; legislated heights, 86-7, n137; dangers, 85-87; Vitruvius on, 87-8; advantages, 93; Ephesian examples, 213-17; Tyre, Aradus, 217; Ptolemais, 225
Insula Orientalis, *see* Herculaneum
Isis, Hall of, 75
Italic houses, prototype farmhouse, 17-18, 34, figs 3, 4; *domus Italica*, 17-18, 22, 34, figs 6, 7
Istacidius Zosimus, L., 111
Item, Villa, *see* Pompeii, Villa of the Mysteries
Izmit, *see* Nicomedia

Jefferson, Thomas, 101
Jerash, 220
Jericho, 219; Villa of Herod, 230, n389
Jerusalem, 218
Josephus, 218
Jucundus, Caecilius, L., House of, *see* Pompeii
Judaea, 217-19
Julia Felix, Villa of, *see* Pompeii
Julii, Mausoleum of (Glanum), 161
Julius Mosaic, *see* Carthage
Juvenal, 7, 85, 89, 99, 136

Katsch (Austria), villa, 204
keys, water system, 48; locks, 32
kitchens, 49-50, 86, 93, 94, 107, n171
Kleberg, T., 94
Köln-Müngersdorf, walled estate, 174-5, fig. 58
Konz (Contionacum), corridor style villa, 175, fig. 59

Laelius, C., 101
Laodicea (Syria), 220
Larario, Caseggiato del, *see* Ostia
lararium, 37, 43
Last Supper, The, n383

Latin words, n361
latrines, 161
Laurentine villa, Pliny the Younger, 115
Laurentum, 78
Laviosa, C., 25
Lehmann, P., 149
Lepcis Magna, 220-31
Lepidus, M. Aemilius, 68, 84, 101, House of, *see* Rome
Lepidus, triumvir, 131
Lesbia, 67
Licenza, Sabine Farm, 112, pl. 40, fig. 43
lighting, Etruscan, 27; Roman, 140, 200
Lincoln (Lindum), 180, 200
Liternum (Campania), Scipio's villa, 101, 103, 106, 236
Little Woodbury, Wiltshire, 183
Livia, House of, *see* Rome; Villa of, *see* Prima Porta
Livy, 35, 66, 86
liwan-style architecture, 15
Ljubljana, 202
Ljušina (Illyricum), 205
Llantwit-Major, Glamorgan, 185, villa, aisled house, 193-4, 198
Lockleys, Hertfordshire, 184, 185, 186
locks, bolts, 32, 107
London (Londinium), 180, 188
Low Ham, Dido and Aeneas mosaic, 199
Lucilius, 142
Lucretius, 100
Lucrine Lake (Lacus Lucrinus). 102; Villas, 140
Lucullus, Varro, 223
Lucullus, L., 143, 145 (black marble)
lucumones, 14, 23, 25
Lugdunensis (Gallia), 158
Lugdunum Convenarum, 170
Lugli, G., 40
Lullingstone Villa, Kent, 167, 174, 191-3, 196, 198, pl. 69, fig. 65
lupanaria, 94

Macedonia, 211
MacKendrick, P. L., 135, 157, 159
Maecenas, 29, 72, 73, 112

Maiuri, A., 111
Malibu (California), n5
Mamurra, 68, 143, 145
Manlius, Gn., 138, 139
Mannicius, M., 94
Mansfield Woodhouse, Nottinghamshire, 185
Mansuelli, G., 19, 21-2
marble, Roman, Hymettan, 68; Lucullan (Melian) 68; Numidian, 68, 75; Phrygian, 75; Carrara, 68; Carystus, 68; Porta Santa, 75
Marcomanni, 204
Marcus Aurelius, Emperor, 208
Marius, M., Villa of, *see* Pompeii
Marius, C., 102
Marta, River, 24
Martial, 89
Marzabotto, 19-22, 210, n25, pl. 6, fig. 5
Masada, palaces, 218-19, pl. 74
Mauretania Tingitana, 208
Mausolus, palace, 145
Maximian, 133, 135, 206
Maximus, Trebellius M., 186
Mayen, 171
Mazois, 43
megaron, megara, 12, 15, 210
Meiggs, R., 83
Menander, House of, *see* Pompeii
Mesopotamia, 221
Messalla, 73, n101
Messii, House of the, *see* Vasio
Metellus Celer, Q. Caecilius, 67
Metropolitan Museum, New York, reconstructed *cubiculum*, 6
Middle East, 221, n395
Milan 206
Mildenhall, Suffolk, silver treasure, n361
Miletus, 212
Milo, T. Annius, 67
Minori (Reginna Minor), 121
Miriamne, n389
Misenum, 30, 31
Moesia, 202
Montmaurin, villa, 168-70, pl. 65
Mosaic Atrium, House of the, *see* Herculaneum

mosaics, Campanian, 44, 55, 56, 60, 142–5; Sicily, 135; Britain, 191–2, 195, 199; North Africa, 233–5; Pliny the Elder on, 142, 143

Moselle, River, 172, 173, 180

Motya (Sicily), 224

Müngersdorf, see Köln-Müngersdorf

Mysteries, Villa of he, see Pompeii

Namur (Belgium), Anthée villa, 165

Naples, 91, 114, 122

Narcissus, Claudius' freedman, 118

Narona, 202

Nébouzan, see Nepotianus

Nemi, Lake, 128

Nennig, villa, 173–4, fig. 57

Nepos, Cornelius, 68

Nepotianus, 168

Neptune and Amphitrite Mosaic, House of the, see Herculaneum

Nero, 7, 73–4, 86–7, 128–31

Neumagen, reliefs, 179

Neusiedel, Lake, villas, 203, 204

Nicomachus Flavianus, n235

Nicomedia, 206

Norchia, 24

Noricum (Austria), 201, 202

Norton Disney, Nottinghamshire, 185

Notitia (Rome), 77, 83

Noviomagus, see Neumagen

Nuceria (Nocera), 40–1

Numa Pompilius, 15, 65

nymphaea, 44, 76, 69, 119, 126–8, 131, 144–5, 225, pl. 51, fig. 49

Odyssey landscapes, 147, 152, 153

oecus, oeci, 34; vaulted, 42; tetrastyle, 42, pl. 15; Cyzicene, 53; Aegyptius, 51, fig. 18; Corinthius, 50, 59

Oplontis (Campania), 155

Oppianicus, 102

opus caementicium, 40, 67, 84, 87, 101

opus craticium, 66, 82, 86

opus incertum, 40

opus latericium, 89

opus quadratum, 104

opus reticulatum, 40, 89

opus signinum, 56, 142

opus spicatum, 96, 125, 142

opus vitattum, 90

Orata, Sergius, 122, 140

Orontes, River, 99

Orvieto, 15, 20, 210

Ostia, 76–9, 89–99; property numbers and blocks, n43; insulae, 83–4, 89–99; evolution, 83–4; construction, style, 89–90; tabernae, 89, 90, pl. 36, fig. 28; vaulted arcade, 90–1; categories of Boëthius, 91; numbers, 91; accommodation, 91–3; builders, 93; kitchens, latrines, drains, 93–4; guildhouses (collegia), 94–5; hotels, taverns, 94, n148; decoration, 95; baths, 95; population figures, 98, n155; House of the Round Temple, 78, fig. 27; House of Fortuna Annonaria, 78, 79; House of Cupid and Psyche, 79, 220, n113, pl. 24; Domus of the Dioscuri, 95; Caseggiato del Larario, 96, fig. 32; Caseggiato di Diana (House of Diana), 96–7, pls 32, 33, 34, figs 33, 34; Casa dei Dipinti (House of the Paintings), 97, pl. 31; Casa delle Volte Dipinte (House of the Painted Vaults), 97–8, pl. 35, fig. 35; House of the Columns, 226; House near the Round Temple, 226, pl. 30

Painted Stuccoes (Reliefs), Tomb of the, see Caere

Painted Vaults, House of the, see Ostia

painting, painters, techniques, 145; Etruscan, 14, 27; Pompeian Styles, I, 146; II, 146–7, 148–9, pl. 59; III, 50, 154; IV, 150, 151, pls 62, 63; programmatic, cyclical, 151, 152, 153, 154, pls 62, 63; Delian, masonry style, 63, 146; Odyssey landscapes, 147, 152, 153; House of Livia

(Rome), 147; Prima Porta, 147; Stabiae, 119–21, 122, 154, pls 44, 45; Boscoreale, 149, pl. 60, 61; Britain, 197–8, pl. 72; Trier, 178–9; Ephesus, 215–17

Paintings, House of the, see Ostia

Palaces, Rome: see under Regia, Domus Aurea, Domus Flavia, Domus Tiberiana, Domus Transitoria; Italy: see under Baiae, Villa Jovis, Capri; provinces: Aquincum, Dura-Europos, Fishbourne, Masada, Split; Etruscan, see under Regia; ash urn (Florence), 24, Tomb of the Volumnii, 23, pl. 8

palaestra, palaestrae, 33, 110

Palatine Hill (Mons Palatinus), 77; residences 147

Palatine village, Iron Age, 13; huts, 64–5, pl. 1

Palatiolum, see Pfalzel

Papyri, Villa of the, see Herculaneum

Pandateria (Campania), 115

Pannonia (Hungary), 201, 202, 203, 204, 205, 220

Pansa, House of, see Pompeii

Parioli (Rome), 97

Park Street, Hertfordshire, 184, 185, 186

Parndorf (Hungary), villa, 204

Patroni, G., 17, 18, 34, figs 3, 4

patronus, 34, 66, 73, 74

Pauliacus (Gallic name, derivatives), 159

Paullus, L. Aemilius, 101

Peloponnese, 211

pensione, pensioni, see insulae

peperino, 72, 87

peregrinatio, 115

peristyle, 34, 35, 41; and palaestrae, 35; and gymnasia, 44; Rhodian, 41; affects atrium, 45–6; gardens, 53, 58, 61; size, 73; advantages, 226

Persius, 29

Perugia (Umbria), Tomb of the Volumnii, 23, pl. 8

Petra, 220

Petronius, 94, 113–14, 138

Pfalzel (Germany), 175–6, fig. 60

Philadelphia (Egypt), 224
Philippi, 211
Philippopolis (Syria), Governor's Palace, 208
Philip the Arab, Emperor, 208
Philodemus, 111
philology, Gallo-Roman properties, 159
Philostratus, Neapolitan villa, 122
Philoxenus of Eretria, 144
Piazza Armerina (Casale), 133, 135, n235, pl. 54, fig. 52
Picardy, air photography, 159, 166
picture galleries, see art galleries
Pilate, Pontius, 217
Pillig, 172, pl. 66
pinacotheca, see art galleries
piscinarii, 115
Piso, L. Calpurnius, 111
Pliny the Elder, 32, 128, 138, 142, 143, 145
Pliny the Younger, 30–1, 78, 115, 156
Plutarch, 66
plumbing, toilets, latrines, 200
Pollius Felix, villa, 121–2
Pompeii, 30–1, 80–1; regions, blocks, house numbers, n43; Houses: of L. Caecilius Jucundus, 150; of Caetronius, 47; of the Cryptoporticus, n251; of the Dioscuri, 47–50, n54, pl. 16; of Epidius Rufus, 51, n61; of the Faun (or Goethe), 43–5, 143–4, 146, fig. 14; of the Gilded Amorini (or Golden Cupids), 58–9, 150; of M. Loreius Tiburtinus, 44–5, fig. 15; of M. Lucretius Fronto, 129, 130; of Menander, 53–5, nn61, 251; of Pansa, 42–3, 46, 82, 139–40, figs 8, 13; of Sacerdos Amandus, 150; of Sallust, 23, 38–40, 108, 146, fig. 12; of the Silver Wedding, 41–2, n62, fig. 9; of the Surgeon, 23, 36–8, fig. 11; of the Tragic Poet, 55–6; of the Vettii, 56–8, 151, 152, 153–4, pl. 22, figs 21, 22; Villas: of Cicero, 150; of

Diomedes, 106, 111; of Julia Felix, 53, 82, n67, pl. 18; of Marcus Marius, 124; of the Mysteries, 106, 108–10, 111, 114, 116, 145, 148, pl. 59, figs 40, 41; terrace housing, 39, 69, 112, n95; Forum baths, insula, 80–1; hotels, bars, 94; tabernae, 80–1, 94
Pompey the Great, 131
Pontiae (Ponza), 115
Pontifex Maximus, 15, 65
Poplicola, P. Valerius, House of, see Rome
Porta Nigra (Trier), 209
porticus triplex, 110, 119
Posillipo (Naples), 121
Posto Villa, see Francolise
pozzolana (pulvis Puteolanus), 40, 67, 114, 124
Praeneste (Palestrina), sanctuary, 122; row shops, cenacula, 80; chests, 26–7; mosaic, 223–4, pl. 75
Priene, 212
Prima Porta, Villa of Augustus, 124; Villa of Livia, 124, 147, 190, pl. 49
Provence, 158
Ptolemais (Libya), 225, 226–8, 230; Palazzo delle Colonne, 228, 230, figs 72, 73; Villa, 227–8, fig. 71
Puteoli (Pozzuoli), 101, 113–14, 153

Quirinal Hall (Rome), 86

Rabirius, 74, 76, 77, 131
Raetia-Vindelicia, 201
Ravenna, 206
Reate (Sabinum), 102
Regensburg, 202
Regia, 15, 65, fig. 2
relief work, 59, 161
Richardson, L., 48, 49, 50
Richmond, Sir Ian, 234, n348
Rider, B. C., 6
Rivet, A. L. F., 190–1
Romania, see Dacia
Rome, 64–77; Regia, 15, 65, fig. 2; Evander's settlement, 64; Romulus' hut, 36, 64–5, n82; Palatine huts, 64–5;

Cloaca Maxima, 65; Gallic destruction, 66; Germalus mansions, 67; insulae, domus, 77; domus, tabernae, 80; insulae, 83–9, 98–9; Great Fire, protective measures, 7, 86, 88; slums, congestion, 98–9; population figures, 98, n155; Houses: of the Griffins (Casa dei Grifi), 69, 75, 124, n95; of Augustus, 70–2, n101, figs 25a, 25b; of Livia, 69–70, 147, n99, pl. 25, fig. 24; of M. Aemilius Lepidus, 84; of P. Valerius Poplicola, 65–6; of the Scipios, 66; Villa Farnesina, 130, n224; of Sette Bassi, 133; Tabernae Veteres, 66; Temple of Venus and Roma, 130; Arch of Titus, 218; see also under Palaces
roofing, Etruscan 14, Roman, 197, 223–7; see also under atrium
Roscius, 102
Round Temple, House near the, see Ostia
Round Temple, House of the, see Ostia
Rubra, 124
Rufus, Caelius M., 67–8
Ruggiero, M., 120
Rusellae (Roselle), 25
Rutilius, 88

Saalburg, 200, n358
Sabine Farm, 112–13
Sabratha (Libya), 231
Sacerdos Amandus, House of, see Pompeii
St Albans, see Verulamium
Saint Augustine, 223
St - Bertrand - de - Comminges, see Lugdunum Convenarum
St-Rémy, see Glanum
Salerno (prov.), 108
Sallust, House of, see Pompeii
Salona (Illyricum), 202, 205
Samnite House, see Herculaneum
Samnite housing, 38–40
San Giovenale, 23, 24, 103–4; figs 36, 37
San Giuliano, 24

San Rocco Villa, *see* Francolise
Satyricon, 113
Sauer, River, 172
Sautel, J., 163
Save, River, 202, 203, 205
Saxa Rubra, *see* Prima Porta
Scaurus, M. Aemilius, 67, 68
Scipios, House of the, *see* Rome
Scipio Africanus Maior, 101, 236
Scribonia, 70
Seius, 67
Sejanus, 127
Seleucia-Pieria, 220
Sella di Baia, *see* Baiae
Seneca, L. Annaeus, 86, 103, 140, 185
Septimius Severus, 77, 220–1, n371
Sette Bassi, House of the, *see* Rome
Severn area, Celtic homes, 182
Severus, architect, 73, 129
Severus Alexander, 221
Severus, imperial villa, Baccano, n394
Sheba (Shehba), *see* Philippopolis
Shields and Chairs, Tomb of the, *see* Caere
Sicily, 133, 135
Side (Turkey), 210
Sidonius Apollinaris, 170–1
Silchester, Hampshire (Calleva Atrebatum), 162, 181, 187, 188, 199–200
Silver Bust, House of the, *see* Vasio
silver service, 55, n361
Silver Wedding, House of the, *see* Pompeii
Simpelveld, sarcophagus, 138, 139, 179, pls 56, 57
Siren Land (Sorrentine peninsula), 121
Sirmione (Lake Garda), villa, 132–3, fig. 51
Sirmium (Illyricum), 202, 204, 206
Siscia (Sisak), 202
Somerset, ranches, 183
Somme, 159, 164
Sopianae (Hungary), 205
Sorrell, Alan, 193

Sorrento, 115; Pollius Felix, 121–2; Augustan villa, 121; Strabo on, 121
Sosus, mosaicist, 141
Spain, 158
Spalato, *see* Split
Sperlonga (Spelunca), 127–8, pl. 51, fig. 49
Spina, 24–5
Split, Diocletian's palace, 135, 206, 296–9, pl. 73, fig. 67
Squire Julius, mosaic, *see* Carthage
Srimska Mitrovica, *see* Sirmium
Stabiae, villas: of Ariadne (formerly Villa della Venditrice di Amori, of the Cupid Seller), 120–1; Villa San Marco (or Edificio Porticato, or of the Obsidian Vases), 118–21, 154, n384, pls 44, 45, fig. 45
stables, 50
Stags, House of the, *see* Herculaneum
Statius, 121–2
Stein, Gertrude, 99
stibadia, 148, 171
Strabo, 14, 85, 114, 121, 217
streets, 47, 85, 86, 206, 213–14
Strupnić (Hungary), 205
stucco work, 130, 198, pl. 50
Styria, 202, 204
Subiaco (Sublaqueum), Nero's villa, 138
Subura (Rome), 86
Suetonius, 72, 128, 129
Sulla, P. Cornelius, 67, 143, 223; House of, *see* Glanum
Sümeg (Lake Balaton), 203
SUNY House, *see* Cosa
Surgeon, House of the, *see* Pompeii
Surrentum, *see* Sorrento
Sussex Downs, Celtic homes, 182
Swoboda, K. M., 117
Synistor, Fannius, Villa of, *see* Boscoreale
Syria, 219–20

Tabarka, villa mosaic, 234–5, fig. 75
tabernae, 21, 23, 38, 66, 80, 86, 89, 90, nn115, 148

tables, Etruscan, 26, 28; Roman, 136, 137
tablinum, 17, 21, 23, 33–4, 49, *passim*
Tac-Fövenypuszta (Hungary), 203
Tacitus, Cornelius, 88, 127, 162, 200
Tamphilus, 68
Taqle (Syria), 219
Tarquinii, 14, 16, 27, pl. 7
Tarquins, 25
Tastovčići (Hungary), 205
Tebtunis, 224
Telephus Relief, House of the, *see* Herculaneum
Termessos, 212
terrace houses, 23, 24, 39, 69, n95; terrace villas, 105, 124–6, 130–1, 231
Terracina, 101
Tetrarchic Period, 206
Thabraea, *see* Tabarka
Thames Valley, Celtic homes, 182
Thamugadi, *see* Timgad
thermae, *see* baths, public and private
Thessalonica, 215
Thouvenot, R., 226
thresholds, 197
Tiber, River, 99
Tiberius, 73, 124–7, 201, fig. 48
Tibertinus, Loreius, House of, *see* Pompeii
Tibur (Tivoli), Hadrian's villa, 131–2, 135, pl. 52
tiles, 95, 197
Timgad, 231, fig. 74
Tipasa, 231
Titus, Arch of, 75, 218
Tivoli, *see* Tibur
tombs, Etruscan, 14, 15, 20, 23, 24, 25–9
tools, 182
Torre Annunziata, *see* Oplontis
Torre del Greco, 121
towers, 103, 219, 220, 224, nn6, 418
town house, *see* domus
town-planning, 6, 7, 15, 20, 25, 162, 186–7, 188, 205
Trajan, 93, 196, 202
Tragic Poet, House of the, *see* Pompeii

triclinia, 34, 41, 44, 45, 60, 69, 127, 135 (*triconchos*), 141–5, 153–4, 220, *passim*
Trier, 173, 180, 208, pl. 68
Trimalchio, 113–14, 137, 142, 151, 153
tufa, 14, 17, 23, 66
Tunisia, 224
Turkey, 210–17
Tuscan atrium, 16, 17
Tuscanicae dispositiones, 13
Tyre, 217

Ucalegon ('care-free'), 85
Umbricius ('shadowy'), 7
Uthina, 231
Utica, 231

Vasion-la-Romaine, *see* Vasio
Val de Catena, 122
Valentinian, Emperor, 173, 175
Valerian, Emperor, 208
Varano, Mount (Campania), 118, 120
Varro, M. Terentius, 16, 28–9, 100, 102, 116, 130, nn115, 165
Varus, Quinctilius, 201, n362
Vasio, 162–3; House of the Silver Bust, 162; House of the Messii, 163; House of the Dolphin, 162
vats, 104, 108
Veii, 15, pl. 3
Velia (Lucania), 101
Venafrum, 101
Venice, 91
Venusia, 112
Vergil (or Virgil), 8, 64, 65, 103, 147, 152, 156, 192, 223
Verulamium, 162, 181, 187, 200, n335; paintings, 197–8

Vespasian, 74, 75, 157, 218
Vesuvius, 30–1, 61
Vetera (Germany), 208
Vettii, House of the, *see* Pompeii
Vetulonia, 106
Vicus Belgica, 162
villas, 100–35; *rustica*, 100, 101, 104–8, 133, 179, 205, fig. 39; *suburbana*, 100, 108–10, 114, 124, 128–31, pl. 37, figs. 40, 41, 42; *maritima*, 115–28, 131, 132–3, 228; pls 41, 42, 46, 47, 48; and *passim*; archetypal farmhouse, 17–18, 38, figs 3, 4
Villa Aldobrandini, 130
Villa Borghese, 130
Villa d'Este, 44, 130
Villa Farnesina, *see* Rome
Villa Gradola, *see* Capri
Villa Jovis, *see* Capri
Villa Rustica, *see* Boscoreale
Villa San Marco, *see* Stabiae
Villanovans, 12–13, 64–5, pl. 1
Vindelicia, 201
Viroconium Cornoviorum, *see* Wroxeter
Vitruvius Pollio, architect, 13, 14, 16–17, 32, 37–8, 40, 41, 61, 69, 72–3, 82, 86, 87, 100, 110, 142, 146–7, 148–9, 151
Vittimose, 108
vocabulary, Latin-English, n361
Volte Dipinte, Casa delle, *see* Ostia
Volubilis, 208, 225–6
Volumnii, Tomb of the (Perugia), 23, pl. 8
Vulci, 146

Wadi-Qelt, 219
walls, estates, 103, 167, 174, 203, 204, 206–8, 235–6; house walls (Britain), 196–7
Ward-Perkins, J. B., 130, 204, 219
warehouse architecture, *see* horrea
water-organ, 174, n307
water-supply, 32, 38, 48, 49, 97, 183, 200, 213
Webster, G., 184
Weilerbüsch, 176, fig. 61
Weitersbach, 172
wells, 20, 22, 38–9, 183; Regia, 15
Welschbillig, 179–80
Wheeler, Sir M., 79
Wilkes, J. J., n372
windows, Etruscan, 14; Roman, 48, 50, 61, 90, 95–6, 101, 124, 139–40, 197, 200, 204, 214
Wittlich, 175
women, roles of, Etruscan, 26; Roman, 170, 233, 234
Woodchester, Gloucestershire, 195
Wooden Partition, House of the, *see* Herculaneum
Wroxeter, Shropshire (Uriconium), 181, 200

Xanten, *see* Vetera

Yadin, Y., 218
Yale University, 221

Zadar, *see* Iader
Zosimus, L. Istacidius, 111
Zotikos, 208